PALESTINIAN REFUGEES

Pluto Middle East Studies
Nur Masalha
General Editor

PALESTINIAN REFUGEES
The Right of Return

Edited by
NASEER ARURI

Pluto Press
LONDON • STERLING, VIRGINIA

First published 2001
by PLUTO PRESS
345 Archway Road, London N6 5AA
and 22883 Quicksilver Drive,
Sterling, VA 20166–2012, USA

www.plutobooks.com

British Library Cataloguing in Publication Data
A catalogue record for this book is available from
the British Library

Library of Congress Cataloging in Publication Data
Palestinian refugees : the right of return / edited by Naseer Aruri.
    p. cm.
Includes bibliographical references and index.
    ISBN 0–7453–1777–4 (hardback) — ISBN 0–7453–1776–6 (pbk.)
    1. Refugees, Palestinian Arabs. 2. Refugees, Palestinian
Arabs—Government policy—Israel. 3. Repatriation—Israel. 4.
Arab–Israeli conflict—1993—Peace. I. Aruri, Naseer Hasan, 1934–
    HV640.5.P36 P35 2001
    362.87'089'9274—dc21
                                                           2001000620

ISBN 0 7453 1777 4 hardback
ISBN 0 7453 1776 6 paperback

Reprints: 10   9   8   7   6   5   4   3   2   1

Designed and produced for Pluto Press by
Chase Publishing Services, Fortescue, Sidmouth EX10 9QG
Typeset from disk by Stanford DTP Services, Northampton
Printed in the European Union by Antony Rowe, Chippenham, England

CONTENTS

Part IV   Refugee Claims and the Search for a Just Solution

PREFACE

Elaine C. Hagopian

Looking at the issue of the Palestinian right of return from the viewpoint of autumn 1999, it appeared that the PLO Chairman, Yasir Arafat, was on the point of signing away that right in exchange for a truncated Palestinian 'state'. Final status negotiations were imminent. For this reason, elements of the Palestinian refugee population in Occupied Palestine stepped up their efforts to publicize their just and legal right to the international community. As early as 1996, they had informed Arafat that he had no mandate to compromise their absolute and inalienable right of return to their homes and property in Israel proper, and to receive full compensation for losses and damages that had been incurred. Although Arafat attempted to defuse their anger by establishing a Department for Refugee Rights, headed by Dr As'ad Abdul Rahman, the refugee organizational effort continued. In the forefront was the Union of Youth Activities Centres, based in the West Bank camps, whose activities began three years after the Oslo Declaration of Principles was signed in September 1993. It had become obvious to them that the refugees' right of return under the Declaration was to be nullified, and in its place a 'humanitarian', phased family reunification programme for very limited numbers was being discussed. Clearly, Israel was refusing to accept any responsibility for the expulsion of Palestinians from Palestine.

At the same time a number of non-governmental organizations (NGOs) for refugee rights, as well as research centres, were being established. Foremost among these is the BADIL Resource Centre for Palestinian Residency and Refugee Rights, which is based in Bethlehem. Informed by the work of Professors Susan Akram, Guy Goodwin-Gill and John Quigley, but especially of Akram, BADIL pursued a solid campaign for publicizing refugee rights in various international fora. Joining those efforts was a Palestinian researcher, Salman Abu-Sitta, whose work resulted in an analysis of the outcome of confiscated Palestinian land in Israel proper, and a detailed map of the depopulated villages and their present status. His work was published by the Palestinian Research Centre in London. Abu-Sitta's studies also inform BADIL's campaign.

Independently, other refugee right of return organizations had been established throughout the Arab region. These included: A'idun ('We Will

Return') in Lebanon and Syria; several committees in Jordan; refugee advocates for Palestinians in Israel whose homes and property were confiscated by Israel, making them internal refugees; *Shaml*, the Palestinian Diaspora and Refugee Centre, founded in 1994 in Jerusalem; and numerous Arab popular committees supporting refugee rights. In addition, various local and national Arab-American organizations, such as the American Arab Anti-Discrimination Committee, the Association of Arab-American University graduates, national Muslim groups and numerous local groups, have long supported Palestinian refugees' right to return. However, most of these groups, scattered as they are across North America, Europe and elsewhere, were unaware of each other's work, nor did they follow a common programme or strategy.

As final status negotiations drew ever closer, the Board of Directors of the Trans-Arab Research Institute, Boston, recognized the need to hold a conference on the right of return. Their thinking was based on the conviction that any agreement that attempted to nullify the inalienable Palestinian right of return would result in greater instability in the area, rather than the expected closing of the refugee file. They therefore felt a responsibility to publicize this matter as part of the Institute's educational mission.

'The Right of Return: Palestinian Refugees and Prospects for a Durable Peace' conference was held on 8 April 2000 at the Boston University Law School. It brought together scholars, journalists, individuals and representatives of some of the Palestinian refugee advocacy organizations listed above. The papers presented at that conference make up the chapters of the present volume, to which are added chapters by Michael Prior, Nur Masalha, Joseph Massad and Jan Abu Shakrah, which complement the comprehensive coverage of this core issue topic.

Crucially, the various individual and refugee organizational advocates met on their own initiative the day following the conference to begin to coordinate their efforts. The meeting had two outcomes: the establishment of a Palestinian right of return grassroots activist organization in North America and Europe, Al-Awda (Return); and an opportunity for the representatives of refugee organizations from abroad to meet and develop a refugee network.

Subsequently, Al-Awda North America and Europe set up a Palestine Right to Return Coalition, which organized massive marches and rallies in September 2000 in Washington and London, complemented by similar events in Lebanon, Palestine, Israel and Jordan. Their activities are continuing, and their spokespeople have declared that they will go on until the Palestinians' right to return to their homes and property in Israel proper with full compensation is recognized and implemented. The network of refugee right of return organizations abroad not only sponsored and held their complementary marches and rallies, but also ran a coordinating workshop in October 2000 to further their common efforts to secure the right of return under international law. A British Commission of Inquiry on

Palestinian Refugee Choice interviewed refugees on site in the Israeli-occupied Palestinian territories, as well as organizational leaders and Palestinian legislators. They determined that the refugees want repatriation to their original homes or property in Israel proper, and compensation for material losses and damages, and for the suffering caused by the years of exile. The Commission was an initiative of the Joint British Parliamentarian Middle East Council and was premised on the recognition of Britain's historical responsibility for the creation of the Palestinian refugee problem.

By the time President Clinton organized Camp David II in July 2000 – presumably with a view to completing all final status negotiations – a viable and vociferous right of return movement had made its voice heard. Although other issues, particularly Jerusalem, were considered thorny, the right of return was the thorniest and most threatening to Israel. Arafat – and as PLO chairman, he is supposed to represent all Palestinians – understood that he could not do what the Americans and Israelis wanted him to do: that is, encompass refugee individual rights within the collective right of a promised Palestinian 'state'. Arafat himself did not want to go to Camp David II, but went nevertheless. On his arrival, he was made aware of a Joint Statement of the Popular Organizations of the Refugee Camps in the West Bank. The Statement affirmed:

that the negotiators should not bother returning if they bring anything less than the right of return. 'We are going home – home to Palestine. Our olive trees and oranges await us. We will not accept anything less no matter who signs the next of the infinite agreements.' (*News from Within*, September 2000, p. 20)

Camp David II was a failure for Clinton and the Israeli prime minister, Ehud Barak. They failed to make Arafat capitulate to their terms, which were neither based on minimal justice, nor applicable to international law or UN Security Council Resolution 242 – the very basis of the Oslo process.

Clearly, the activities after the Right of Return Conference had had a sobering effect on Arafat's freedom to sign away the refugees' rights. Although he reportedly attempted to finesse this issue at Camp David, Israel did not cooperate. He sought to have Israel admit responsibility for the refugee problem, following which the 'modalities' of a solution could be worked out. He believed that Israel's acknowledgement would compensate for the expected inadequate 'modalities'. But whatever the case, anything short of implementation of UN General Assembly Resolution 194 (III) would not be acceptable nor lead to a lasting peace. After all, the Palestinian refugees constitute 70 per cent of the Palestinian population, the largest single Palestinian constituency and the most destitute; and the unresolved refugee issue, coupled with all the Oslo 'peace' process-induced and intensified Palestinian suffering in the Israeli-occupied Gaza, West Bank and East Jerusalem had led inexorably to the *al-Aqsa Intifada*.

The chapters presented in this book represent the most comprehensive coverage of the various facets of the refugee issue to date and recognize the compelling human and legal case of Palestinian refugee rights. The book is divided into an introductory essay and four parts: the urgency of the re-emergence of the refugee right of return (E. Said, Aruri); the historical roots and context (Masalha, Prior, W. Said); the interests and behaviour of the major actors – Israel, the United States, the European Union and the PLO (Pappe, Chomsky, Gresh, Suleiman); the conditions of diaspora refugees (Massad, Ghandour); and the legal case and strategy for a just solution (Akram, Abu-Sitta, Finkelstein, Abu Shakrah, Kubursi and Jaradat Gassner).

The Trans-Arab Research Institute is pleased to have provided the important information and analyses presented in the chapters in the hope that they may enlighten solutions that lead to a durable peace.

ACKNOWLEDGEMENTS

This book would not have been possible without the help of many individuals, who participated in preparing the conference on the 'Right of Return' held at Boston University Law School under the auspices of the Trans-Arab Research institute (TARI) on 8 April, 2000. Most of the chapters in this book were the product of that conference. Two persons, in particular, made that conference possible through consistent voluntary work throughout the largest part of the year 1999 and the first quarter of 2000. Not only did Dr Elaine Hagopian conceptualize the conference, identify potential speakers, extend the invitations, raise funds, handle the voluminous correspondence, and finalize the programme in a most professional manner, but she also handled most of the arrangements, normally carried out by paid staff, such as monitoring and recording registrations, and dealing with all tedious tasks, including meals, projectors, and book-sale tables at the conference, among many other chores. Beyond all that, she offered financial support and she planned a conference in Siracusa, Italy three years earlier, which had in effect given birth to TARI. Her dedication is, indeed, very rare and her commitment to justice in Palestine has been a lifetime endeavour. The second person is Dr Nancy Murray, who was the first to propose holding this conference, and who assumed many tasks, which were indispensable to the success of the conference. Her counsel, wisdom, and hard work, ever-present throughout the long conference preparation period, made it possible to convene the conference.

I am grateful for the commitment and support of organizations and individuals who contributed to the success of the Conference of Return, including the Jerusalem Fund, the Canadian Arab Society, National Council on Canadian-Arab Relations, Americans for Middle East understanding, Genevieve McMillan, Maha Kaddoura, Marwan Taqtaq, Elise Young, Rhonda and Shukri Khouri, Katha Kissman and Samih Farsoun, Nazik and Mujid Kazimi, Rima and Ghaleb Daouk, Robert Bateh, Susan Akram and Jeff Boshar, Maysoon and Subhi Ali, Najwa and Rifaat Dweik, Anthony Sahyoun, Margaret and Omar Khudari, Eid Mustafa, Baker Azzam, Said Abu-Zahra, Tareef Kawaf, Lucie and Charles Hagopian, Ahmad Kawash and Cheryl and Martin Rubenberg.

I wish to express my deep gratitude to the Boston University Arab Students, who hosted the conference, and in particular to Nedal Awde, who organized the students and opened the conference. An incredible number of Boston University students assembled the conference packets, served as ushers at the conference, and spread the word on their campuses. I am also grateful for the help provided by the many students and volunteers from Boston's surrounding universities and associations. Among them I would like to thank Mona Fawaz (MIT), Maysa Sabah (MIT), Nasser Sharara, Yasmin Khayal, Mera Eftaiha, Professor Betty Anderson, of the History Department at Boston university, Hannah Schuller (Friends of Sabeel), Mark Wolff (Boston Committee on the Middle East), and Hussein Ibish.

Many colleagues and friends have helped in various capacities, offering suggestions, ideas and voluntary services during the planning stage of the conference as well as organizing the book. Among them, I would like to thank Merrie Najimy, Leila Farsakh, and Lamis Andoni. I would like to thank Nur Masalha, for adding to the original conference essays a prime chapter that provided a much needed historical background. He also introduced me to the work of Michael Prior and persuaded him to write the seminal chapter on ethnic cleansing and the Bible. Both of these chapters, based largely on original sources in Hebrew and English, have enriched the volume and made it more complete. My colleague and friend Professor Samih Farsoun read many drafts of the outline and a number of the chapters, and offered valuable commentary. I am truly grateful for his sustained support.

My friend Tamara Kohns read my own chapter 15, offered valuable comments, and did excellent editorial work. I am most grateful for her helpful counsel over the years.

My wife Joyce provided invaluable assistance throughout the long process during which this book was in preparation. She was generous with ideas, discussions, and logistics, in addition to assuming my share of the duties in the household. My son, Jamal and his wife Mona Igram offered assistance in maintaining the financial records of the conference and assisted in other capacities at the conference.

I wish to thank the editors of the *Columbia Human Rights Law Review* and the journal *Critique* for granting permission to reprint articles by Wadie Said and Joseph Massad in this volume.

Last but not least, Roger van Zwanenberg and Robert Webb of Pluto Press have been a continued source of support in handling logistics and dealing with complex issues related to the realization of this project. I wish to also thank Ruth Willats, the copy-editor, Melanie Patrick, Tracey Day and Ray Addicott of Chase Publishing Services. My thanks also go to the authors, without whose hard work and cooperation this volume would not have been possible.

                                                            NASEER ARURI

INTRODUCTION: THE RIGHT OF RETURN AT LAST
Edward W. Said

The issue in the by now notorious peace process finally has come down to one issue, which has been at the core of Palestinian depredations since 1948: the fate of the refugees who were displaced in 1948, again in 1967 and again in 1982 by naked Israeli ethnic cleansing. Any other description of those acts by the Israeli army is a travesty of the truth no matter how many protestations are heard from the unyielding Zionist right-wing (assuming that the left is more likely to accept the truth). That the Palestinians have endured decades of dispossession and raw agonies rarely visited on other peoples – particularly because their agonies have either been ignored or denied and, even more poignantly, because the perpetrators of this tragedy are celebrated for social and political achievements that make no mention of where those achievements began – is of course the locus of the 'Palestinian problem', but it has been pushed very far down the agenda of negotiations until finally it has popped up to the surface.

For Palestinians, a vast collective feeling of injustice continues to hang over our lives with undiminished weight. If there has been one thing, one particular delinquency committed by the present Palestinian leaders for me, it is their supernally gifted power of forgetting. When one of them was asked what he felt about Ariel Sharon's accession to the Foreign Ministry, given that he was responsible for shedding so much Palestinian blood, this leader replied blithely, 'We are prepared to forget history.' That is a sentiment I can neither share nor, I hasten to add, easily forgive.

One needs to recall, by comparison, Moshe Dayan's statement in 1969:

We came to this country which was already populated by Arabs and we are establishing a Hebrew, that is a Jewish, state here. In considerable areas of the country [the total area was about 6 per cent], we bought land from the Arabs. Jewish villages were built in the place of Arab villages, and I do not even know the names of these Arab villages, and I do not blame you, because these geography books no longer exist; not only do the books not exist, the Arab villages are not there either. Nahalal [Dayan's own village] arose in the place of Mahalul, Gevat – in the place of Jibta, [Kibbutz] Sarid – in the place of Haneiofs and Kefar Yehoshua – on the place of Tel Shaman. There is not one place built in this country that did not have a former Arab population. (*Ha'aretz*, 4 April 1969)

1

What strikes me about early Palestinian reactions is how largely unpolitical they were. For 20 years after 1948, Palestinians were immersed in the problems of everyday life with little time left for organizing, analysing and planning. With the exception of the kind of work produced in Mohammed Hassanein Haykal's *Ahram* Strategic Institute, Israel to most Arabs – and even to Palestinians – was a cipher, its language unknown, its society unexplored, its people and the history of their movement largely confined to slogans, catch-all phrases, negation. We saw and experienced its behaviour towards us, but it took us a long time to understand what we saw or what we experienced.

The overall tendency was to think of military solutions to that scarcely imaginable country, with the result that a vast militarization overtook every society almost without exception in the Arab world; coups succeeded each other more or less unceasingly and, worse yet, every advance in the military idea brought an equal and opposite diminution in social, political and economic democracy. Looking back on it now, the rise to hegemony of Arab nationalism allowed for very little in the way of democratic civil institutions, mainly because the language and concepts of that nationalism devoted little attention to the role of democracy in the evolution of those societies. Until now, the presence of a putative danger to the Arab world has engendered a permanent deferral of such things as an open press, or unpoliticized universities, or freedoms to research, travel in and explore new realms of knowledge. No massive investment was ever made in the quality of education, despite on the whole successful attempts on the part of the Nasser government in Egypt as well as other Arab governments to reduce the rate of illiteracy. It was thought that given the perpetual state of emergency caused by Israel, such matters, which could only be the result of long-range planning and reflection, were luxuries that were ill afforded. Instead, arms procurement on a huge scale took the place of genuine human development with the negative repercussions that we live with to this day. Thirty per cent of the world's arms were bought by Arab countries in 1998–99.

Along with the militarization went the wholesale persecution of communities, pre-eminently but not exclusively the Jewish ones, whose presence in our midst for generations was suddenly deemed to be dangerous. I know that there was an active Zionist role in stimulating unrest amongst the Jews of Iraq, Egypt and elsewhere on the one hand, and the governments of those Arab countries were scarcely democratic on the other, but it seems to me to be incontestable that there was a xenophobic enthusiasm officially decreeing that these and other designated 'alien' communities had to be extracted by force. Nor was this all. In the name of military security in countries such as Egypt, there was a bloody-minded, imponderably wasteful campaign against dissenters, mostly on the left, but against independent-minded people too, whose vocation as critics and skilled men and women was brutally terminated in prisons, by fatal torture and summary executions. As one looks back at these things in the context of 1948, it is the immense panorama of waste and cruelty that stands out as the immediate result of the war itself.

Along with that went the scandalously poor treatment of the refugees themselves. It is still the case, for example, that the 40,000–50,000 Palestinian refugees resident in Egypt must report to a local police station every month; vocational, educational and social opportunities are curtailed; and a general sense of not belonging adheres to them, despite their Arab nationality and language.

In Lebanon the situation is even more dire. Almost 400,000 Palestinian refugees have had to endure not only the massacres of Sabra, Shatila, Tel al-Za'atar, Dbayyeh and elsewhere, but have remained confined in hideous quarantine for almost two generations. They have no legal right to work in at least 60 occupations; they are not adequately covered by medical insurance; they cannot travel and return; they are the objects of suspicion and dislike. In part – and I shall return to this – they have inherited the mantle of opprobrium draped round them by the PLO's presence (and since 1982 its unlamented absence) there, and thus they remain in the eyes of many ordinary Lebanese a sort of house enemy to be warded off and/or punished from time to time.

A similar situation exists in kind, if not in degree, in Syria. As for Jordan, although it was – to its credit – the only country where Palestinians were given naturalized status, a visible fault line exists between the disadvantaged majority of that very large community and the Jordanian establishment for reasons that scarcely need to be spelled out. I might add, however, that for most of these situations where Palestinian refugees exist in large groups within one or another Arab country – all of them the direct consequence of 1948 – no simple, much less elegant or just, solution exists in the foreseeable future. It is also worth mentioning, or rather asking, why it is that a destiny of confinement and isolation has been imposed on a people who quite naturally fled to neighbouring countries when driven out of their own, countries that everyone believed would welcome and sustain them. More or less the opposite occurred: except in Jordan, no welcome was given them – another unpleasant consequence of the original dispossession.

Recently, two contradictory sets of happenings have occurred which, in their stark, irreconcilable antithesis, tell almost the whole story of what is wrong with an unevolved Zionism on the one hand, and what is just as seriously wrong with the peace process on the other. Ehud Barak and several of his faceless underlings have tirelessly been on record in Israel, in Europe and elsewhere to affirm their increasingly strident disavowal of any responsibility for Palestinian dispossession. Here and there, a more humane Israeli official will, for example, temper these disavowals with an acknowledgement that Israel bears some responsibility for the 'transfers' that took place in 1948 and 1967, but that 'the Arabs' – who presumably are supposed to have evicted Palestinians too (the notion is too preposterous to require rebuttal) – are also responsible, thereby preparing the way for a magnanimous offer for Israel to take back 100,000 of the nearly 4.5 million refugees who now exist in the Arab world and beyond. But such individual declarations are remarkable for their infrequency and the lack of response they have engendered in Barak and his entourage, to say nothing of the Knesset majority, the settlers and a dispiritingly large number of ordinary Israelis, who seem to believe that whatever happened in 1948 they will have nothing to do with it. It is not their problem, so why should they have anything to say? That, of course, has precisely been Barak's negotiating strategy: to refuse any discussion at all of the refugees' claim to return, repatriation and/or compensation. Recent revelations by an Israeli researcher that a bigger 15 May 1948 massacre than the notorious one at Deir Yassin took place in Tantura, in which more than 200 Palestinian civilians were shot by Zionist soldiers has not shaken Barak's rejectionism one iota.

The contradictory part of the issue is the snowball effect of what is now a universal Palestinian demand heard all over the globe for the right to return. Petitions have been signed by the dozen, thousands of names in the Arab world, Europe, Africa and the Americas have been added to these lists daily, and for the first time, the right of return has been put squarely on the political agenda. As'ad Abdul Rahman, the PLO's minister in charge of the refugee question for the peace process, has recently made some excellent strong statements about the absolute right of return for Palestinians evicted by Israel. These statements express the right kind of resolve and the right kind of moral indignation. After all, Abdul Rahman says, UN Resolution 194 has been affirmed annually since 1948 and allows the Palestinians the right of return and/or compensation. Why should there be a compromise given the world's unanimity? Even the United States has supported the resolution, with Israel the lone dissenter. The troubling thing, however, is that Abdul Rahman hints that the PLO leadership may do a deal with Israel on the refugees behind his back. In view of the long history of shabby Arafatian compromises, whose effect has been to sell out his people, this is an allowable – not so say well-founded – worry.

The one certain thing is that it is going to take a great deal of ingenuity, public relations spin-doctoring and specious logic to convince any Palestinian that the deal to be made (as it will be) by the PLO is not an abrogation of the right to return. Consider the logic of what has happened since 1991. On every major issue separating Palestinians from Israelis, it is the Palestinians who have given way. Yes, they have achieved small gains here and there, but all one needs to do is look at a map of Gaza and the West Bank, then visit those places, then read the agreements, then listen to Israelis and Americans, and one will have a fair idea of what has happened by way of compromise, flawed arrangements and a general abrogation of full Palestinian self-determination. All this has happened because the Palestinian leadership has selfishly put its self-interest, its over-inflated squadrons of security guards, its commercial monopolies, its unseemly persistence in power, its lawless despotism, its anti-democratic greed and cruelty, before the collective Palestinian good. Until now it has connived with Israel to let the refugee issue slither down the pole, but now that the final status era is upon is there is no more room down there. And so we are back to the basic, irreconcilable, the irremediably interlocked contradiction between Palestinian and Israeli nationalism. Unfortunately, I have no faith that our leadership will maintain the façade of resistance and continue to let Abdul Rahman and others like him carry the message forward. There is always another Abu-Mazin–Yossi Beilin arrangement to be made, and if the Israelis can 'persuade' Arafat's men that Abu Dis is in fact Jerusalem, why can they not also persuade them that the refugees will have to remain refugees for a bit longer? Of course they can – and will.

So that leaves the unanswered question: will Palestinian people as a whole accept the final card being played, or not? The short-run prognosis is not good, as witness the wasted opportunity to impeach the Authority in November 1999. Several of the 20 petitioners were unlawfully imprisoned, the rest threatened, Very little happened by way of repercussion, and the Authority got away with its brazen strong arm tactics. Arafat survives inside the Palestinian territories for two main reasons: he is needed by the inter-national supporters of the peace process – Israel, the United States and the European Union chief among them; he is needed to sign and that, after all, is what he is good for. Nothing else. Everyone knows this. He can deliver his people. The second reason is that because he is a master at corrupting even the best of his people he has bought off or threatened all organized opposition and therefore removed them as a threat. The rest of the population is too uncertain and discouraged to do much. The Authority employs 140,000 people. Multiply that by five or six (the number of dependants of each employee) and you get close to one million people whose livelihoods hang by a thread offered by Arafat. Much as he is disliked, disrespected or feared, he will remain while he has this leverage over an enormous number of people who will not jeopardize their future simply because they are ruled by a corrupt, inefficient and stupid dictatorship, which cannot even deliver the essential services for daily civil life: water electricity, health care, food, etc.

That leaves the Palestinian diaspora, which produced Arafat in the first place. It was from Kuwait and Cairo that he emerged to challenge Shuqairi and Haj Amin al-Husseini. A new leadership will almost certainly appear from the Palestinians who live elsewhere: they are a majority and none of them feels that Arafat represents them. All of them regard the Authority as without real legitimacy, and they are the ones with the most to gain from the right of return, on which Arafat and his men will be forced to back down.

We must encourage ourselves to do the work of collating the desires and the numbers of refugees, cataloguing property losses, compiling the list of destroyed villages, carrying forward the claims – such as the petition circulated by the BADIL Resource Centre. The extraordinary engineer and scholar Salman Abu-Sitta has done a lot of the work on property and demo-graphics; and others are following his lead or supporting him. He works independently or with the support of friends. To expect Arafat to take advantage of all this loyal expertise and authentic commitment is, of course, a pipe dream. What he has done is to contract out the final status negotiations to a right-wing London think tank, the Adam Smith Institute, which is paid for its services by the British Foreign Office, and has retained an American consulting firm, Arthur Andersen, to advertise its investment attractions. No other liberation group in history has sold itself to its enemies in this way. We all have a stake in making sure that these shabby diversions fail and that the handful of expert Palestinians who are now complicit in these arrangements come to their senses and leave the Authority to sink terminally into the mud that surrounds them. Then we will press the claims for return and compensation in earnest with new leaders.

Part I

The Historical Context

1 THE RIGHT TO EXPEL: THE BIBLE AND ETHNIC CLEANSING

Michael Prior

Since, as Joseph Conrad's Marlow notes, 'the conquest of the earth is not a pretty thing when you look into it too much', colonizers invariably seek out some ideological principle to justify their actions, and when these involve dubious deeds of exploitation, the search is all the more intense. Appeal to the Bible to justify inhumane behaviour is not uncommon in the history of imperialist colonialism emanating from Europe. Indeed, whether deployed honestly or cynically, the Bible frequently has been used as *the idea* that *redeems the conquest of the earth*.[1] It is also the potentially most convincing *apologia* legitimizing the Zionist enterprise of establishing a state for Jews at the expense of an indigenous population. For David Ben-Gurion, the Bible is the 'Jews' sacrosanct title-deed to Palestine ... with a genealogy of 3,500 years'.[2] It, allegedly, underpins the Jewish right of return. Such claims are not above reproach.

The status of the land of Israel in (religious) Jewish thought is integrally linked with the biblical narrative. According to that narrative, the land was promised to Abraham and his descendants, a promise realized in the almost punctiliar military campaign described in Joshua or, if one prefers the narrative of Judges, in the gradual extension over a period of time of Israelite hegemony by the 'judges'. We shall see that that biblical paradigm, with the Exodus narrative at its core, is a major element in the justification for enterprises of colonization in general, as well as for the establishment of the state for Jews in 1948.[3] The Zionist enterprise of 'return' demanded the expulsion of the indigenous non-Jewish population, a fact realized from the beginning.

RETURNING TO EXPEL

The 'Law of Return', enacted by the Israeli Knesset on 5 July 1950, gives legal substance to the Jewish 'right to return', permitting any Jew, simply in virtue of being a Jew, to settle in the State of Israel. Despite its claims to legitimacy, however, the Jewish 'right to return' is questionable. For one, a communal right of return operates in the wider world only when a defined community has been subjected to recent expulsion. Such an arrangement is a *sine qua non* for orderly international behaviour. But there is a yet more problematic element in the 'right of return'.

The realization of the Zionist programme as outlined in Theodor Herzl's *Der Judenstaat* (the State for Jews)[4] involved more than a return of Jews: it required the dislocation of an identifiable indigenous population. Although he did not use the language of a right of return Herzl spoke of 'the distinctive nationality of Jews' (pp. 76, 79),[5] and of 'the restoration of the Jewish State' (p. 69). Although he aspired to construct a separate state 'like every other nation', Herzl's enterprise would require special pleading, since the basic assumption of European nationalisms was the indigenous nature of a specific community, and its desire for independence from the relevant imperial power.

Although in his pamphlet Herzl gave no indication of the adverse effect his enterprise would have on the indigenous Arab population of Palestine – on the contrary, he gave the impression that it would be beneficial all round – he was in no doubt as to what was needed to establish a state for Jews in a land already inhabited. An item in his diary entry for 12 June 1895 shows that he was aware of the demographic realities of Palestine and knew what would be necessary to achieve the Zionist goal.[6] The transition from a Jewish society to the state for Jews would require the occupation of the land and the expropriation of the private property, after which, 'We shall endeavour to expel the poor population across the border unnoticed, procuring employment for it in the transit countries, but denying it any employment in our own country.'[7] He added that both 'the process of expropriation and the removal of the poor must be carried out discreetly and circumspectly'. This diary entry confirms Herzl's real intentions, despite his public pretence of wishing to further the interests of the native population. This kind of duplicity was a characteristic of Zionist discourse, producing 'a not-undeserved reputation in the world for chronic mendacity',[8] with respect to both true Zionist intentions and the distortion of what was done in their execution. After his death in 1904, Herzl's diaries were held by the Zionist movement, and until 1960 only edited versions were released, carefully omitting his 'population transfer' plans.

In bypassing the question of the impact of his plans on the indigenous people, Herzl reflected stereotypical nineteenth-century European colonialist prejudices. In addition to providing 'a house to shelter the Jewish nation', the project would 'advance the interests of civilization, by establishing a cultural station, on the shortest road to Asia, a task Jews were ready to undertake as the bearers of culture'.[9] Herzl presented the proposed state for Jews as 'a portion of the rampart of Europe against Asia, an outpost of civilization [Herzl's term was *Kultur*] opposed to barbarism'.[10] He reflected elsewhere also the typical world-view of European racist superiority. He assured the Grand Duke of Baden that Jews returning to their 'historic fatherland' would do so as representatives of Western civilization, bringing 'cleanliness, order and the well-established customs of the Occident to this plague-ridden, blighted corner of the Orient'.[11] As Joseph Conrad might have put it, Herzl's Jewish state would be an 'outpost of progress' in 'the heart of darkness'.

It was inevitable from the beginning that the relationship between the immigrant Zionist Jews and the indigenous Palestinian Arabs would result in conflict, since the Zionist movement was determined to establish a state for Jews in a territory which was already inhabited,[12] and in which Jews constituted less than 5 per cent of the total population.[13] Contrary to the sanitized version of Zionist intentions promoted by the State of Israel until recently, the Zionist archives themselves confirm that 'ethnic cleansing' was foreseen as necessary, was planned for and was put into operation at the first opportunity in 1948–49, and again in 1967. Despite public protestations to the contrary, the major Zionist ideologues were well aware of the demographic realities in Palestine, and recognized from the beginning that their determination to establish a state for Jews would require the expulsion of the indigenous non-Jews.[14] Military conquest, rather than a moral appeal to a 'right of return', then, was the order of the day among the Zionist ideologues prior to the establishment of the State of Israel. The expulsion of the Palestinian Arabs would of necessity be a direct consequence of the Jewish 'right of return'.

What makes the case of Israel-Palestine unique is the claim that the consequential expulsion of the indigenous non-Jewish population belongs within the domain of the 'rights' of those perpetrating the expulsion, rather than being merely the fruit of force. The designation 'right' implies the support of a moral framework bestowing 'legitimacy', while conquest is conquest, the product of military might, which, in the eyes of the victims at least, lacks legitimacy.

For the Zionist 'right' to establish a state in Palestine to prevail in the moral domain it would need to be shown to be of superior authority to the 'right' of the indigenous Palestinian Arabs to remain undisturbed in their own homeland. In the absence of a 'human right' to justify the expulsion of the indigenous population of Palestine appeal would have to be made to an altogether higher authority, to claim any level of moral approval. Thus appeal is made to the land narratives of the Bible, since they appear to bestow no less than divine authority on the promise of land to one people, with the concomitant mandate to cleanse it of its indigenous people.

THE BIBLE AND THE REDEEMING IDEA OF COLONIALISM

Awaiting the turn of the tide on the Thames as he embarked on another colonial expedition, Joseph Conrad's Marlow muses on the whole enterprise of imperial conquest, whether in Roman Britain or in the European Congo:

They were conquerors, and for that you want only brute force – nothing to boast of, when you have it, since your strength is just an accident arising from the weakness of others. They grabbed what they could get for the sake of what was to be got. It was just robbery with violence, aggravated murder on a great scale, and men going at it blind – as is very proper for those who tackle a darkness. The conquest of the earth, which mostly means the taking it away from those who have a different complexion or slightly flatter noses than ourselves, is not a pretty thing when you look into it too much. What redeems it is the idea only. An idea at the back of it; not a sentimental pretence but an idea; and an unselfish belief in the idea – something you can set up, and bow down before, and offer a sacrifice to. (Conrad, *Heart of Darkness*)

Whatever pangs of conscience one might have about the expulsion of three-quarters of a million Palestinian Arabs, and the destruction of their villages to ensure they would not return, the Bible can be appealed to salve it. Ironically, although a programme originally despised by both wings of Judaism, Orthodox and Reform, as being anti-religious (by the Orthodox) and contrary to the universal mission of Judaism (by Reform Jewry), Zionism is now at the core of religious Jewish self-identification. And not a few credulous Christians allow themselves to be sucked into the vortex. Indeed, in evaluating Zionism, the normal rules of morality are suspended: only in this instance is ethnic cleansing applauded by the religious spirit.

The link between the Zionist conquest and the Bible is reflected widely in both the mainstream theology of the Jewish religious establishment, and in much Christian ecclesial and theological opinion. Indeed, some Christians and Jews see Zionism as the instrument of God promoting the ingathering of Jews, and in such circles anyone who opposes Zionism is considered to oppose God himself.[15] Indeed, the view that the Bible provides the title-deed for the establishment of the State of Israel and for its policies since 1948 is so pervasive, not only in Christian Zionist and Jewish Zionist circles but even within mainstream Christian theology and university biblical studies, that any attempt to raise the issue is sure to elicit opposition. The disfavour usually takes the form of personal abuse and the intimidation of publishers. One is seldom honoured by having the substantive moral issues addressed in the usual academic fashion. However, such issues must be raised, if only because the integrity of the scholastic enterprise itself is at stake: Zionism has left its mark even on the biblical academy.

That the Bible provides an imperative for Jews to return to *Eretz Yisrael* is not well attested by the theory or the practice of Jewry. Indeed, when Zionism established itself as a political programme in 1897, it had the support of only a minuscule percentage of Jews and was disdained by virtually all sides of religious Jewry. The majority of Jews world-wide did not share the enthusiasm of the Bible for *Eretz Yisrael* to the point of wanting to live there, and neither Jewish nor Christian scholars considered the subject to be a burning issue. Perceptions changed only in the course of the twentieth century, especially with the establishment of the State of Israel.[16] The planned and executed expulsion of the indigenous Arab population of what became the state, exacerbated by the aftermath of Israel's victory in the 1967 war, required a formidable *apologia*. Hence the new interest in the biblical legend.

Given its alleged centrality in Old Testament covenant theology, it is indeed surprising that 'the land', which occurs some 1,705 times in the English Bible, had attracted so little scholastic attention until recently. Gerhard von Rad lamented in his 1943 pioneering essay that, despite the importance of the theme in the Bible from Genesis to Joshua, no thorough investigation had been made.[17] More recently, James M. Scott finds it surprising that the biblical academy had not done more work on 'the exile'.[18] However, no explanation is offered for the previous lack of interest.

I take the view that the recent interest in 'the land' and 'the return from exile' is intimately related to the Zionist programme. Even after von Rad's comment no serious study of 'the land' was undertaken for another 30 years, and the timing of that work was no coincidence. W.D. Davies acknowledged that he had written his seminal *The Gospel and the Land* (1974)[19] at the request of friends in Jerusalem, who just before the 1967 war urged his support for the cause of Israel.[20] In his 1982 work, Davies publicized his hermeneutical key: 'Here I have concentrated on what in my judgement must be the beginning for an understanding of this [Israeli-Palestinian] conflict: the sympathetic attempt to comprehend the Jewish tradition.'[21] Moreover, while Davies considers 'the land' from virtually every conceivable perspective, little attention is given to broadly moral and human rights' issues. Furthermore, he excluded from his concern, 'What happens when the understanding of the Promised Land in Judaism conflicts with the claims of the traditions and occupancy of its other peoples[.]' He excuses himself by saying that to engage that issue would demand another volume,[22] without indicating his intention to embark upon such an enterprise.

ARCHAEOLOGY, THE BIBLE AND STATE FORMATION

Political interests also spurred on the new fascination with the archaeology of the region. From the beginning, the Western Christians who established the discipline of archaeology in Palestine were determined 'to prove the veracity of Scripture'. On the political front, the race for choice archaeological sites became an index of diplomatic prestige for the European nations in their scramble for Palestine in the nineteenth century. Since the establishment of the State of Israel in 1948, archaeology has become a cornerstone of Israel's civic religion, testifying to exclusively Jewish claims to the land, with the biblical narrative providing legitimacy for cleansing it of its indigenous Arab population. Archaeology's intensive search for 'ancient Israel' has been driven by the desire to uncover the taproot of Western (Christian) civilization, and, more recently, to underpin Israeli national identity. Digging in the region from the beginning of the modern interest in archaeology, then, has been Bible study, or politics by other means.

Hebrew archaeology from the 1920s was nationalist, and became more so with the foundation of the State of Israel. The biblical narrative functioned as the objective historical account of Jews' title to the land, a claim borne out by archaeological findings. This was the case even for secular nationalists uninterested in the Bible as the repository of a theological claim to Palestine. Zionism, then, was a return to the Bible no less than to the land.

One notes also the changing function of the more popular archaeological sites in the attempt to make essentially modern, politically rooted assumptions appear timeless and inevitable. Moreover, concentration on the archaeological past was marked by a decided detachment from the lives of the people of the modern cities and villages. The lifeless mounds veiling earlier civilizations were interpreted as illustrating a continuous process of racial conquest, in which more 'vigorous' races had always overcome the more 'passive' ones.

Indeed, William Foxwell Albright, the doyen of biblical archaeologists in the twentieth century, had no qualms about the plunder attendant upon Joshua's enterprise, which he understood in a largely historically reliable way:

> From the impartial standpoint of a philosopher of history, it often seems necessary that a people of markedly inferior type should vanish before a people of superior potentialities, since there is a point beyond which racial mixture cannot go without disaster ... Thus the Canaanites, with their orgiastic nature worship, their cult of fertility in the form of serpent symbols and sensuous nudity, and their gross mythology, were replaced by Israel, with its pastoral simplicity and purity of life, its lofty monotheism, and its severe code of ethics.[23]

Albright wrote thus only a decade after the full horrors of the Nazi 'ethnic cleansing' had been revealed. Yet, prior to Keith Whitelam's critique,[24] no commentator had drawn attention to Albright's undisguised racist attitudes, which were typical of virtually every western colonial enterprise, which predicated that the 'superior' peoples of the West had the right to exploit, and in some cases exterminate, the 'natives'. Reflecting these conventional values, Albright also judged that through Zionism Jews would bring to the Near East all the benefits of European civilization.[25] In a similar vein, George E. Wright, another distinguished American biblical scholar, justified the genocide of the narrative of Joshua in terms of the inferiority of the indigenous culture.[26]

It is all the more urgent, then, that the academy responsible for the exegesis of texts of such rhetorical moral problematic, texts carrying the additional moral burden that they have been employed as instruments of oppression for centuries beyond their compositions, should subject them to a thorough moral investigation. The academy should not encourage biblical scholars to continue to seek refuge by expending virtually all their intellectual energies on an unrecoverable past, thereby releasing themselves from the obligation of engaging in contemporary discourse. It is not morally acceptable to maintain an academic detachment from significant engagement in current, real issues, with the excuse that modern life is beyond the period of inquiry, and that, in any case, such critical moral questions can comfortably be left to specialists in political ethics. Responsibility for moral judgement and action rests with the individual, and cannot be exercised vicariously, even when shifted to others more gifted, learned and morally upright than oneself. The Exodus narrative is an appropriate starting point for investigation.

THE PROBLEM OF THE EXODUS PARADIGM

The biblical paradigm of the Exodus is well known. Within the Old Testament itself it reappears in the credos of the Israelites, in their historical, legal and prophetic texts, and in their celebration of Passover. Moreover, much of the imagery of Passover is taken up in the New Testament interpretation of the death and resurrection of Jesus and salvific consequences that followed. Moreover, it has served as an inspiration and ideological foundation document for liberation movements, and as a model for virtually all expressions of liberation theology in cultures influenced by the Bible (Latin America, Africa, South Africa, South Korea, the Philippines). So profound has been the impact of the Exodus narrative that its portrayal of Yahweh's 'option for the oppressed' gives it a virtually perennial and ubiquitous relevance, making it into a paradigm of all liberation.[27] However, the use of the biblical narrative in such circles is selective and naive. Invariably, it is only the deliverance from Egypt of the enslaved Israelites and their entrance into the land 'flowing with milk and honey' to which allusion is made.[28] Readers are easily impressed and consoled by that story's capacity to lift the spirits of the oppressed.

But, in addition to predicating a message of deliverance from slavery in Egypt, the Exodus narrative posits the ethnic cleansing of the Promised Land as not only legitimate but as being in conformity with the demands of the divinity. One's perspective on the story takes on a different complexion when it is 'read with the eyes of the Canaanites'. The problematic of the text appears in even sharper relief when it is acknowledged that it has been used as part of the justification for exploiting various native peoples. In addition to being 'read with the eyes of the Canaanites', then, the text should be read with the eyes of any of several cultures that have been victims of a colonialism fired by an imperialism fuelled by religious fervour, whether the native peoples of North or Latin America, the Maoris in New Zealand, the Aborigines in Australia, the Khoikhoi and San in southern Africa or, more recently, the Palestinians in Palestine.

The Exodus narrative does indeed portray Yahweh as having compassion for the misery of his people, and as willing to deliver them from the Egyptians and bring to a land flowing with milk and honey (Exodus 3.7–8). However, though the reading of that text, both in the Christian liturgy and in the classical texts of liberation theologies, halts abruptly in the middle of v. 8, at the description of the land as one 'flowing with milk and honey', the biblical text itself continues, 'to the country of the Canaanites, the Hittites, the Amorites, the Perizzites, the Hivites, and the Jebusites'.[29] While the promised land of the narrative indeed flowed with milk and honey, it had no lack of indigenous peoples, and, guaranteed by the divine promise, would soon flow with their blood:

> ... for I will hand over to you the inhabitants of the land, and you shall drive them out before you. You shall make no covenant with them and their gods. They shall not live in your land, or they will make you sin against me; for if you worship their gods, it will surely be a snare to you. (Exodus 23.27–33)

Yahweh's mandate to cleanse the land is made even more explicit in Deuteronomy:

> When Yahweh your God brings you into the land that you are about to enter and occupy, and he clears away many nations before you – the Hittites, the Girgashites, the Amorites, the Canaanites, the Perizzites, the Hivites ... and when Yahweh your God gives them over to you and you defeat them, then you must utterly destroy them. Make no covenant with them and show them no mercy ... Break down their altars, smash their pillars, hew down their sacred poles, and burn their idols with fire. For you are a people holy to Yahweh your God; Yahweh your God has chosen you out of all the peoples on earth to be his people, his treasured possession. (Deuteronomy 7.1–11; see also 9.1–5; 11.8–9, 23, 31–2)

Moreover, in the rules for the conduct of war, when a besieged town surrenders, all its inhabitants shall serve as forced labour; if not, the Israelites shall kill all its males and take as booty the women, children, livestock and everything else in the town (Deuteronomy 20.11–14). The narrative, then, presents 'ethnic cleansing' as not only legitimate, but as required by the divinity:

> But as for the towns of these peoples that Yahweh your God is giving you as an inheritance, you must not let anything that breathes remain alive. You shall annihilate them – the Hittites and the Amorites, the Canaanites and the Perizzites, the Hivites and the Jebusites – just as Yahweh your God has commanded, so that they may not teach you to do all the abhorrent things that they do for their gods, and you thus sin against Yahweh your God. (Deuteronomy 20.16–18)

Mercifully, in a gesture of ecological indulgence, fruit-bearing trees are to be spared, as is a captive 'beautiful woman whom you desire and want to marry' (Deuteronomy 21.11).

Despite the inextricable link in the biblical narrative between extrication from slavery and the mandate to commit genocide, in the case of liberation movements the oppressed are encouraged to assume the fortunes of the liberated Israelite slaves only, and are not burdened with the guilt of dispossessing or annihilating others. Thus, Gustavo Gutiérrez, the father of liberation theology, portrays the Exodus event as 'the breaking away from a situation of despoliation and misery and the beginning of the construction of a just and comradely society. It is the suppression of disorder and the creation of a new order.' Following his literalist reading of the Exodus narrative, Gutiérrez shifts to the text of Isaiah 42.5–7, implying that the act of liberation from Egypt ended with such an idyllic scene: 'The God who makes the cosmos from chaos is the same God who leads Israel from alienation to liberation.' In line with the general thrust of liberation theology, Gutiérrez excludes the reference to the original inhabitants of Canaan in his summary of Exodus 3.7–10, making no reference to the plight of those whom, in the biblical legend, God reduces from order to chaos. Instead he agrees that,

With the Exodus a new age has struck for humanity: redemption from misery. If the Exodus had not taken place, marked as it was by the twofold sign of the overriding will of God and the free and conscious assent of men, the historical destiny of humanity would have followed another course.[30]

It seems not to have occurred to Gutiérrez that the indigenous population might have been quite pleased had the destiny of humanity indeed taken another direction.

James Cone, the father of Black Theology, also is seduced by a partial reading of the Exodus motif. Although particularly sensitive to a reading of the Bible, which sees it as a document giving preference to the poor, he, and other proponents of Afro-American Theology, fail to deal with the destruction of the people who pay the price for the liberation and settlement of the Israelites.[31] *Pace* Gutiérrez and others, it is not the case that 'the entire Bible ... mirrors God's predilection for the weak and abused of human history'.[32] The real poor of the Exodus narrative are the ones forgotten in the victory, the Canaanites and others, who are to be pushed aside or exterminated by the religious zeal of the invading Israelites with God on their side. Combining the Exodus from Egypt with the Eisodus (entry) into the land of the Canaanites and others, as the narrative requires, the biblical paradigm appears to legitimize, if not indeed demand, the behaviour of the *conquistadores* and other perpetrators of colonialist imperialism, including those in North America.

Many Puritan preachers referred to the Native Americans as Amalekites and Canaanites, who, if they refused to be converted, were worthy of annihilation. Thus Cotton Mather (1648–1728), author of *Magnalia Christi Americana* (1702), delivered a sermon in Boston in September 1689, charging the members of the armed forces in New England to consider themselves to be Israel in the wilderness, confronted by Amalek: pure Israel was obliged to 'cast out [the Indians] as dirt in the streets' and eliminate and exterminate them.[33] In a similar vein, Herbert Gibbs, an eighteenth-century preacher, thanked the mercies of God for extirpating the enemies of Israel in Canaan (that is, Native Americans).[34] The mythology is deeply rooted. Even at a time when former colonial peoples are embarrassed by their past, the Catholic dioceses of the United States draw a parallel between the Israelite and European conquests in the special Preface to the Eucharistic Prayer for the liturgical celebration of Thanksgiving Day:

Once you chose a people and gave them a destiny and, when you brought them out of bondage to freedom, they carried with them the promise that all men would be blessed and all men could be free. What the prophets pledged was fulfilled in Jesus

Christ ... It has come to pass in every generation ... It happened to our fathers, who came to this land as if out of the desert into a place of promise and hope ...

The Exodus/Eisodus narrative, then, poses difficulties for any reader who is neither naive nor amoral.[35] While the Exodus motif might be perceived as a paradigm for liberation for the former victims, it is one of colonial plunder for the indigenous population. That is not only the plain sense of the biblical narrative, but also the way the text has been used in a range of colonial enterprises.

While it may be plain to modern readers of the Bible that some of the narratives of the Bible have played a huge part in the imperializing impulse, it appears not to bother biblical scholars to the point of critical opposition. Deuteronomy, for example, despite its requirement of the genocide of the indigenous population of Canaan, is held in the highest esteem in the biblical academy. Commentators conventionally assess it to be a theological book *par excellence*, and the focal point of the religious history of the Old Testament. In the 1995 Lattey Lecture in Cambridge University, Professor Norbert Lohfink interpreted the laws of Deuteronomy in terms of defining a utopian society in which there would be no poor.[36] Naturally, one found the prospect inviting and was pleased to reflect upon 'Mount Zion as the place where they [the nations] can learn how a better society functions'. Moreover, Lohfink dealt with Exodus only in terms of the delivery from Egypt of a marginalized and exploited group, without any reference to what was to follow. In my role as the formal proposer of a vote of thanks, I invited Professor Lohfink to consider whether, in the light of the insistence on a mandate to commit genocide, the utopian society would be possible only after the invading Israelites had wiped out the indigenous inhabitants. The protocol left the last word with me, and subsequently I was given a second word, being invited to deliver the 1997 Lattey Lecture, for which I chose the title, *A Land Flowing with Milk, Honey, and People*.[37]

The biblical text is problematic, not only because of its reception history, but also in virtue of its content. G.E.M. de Ste. Croix, an expert on class politics in the ancient world, asserted that the Israelites were the one people who felt able to claim that they had a divine command to exterminate whole populations among those they conquered. There is no text in ancient culture, he added, which matches the Bible in terms of ferocity, a detail seldom dwelt on today by Christians or Jews, despite the fact that such incomparable ferocity is revealed not by hostile sources but by the very literature they themselves regard as sacred.[38] The conceptual moral problem of the relevant biblical narratives is exacerbated by the fact that their value system, with all the authority their religious provenance can confer, has been incorporated as a 'legitimizing' agent in the ideologies of virtually all European imperialist enterprises, the consequences of which have been the irreversible suffering of entire indigenous communities and, in some cases, their virtual annihilation as a people.[39]

The question is not without contemporary relevance. The establishment of the State of Israel is portrayed not infrequently as virtually a re-enactment of the first Exodus from slavery in Egypt to freedom in the Promised Land, usually ignoring the narrative's portrayal of the Israelite ethnic cleansing of the land of Canaan, as well as maintaining innocence of the dispersal of the indigenous Arab population in 1948. Thus Lapide sees in the 'present-day return of the Jews to the land of their fathers' the culmination of the historical connection between Israel's persecution and its persistence through trust in God.[40] Such assignations are also a feature of the Jewish religious settlers in the Occupied Territories to this day, for whom the biblical narrative is the core factor legitimizing the Zionist conquest. Such use of the narrative demands close attention, not least against the background of its current application.

BIBLICAL RESONANCES OF ZIONISM

Despite the non- and frequently anti-religious dispositions of the major Zionist ideologues, the biblical narrative was available in the background as a support. In *Der Judenstaat,* Herzl showed that, while his motivation was not dictated by a religious longing for the ancient homeland, nor by appeal to biblical injunctions, for example, to go to the Promised Land in order to observe the *Torah*,[41] his enterprise was replete with religious overtones. Concerning whether the state should be established in Argentina or Palestine, he said, 'Palestine is our ever-memorable historic home. The very name Palestine would attract our people with a force of marvellous potency' (p. 96). He promised that 'The Temple will be visible from long distances, for it is only our ancient faith that has kept us together' (p. 102). He appealed for the support of the rabbis (p. 129), and asserted, 'our community of race is peculiar and unique, for we are bound together only by the faith of our fathers' (p. 146). Herzl ended his pamphlet with an evocation of the exploits of biblical heroes:

A wondrous generation of Jews will spring into existence. The Maccabeans will rise again ... The Jews who wish for a State will have it. We shall live at last as free men on our own soil, and die peacefully in our own homes. The world will be freed by our liberty, enriched by our wealth, magnified by our greatness. And whatever we attempt there to accomplish for our own welfare, will react powerfully and beneficially for the good of humanity. (pp. 156–7)

Little wonder, then, that at various times people referred to Herzl as the Messiah, or King of Israel, and as the fulfilment of the prophecies of the Jewish Scriptures. Nevertheless, the Jewish state would not be a theocracy: 'We shall keep our priests within the confines of their temples in the same way as we keep our professional army within the confines of their barracks' (p. 146).

While Herzl acknowledged that the notions of 'Chosen People', and 'return' to the 'Promised Land' would be potent factors in mobilizing Jewish opinion – despite the fact that he himself,[42] as well as the leading Zionists were either non-religious, atheists or agnostics – rabbis representing all shades of opinion denounced Zionism as a fanaticism and contrary to the scriptures, and affirmed their loyalty to Germany or elsewhere.[43]

The hostile attitude of the religious establishments of both Orthodox and Reform Judaism gradually changed in the course of the 1930s and 1940s, and almost disappeared in the wake of the 'miraculous victory' of 1967. Indeed, in most Jewish religious circles today the existence of the state is at the core of the Jewish credo.[44] Moreover, the religious wing in Israel-Palestine is at the forefront of the opposition to political 'compromise' with the Palestinians, with very few Orthodox rabbis supporting it, and many at the vanguard of its destruction. That secular Zionism, largely agnostic and even atheistic was able to engage the support of religious Jews, both Orthodox and Reform, who bitterly opposed its programme for most of the period prior to the creation of the state, is one of the most remarkable ideological coalitions of the twentieth century.

The role of the biblical narrative within the Zionist ideology increased significantly in the wake of the 1967 war and the rise of *Gush Emunim*. The biblical paradigm was the backdrop for the Zionist self-portrayal as the (sole) 'descendants of the biblical children of Israel', while the natives were 'Canaanites'. This introduced into the discourse a religious authority justifying the new conquest of the land and the maltreatment of its population. Measured against the divine right of the colonizers, appeal to the human rights of the local population, who were considered to be interlopers and obstacles to the divine plan, carried no conviction.

Historically, however, the Palestinian Arabs are likely to have been descendants of the inhabitants of the region from the earliest times. Indeed, Palestine has been multicultural and multi-ethnic from the beginning, as one can read between the lines even in the biblical narrative.[45] Its 'ethnic markers' of the diverse inhabitants of Bronze or Iron Age Palestine ('Canaanite' during the Bronze Age, 'Israelite' and 'Philistine' in the Iron Age period) do not correspond to the social realities of those periods. Moreover, the concept of 'children of Israel' as a self-identifying metaphor of early Judaism was created in the process of the Bible's formation.

Moreover, while population transfers were effected in the Assyrian, Babylonian and Persian periods, most of the indigenous population remained in place. Indeed, after Jerusalem was destroyed in AD 70 the population by and large remained *in situ*, and did so again after the suppression of Bar Kochba's revolt in AD 135.[46] Similarly during the Byzantine period, there was no question of the majority population being driven out. Likewise in the seventh century, when the majority became Muslim, few were driven from the land. Thus, many Palestinian Jews became Christians, and in turn Muslims. Ironically, many of the forebears of Palestinian Arab refugees may well have been Jewish.

THE UBIQUITOUS AND PERENNIAL DIASPORA LONGING FOR THE LAND OF ISRAEL

The biblical narrative has been determinative in other ways as well, and has established the parameters within which much popular opinion expresses itself. The Hebrew word for 'exile' (*golah*, or its derivative *galut*) is invariably associated with being under the curse of the divine banishment from the homeland which some of the Old Testament prophets predicted. Nevertheless, in rendering *golah*, the Greek (Septuagint) translators of the Hebrew Bible chose the language of emigration or colonization (*apoikia, aichmalosia,* etc.), rather the standard Greek word for 'exile' or 'banishment' (*phuge*). No less intriguing is the fact that while the Septuagint translators chose a rare Greek noun *diaspora* and its cognate verb *diaspeirein* to render a variety of Hebrew terms, it never does so for *golah* and its derivatives. While these facts are indisputable, there are two poles of interpretation.

One argues that the change in terminology from that of exile to emigration or colonization reflects a shift from an ideology or theology of 'exile'. In such a view, displacement from the land was considered no longer to be the result of divine punishment, nor did returning to the land constitute the great hope of the people. Rather, due not least to the flourishing of the institution of the synagogue, which brought cohesion to Jewish religious and social identity away from the land, Jewish identity could be safeguarded in an accommodation with Greco-Roman social organization, reflecting a confident diaspora ideology or theology. As a result, the impetus to return to the land receded and was replaced by a more positive attitude to living outside of the land.

The second, contrasting interpretation counters such a benevolent assessment of living outside the land. It argues that *diaspora* and *diaspeirein*, whether in classical Greek literature, the Septuagint, Jewish literature of the Greco-Roman period, the New Testament or the patristic writings, are frequently used in the negative sense of destructive decomposition into individual parts. In the Septuagint itself, the terms are used in the context of the covenant between Yahweh and his people, in which dispersion is seen as the final punishment for disobedience, which will be reversed in a return to the land only when the nation repents. At this juncture Yahweh in his mercy will regather them into the land.

We can detect in these two conflicting attitudes some of the differences marking Orthodox and Reform Judaism before the advent, and in the early decades of political Zionism. What is clear, however, is that the negative assessment of the diaspora results from a theological position that is well supported within the biblical narrative: dispersion is the divine punishment for the people's sin, endangers the existence and identity of Jews and will be brought to an end by God himself, who will bring the people back to the land. But once one examines the social realities other than through the lens of the biblical ideologues a different picture emerges.

From the ideological/theological perspective of the biblical authors, the period in Babylon (586–538 BC) was one of unrelieved lament for the homeland (see, for example, Psalm 147). In reality, the evidence for the severity of the conditions in Babylon is by no means uniform – some implying no overt oppression or loss of identity – suggesting that the exile was not quite the catastrophe the biblical authors intimate. Indeed, it is not easy to reconcile the view that Babylonian exile was an enormous physical, social and psychological trauma with the reality that many Jews remained in Babylon after permission in 538 BC allowed them to return to Zion. In fact, it was held in antiquity that the 'ten tribes' had never returned (for example, Josephus, *Antiquities* 11.133; 4 Ezra 13. 39–47; *Mishnah Sanhedrin* 10.3 V). Moreover, documents from the Persian period show clearly that deported Judahites remained in Babylon, and the region became the home of the majority of world Jewry from the exile to the end of antiquity.[47]

Of course, Israelites/Jews were expelled and deported, whether by the Assyrians (721 BC), the Babylonians (586 BC), Artaxerxes Ochus (345–343 BC?), or Tigranes (83–69 BC), and we know that the Romans carried off hundreds of prisoners of war to Rome after Pompey's conquest of Jerusalem in 63 BC. Moreover, some deportation of Jews followed the defeat of the Jewish rebellion of AD 70, but there was no mass exodus and the community reorganized itself under the leadership of the body of rabbis operating from Yavneh.[48] Moreover, after the defeat of Bar Kochba's revolt (AD 135), Hadrian expelled Jews from the territory of Jerusalem only (Eusebius, *Ecclesiastical History* 4: 6.3).

It is no less true that there was a widespread Jewish diaspora in the Hellenistic period that was altogether unrelated to expulsion. Voluntary emigration of Jews from Palestine into the cities of the 'civilized world' was widespread, and there is evidence of Jewish communities outside Palestine long before Alexander the Great. Alexander himself encouraged the foundation of new cities and invited new settlers on whom he bestowed various privileges and even citizenship. Jews answered the call in considerable numbers, going to Syria, Egypt and other newly founded Hellenistic cities.

In fact, Jewish voluntary emigration extended to Mesopotamia, Media, Babylonia, Dura-Europos, the Arabian Peninsula, Asia Minor, the north coast of the Black Sea, Cyrenaica, the North African provinces of Africa proconsularis, Numidia and Mauretania, Macedonia and Greece, the Greek Islands, Cyprus, Crete, Rhodes, Delos, Euboea, Cos, the Balkans, Italy and Rome, and in the Christian period to Spain, southern Gaul and Germany.[49] There were colonies of Jews throughout most of the inhabited world, as known by people in the West. Indeed, the picture one gets is that of Jews founding a colony, after the fashion of the Athenians founding colonies. Salo W. Baron estimates that Jews in the middle of the first century AD numbered more than eight million, most of whom lived in the diaspora.[50] However acute the theoretical question of whether religious Jews could live other than in *Eretz Yisrael*, the communities of Jews who settled throughout Europe, North Africa and east of Palestine gave a pragmatic answer.

Despite the voluntary nature of much Jewish emigration, the common use of the term 'the Jewish diaspora' establishes an artificial dichotomy between 'the land of Israel' and everywhere else. The polarity also suggests that conditions in the widespread 'diaspora' were consistent, uniform and, invariably, altogether disadvantageous to Jews. However, in reality, in antiquity as today, not every Jew in 'the diaspora' experienced alienation.[51]

Indeed, the portrayal of the conditions of Jews in the diaspora has been marked by overarching generalizations and extrapolations,[52] heavily influenced by biblical texts, and the predominantly negative attitude of the (Palestinian) rabbis to the diaspora. Much of the attitude towards exile is strongly influenced by the biblical narrative, read in the synagogues of the diaspora (Leviticus 26; Deuteronomy 28; 30; 2 Kings 23–5; and Jeremiah 32–45), which, in its turn, provided occasion for reflection by the rabbis, and found its way into the rhythm of Jewish prayer. Jewish works of the Second Temple period written in Judea insisted that the diaspora was the result of sin.[53] Just as Adam had transgressed and was cast out of the Garden, so his transgressing descendants were exiled from Jerusalem (see 2 Esdras 3.24–28). The equiparation of diaspora living with sin was challenged, of course, by rabbis living outside the land, some of whom viewed dispersion as part of the universal mission of Jews.

Furthermore, the destruction of the Temple in AD 70 and the Bar Kochba débâcle of AD 135 induced the Palestinian rabbis to demand even greater attachment to *Eretz Yisrael*. This reflected the challenge to their authority, which the Jews across the Euphrates in particular presented. The two, rival centres of Jewish authority had different views on who was to guide the religious life of the Jewish people: who constituted the central *halakhic* authority? For the Palestinian Jews life outside the land was futile, while for those in Babylonia the benefits of 'Zion' and 'the Land' were already to hand: Davidic leadership, remnants of the Temple, links with the Patriarchs, etc. Indeed, the Jews of Talmudic Babylonia (third–fifth century AD) displayed a distinctive, militantly pro-Babylonian 'local patriotism' and a definite sense of being at home within the Persian Empire.

In fact, the Babylonian Talmud projects the Babylonian diaspora as akin to a second Jewish homeland, with roots going back to the formative years of Israelite nationhood. This attitude, in turn, evoked censure from the rabbinic establishment in *Eretz Yisrael*. These Palestinian rabbis, for the first time in Jewish history, generated an ideology of disdain for Jewish life in the diaspora (for example, Tosefta, *'Aboda Zara* 4.5). Nevertheless, despite the strain, the rabbis in the two regions reached an accommodation whereby the Jews of Babylonia could remain loyal to Palestine, while modifying patterns of behaviour to enable them to continue to thrive outside it. With respect to *halakhic* authority, while their Palestinian counterparts referred to the authoritative status of only those living in *Eretz Yisrael,* the Babylonian sages show a preference for the foremost scholars of their generation.

Furthermore, the notion of Israel as separate also has a long, but by no means uniform history.[54] The famous prediction in Balaam's oracle, that Israel would not be reckoned among the nations (Numbers 23.9), was assessed variously by divers Jewish communities in the different areas of the widespread diaspora in the Hellenistic period alone. Philo, living contentedly in Alexandria in the first half of the first century AD, interpreted the oracle as indicative of a demarcation on the basis of the exceptional ancestral customs of Jews, and 'not because their dwelling-place is set apart and their land severed from others' (*De Vita Mosis* I.278). The Jewish community had lived in Alexandria for centuries alongside Greeks and Egyptians, and he had no reason to doubt that it would continue to do so for centuries to come. For his part, Josephus, in commenting on Balaam's oracle, stressed not merely the social distinctiveness of Jewish customs, but the ethical superiority of their virtue and their customs (*Antiquities* 4.114). The perspectives reflected in these two first-century Jews, one in Alexandria and the other in Rome, invites inquiry into the social and cultural strategies of Jews in the Mediterranean diaspora – not in an undifferentiated 'diaspora', but in the quite diverse geographical locations, and changing political fortunes that marked the actual conditions of Jewish communities scattered throughout the Mediterranean world.

There is abundant evidence of Jews being firmly and contentedly rooted in communities throughout the diaspora, and, as Philo expresses it, taking a certain pride in the ubiquity of Jews throughout Europe and Asia, encouraging them to see their 'new locations' as their fatherland (*In Flaccum* 46). However, those who found themselves in the diaspora against their wills eagerly awaited return to the 'holy land' (for example, *Sibylline Oracles* 5.260–85). Some may even have considered themselves to be 'perishing as foreigners in a foreign land', living lives that 'have become entangled in impieties in our exile' (3 Maccabees 6. 3, 10).

In the centuries just before and after the inauguration of the Christian era, travel of Jews, whether soldiers, slaves, refugees or economic migrants, between Palestine and Egypt is well documented, and physical proximity ensured easy contact between Syrian Jews and Palestine. Apart from the religious attachment to the Temple, and pilgrimage thereto, however, there is little evidence that there was any substantial link between Jews in the diaspora and in Palestine. The Jewish Scriptures and festivals, of course, reinforced the significance of the land, and the promised return to it, and diaspora Jews wrote in glowing terms about the beauties of Jerusalem and its temple (for example, Aristeas 83–120; Philo, *Legatio* 157; Josephus, *Wars* 5.184–247). But they chose to remain elsewhere.

ZIONISM AND THE RELIGIOUS SPIRIT

From its very inception, Zionism was a secular ideology, which was bitterly opposed by the Jewish religious establishment, since it was an extension into a nationalist mode of the Enlightenment spirit, which threatened religious particularism. Diaspora living was not a problem for religious Jews, since the diaspora was a condition ordained by God, who alone would bring it to an end. To describe it as a problem was to verge on the blasphemous.

Until the modern period, the predominant view among religious Jews was that Jews were living in exile because of their sins. Eventually, in the New Age of his own making, God would restore them to their land through the Messiah, who would conquer the land, rebuild the Temple and reconstitute a Jewish society in *Eretz Yisrael* based on the *Torah*. God would grant glory to Israel, and all peoples would acknowledge his dominion, at which point there would be universal peace (see, for example, Tobit 14.4–7). The predominantly secular Zionist movement was a rebellion against and a conscious repudiation of classical Judaism and its theological tenets. Nevertheless, political Zionists with some sensitivity to the religious element in Judaism could tap into the ancient symbols of the Promised Land and the Covenant, and give them a new significance, refracted through the modern conditions of the Jewish people. Hence, Zionism could be endowed with particular religious significance, if not immediately, at least *post factum*.

Classical religious, messianic Zionism contrasted sharply with the political Zionism, which ultimately fashioned the State of Israel. Moreover, the religious Jews who came to Palestine before the advent of Zionism did so without any political aspirations, considering all efforts to create a Jewish state to be sinful interference with the messianic time-table of Almighty God. The pietists who made up the old Jewish settlements in Palestine were bitterly opposed to the newly arrived secularists, who systematically violated the *Torah*. The newcomer Zionists, for their part, considered the pietists to be decadent parasites who were blind to the vision of Jewish redemption. This state of affairs was to change.

Reform Judaism, for its part, rejected all forms of Jewish nationalism and utterly repudiated Zionism. In highlighting the universalist values of the unity of the human family, and the ideals of liberty, equality and fraternity, it sought to wean Judaism away from its parochialist features and insert it into the liberal spirit of the day. Whereas traditional Judaism viewed practices, which required residency in Palestine (for example, agricultural and Temple rituals) as merely in suspension, the Reform leaders regarded them as no longer valid. Viewing Jewish history as evolutionary and dynamic, and according no essential significance to any one period, Reform Judaism rejected the notion that Jews outside of Palestine were 'in exile', and insisted that Jews constituted a religious community, not a nation. They had made their homes in and had become citizens of many states. For the American Reformers, the majority of American Jewry in the 1880s, living among other peoples provided Jews with an opportunity to let their light shine among the nations. American Jews were Americans of Mosaic persuasion. The establishment of a separate Jewish state was unnecessary and was a hindrance to Judaism's world-wide mission. Accordingly, the first prayer book of the movement removed all references to Jews being in exile and to the traditional hope that a Messiah would miraculously restore Jews to the homeland and rebuild the Temple in Jerusalem. It also eliminated all prayers for a return to Zion.

By the 1930s and 1940s, however, religious opposition to Zionism was on the wane, with both major camps beginning to put their energies behind the movement. Whatever hesitations attended the project, Israel's 'miraculous victory' in the 1967 war convinced many religious Jews that the Zionist enterprise was at the core of religious Judaism. Thus, Zionism, an essentially secular and mostly anti-religious enterprise, was endowed with particular religious significance. Although vehemently opposed to its programme from the beginning, nobody now is more supportive of its achievement than the religious establishment. The secular movement of Zionism, whose tenets diverged fundamentally from rabbinic eschatology, has been transposed into an ideology, which the majority of religious Jews regard as of divine origin. We are witnessing a process of resacralization, whereby irreligious, secular, nationalist salvation has been endowed with the mythology of traditional Jewish soteriology. Paradoxically, today, religious nationalism has rekindled the fire of the jaded secular nationalism that brought the state into existence, a phenomenon recognized as the most important ideological development in the history of the state. Clearly, in such a context the biblical narrative would be at the core of the justification for the Zionist project.[55]

CONCLUSIONS

Manifestly, 'right', 'conflicting rights' and 'conquest' feature in the discourse concerning Israel-Palestine. The exercise by the Zionists' of the Jewish 'right of return' to enter Palestine and conquer it prevailed over the 'right' of the indigenous Arab population to remain in their own homeland. However, in order to establish a 'right' to return, in contrast to having the military might to affect it, all the Jews of the world would have to constitute a clearly defined community, which could demonstrate its recent collective expulsion. Notwithstanding clear evidence to the contrary, there is a widespread assumption that the diaspora condition of Jews was invariably the result of their being expelled from their homeland, usually predicated as having happened in AD 70.

The Zionized expression of Jewish history takes the following popular form: the destruction of the Temple by the Romans in AD 70 symbolized the start of the long Jewish exile and ended with the Holocaust, the creation of Israel in 1948 and the conquest of the Six-Day War. In such a reading, all Jewish residence outside *Eretz Yisrael* is the result of forced expulsion and is inherently alienating. Jewish history and demographic realities in Palestine and elsewhere between AD 70 and the beginning of the nineteenth century are ignored, and the claim is made that the attachment to the land of Israel attributed to diaspora Jews, predicated as perennial and ubiquitous, found its appropriate realization in the achievement of the Zionist project. As we have seen, there never was a unified Jewish community which was exiled at one time, or even over a definite period.

While some Jews on occasion were forced into exile, others voluntarily emigrated. Indeed, modern scholarship on the fate of Jews in antiquity has shown that, while those with shallow roots in their environment bemoaned the conditions of their 'sojourn' away from home, others considered their diaspora position to be a real achievement, and, in the case of Josephus, viewed the whole world as their eternal home (*Antiquities* 4.115–16). Writing in Rome some two decades after the fall of Jerusalem in AD 70, he does so from the perspective of one fully committed to the diaspora. For Josephus the diaspora was a blessing (*Antiquities* 1.282). More widely, while 'the holy land' retained religious significance for diaspora Jews, whatever nostalgia they had towards Palestine reflected their social and political conditions, and was never sufficiently vigorous to induce more than a handful to 'return' even when the circumstances in the diaspora were difficult.

Moreover, the moral case for return of Jews is undermined where there is a considerable time-span between the expulsion and the determination to resettle. Indeed, the right to return dissolves into desuetude as that time-span exceeds reasonable limits; otherwise, international order would collapse. To concede the legitimacy of a Jewish law of return would open the floodgates for bizarre returns to ancestral homes at the expense of people in place for thousands of years.

In addition, no group has a right in customary international law to conquer and annex the territory of another people and expel its population. Furthermore, return to the land from which one has been expelled is a two-fold right under customary international law. The body of law on nationality requires a country to allow its nationals to reside within its territory, while the 'host' country has the right to demand that an expelled person be re-admitted to his/her own country. Moreover, individual rights require that each person has the right to reside in his/her own country. This right has a universally valid moral quality, and obtains for all peoples and for each individual person who experience expulsion.[56]

The exiled Palestinians constitute a quintessential example of a people with a right to return, since, in 1948, a clearly identified population was expelled by their Zionist conquerors, and has never renounced its rights. Nevertheless, Israel continues to deny the displaced Arabs' right of return, whether on the basis that they are not nationals of Israel or that Israel is not responsible for their displacement. Thus, by a legal subterfuge, which lacks any semblance of morality and satisfies only the self-delusion of the nation, Israel exculpates itself from the crime of displacing another people.

But a discourse based on considerations of human rights, respect for international law and conformity with UN resolutions[57] counts for little against a naive reading of the biblical narrative which is difficult to dislodge, even if, as we have seen, some of that narrative is problematic, containing texts of unsurpassed violence which are an affront to moral sensitivities. Moreover, the problem is not only theoretical. In addition to being morally reprehensible, some of these texts have fuelled gross injustices not least through colonialist enterprises. The Holy War traditions of the Old Testament pose an especially difficult moral problem. In addition to portraying God as one who cherishes the slaughter of his created ones, they acquit the killer of moral responsibility for his deeds, presenting them as a religious obligation. Every effort should be made to rescue the Bible from being a blunt instrument in the oppression of one people by another. If a naive interpretation of the Bible leads to such unacceptable conclusions, what kind of exegesis can rescue it?[58]

The view that the Bible can be understood in a straightforward, literal way must be surrendered. The first task of biblical exegesis is to respect the distinctive literary forms within the biblical narrative: history, epic, legend, fabricated myths of the past, prophecy and apocalyptic, and so on. In general, narratives purporting to describe the past cannot be assumed to be accurate records of it.

In particular, the biblical narratives pertaining to the divine promise of land to the Israelites and its conquest are not simple history, but reflect the religious and political ideologies of their much later authors. It is now part of the scholarly consensus that the patriarchal narratives of Genesis do not record events of an alleged patriarchal period, but are retrojections into a past about which the writers knew little, reflecting the author's intentions at the later period of composition. It is naive, then, to cleave to the view that God made the promise of progeny and land to Abraham after the fashion indicated in Genesis 15.

As we have seen, the Exodus narrative poses particular difficulties for any reader who is neither naive nor amoral. It is the entrance (Eisodus) into the land of milk and honey, which keeps the hope of the wandering Israelites alive. Without the anticipation of entering the land the Israelites of the biblical narrative would have languished in the desert or reverted to the less intolerable life in Egypt. Man does not live on manna and quails alone. However, that entrance presaged the divinely mandated slaughter of the indigenous people, according to several traditions within the biblical narrative.

The narratives of Genesis–Deuteronomy are best understood as common traditions of Judah sometime after 600 BC, and should not be used as historiographical sources for the period before 1000 BC, but used only very cautiously for the period of the monarchy itself. Moreover, there is virtual unanimity among scholars that the model of tribal conquest as narrated in Joshua 1–12 is unsustainable. Leaving aside the witness of the Bible, we have no evidence that there was a Hebrew conquest.

The Exodus-Settlement accounts reflect a particular genre, the goal of which was to inculcate religious values, rather than merely present empirical facts of history. The modern historian must distinguish between the actual history of the peoples and the history of their self-understanding. The archaeology of Palestine must be a primary source for tracing the origins of Israel, and it shows a picture quite different from that of the religiously motivated writings. The evidence from archaeology, extra-biblical literature, supplemented by insights from the independent methodologies of geography, sociology, anthropology, historical linguistics, Egyptology, Assyriology, etc., points in an altogether different direction from that propounded by Joshua 1–12. It suggests a sequence of periods marked by a gradual and peaceful coalescence of disparate peoples into a group of highland dwellers whose achievement of a new sense of unity culminated only with the entry of the Assyrian administration. The Iron Age settlements on the central hills of Palestine, from which the later kingdom of Israel developed, reflect continuity with Canaanite culture and repudiate any ethnic distinction between 'Canaanites' and 'Israelites'. Israel's origins, then, were within Canaan, not outside it. There was neither invasion from outside, nor revolution within. An historiography of Israelite origins based solely, or primarily on the biblical narratives, then, is an artificial construct influenced by certain religious motivations obtaining at a time long postdating any verifiable evidence of events.

Moreover, subsequent Jewish writers adapted the biblical traditions of land to their own historical contexts and contemporary interests in such a way that the land no longer functioned as the key signature of covenantal history. They developed new narratives which de-emphasized the theological significance of land. In each reworking of the tradition, the concept of the covenant was reformulated so that a promise other than land assumed the pivotal position.[59] That remained the case with the majority of Jews until the success of nineteenth-century Zionism, and remains true today of the majority of the world's Jews who choose not to live in Israel.

But even the biblical narrative would not be sufficient to transform the barbarism of ethnic cleansing into piety, unless one approaches it in a spirit of literalism and with scant regard for its moral character. One is left with an appeal to perceived self-interest and need, and the exercise of superior military might to justify the cleansing of the land of its indigenous people. At that point one has abandoned the rhetoric of rights.

NOTES

1. For a fuller discussion of the link between the two, see my *The Bible and Colonialism. A Moral Critique* (Sheffield: Sheffield Academic Press, 1997), in which I exemplify the matter by reference to three different regions and periods (Latin America, South Africa and Palestine). See also my 'The Bible and Redeeming Ideas of Colonialism', *Studies in World Christianity* 5 (1999), pp. 125–55; and my 'Zionist Ethnic Cleansing: The Fulfilment of Biblical Prophecy', *Egworth Review* 27 (2000), pp. 49–60.
2. *The Rebirth and Destiny of Israel* (New York: Philosophical Library, 1954), p. 100.
3. It was deployed in support of most of the colonizing enterprises emanating from 'Christian' Europe in the nineteenth and twentieth centuries (see my

The Bible and Colonialism). Indeed, the term 'ethnic cleansing' itself, I suggest, is related to a conflation of the biblical notions of 'unclean'/'profane' with the command to 'drive out' the inhabitants of Canaan (Exodus 23–24; Numbers 33; Deuteronomy 33 and Joshua), because, according to the biblical legend, they had defiled themselves by their evil practices (Leviticus 18.24). Uniquely in ancient literature, the biblical legend projects the extermination of the defiled indigenes as a divine mandate. With the authority of its religious provenance that value system has been incorporated into European imperialist ideologies, 'legitimizing' the destruction or displacement of indigenous peoples.

4. *Der Judenstaat. Versuch einer Modernen Lösung der Judenfrage* (Leipzig und Wien: M. Breitenstein's Verlags-Buchhandlung, 1896) was translated into English by Sylvie d'Avigdor as *A Jewish State*, and in 1946 as *The Jewish State*, and published by the American Zionist Emergency Council. *Der Judenstaat* might be translated more appropriately by 'The State for Jews', to distinguish it from the implications of a Jewish state (*Jüdischer Staat*).

5. Quotations and page references in what follows are from *The Jewish State* (New York: Dover Edition, 1988).

6. Herzl began his Diaries in 1895, and continued until shortly before his death. Seven volumes of the Letters and Diaries have been published: Vol. I, 1983, *Briefe und Autobiographische Notizen. 1886–1895*; Vol. II: 1983, *Zionistiches Tagebuch 1895–1899*; Vol. III, 1985: *Zionistiches Tagebuch 1899–1904* (Vols I–III, ed. Johannes Wachten, *et al.*); Vol. IV, 1900, *Briefe 1895–1898*; Vol. V, 1993, *Briefe 1898–1900*; Vol. VI, 1993, *Briefe Ende August 1900–ende Dezember 1902*; Vol. VII, 1996, *Briefe 1903–1904* (Vols IV–VII, ed. Barbara Schäfer, *et al.*) (Berlin: Propylaen Verlag). Raphael Patai edited an English translation of the diaries in five volumes: *The Complete Diaries of Theodore Herzl*, trans. Harry Zohn (New York: Herzl Press, 1960). In general, I quote from Patai's edition (rendered Herzl 1960), which I have checked against the original in Wachten and Schäfer. Where I judge it to be important, I give the original German (or other language) from the latter (rendered Herzl 1983–96). I indicate the volume number of the English translation by 1, 2, etc., and the German ones by I, II, etc.

7. I offer this translation of 'Die arme Bevölkerung trachten wir unbemerkt über die Grenze zu schaffen, indem wir in den Durchzugsländern Arbeit verschaffen aber in unserem eigenen Lande jederlei Arbeit verweigern' (Herzl 1983, II: 117–18), in preference to Zohn's translation, 'We shall try to spirit the penniless population ...' (*The Complete Diaries ...*, 1: 87–8).

8. Christopher Sykes, *Crossroads to Israel. Palestine from Balfour to Bevin* (London: Collins, 1965), p. 26.

9. *Protokoll des I. Zionistenkongresses in Basel vom 29. bis 31. August 1897* (Prag: Selbstverlag –Druck von Richard Brandeis, 1911), p. 15.

10. *The Jewish State*, p. 96.

11. *The Complete Diaries*, 1: 343.

12. Herzl visited Rome on 23 January 1904, and met Victor Emmanuel III and Pius X. To Herzl's request for a Jewish state in Tripoli, the king replied, '*Ma è ancora casa di altri*' ('But it is already the home of other people') (Herzl, 1985, III: 653).

13. There are no exact figures for the number of Jews in Palestine before the First World War. Justin McCarthy estimates that in 1880 there were some 15,000 Jews in a total population of approximately 450,000. By 1914 the

population of Palestine was c. 710,000, of which some 38,000 (still 5 per cent) were Jews. See further my *Zionism and the State of Israel: A Moral Inquiry* (London: Routledge, 1999), p. 12 n10.

14. As early as November 1882 the use of arms was envisaged: 'The Jews, if necessary with arms in their hands, will publicly proclaim themselves masters of their own, ancient fatherland' (see Walter Lehn, in association with Uri Davis, *The Jewish National Fund* (London and New York: Kegan Paul International, 1988), p. 10). Nahman Syrkin, the ideological founder of Socialist Zionism, too, insisted in 1898 that Palestine must be evacuated for the Jews (in Nur Masalha, *Expulsion of the Palestinians: the Concept of 'Transfer' in Zionist Political Thought, 1882–1948* (Washington, DC: Institute for Palestine Studies, 1992), pp. 9–11). The Jewish leadership in Palestine began already in 1937 to plan systematically for 'population transfer', and executed it at the first opportunity in 1948, and at the second in 1967. Privately, Theodor Herzl and the majority of Zionists after him were in no doubt that the realization of the Jewish dream would require a nightmare for the indigenous population.

15. For a discussion of the role of the Jewish–Christian dialogue in western Christian support see my *Zionism and the State of Israel ...*, pp. 123–36.

16. Although Zionism had made little headway before the 1930s when considerable numbers of Jews went to Palestine from Germany, the *Shoah* played a significant part in illustrating its thesis that Jews could not live safely other than in a Jewish nation state.

17. Gerhard von Rad, 'The Promised Land and Yahweh's Land in the Hexateuch', in *The Problem of the Hexateuch and Other Essays* (London: SCM and Philadelphia: Fortress, 1966, repr. 1984), p. 79.

18. James M. Scott (ed.), *Exile: Old Testament, Jewish and Christian Conceptions* (Leiden: Brill, 1997), pp. 2–3.

19. *The Gospel and the Land. Early Christianity and Jewish Territorial Doctrine* (Berkeley: University of California Press, 1974).

20. W.D. Davies, *The Territorial Dimensions of Judaism* (Berkeley: University of California Press, 1982), p. xiii.

21. *The Territorial Dimensions of Judaism ...* (pp. xiii–xiv). He wrote this book under the direct impact of the 1967 war, and its updated version in 1991 after the Gulf War (*The Territorial Dimensions of Judaism. With a Symposium and Further Reflections* (Minneapolis: Fortress, 1991)).

22. *The Territorial Dimensions of Judaism. With a Symposium and Further Reflections*, p. xv.

23. William F. Albright, *From the Stone Age to Christianity: Monotheism and the Historical Process* (New York: Doubleday, 1957), pp. 280–1.

24. Keith W. Whitelam, *The Invention of Ancient Israel. The Silencing of Palestinian History* (London and New York: Routledge, 1996), p. 88.

25. William F. Albright, 'Why the Near East Needs the Jews', in *New Palestine* 32 (1942), pp. 12–13. In reflecting recently upon the ideological baggage of the individual researcher (in archaeology), Burke O. Long situates Albright's work in the apologetic context of protecting western values from the threat of Communism and totalitarianism. Christianity and 'the Jewish–Christian tradition' were the pinnacle of all religious reflection, and, of course, were enshrined within the American way of life ('Historical Imaginings, Ideological Gestures: W.F. Albright and the "Reasoning Faculties of Man"', in Neil Asher Silberman and David B. Small, *The*

Archaeology of Israel. Constructing the Past, Interpreting the Present (Sheffield: Sheffield Academic Press, 1997), pp. 82–94).

26. In G.E. Wright and R.H. Fuller (eds), *The Book of the Acts of God: Christian Scholarship Interprets the Bible* (London: Duckworth, 1960), p. 109.

27. For Pinhas Lapide, the Exodus narrative is not only the core document of Israelite liberation but 'the epitome of all liberation', and 'a turning-point in world history', which has provided the inspiration, vocabulary and legitimization for most freedom movements inside and outside the churches ('Exodus in the Jewish Tradition', in *Exodus – A Lasting Paradigm*, pp. 47–55, pp. 49, 52). In any discussion of liberation enterprises, of course, one should distinguish between groups who seek freedom in their own place, and those who exact payment for their achievement from the native peoples of their land of freedom.

28. Thus, in her chapter 'The Book of Exodus', introducing the biblical data in the volume *Exodus – A Lasting Paradigm*, ed. Bas van Iersel and Anton Weiler (Edinburgh: T&T Chark, 1987), pp. 11–21, Rita Burns makes no mention of the divine mandate to exterminate the inhabitants of Canaan. Similarly, sympathetic of the approach of liberation theology, the title page of Esther and Mortimer Arias's study, *The Cry of My People. Out of Captivity in Latin America* (New York: Friendship Press, 1980) reproduces Exodus 3.7–8, but ends with, 'a land of milk and honey ...'

29. See my discussion of the 'liturgical censoring' of the Word of God, and of the ambivalence of the Exodus paradigm in *The Bible and Colonialism* (pp. 273–84).

30. Gustavo Gutiérrez, *A Theology of Liberation. History, Politics, and Salvation* (London: SCM, 1988, revised with a new Introduction), pp. 88–90.

31. See his *God of the Oppressed* (New York: Seabury Press, 1975).

32. *A Theology of Liberation*, p. xxvii.

33. Susan Niditch, *War in the Hebrew Bible. A Study of the Ethics of Violence* (Oxford: Oxford University Press, 1993), p. 3.

34. Roland H. Bainton, *Christian Attitudes toward War and Peace* (Nashville: Abingdon, 1960), pp. 112–33, 168. One recalls also that although Hitler's *Lebensraum* policy was not derived from the biblical narrative, it was inspired by the European conquest of North America and he saw himself in the line of European colonizers, whose racial superiority conferred on them the right to dominate.

35. Michael Walzer's exegetical appetite also is exhausted simply by his comments on 'the land of milk and honey'. His mellifluous prose obscures the problem raised by the presence of the indigenes, and the requirement of exterminating them in order to be a kingdom of priests and a holy nation (*Exodus and Revolution* (New York: Basic Books, 1985), pp. 101–30). As the first description of revolutionary politics (p. 134), Exodus provides the paradigm for political Zionism, with the Canaanites explicitly excluded from the world of moral concern (p. 142). Their extermination, gratefully, was effectively rescinded by Talmudic and medieval commentators (pp. 143–4). See also Edward W. Said, 'Michael Walzer's *Exodus and Revolution*: A Canaanite Reading', in Edward W. Said and Christopher Hitchens (eds), *Blaming the Victims. Spurious Scholarship and the Palestinian Question* (London and New York: Verso, 1988), pp. 161–78.

36. 'The Laws of Deuteronomy. A Utopian Project for a World without any Poor?' (St Edmund's College, Cambridge: Von Hügel Institute, 1996),

published also as 'The Laws of Deuteronomy. A Utopian Project for a World without any Poor', in *Scripture Bulletin* 26 (1996), pp. 2–19.

37. Cambridge: Von Hügel Institute, 1997, and in *Scripture Bulletin* 28 (1998), pp. 2–17.

38. G.E.M. de Ste. Croix, *The Class Struggle in the Ancient Greek World from the Archaic Age to the Arab Conquest* (London: Duckworth, 1981), pp. 331–2.

39. For a discussion of how the biblical narrative provided moral authority for the Iberian devastation of 'Latin America' in the late mediaeval period, for the Afrikaner exploitation of non-whites in southern Africa in the apartheid era, and for the ongoing exspoliation of the Arabs of Palestine at the hands of Zionists, see my *The Bible and Colonialism*.

40. Lapide sees in Israel's contemporary history also 'an optimistic indicator for every as yet unliberated nation everywhere' ('Exodus in the Jewish Tradition', pp. 53–4). How that consideration might extend to the Palestinians he does not discuss.

41. Rather, Herzl's Zionism had much in common with 'Pan-Germanism', with its emphasis on *das Volk*: all persons of German race, blood or descent owed their primary loyalty to Germany, the *Heimat*. Jews, wherever they lived, constituted a distinct nation, whose success could be advanced only by establishing a Jewish nation-state.

42. At his graveside, Martin Buber did not hide the fact that Herzl had no sense of Jewish national culture, and no inward relationship to Judaism or to his own Jewishness (Robert Wistrich, 'Theodor Herzl: Zionist Icon, Myth-Maker and Social Utopian', in Robert Wistrich and David Ohana (eds), *The Shaping of Israeli Identity: Myth, Memory and Traum* (London: Frank Cass, 1995), pp. 30–1).

43. On 6 March 1897, the *Zionsverein* decided upon a Zionist Congress in Munich for August, but the Munich Jews refused to host it. Moreover, the executive committee of the German Rabbinical Council 'formally and publicly condemned the "efforts of the so-called Zionists to create a Jewish national state in Palestine" as contrary to Holy Writ' (David Vital, *The Origins of Zionism* (Oxford: Clarendon, 1975), p. 336).

44. According to Jonathan Sacks, Chief Rabbi of the United Hebrew Congregations of the Commonwealth, the State of Israel for many religious Jews is 'the most powerful collective expression' of Jewry, and 'the most significant development in Jewish life since the Holocaust' (*Daily Telegraph*, 31 December 1993, p. 21). The degree to which the mixed marriage between irreligious political Zionism and religious Judaism has been consummated can be seen in Michael Rosenak's assertion that for most modern Jews, 'the emergence of the State of Israel is the central positive event in two millennia of Jewish history' ('State of Israel', in Arthur A. Cohen and Paul Mendes-Flohr (eds), *Contemporary Jewish Religious Thought. Original Essays on Critical Concepts, Movements and Beliefs* (New York: The Free Press/ London: Collier Macmillan, 1987), p. 910).

45. See Thomas L. Thompson, 'Hidden Histories and the Problem of Ethnicity in Palestine', in Michael Prior (ed.), *Western Scholarship and the History of Palestine* (London: Melisende, 1998), pp. 23–39.

46. In providing an overview of Jews and Christians in Palestine in a period of seminal importance for the two communities, Günther Stemberger overturns many of the assumptions that many non-specialists apply to the period. These include the presumed absence of Jews from Palestine after the

defeat of the Bar Kochba revolt and the alleged hostile attitude of Emperor Constantine to Jews (*Jews and Christians in the Holy Land. Palestine in the Fourth Century*, Edinburgh: T&T Clark, 2000). He estimates that there were c. 2.5 million inhabitants in Palestine (including east of the Jordan) in AD 140, of which some 700,000–800,000 were Jews, down from c. 1.3 million before the Bar Kochba revolt. By the fourth century, the population west of the River Jordan may not have been more than 500,000, and this was made up of Jews who were in a majority, then pagans, Samaritans and Christians, the smallest of the four. Jews were forbidden entry into Aelia Capitolina, and had their strongest presence in Sepphoris, Tiberias, Safed, the Jezreel Valley and on the Golan Heights, as well as in Caesarea Maritima where there was a rabbinic school. Synagogue remains of the period also attest a significant Jewish presence in a line from En Gedi by the Dead Sea to Ashkelon.

47. See E.J. Bickerman, 'The Babylonian Captivity', in W.D. Davies and L. Finkelstein (eds), *The Cambridge History of Judaism* (Cambridge: Cambridge University Press, 1984), I, pp. 342–58.

48. Isaiah M. Gafni, 'The Historical Background', in Michael E. Stone (ed.), *Jewish Writings of the Second Temple Period. Apocrypha, Pseudepigrapha, Qumran Sectarian Writings, Philo, Josephus* (Assen: Van Gorcum/Philadelphia: Fortress Press, 1984), p. 28.

49. An abundance of evidence witnesses to a widespread Jewish diaspora (1 Maccabees 15.22–23; the *Sibylline Oracles* iii: 271; Strabo, according to Josephus, *Antiquities* 14.115; Philo, *Flaccus* 46 and *Legatio ad Gaium* 281–2; Josephus, *Wars* 2.398; 7.43; Acts 2.5–11; and so on).

50. *A Social and Religious History of the Jews*. Vol. I, *To the Beginning of the Christian Era* (2nd edition, New York: Columbia University Press; Philadelphia: The Jewish Publication Society of America, 1952), p. 170.

51. In the modern period, the Balfour Declaration was careful to insist that the drive to establish a Jewish homeland would not prejudice 'the rights and political status enjoyed by Jews in any other country'. In Britain itself at that time the leadership of the Jewish community, being in no mood to throw away its gains from assimilation into English culture for which it had been duly honoured by the establishment, had little time for Herzl's insistence that Jews could live authentically only in their own state.

52. See John M.G. Barclay, *Jews in the Mediterranean Diaspora from Alexander to Trajan (323 BCE–117 CE)* (Edinburgh: T&T Clark, 1996), pp. 1–9.

53. For example, Sirach 48.15, as well as the Apocrypha and Pseudepigrapha: for example, the *Testament of Levi* 10.3–4; the *Testament of Asher* 7.2–7.

54. Note the title of David Vital's recent study, *A People Apart. The Jews in Europe 1789–1939* (Oxford: Oxford University Press, 1999).

55. See further my *Zionism and the State of Israel*, pp. 67–102.

56. 'No one shall be arbitrarily deprived of the right to enter his own country' (International Covenant on Civil and Political Rights, art. 12), and the Universal Declaration of Human Rights states that everyone has a right 'to return to his own country' (art. 13).

57. For example, UN General Assembly Resolution 194 (III) of 11 December 1948 '*Resolves* that the refugees wishing to return to their homes and live at peace with their neighbours should be permitted to do so at the earliest practicable date, and that compensation should be paid for the property of those choosing not to return and for loss of or damage to property which,

under principles of international law or in equity, should be made good by the Governments or authorities responsible' (11).

58. Christians read the Old Testament in the light of the life, death and resurrection of Christ. In such a perspective, the writings of the Old Testament contain certain 'imperfect and provisional' elements, which the divine pedagogy could not eliminate right away. The Bible, in such a view, reflects a considerable moral development, which finds its completion in the New Testament. I do not find this explanation satisfactory. Nor do the attempts of the Fathers of the Church to eliminate the scandal caused by particular texts of the Bible impress me. Neither is the allegorical presentation of Joshua leading the people into the land of Canaan as a type of Christ, who leads Christians into the true promised land convincing. There is, however, another method, which is more amenable to modern sensibilities, one that takes seriously the literary forms of the materials, the circumstances of their composition, and relevant non-literary evidence.

59. In each of the four examples she examines, Betsy Halpern-Amaru shows how the author reconstructed the biblical narrative (*Rewriting the Bible: Land and Covenant in Post-Biblical Jewish Literature* (Valley Forge: Trinity Press, 1994)).

2   THE HISTORICAL ROOTS OF THE PALESTINIAN REFUGEE QUESTION

Nur Masalha

The primary aim of this chapter is to show that the Palestinian refugee exodus of 1948 was the culmination of over half a century of efforts, secret (Zionist) plans and, in the end, brute force; and that the Zionist (Jewish) leadership, especially David Ben-Gurion and the military commanders, were primarily responsible for the displacement and dispossession of three-quarters of a million Palestinian refugees in 1948. Furthermore, it was mainly the Palestinian refugees themselves who publicly resisted and opposed resettlement schemes in Arab countries. The refugees clung to the 'right of return', enshrined in UN General Assembly Resolution 194 of December 1948. Israeli resettlement schemes after 1948 were aimed at 'dissolving' the refugee problem, not resolving it. Israel's need to 'dissolve' the refugee problem stemmed from the deep fear of refugee return and the determination to extirpate the problem from the heart of the Arab-Israeli conflict. But that is where the Palestinian refugee problem has remained. A comprehensive and durable settlement depends on addressing the refugee problem seriously. For over five decades the Palestinians' 'right of return' ('*Haq al-Awda*') has been central to their struggle against dispossession and expulsion from their ancestral homeland, and for national reconstitution. Only by understanding the centrality of the *nakba* is it possible to understand the Palestinians' sense of the right of return. The wrong done to the Palestinians can only be righted, and the disasters ended, by a return to their homeland and restitution of property.

Since the mass expulsions of 1948 the Palestinians and the Arab states have demanded that the Palestinian refugees be given a free choice of repatriation and/or compensation, in line with Resolution 194. The catastrophe of the *nakba* (expulsion of the Palestinians in 1948, the deliberate destruction of hundreds of Palestinian towns and villages, the numerous massacres of 1948; and acknowledging the enormous suffering of the refugees for over half a century) has remained central to Palestinian society (in the same way that the Holocaust has been central to Israeli society and Jewish communities). Today, the aspirations of millions of Palestinian refugees – in the diaspora, in the West Bank and Gaza and even among some 250,000 'internal refugees' in Israel – are linked to the catastrophe of 1948. Since the mid-1950s successive Israeli governments have, in effect, refused to acknowledge any responsibility for monetary compensation to the Palestinian refugees. Any genuine reconciliation between the two peoples – peace between peoples as opposed to a political settlement achieved by leaders – can begin only by Israel and most Israelis taking responsibility for the displacement and dispossession of the refugees. Holocaust denial is abhorrent; in some European countries it is a crime. Acknowledging the *nakba* and an official apology by Israel would be very helpful, but it would not be sufficient. Taking responsibility also means admitting responsibility for monetary compensation, including restitution of property and making reparation.

THE CONCEPT OF 'POPULATION TRANSFER' IN MAINSTREAM ZIONISM, 1882–1948

For the Jewish settlers coming 'to redeem the land', the indigenous inhabitants earmarked for dispossession are usually invisible. They simultaneously are divested of their human and national reality and classed as a marginal nonentity. Indeed, Zionist historiography provides ample evidence to suggest that from the outset of the Zionist *Yishuv* (settlement) the attitude of the majority of the Zionist groups towards the Arab population ranged from indifference and patronizing superiority, to outright denial of their national rights. Uprooting and transferring them to neighbouring countries followed. Leading figures such as Israel Zangwill, a prominent Anglo-Jewish writer, a close associate of Theodor Herzl (the founder of political Zionism) and propagator of the transfer solution, worked relentlessly to propagandize the slogan that Palestine was 'a land without a people for a people without a land'. A similar reference to an 'empty country' was made in 1914 by Chaim Weizmann, later president of the World Zionist Congress and the first president of the state of Israel:

In its initial stage, Zionism was conceived by its pioneers as a movement wholly depending on mechanical factors: there is a country which happens to be called Palestine, a country without a people, and, on the other hand, there exists the Jewish people, and it has no country. What else is necessary, then, than to fit the gem into the ring, to unite this people with this country?'[1]

More revealing, however, is an anecdote Weizmann once told Arthur Ruppin, the head of the colonization department of the Jewish Agency, about how he (Weizmann) had obtained the Balfour Declaration in 1917. When Ruppin asked what he thought about the indigenous Palestinians, Weizmann replied: 'The British told us that there are some hundred thousand negroes ['*kushim*'] and for those there is no value.'[2] A few years after the Balfour Declaration, Zangwill wrote: 'If Lord Shaftesbury was literally inexact in describing Palestine as a country without a people, he was essentially correct, for there is no Arab people living in intimate fusion with the country, utilizing its resources and stamping it with a characteristic impress; there is at best an Arab encampment.'[3] This and other pronouncements by Weizmann and leading Zionists embodied European supremacy which planted in the Zionist mind the racist notion of an empty territory – empty not necessarily in the actual absence of its inhabitants, but rather in the sense of civilizational barrenness. It justified Zionist colonization and engendered obliviousness to the fate of the native population.

The United States Ambassador to Israel, James McDonald, in his book *My Mission in Israel, 1948–1951*,[4] recalls a conversation he had with Weizmann, in the course of which Weizmann spoke in 'messianic' terms about the 1948 Palestinian exodus as a 'miraculous simplification of Israel's tasks'. McDonald added that not one of the 'big three' – Weizmann, Prime Minister and Defence Minister David Ben-Gurion and Foreign Minister Moshe Sharett – and no responsible Zionist leader had anticipated such a 'miraculous clearing of the land'. In fact, the evidence (from Israeli archival documents) shows that the 'big three' endorsed 'transfer' in the period between 1937 and 1948 and had anticipated 'the clearing of the land' in 1948. They enthusiastically endorsed the Peel Commission's transfer proposal, which would have partitioned the British Mandate territory into an Arab state, a Jewish state and a British zone in and around Jerusalem. The importance Ben-Gurion attached not merely to transfer but 'forced transfer' is seen in his diary entry of 12 July 1937:

The compulsory transfer of Arabs from the valleys of the proposed Jewish state could give us something which we never had, even when we stood on our own feet during the days of the First and Second Temple [a Galilee free of Arab population].[5]

Ben-Gurion was convinced that few, if any, Palestinians would 'voluntarily' transfer themselves to Transjordan. He also believed that if the Zionists were determined in their effort to put pressure on the British Mandatory Authorities to carry out a 'compulsory transfer', the plan could be implemented:

We have to stick to this conclusion in the same way we grabbed the Balfour Declaration, more than that, in the same way we grabbed Zionism itself. We have to insist upon this conclusion [and push it] with our full determination, power and conviction ... We must uproot from our hearts the assumption that the thing is not possible. It can be done.

Ben-Gurion went as far as to write: '*We must prepare ourselves to carry out* [the transfer]' (emphasis in the original).[6]

A letter to his son, Amos, dated 5 October 1937, reveals the extent to which transfer had become associated in his mind with expulsion:

We must expel Arabs and take their places ... and, if we have to use force – not to dispossess the Arabs of the Negev and Transjordan, but to guarantee our own right to settle in those places – then we have force at our disposal.[7]

At the Twentieth Zionist Congress (3–21 August 1937), Ben-Gurion emphasized that transfer of Arab villagers had been practised by the *Yishuv* all along:

Was the transfer of the Arabs ethical, necessary and practicable? ... Transfer of Arabs had repeatedly taken place before in consequence of Jews settling in different district.[8]

A year later, at the Jewish Agency Executive's transfer discussions of June 1938, Ben-Gurion put forward a 'line of actions' entitled 'The Zionist Mission of the Jewish State':

The Hebrew State will discuss with the neighbouring Arab states the matter of voluntarily transferring Arab tenant farmers, workers and *fellahin* [peasants] from the Jewish state to neighbouring states. For that purpose the Jewish state, or a special company ... will purchase lands in neighbouring states for the resettlement of all those workers and *fellahin*.[9]

He returned to the transfer solution in his 'Lines for Zionist Policy' of 15 October 1941:

We have to examine, first, if this transfer is practical, and secondly, if it is necessary. It is impossible to imagine general evacuation without compulsion, and brutal compulsion ... The possibility of a large-scale transfer of a population by force was demonstrated, when the Greeks and the Turks were transferred [after the First World War]. In the present [Second World] war the idea of transferring a population is gaining more sympathy as a practical and the most secure means of solving the dangerous and painful problem of national minorities. The war has already brought the resettlement of many people in eastern and southern Europe, and in the plans for post-war settlements the idea of a large-scale population transfer in central, eastern, and southern Europe increasingly occupies a respectable place.[10]

Ben-Gurion went on to suggest a Zionist-inspired campaign in Britain and the United States that would aim at 'influencing' neighbouring countries, especially Syria and Iraq, to 'collaborate' with the Jewish *Yishuv* in implementing transfer schemes of Palestinian Arabs from Palestine in return for economic gains.[11] Moreover, Ben-Gurion entered the 1948 war determined to expel the Palestinians. He advised on 19 December 1947 that:

[the Haganah should] adopt the system of aggressive defence; during the assault we must respond with a decisive blow: the destruction of the [Arab] place or the expulsion of the residents along with the seizure of the place.[12]

In early February 1948 Ben-Gurion told Yosef Weitz:

The war will give us the land. The concepts of 'ours' and 'not ours' are peace concepts, only, and in war they lose their whole meaning.[13]

From the beginning of the Zionist enterprise to found a Jewish national home, or state, in Palestine, the Zionists had been confronted with what they termed the 'Arab problem'– the fact that Palestine was already populated. One of the proposed solutions was the 'transfer' solution – a euphemism

denoting the organized removal of the Palestinian population to neigh-
bouring Arab lands. Before 1948 the transfer concept was embraced by the
highest level of leadership, including virtually all the founding fathers of the
Israeli state and representing almost the entire political spectrum. Nearly all
the founding fathers, including Theodor Herzl, Leon Motzkin, Nahman
Syrkin, Menahem Ussishkin, Chaim Weizmann, David Ben-Gurion, Yitzhak
Tabenkin, Avraham Granovsky, Israel Zangwill, Yitzhak Ben-Tzvi, Pinhas
Rutenberg, Aaron Aaronson, Ze'ev Jabotinsky and Berl Katznelson,
advocated transfer in one form or another. Katznelson, who was one of the
most popular and influential leaders of the Mapai Party (later the ruling
Labour Party), had this to say in a debate at the World Convention of Ihud
Po'alei Tzion (the highest forum of the dominant Zionist world labour
movement), in August 1937:

The matter of population transfer has provoked a debate among us: Is it permitted or
forbidden? My conscience is absolutely clear in this respect. A remote neighbour is
better than a close enemy. They [the Palestinians] will not lose from it. In the final
analysis, this is a political and settlement reform for the benefit of both parties. I have
long been of the opinion that this is the best of all solutions ... I have always believed
and still believe that they were destined to be transferred to Syria or Iraq.[14]

A year later, at the Jewish Agency Executive's discussions of June 1938,
Katznelson declared himself in favour of maximum territory and the
'principle of compulsory transfer':

What is a compulsory transfer? ... Compulsory transfer does not mean individual
transfer. It means that once we resolved to transfer there should be a political body
able to force this or that Arab who would not want to move out. Regarding the
transfer of Arab individuals we are always doing this. But the question will be the
transfer of much greater quantity of Arabs through an agreement with the Arab
states: this is called a compulsory transfer ...We have here a war about principles, and
in the same way that we must wage a war for maximum territory, there must also be
here a war [for the transfer 'principle'] ... We must insist on the principle that it must
be a large agreed transfer.[15]

In the early 1940s Katznelson found time to engage in polemics with the
left-wing Hashomer Hatza'ir about the merits of transfer. He told them: don't
stigmatize the concept of transfer and rule it out beforehand.

Has [Kibbutz] Merhavyah not been built on transfer? Were it not for many of these
transfers neither Merhavyah nor [Kibbutz] Mishmar Ha'emek nor other socialist
Kibbutzim would have been set up.[16]

Supporters of 'voluntary transfer' included Arthur Ruppin, a co-founder
of Brit Shalom, a movement advocating bi-nationalism and equal rights for
Arabs and Jews; moderate Mapai leaders such as Moshe Shertok (later
Sharett) and Eli'ezer Kaplan, the first Finance Minister; and Histadrut leaders
such as Golda Meir and David Remez. But perhaps the most consistent,
extremist and obsessive advocate of 'compulsory transfer' was Yosef Weitz,

the director of the Settlement Department of Jewish National Fund (JNF) and the head of the Israeli government's official Transfer Committee of 1948. Weitz was at the centre of the Zionist land purchase activities for decades. His intimate knowledge and involvement made him acutely aware of the limitations of land purchase. As late as 1947, after half a century of tireless efforts, the collective ownership of the JNF – which constituted about half the *Yishuv* total – amounted to a mere 3.5 per cent of the land area of Palestine.

A summary of Weitz's political beliefs is provided by his diary entry dated 20 December 1940:

Amongst ourselves it must be clear that there is no room for both peoples in this country. No 'development' will bring us closer to our aim to be an independent people in this small country. After the Arabs are transferred, the country will be wide open for us; with the Arabs staying the country will remain narrow and restricted ... There is no room for compromise on this point ... land purchasing ... will not bring about the state ... The only way is to transfer the Arabs from here to neighbouring countries, all of them, except perhaps Bethlehem, Nazareth, and Old Jerusalem. Not a single village or a single tribe must be left. And the transfer must be done through their absorption in Iraq and Syria and even in Transjordan. For that goal, money will be found – even a lot of money. And only then will the country be able to absorb millions of Jews ... there is no other solutions.[17]

A tour of the country in the summer of 1941 took Weitz to a region in central Palestine. He recorded in his diary seeing

large [Arab] villages crowded in population and surrounded by cultivated land growing olives, grapes, figs, sesame, and maize fields ... Would we be able to maintain scattered [Jewish] settlements among these existing [Arab] villages that will always be larger than ours? And is there any possibility of buying their [land]? ... and once again I hear that voice inside me called: *evacuate this country.* (emphasis in the original)[18]

Earlier in March 1940, after touring Jewish settlements in the Esdraelon Valley (Marj Ibn 'Amer), Weitz recorded: 'The complete evacuation of the country from its [Arab] inhabitants and handing it to the Jewish people is the answer.'[19] And in April 1948 he recorded:

I made a summary of a list of the Arab villages which in my opinion must be cleared out in order to complete Jewish regions. I also made a summary of the places that have land disputes and must be settled by military means.[20]

WEIZMANN'S PROPOSAL TO TRANSFER PEASANTS TO TRANSJORDAN, 1930

In 1930, against the background of the 1929 disturbances in Palestine, Weizmann, then President of both the World Zionist Organization and the Jewish Agency Executive, actively began promoting the idea of Arab transfer in private discussions with British officials and ministers. In the same year Weizmann and Pinhas Rutenberg, who was chairman of the Yishuv's

National Council and a member of the Jewish Agency Executive, presented the Colonial Secretary Lord Passfield with an official, albeit secret, proposal for the transfer of Palestinian peasants to Transjordan. This scheme proposed that a loan of £P1,000,000 be raised from Jewish financial sources for the resettlement operation. This proposal was rejected. However, the justification Weizmann used in its defence formed the cornerstone of subsequent Zionist argumentation. Weizmann asserted that there was nothing 'immoral' about the concept of transfer; that the 'transfer' of Greek and Turkish populations in the early 1920s set a precedent for a similar measure for the Palestinians; and that the uprooting and transportation of Palestinians to Transjordan, Iraq, Syria or any other part of the vast Arab world would merely constitute a relocation from one Arab district to another. Above all, for Weizmann and other leaders of the Jewish Agency, the transfer was a systematic procedure, requiring preparation, money and a great deal of organization, which needed to be planned by strategic thinkers and technical experts.[21]

EMERGING CONSENSUS, 1937–48

While the desire of the Zionist leadership to be rid of the 'Arab demographic problem' remained constant until 1948, the extent of preoccupation with, and the envisaged modalities of, transfer changed over the years according to circumstances. Thus the wishful and rather naive belief in Zionism's early years that the Palestinians could be 'spirited across the border', in the words of Herzl, or that they would simply 'fold their tents and slip away', to use the formulation of Zangwill, soon gave way to more realistic assessments. From the mid-1930s onwards the transfer solution became central to the assessments of the Jewish Agency (then effectively the government of the *Yishuv*).

Three (Semi-Official and Official) Transfer Committees, 1937–48

Jewish Agency assessments required strategies and planning that produced a series of specific plans, generally involving Transjordan, Syria or Iraq. Some of these plans were produced by three 'transfer committees': the first two, set up by the *Yishuv* leadership, operated between 1937 and 1944 and the third was officially appointed by the Israeli cabinet in August 1948. As of the late 1930s some of the transfer plans included proposals for agrarian legislation and citizenship restriction and various taxes designed to encourage Palestinians to 'transfer voluntarily'.[22] However, in the 1930s and early 1940s Zionist transfer proposals and plans remained largely confined to private and secret talks with British (and occasionally American) senior officials; the Zionist leadership generally refrained from airing the highly sensitive proposals in public. On one occasion, in February 1941, Weizmann, in a secret meeting with Ivan Meiski, the Soviet ambassador to London, proposed a transfer of one million Palestinians to Iraq in order to settle Polish Jews in their place. More importantly, however, during the British Mandate period, for reasons of political expediency, the Zionists calculated that such proposals could not be carried out without Britain's active support and even British implementation. Moreover, the Zionist leadership was tireless in trying to shape the proposals of the Royal (Peel) Commission of 1937. It has generally escaped the attention of historians that the most significant proposal for transfer submitted to the Commission – the one destined to shape the outcome of its findings – was put forward by the Jewish Agency in 1937 in a secret memorandum containing a specific paragraph on Arab transfer to Transjordan.

Between 1937 and 1948 very extensive secret discussions concerning Arab transfer were held in the Zionist movement's highest bodies: the Zionist Agency Executive; the Twentieth Zionist Congress; the World Convention of Ihud Po'alei Tzion; and various official and semi-official 'transfer committees'. Many leading figures justified Arab removal politically, morally and ethically as the natural and logical continuation of Zionist colonization in Palestine. There was a general endorsement of the 'moral' justification of the transfer concept; the differences centred on the question of 'compulsory transfer' and whether such a course would be practicable without Britain's support.

THE ISSUES OF LAND AND DEMOGRAPHY

Demography and the land issue were at the heart of the Zionist transfer mentality and secret transfer plans of the 1930s and 1940s. In 1947 the Palestinians were the overwhelming majority in the country and owned much of the land; the Jewish community was about a third of the total population and owned about 6 per cent of the land. In the 1930s and the 1940s the general endorsement of transfer – whether voluntary, agreed or compulsory – had been designed to achieve two crucial objectives: to clear the land for Jewish settlers and would-be immigrants; and to establish a fairly homogeneous Jewish state. Ben-Gurion strongly believed that Zionism would not succeed in establishing a homogeneous Jewish state and fulfilling its imperative of absorbing the expected influx of Jewish immigrants if the indigenous inhabitants were allowed to remain.

THE 1948 EXODUS

On the Connection between Premeditation and Action

Evidence suggests that as early as the beginning of 1948 Ben-Gurion's advisers were counselling him to 'wage a total war' against the Palestinians; and, importantly, Ben-Gurion entered the 1948 war determined to expel Palestinians. In early 1948 he wrote in his *War Diary* (*Yoman Hamilhamah*): 'During the assault we must be ready to strike a decisive blow; that is, either to destroy the town or expel its inhabitants so our people can replace them.'

Plan Dalet, a straightforward Haganah document, of early March 1948, was in many ways a master plan for the expulsion of as many Palestinians as possible. The plan constituted an ideological-strategic anchor and basis for expulsion by Jewish commanders and the destruction of Arab localities. In conformity with the plan the Haganah cleared various areas (including the Jerusalem corridor, the coastal plain and the area around Mishmar Ha'emek) completely of Arab villages.

The general endorsement of the 'transfer' schemes and the attempt to promote them secretly by mainstream Labour leaders (some of whom played a decisive role in the 1948 war) highlight the ideological intent that made the 1948 refugee exodus possible. Ben-Gurion in particular emerges from my book *Expulsion of the Palestinians: The Concept of 'Transfer' in Zionist Political Thought, 1882–1948* and several other books published in recent years by Israeli revisionist historians, including Benny Morris, Ilan Pappe, Avi Shlaim, Simha Flapan, Tom Segev and Uri Milstein, as both an 'obsessive' advocate of 'compulsory transfer' in the late 1930s and the great expeller of the Palestinians. In 1948 there was no need for any cabinet decision to drive the Palestinians out; Ben-Gurion and his close associates, including the key military commanders of the army (Palmah/Haganah/IDF), notably Yigal Allon, Moshe Carmel, Yigal Yadin, Moshe Dayan, Moshe Kalman and Yitzhak Rabin, played a key role. Everyone, at every level of military and political decision-making, understood that the objective was a Jewish state without a large Arab minority.

In the 1948 war, the Zionists succeeded in many of their objectives; above all they created a vastly enlarged Jewish state (out of 77 per cent of historic Palestine) in which the Palestinians were forcibly reduced to a small and manageable minority. Over the last 15 years, Israeli revisionists ('new historians') as well as Palestinian historians and scholars (including Nur Masalha, Walid Khalidi, Sharif Kana'aneh, Nafez Nazzal) have extensively documented the expulsion of the Palestinians in 1948. The evidence shows that the evacuation of some 750,000 Palestinians in 1948 can only be ascribed to the culmination of Zionist expulsion policies and not to (mythical) orders issued by the Arab armies. Aharon Cohen, who in 1948 was the Director of the Arab Department of Mapam, wrote in a memorandum dated 10 May 1948:

There is reason to believe that what is being done ... is being done out of certain political objectives and not only out of military necessities, as they [Jewish leaders] claim sometimes. In fact, the 'transfer' of the Arabs from the boundaries of the Jewish state is being implemented ... the evacuation/clearing out of Arab villages is not always done out of military necessity. The complete destruction of villages is not always done because there are 'no sufficient forces to maintain garrison.[23]

Yosef Sprintzak, at the time Secretary-General of the Histadrut, stated in a debate at the Mapai Centre on 24 July 1948 – a debate held against the background of the Ramle and Lydda expulsions of 12–13 July:

There is a feeling that *faits accomplis* are being created ... The question is not whether the Arabs will return or not return. The question is whether the Arabs are [being or have been] expelled or not ... I want to know, who is creating the facts [of expulsion]? And the facts are being created on orders.[24]

Sprintzak added that 'a line of action ... of expropriating and of emptying the land of Arabs by force' is in force.[25]

According to Morris, 282 of the 330 villages (85 per cent) evacuated were depopulated as a result of direct Jewish attack. However, based on several books published in the last 15 years we have calculated that:

- at least 122 Arab localities were expelled at gunpoint by Jewish forces;
- 270 localities were evacuated under assault by Jewish troops; the tactic of attacking a locality from two directions, but leaving 'escapes routes' was particularly perfected by Yigal Allon as a deliberate method to ensure Arab evacuation;
- 38 localities were evacuated out of fear of attack or being caught in the cross-fire;
- 49 localities were vacated under the influence of the fall of a neighbouring town;
- 12 were evacuated as a result of psychological warfare methods, spreading rumours and whispering campaigns.

'THE SMOKING GUN': LYDDA AND RAMLE, 12–13 JULY 1948

Some 90 per cent of the Palestinians living in territory occupied by the Israelis in 1948–49 were driven out, many by psychological warfare and/or military pressure. In addition, a very large number were expelled at gunpoint. Examples of 'outright expulsions' include the widely documented cases of Lydda and Ramle in July 1948 – two very large expulsions which account for nearly 10 per cent of the total exodus; the expulsion from the town of al-Faluja and the remaining inhabitants of Beisan and of al-Majdal (in 1950); the expulsion of the villages of Safsaf, Sa'sa', al-Mansura, Tarbikha, Nabi Rubin, Kafr Bir'im, Suruh, Iqrit, Farradiya, Kafr 'Inan, al-Qudayriya, 'Arab al-Shamalina, Zangariya, 'Arab al-Suyyad, al-Bassa, al-Ghabisiya, Danna, Nuris, Tantura, Qisarya, Khirbet al-Sarkas, al-Dumayra, 'Arab al-Fuqara, 'Arab al-Nufay'at, Miska, Tabsar (Khirbet 'Azzun), Zarnuqa, al-Qubayba, Yibna, Zakariya, Najd, Sumsum, 'Iraq al-Manshiya, al-Dawayma, Deir Yassin and al-Majdal. In the cases of Lydda and Ramle, over 60,000 Palestinians were expelled. Ben-Gurion and three senior army officers, Yigal Allon, Yitzhak Rabin and Moshe Dayan, were directly involved, with Allon in command of the operation. Morris writes:

At 13.30 hours on 12 July ... Lieutenant-Colonel Yitzhak Rabin, Operation Dani head of Operations, issued the following order: '1. The inhabitants of Lydda must be expelled quickly without attention to age. They should be directed to Beit Nabala ... Implement immediately.' A similar order was issued at the same time to the Kiryati Brigade concerning the inhabitants of the neighbouring town of Ramle, occupied by Kiryati troops that morning ... On 12 and 13 July, Yiftah and Kiryati brigades carried out their orders, expelling the 50–60,000 remaining inhabitants of and refugees camped in and around the two towns ... About noon on 13 July, Operation Dani HQ informed IDF General Staff/Operations: 'Lydda police fort has been captured. [The troops] are busy expelling the inhabitants [*oskim begeirush hatoshavim*].' Lydda inhabitants were forced to walk eastwards to the Arab Legion lines; many of Ramle's inhabitants were ferried in trucks or buses. Clogging the roads ... the tens of thousands of refugees marched, gradually shedding their worldly goods along the way. It was a hot summer day. Arab chroniclers, such as Sheikh Muhammad Nimr al Khatib, claimed that hundreds of children died in the march, from dehydration and disease. One Israeli witness described the spoor: the refugee column 'to begin with [jettisoned] utensils and furniture and, in the end, bodies of men, women and children ...'[26]

THE MASSACRES FACTOR

According to the Israeli military historian Arieh Yitzhaki, about ten major massacres (defined as more than 50 victims in each massacre) and about 100 smaller massacres (of individuals or small groups) were committed by Jewish forces in 1948–49. The massacres, according to Yitzhaki, had a devastating impact on the Palestinian population, inducing and precipitating the exodus. Yitzhaki went further to suggest that murders were committed in almost every village.[27] Another Israeli historian, Uri Milstein, a myth-shatterer, corroborates Yitzhaki's estimate of the extent of massacres and goes even further to suggest that each battle in 1948 ended with a massacre: 'In all Israel's wars massacres were committed but I have no doubt that the war of Independence was the dirtiest of them all.'[28]

Deir Yassin, 9 April 1948

Deir Yassin was the site of the most notorious massacre perpetrated against Palestinian civilians in 1948, a massacre that became the single most important contributory factor to the 1948 exodus. On 9 April over 250 unarmed villagers, including women, the elderly and children, were murdered. There were also cases of rape and mutilation. Most recent Israeli writers have no difficulty in acknowledging the Deir Yassin massacre and its effect, if not intention, of precipitating the exodus. However, most of these writers take refuge in the fact that the Deir Yassin atrocities were committed by the 'dissidents' of the Irgun Tzvai Leumi (Irgun, then commanded by Menahem Begin) and Lehi (the Stern Gang, then co-commanded by Yitzhak Shamir), thus exonerating Ben-Gurion's Haganah, the military forces of mainstream Zionism. Recently published Hebrew material, however, shows that:

1. in January 1948 village *mukhtar* (selectman) and notables had reached a non-aggression agreement with the Haganah and the neighbouring Jewish settlements of Giva't Shaul and Montefiori;
2. the Irgun's assault on the village on 9 April had the full backing of the Haganah commander of Jerusalem, David Shaltiel. The latter not only chose to break his agreement with the villagers, but also provided rifles and ammunition for the Irgunists;

3. the Haganah contributed to the assault on the village with artillery cover from a Palmah company;
4. a Haganah intelligence officer in Jerusalem, Meir Pa'il, was dispatched to Deir Yassin to assess the effectiveness and performance of the Irgun forces.[29] Although the actual murders were carried out by the Irgun and Lehi, the responsibility for the slaughter of the villagers must be shared by the Haganah and Irgun/Lehi.

More significantly, recently published Israeli material shows that Deir Yassin was only one among many massacres carried out by Jewish forces (mainly by the Haganah and the IDF) in 1948. Recent research proves that the Palestinians were less likely to evacuate their towns and villages in the second half of the war. Hence the numerous massacres committed from June 1948 onwards, such as those of Lydda, Khirbet Nasir al-Din, 'Ayn Zaytun, 'Aylabun, Sa'sa', Jish, al-Dawayma, al-Tira (near Haifa), Safsaf, Sha'ib, Saliha and Hulam, were all designed to force mass evacuations.

Al-Dawayma, 28–29 October 1948

In 1948 al-Dawayma, situated in the western Hebron hills, had a population of some 3,500. Like Deir Yassin, it was unarmed and was captured on 29 October 1948 without a fight. The massacre of 80–100 villagers was carried out at the next day, not in the heat of the battle but after the Israeli army had clearly emerged victorious in the war. The testimonies of Israeli soldiers who witnessed the atrocities and took part in the overrunning of the village by Moshe Dayan's 89th Battalion reveal that the IDF troops entered the village, carried out the liquidation of civilians and then threw their victims into pits. 'The children they killed by breaking their heads with sticks. There was not a house without [its] dead.' The remaining Arabs were then sealed in houses 'without food and water', as the village was systematically razed. 'One commander ordered a sapper to put two old women in a certain house ... and blew up the house with them [inside] ... One soldier boasted that he had raped a woman and then shot her. One woman, with a newborn baby in her arms, was employed to clear the courtyard where the soldiers ate. She worked for a day or two. In the end they shot her and her baby.' Other sources indicate that the atrocities were committed in and around the village, including in the mosque and in a cave nearby, that houses with old people locked inside were blown up, and that there were several cases of the shooting and raping of women.[30]

In *The Birth of the Palestinian Refugee Problem, 1947–1949*, Morris documents the following (partial) inventory of IDF massacres committed in Galilee in October 1948:

- Safsaf, a village in the Safad area, was occupied on 29 October. The Jewish forces assembled all the inhabitants of the village (who numbered approximately 1,000) and killed between 50 and 70 men.

'52 men [were] tied with a rope and dropped down a well and shot. 10 were killed. Women pleaded for mercy. [There were] 3 cases of rape... a girl aged 14 was raped. Another 4 were killed.'

- Jish: 'a women and her baby were killed. Another 11 [were killed?].'
- Sa'sa': cases of 'mass murder [though] a thousand [?] raised white flags [of surrender and] a sacrifice was offered [to welcome] the army. The whole village was expelled.'
- Saliha: '94 ... were blown up with a house.'[31]
- 'Aylabun, October 1948: after the capture of the village on 30 October, twelve youngsters were murdered.[32]
- Majd al-Kurum, November 1948: seven men and two women were murdered.[33]
- Deir al-Asad and al-Bi'ene, 3 October 1948: two men from each village were taken and publicly executed by IDF soldiers.[34]
- Abu-Zurayk: IDF soldiers executed several Arabs several hours after the capture of the village.
- Um al-Shuf: seven youngsters were murdered after the capture of the village.[35]
- Hula, 31 October: a senior IDF officer, Shmuel Lahis, murdered several dozen Arab civilians (up to 80 people); he was on guard in a mosque in the undefended south Lebanese village of Hula during the land clearing operations of October.[36]

Other atrocities carried out earlier in 1948 were reported by Morris and other researchers:

- Khirbet Nasir al-Din, 12 April: (near Tiberias) a Haganah force 'captured the village of Khirbet Nasir al-Din ... some non-combatants were apparently killed and some houses destroyed'.[37]
- Nasr-ed Din: 'Zionists attacked the village of Nasr-ed Din (with 90 Arab inhabitants) and destroyed all its houses, killing some of its inhabitants, including women and children, and expelling all the rest' (Nafez Nazzal, *The Palestinian Exodus from Galilee, 1948*, p. 29).
- 'Ayn Zaytun, 3–4 May: a few days before the conquest of Safad, some 37 young men were rounded up from the neighbouring village of 'Ayn Zaytun after its occupation by the Haganah. They were among the 70 Arab detainees massacred by two Palmah 3rd Battalion soldiers, on Battalion commander Moshe Kalman's orders, on 3 or 4 May in the gully between 'Ayn Zaytun and Safad.[38]
- Tantura, 22–23 May: in the case of Tantura, the large-scale massacre was planned well in advance. Tantura and about four coastal villages south of Haifa were targeted by the Israelis for expulsion. The villagers refused to surrender. On 9 May, local Haganah Intelligence and Arab 'experts held a meeting in Netanya to find the best way to "expel or subdue" these coastal villages'.[39] The meeting had been 'preceded by a Haganah effort to obtain the village's surrender without a fight; the

village elders refused, rejecting the Haganah terms which included the surrender of arms ...'[40] Recently Israeli researchers uncovered the Tantura blood-bath, in which scores of Arab civilians were murdered.[41]

- Lydda, 11–12 July: dozens of unarmed civilians who were detained in a mosque and church premises in the town were gunned down. One official Israeli source put the casualty figures at 250 dead and many injured. It is likely, however, that between 250 and 400 Arabs were killed in the large-scale IDF massacre at Lydda and an estimated 350 more died in the subsequent expulsion and forced march of the townspeople.[42]

- Tel Gezer (in the south): a soldier of the IDF Kiryati Brigade testified that his colleagues got hold of ten Arab men and two Arab women, one young one, the other old. All the men were murdered; the young woman was raped; the old woman was murdered.[43]

- Khisas, 12 December 1947: twelve Arab villagers were murdered in cold blood in a Haganah raid.

- Asdud (in the south), end of August 1948: IDF Giv'ati Brigade soldiers murdered ten Arab *fellahin* in cold blood.[44]

- Qisarya (Caesarea), February 1948: the Fourth Battalion of the Palmah forces, under the command of Yosef Tabenkin, conquered Qisarya. According to Uri Milstein, all those who did not escape were murdered.[45]

- Kabri: on 20 May the Carmeli Brigade conquered the village. One of the Israeli soldiers, Yehuda Rashef, got hold of a few (probably seven) youngsters, ordered them to fill up some ditches and then lined them up and fired at them with a machine gun. A few died.[46]

- Abu Shusha, 14 May 1948: evidence of a large-scale massacre.[47]

THE SYSTEMATIC DESTRUCTION OF 418 VILLAGES

Mountains of archival documents and other evidence show a strong correlation between the Zionist 'transfer' solution (which became central to Jewish strategy in the 1930s and 1940s) and the Palestinian *nakba*, the creation of the Palestinian refugee problem, the wilful and systematic destruction of hundreds of Arab villages. By the end of the 1948 war, hundreds of villages had been completely depopulated. Their houses were blown up or bulldozed, with the main objective of preventing the return of the refugees to their homes and villages (in addition to helping perpetuate the Zionist myth that Palestine was virtually an 'empty territory' before the Jews entered it) The exhaustive study by a team of Palestinian field researchers and academics under the direction of Professor Walid Khalidi details the destruction of each village, supplying statistical, historical, topographical, archaeological, architectural and economic material, as well as the circumstances of each village's occupation and depopulation, and a description of what remains. Khalidi's research team visited all but 14 of the sites, made comprehensive reports and took photographs, recording all the details that remains. *All That Remains*[48] is both a monumental study and a memorial: an acknowledgement of the enormous suffering of hundreds of thousands of Palestinian refugees.

There is an apparent inconsistency in the determination of the number of Palestinian localities depopulated and destroyed in 1948. Morris lists 369 villages and towns, and gives the date and circumstances of their depopulation, relying mostly on Israeli archival and non-archival sources.[49] Khalidi's figure of 418 is based on the villages or hamlets (only) which are listed in the *Palestine Index Gazetteer* of 1945 falling inside the 1949 armistice lines. But Khalidi's figure of 418 amounts to only half the total number of Palestinian villages in Mandated Palestine. More recently, Salman Abu-Sitta has provided an updated register of 531 villages. Abu-Sitta's register includes the localities listed by Morris and Khalidi, as well as those of the tribes in the Beer Sheba District.[50] But while Abu-Sitta adds to the list of destroyed villages, Khalidi's account is the most meticulous and comprehensive. Of the 418 depopulated villages, 293 (70 per cent) were totally destroyed and 90 (22 per cent) were largely destroyed. Seven survived, including 'Ayn Karim (west of Jerusalem), but were taken by Israeli settlers. While an observant traveller can still see some evidence of these villages, in the main all that remains is a scattering of stones and rubble.

THE PRIMARY RESPONSIBILITY OF THE ZIONIST LEADERSHIP FOR THE DISPLACEMENT AND DISPOSSESSION OF THE PALESTINIAN REFUGEES

There is much evidence to show a strong correlation between 'transfer' discussions and ideological intent and actual expulsion orders in 1948. *De facto* 'transfer' or expulsion policies were discussed and adopted in 1948 and carried out. The overwhelming facts show conclusively the primary responsibility of the Zionists for the displacement and dispossession of the Palestinians in 1948. In particular, Ben-Gurion emerges as both an 'obsessive' advocate of 'compulsory transfer' in the late 1930s and the great expeller of the Palestinians in 1948. Israel was primarily responsible for the creation of the Palestinian refugee problem; the exodus was largely the deliberate creation of Jewish leaders (principally Ben-Gurion) and military commanders; it was an outcome of Zionist 'transfer thinking', transfer mentality, transfer predisposition and premeditation. The 1948 war simply provided an opportunity and the necessary background for the creation of a Jewish state largely devoid of Arabs; it concentrated Zionist-Jewish minds, and provided the security, military and strategic explanations and justifications for purging the Jewish state and dispossessing the Palestinians.

THE POST-1948 PERIOD

Preventing the Return of Refugees: Proposals of the Israeli Government's 'Transfer Committee', October 1948

In August 1948 the *de facto* 'transfer committee' was formally and officially appointed by the Israeli cabinet to plan the Palestinian refugees' organised resettlement in the Arab states. The three-member committee was composed of Ezra Danin, a former senior officer of the Haganah Intelligence Service (Shai) (1936–48) and a senior Foreign Ministry adviser on Arab Affairs from July 1948, Zalman Lifschitz, the prime minister's adviser on land matters, and Yosef Weitz, head of the Jewish National Fund's Land Settlement Department, who headed of the committee. Apart from doing everything possible to reduce the Palestinian population in Israel, Weitz and his colleagues sought in October 1948 to amplify and consolidate the demographic transformation of Palestine by:

- preventing the Palestinian refugees from returning to their homes and villages;
- the destruction of Arab villages;
- the settlement of Jews in Arab villages and towns and the distribution of Arab lands among Jewish settlements;
- 'the extrication of the Jews of Iraq and Syria';
- seeking ways that would ensure the absorption of the Palestinian refugees in Arab countries, such as Syria, Iraq, Lebanon and Transjordan, and launching a propaganda campaign to discourage Arab return. Apparently, Ben-Gurion approved these proposals, although he recommended that all the Palestinian refugees be resettled in one Arab state, preferably Iraq, rather than be dispersed among the neighbouring states. Ben-Gurion was also opposed to refugee resettlement in neighbouring Transjordan.[51]

In early 1949 Danin was sent by the Foreign Ministry to England to lobby discreetly for 'initiatives that would assist as many refugees as possible to be absorbed and strike roots in various Arab countries'.[52] Danin firmly believed that money would 'dissolve' the refugee problem.[53] Throughout the 1950s Israel sought western partners for its refugee resettlement projects. From early 1949 onwards Danin, Weitz and other senior Israeli officials spent a great deal of efforts promoting Israeli resettlement schemes. Before leaving for England Danin met Weitz in Jerusalem on 23 January 1949 and expressed the opinion that 'a propaganda [campaign] must be conducted among the Arabs [refugees] that they demand their resettlement in the Arab states'.[54] The reason why Danin, Weitz and their colleagues were preoccupied with refugee resettlement projects outside Palestine stemmed from the fear of refugee return. In a letter to the Cabinet Secretary, Ze'ev Sharef, sent from London on 6 May 1949, Danin wrote about a letter he had received from Weitz in which the latter urged clear 'planning and direction' on the question of refugee resettlement: 'at times' Weitz saw 'a nightmarish picture of long convoys of returning refugees and there is no one to help'.[55]

The Palestinian refugee problem has been at the centre of the Arab-Israeli conflict since 1948. It was mainly the refugees themselves who opposed resettlement schemes in Arab countries. In general Palestinians and Arabs refused to discuss a general settlement of the Arab-Israeli conflict before Israel declared that it accepted the repatriation of the refugees, in accordance with UN General Assembly Resolution 194 (III) of December 1948. That resolution stated that: 'the refugees wishing to return to their homes and live at peace with their neighbours should be permitted to do so at the earliest practicable date'. To Zionist Israelis, on the other hand, the Palestinian 'right of return' appears to entail nothing less than the reversal of Zionism and Israel's transformation into a bi-national state. The official Israeli position has always been that there can be no return of the refugees to Israeli territories, and that the only solution to the problem is their resettlement in the Arab states or elsewhere. Since 1949 Israel has consistently rejected the return of the refugees to their homes and villages; it has always refused to accept responsibility for the refugees and views them as the responsibility of the Arab countries in which they reside. The Israelis did not want the refugees back under any conditions.[56] They did not want them to return because they needed their lands and their villages for Jewish immigrants. Nor did they want the repatriation of an Arab population that would question the Zionist-Jewish character of the state of Israel and undermine it demographically.

Since 1948 successive Israeli governments have refused to discuss any possible return of refugees to the pre-1967 borders. However, between 1949 and 1953 Israel did consider some form of restitution of refugee property in lieu of repatriation.

ISRAELI PROPAGANDA

Since 1948 Israel has continued to claim that the Palestinian refugee exodus was a tactic on the part of the Arabs who launched the war against the Jewish *Yishuv*. In fact, this official version had been cooked up by the Israeli government's Transfer Committee in its report of October 1948, which formulated the main line and arguments of Israeli propaganda in the following decades. It denied any Israeli culpability or responsibility for the Arab exodus – denied, in fact, its own members' roles in various areas and contexts. It also strongly advised against any return of the refugees and proposed that the government play a major role in promoting refugee resettlement in the Arab host countries.[57] Israel has also argued that the Palestinian refugees constituted a population exchange with those Jews who left the Arab world in the 1950s. Although Israel's case was as mendacious as it was misleading, Israeli spokesmen continued to propagate it at home and abroad and many of Israel's friends in the West continued to believe it.

In his book, *The New Middle East*, Shimon Peres repeats the basic points of the Israeli argumentation for rejecting refugee return:

1. the Palestinians fled from their villages and towns in 1948 under orders from their leaders (an allegation that many researchers, including Walid Khalidi, Erskine Childers, Benny Morris, Tom Segev, Simha Flapan, Ilan Pappe and Nur Masalha have shown to be untrue);[58]
2. Peres underestimates the numbers of the 1948 refugees (at 600,000[59]) and equates them with the number of Jews who left Arab countries for Israel;
3. the time has come, Peres argues, to turn away from history and polemics and seek a 'reasonable and fair solution' to the refugee problem, one acceptable to Israelis. According to Peres, the 'right of return' is an unacceptable maximalist position that 'would wipe out the national character of the state of Israel'.[60]

In the 1950s a key slogan coined by senior Israeli Foreign Ministry officials was: 'If you cannot solve it, dissolve it',[61] that is to say, if you cannot solve the Palestinian refugee problem as a political problem, you can try to 'dissolve' the problem and disperse the refugees through economic means and employment projects. In other words, the problem of the Palestine refugees could and should be solved by an economic approach, mainly through their integration into the economies and societies of their countries of residence and/or through their dispersal throughout the interior of the Arab world. This preoccupation with the need to 'dissolve' the refugee problem stemmed from a variety of reasons including the deep fear of Arab 'return' and the determination to remove the problem from the heart of the Arab-Israeli conflict.

EXPULSION OF THE TOWN OF AL-MAJDAL, SUMMER 1950

According to Morris, 'During the immediate post-1948 period, talk of "transferring" Israel's Arab minority was relatively common in Israel.'[62] The Army Chief of Staff, Yigael Yadin, supported implicitly the 'transfer' of Israel's Arabs. In consultation with Ben-Gurion on 8 February 1950, he described the Israeli Arabs as 'a danger in time of war, as in time of peace'.[63] The head of the military government, Lieutenant-Colonel Emmanuel Mor (Markovsky), stated in 1950 ('with probably only marginal exaggeration', according to Morris), that 'the entire nation [i.e. Jews] in Zion [i.e. Israel], without exception, does not want Arab neighbours.'[64] In the summer of 1950, the remaining 2,700 inhabitants of the southern Arab town al-Majdal (now called Ashkelon) received expulsion orders and were transported to the border of the Gaza Strip over a period of a few weeks. The town, which on the eve of the war had 10,000 inhabitants, had been conquered by the Israeli army on 4 November 1948. From that time and throughout 1949, the commanding officer of the Southern Command, General Yigal Allon, had 'demanded ... that the town be emptied of its Arabs'.[65] In February 1949, a government 'Committee for Transferring Arabs' had decided in principle to remove the remaining 2,700 inhabitants of al-Majdal. A year later, in the spring of 1950, Moshe Dayan, Allon's successor in the Southern Command, had decided to direct the clearing of al-Majdal's residents to Gaza. Authorization for this action was given by Ben-Gurion on 19 June 1950.[66] Some 700,000 Jews arrived in Israel between its proclamation as an independent state in May 1948 and the end of 1951. The state's leaders believed that al-Majdal and its lands were needed to rehouse and settle them.

The Israeli state archives in Jerusalem contain dozens of official files with extensive information pertaining to Israel's policies towards the Arab minority, including what usually is described in Israel as 'population transfers'. Although a substantial number of these files are open to researchers and have been used for this chapter, many official files remain classified. However, some idea about the contents of the classified files may be gathered from the archives' index listing those files of the Ministry of Minorities: Expulsion of Inhabitants; Transfer of Inhabitants; Concentration of Arab Residents; Complaints about Police Treatment; Demolition of Arab Houses; and Acts against Civilians.

COMPENSATIONS: ISRAELI PROPOSALS, 1949–53

Israel's economic approach to the Palestinian refugee problem – to try to solve the problem mainly through the integration of the refugees into the economies of various Arab countries and through the initiation of various organized resettlement schemes – also went hand in hand with the Israeli approach to the issue of restitution of refugee property. In October 1948 the official Transfer Committee had recommended that the 'resettlement [costs should come out of] the value of the immovable goods [that is, lands, houses abandoned] in the country (after reparations [for war damages to the *Yishuv*] are deducted), the Arab states will give land, the rest [will come] [from] the UN and international institutions'.[67] The committee had also attempted to work out the monetary value of abandoned Arab property, but was unable to reach any conclusions without further study.[68]

A year later, in October 1949, the Transfer Committee was reconstituted as the Compensation Committee, with the addition of a number of technical advisers and submitted its recommendations six months later. It recommended that in the context of an overall settlement of the Arab-Israeli conflict Israel should make a single, global payment of compensation for rural refugee property, for undamaged urban property and for bank accounts. At the same time, the Compensation Committee advised against the payment of compensation for the Arab share of state land and against making individual restitution payments for individual refugees for two main reasons (according to the committee): first, this would take years to arbitrate, and second, and perhaps more importantly, it would require that refugee owners of property be allowed to return to Israel to take part in the evaluation of their assets. This was considered undesirable.[69] Prime Minister Ben-Gurion, in particular, ruled out the idea of compensating each refugee personally. Israel would not enter into individual claims of compensation.[70]

In June 1953 the Israeli government made another attempt to work out a policy on restitution of refugee property by appointing a new committee, which included senior government officials. The committee's recommendations were submitted in December 1953 and suggested that Israel should contribute $100 million, on account of the overall restitution bill, to an international fund which would be created to initiate collective resettlement projects in Arab countries. This willingness to contribute a share towards the financial cost of compensation was encouraged by the anticipated increase in foreign currency liquidity as a result of the Reparations Agreement with the Federal Republic of Germany, signed earlier in September 1952.[71] At about the same time various Israeli estimates of the global value of total movable and immovable Palestinian refugee property were close to $350 million.[72] Although this figure was close to the United Nations Refugee Office estimate of £120 million, it was only about 16 per cent of the global valuation of Palestinian property losses arrived at in two detailed Palestinian studies.[73]

During the early 1950s the Israeli government signalled its willingness to contribute to any international fund established to resettle Palestinian refugees in Arab countries or elsewhere collectively. However, at the same time, Israel was prepared to shoulder only a share of the total costs of resettling the refugees. Moreover, gradually all Israeli attempts to work out proposals on restitution of Palestinian refugee property were tied to a settlement of abandoned Jewish property in Iraq, and later in other Arab countries.[74] Consequently, since the mid-1950s, all Israeli governments have, in effect, refused to admit any responsibility for monetary compensation to the Palestinian refugees.[75]

'INFILTRATION': REFUGEES ATTEMPTING TO RETURN 1949–56

The Palestinian refugees themselves and their leaders have always demanded repatriation and refused resettlement. In the early 1950s the refugees clung stubbornly to the 'right of return', enshrined in Resolution 194 (III). The refugees believed they would return one day to their homes and villages in what had become Israel. Moreover, large numbers of refugees camped either along, or within a short distance of, Israel's borders, in southern Lebanon, in the West Bank and the Gaza Strip, creating a major 'infiltration' problem for Israel. Between 1948 and 1956, tens of thousands of refugees – mainly peasants deeply attached to the lands – continued to cross the armistice lines, 'infiltrating' (in Israel's terminology) their villages either to slip home, visit relatives, collect possessions, harvest crops or, in some cases, to raid Israeli border settlements. Occasionally, some of these acutely hungry 'infiltrators' robbed or killed Israelis, possibly a personal vengeance for their misfortune.[76] The first Israeli objective was to prevent them and foil the danger of refugees resettling inside Israel.[77] To combat this persistent infiltration, the Israelis carried out vigorous 'retaliatory' attacks against Palestinian targets in general and refugee camps in the Gaza Strip in particular. These attacks resulted in many civilian deaths. Furthermore, between 1949 and 1956, between 2,700 and 5,000 'infiltrators' were killed by the Israeli army, the vast majority unarmed 'economic and social infiltrators'.[78] One major reason for the insistence with which Israel prosecuted its 'retaliatory' policy during these days, according to Livia Rokach,

was the desire of the Zionist ruling establishment to exercise permanent pressure on the Arab states to remove the Palestinian refugees from the 1948 war from the proximity of the armistice lines and to disperse them throughout the interior of the Arab world.[79]

In addition, thousands of refugees who had managed to slip back to their villages were rounded up by the Israeli army and expelled across the border in the early years of the state.

EXPULSION OF THE NEGEV BEDOUIN, 1949–59

The Negev was an early focus of expulsion activities. According to the 1947 UN Partition Plan, the Negev had been included in the areas allotted to the Palestinian Arab state. After its occupation, Ben-Gurion had been anxious to populate the Negev with Jews. In November 1949, some 500 Arab Bedouin families (2,000 people) from the Beer Sheba area were forced across the border into the West Bank. Jordan complained about this expulsion.[80] A further expulsion of 700–1,000 of the 'Azazme or Djahalin tribes to Jordan took place in May 1950.[81] On 2 September 1950 the Israeli army rounded up hundreds of 'Azazme tribesmen (a United Nations Truce Supervision Organization [UNTSO] complaint spoke of 4,000) from the Negev, 'and drove them ... into Egyptian territory'.[82] A week later further expulsion of 'Azazme tribesmen was carried out. UNTSO chief of staff, Major-General William Riley, put the total number of Bedouin at Qusayma in Sinai in mid-September 1950 at 6,200, the majority having been recently expelled by the Israeli army from the Negev. Riley also wrote that the Israeli army killed 13 Bedouin during these expulsion operations.[83] (The Israelis claimed that the 'Azazme tribesmen were crossing back and forth continually between the Negev and Sinai.) In September 1952 the Israeli army expelled some 850 members of the Al-Sani' tribe from the northern Negev to the West Bank. 'Subsequently,' Morris writes, 'several thousand more 'Azazme and other Bedouin tribesmen were expelled to Sinai.'[84]

Morris quotes an Israel Foreign Ministry report as stating that during 1949–53 'Israel expelled all told "close" to 17,000 Negev Bedouin, not all of them alleged infiltrators'.[85] The Arabs of the Negev had been reduced through expulsion and flight from 65,000–95,000, at the end of the British Mandate, to 13,000 by 1951.[86] In fact, the remaining Arabs of the Negev were not granted Israeli identity cards until 1952, a situation which made it easier for the Israeli army to push them out. A year later, in 1953, it was reported in the United Nations that 7,000 Arab Bedouin, approximately half of them from the 'Azazme tribe, had been forcibly expelled from the Negev.[87]

EXPULSION OF GALILEE BEDOUIN BY YITZHAK RABIN, 30 OCTOBER 1956

On 30 October 1956, just one day after the Kafr Qassim massacre, General Yitzhak Rabin, then Commanding Officer of the Northern Command, exploited the tripartite attack against Egypt in the south to carry out a mass expulsion of Israeli Arabs across the northern border into Syria. This little-known episode, which was revealed by Rabin himself in his *Service Notebook*, involved the expulsion of 2,000–5,000 inhabitants of the villages of Krad al-Ghannama and Krad al-Baqqara, to the south of Lake Hula. These people had already been evicted from their native villages by the Israeli army in 1951 in the course of water diversion projects. Then (in 1951) the UN Security Council had passed a resolution calling on Israel to halt work on the water diversion projects to enable the villagers to return to their homes. In the meantime, however, the Israeli army had blown up all the houses in the two villages. In his memoirs, Rabin wrote:

I solved one problem in the north by exploiting the fighting against the Egyptians [in the south] and ... we [the army] transferred about 2,000 Arabs, who had been a burdensome security problem [across the Jordan River into Syria].[88]

Referring to the same episode in an interview in early November 1982, on the 26th anniversary of the Sinai war, Rabin (by then a member of the Knesset) said that 'during Operation Kadesh [the code name of the Sinai operation] in 1956, the IDF expelled between 3,000 and 5,000 Arab villagers, residents of the Galilee, to Syria'. When Rabin was asked what the reaction of the villagers to their expulsion was, he replied: 'I did not take a democratic decision in this matter.'[89] There were no international repercussions to this 1956 episode in Galilee. International attention was focused on the fighting in the south and the Suez Crisis.

TREATMENT OF 'INTERNAL REFUGEES'

In 1948, the Zionist concept of transfer had not been applied universally, and the Israeli army's expulsion policy had failed to rid the new Jewish state of a small Arab minority that remained in situ. However, having expelled 750,000 Palestinian Arabs from the greatly enlarged boundaries of the state and having reduced the Arab population from a large majority to a small minority, the pragmatic Labour leadership believed that it had largely, although not entirely, solved its land/settlement and political/'demographic' problems, and was prepared – albeit reluctantly – to tolerate the presence of a small, politically subordinate and economically dependent Arab minority

– some 150,000 Palestinians of the over 900,000 who used to reside in the areas that became the state of Israel in the aftermath of the 1948 war.

After its establishment, Israel treated the Palestinians remaining within its frontiers almost as foreigners. It swiftly imposed a military government in the areas inhabited by the Arab minority, expropriated over half the lands of this 'non-Jewish' population, and pursued various policies of demographic containment, political control, exclusionary domination and systematic discrimination in all spheres of life. The institution of the military government, together with the imposition of the Defence (Emergency) Regulations promulgated by the British Mandatory Authorities in 1945, empowered the military governors to close off the Arab localities and restrict entry or exit to those who had been issued permits by the military authorities. These regulations also enabled the Israeli authorities to evict and deport people from their villages and towns; to place individuals under administrative detention for indefinite periods without trial; and to impose fines and penalties without due process. The military governors were authorized to close Arab areas in order to prevent internal Arab refugees (also referred to as 'present absentees', estimated at 30,000, or 20 per cent of those remaining) from returning to their homes and lands.

Officially, the purpose of imposing martial law and military government on Israel's Arab minority was security. However, its establishment, which lasted until 1966, was intended to serve a number of both stated and concealed objectives.

The first was to prevent the return of the Palestinian refugees, or 'infiltrators' in Israeli terminology, to their homes. 'In the process other Arabs who had not infiltrated the country were sometimes driven out as well.'[90]

A second goal was to evacuate semi-abandoned (Arab) neighbourhoods and villages as well as some that had not been abandoned, and to transfer their inhabitants to other parts of the country. Some were evacuated from a 'security cordon' along the borders, and others were removed in order to make room for Jews.[91]

The third purpose was to maintain control and supervision over the Israeli Arabs, who were separated and isolated from the Jewish population.[92]

On 24 March 1949, Ben-Gurion appointed a committee directed to submit to him recommendations on whether the military government should be abolished, or whether any changes in its policies toward the Arab minority ought to be carried out. By determining the composition of the committee, Ben-Gurion seems to have ensured the outcome of its investigations. The committee was chaired by General Elimelech Avner, who was the head of the military government; its two other members were Major Michael Hanegbi, the military governor of the Negev, and Yehoshu'a Palmon of the Foreign Ministry. In its report, submitted on 3 May 1949, the committee stressed that the continuation of a forceful military government was essential for security, demographic and land settlement reasons. The committee maintained, *inter alia*, that, a comprehensive and effective supervision over the Arab population was needed in order to: a) prevent it from becoming a fifth column; b) prevent 'infiltration' of Palestinian refugees to their homes and villages; c) find 'a solution to the problem of the Arab refugees who are present within the boundaries of the state [because the problem of internal refugees] requires the transfer [of Arab communities] from one place to another, the concentration of land for their resettlement, the transfer of [Arab] workers to employment centres, [and] directed [Jewish] settlement policies ... The implementation of all these requires a regime with military character, which is not subject to the rules of normal procedures'; d) 'would [facilitate] greatly the implementation of the desired demographic and land policies, and the process of populating [with Jews] the abandoned Arab villages and towns'.[93]

The institution of the military government, together with the imposition of the Defence Emergency Regulations promulgated by the British Mandatory Authorities in 1945, empowered the military governors to close off the Arab localities and restrict entry or exit only to those who had been issued permits by the military authorities. These regulations also enabled the Israeli authorities to evict and deport people; to place individuals under administrative detention for indefinite periods without trial; and to impose fines and penalties without due process.[94] The military governors were also authorized to close Arab areas in order to prevent internal Arab refugees (also referred to as 'present absentees') from returning to their homes and lands that had been confiscated by the state and taken over by new and old Jewish settlements.[95] Palmon suggested in a letter to the Custodian of the Absentees' Property, Zalman Lifschitz of the Prime Minister's Office, and the Attorney-General that 'in the cases in which [internal] refugees want to sell their property in their former place of residence and leave the country, we should encourage them to do that'.[96]

The Israeli state archives in Jerusalem contain files with extensive information pertaining to Israel's policies towards the Arab minority, including what is usually described in Israel as 'population transfers'. Although a substantial part of these files are open to researchers and have been used for this book, many remain classified. However, some idea about the contents of these files may be gathered from the Archives' index.[97] Expulsions of Palestinians, some with Israeli citizenship, across the border continued well into the late 1950s. As late as 1959 – eleven years after the establishment of the state – Bedouin tribes were expelled from the Negev to the Sinai Peninsula in Egypt and to Jordan; only after UN intervention was this action reversed.[98] Thousands of 'Israeli Arabs' were expelled by the Israeli army in the early years of the state (together with many other thousands of Palestinian refugees who had managed to 'infiltrate' their villages and towns).[99]

The Case of Iqrit and Bir'im, November 1948–2000

One of the first evictions of 'Israeli Arabs' from their villages was the forced evacuation of the villages of Iqrit and Bir'im on 6 November 1948. In *Israel's Border Wars, 1949–1956*, Morris discusses the issue of 'Expelling Border Communities [Israeli Arabs] and Nudging Back the Borders':

At the end of 1948 ... Israel decided to clear its border areas of [Israeli] Arab villages, to a depth of five or ten kilometres. The motive of the policy – initially implemented at the beginning of November along the Lebanese border – was military: Arab villages along the border, just behind IDF positions and patrol roads, constituted a threat. They could receive and assist Arab troops and irregulars should the Arabs renew the war; harbour saboteurs and spies; and serve as way stations for infiltrating [Palestinian refugees] returnees, thieves, and smugglers. Partly depopulated villages, such as Tarshiha in the Galilee, beckoned infiltrators [returning refugees] bent on resettlement. And some semi-abandoned border villages, such as Zakariya, in the Jerusalem Corridor, were a socio-economic burden on the state since the young adult males were mostly dead, incarcerated, or had fled to Jordan, while the old, the women, and the children of the village lived off government handouts. Lastly, the authorities wanted as small an Arab minority as possible in the new Jewish state.

In part, these border-area transfers were designed to hamper infiltration [of Palestinian refugees] into Israel.[100]

The struggle of the internal refugees of Iqrit and Bir'im to return to their homes and villages has lasted for more than half a century. In December 1995 (under the pragmatic coalition of Labour-Meretz) a ministerial committee recommended that about 600 families be allowed back and that each village receive 60 hectares of land. Eligibility to return would be restricted to heads of household who lived in one of the villages and owned a house there on 6 November 1948, as well as two adult descendants per household (with their dependants). These recommendations were not implemented. The people of Iqrit and Bir'im demanded more land (having lost more land through expropriation after 1948) and insisted that all their descendants be allowed to return, while Jewish settlements in the area urged that less land be handed to the Arab villagers. A committee of directors-general formed in early 1996, in response to the villagers' campaign, revised the recommendations of December 1995 by removing the two descendants restriction; it also suggested that the government consider expansion of the two villages' boundaries if necessary. No action was taken. A petition filed by the Iqrit villagers in late 1996 was still pending in 1999 before the High Court of Justice: the villagers wanted the Court to order that the ministerial committee recommendations be implemented. On 2 December 1998, the Knesset defeated a private member's bill, submitted by the liberal Knesset member Dedi Tzucker (Meretz), to allow the villagers to return. However, even those liberal Israelis who have supported the villagers' struggle to return Iqrit and Bir'im believe that the case is unique and should not be taken as a precedent to allow other internal refugees (some 250,000) to return to the villages and homes.

WHOLESALE LAND EXPROPRIATION

The outcome of the 1948 war left Israel in control of over five million acres of Palestinian land. After 1948, the Israeli state took over the land of the 750,000 Palestinian refugees, who were barred from returning, while the remaining Palestinian minority was subjected to laws and regulations that effectively deprived it of most of its land. The massive drive to take over Palestinian land has been conducted according to strict legality. Since 1948 Israel has enacted some 30 statutes which transferred land from private Arab to state (Jewish) ownership.[101]

THE 1967 EXODUS: WHY DID THE PALESTINIANS LEAVE?

In his study of the 1967 exodus, William Harris found that the exodus from the West Bank involved up to 250,000 people and was by far the largest out-movement of Palestinians caused by the 1967 hostilities. Harris also estimated the population loss of the Gaza Strip between June and December 1967 at 70,000.[102] In total, some 320,000 Palestinians were expelled from the West Bank and Gaza in the course of the hostilities or shortly after.[103] An important body of new evidence has been unearthed in recent years, much of it appearing in the form of investigative articles in the Hebrew press, which sheds new light on the events surrounding the 1967 exodus.

The 1967 Palestinian exodus has been discussed extensively in a long paper which appeared in 1999 in a collection entitled *The Palestinian Exodus, 1948–1998*.[104] Below is a summary of my conclusions:

1. The 1967 exodus was, in part, a response to the severe situational pressures at the time. The pressures were generated by the Israeli aerial attacks upon these territories, including the extensive use of napalm.
2. The occupation of the West Bank villages and towns by the Israeli army, and the actions of the occupying forces, drove out many Palestinians. Certainly the most drastic of these actions was the evictions of civilians and the deliberate destruction of several villages ('Imwas, Yalu, Bayt Nuba, Bayt Marsam, Bayt 'Awa, Habla, al-Burj and Jiftlik), and the initial and partial destruction of Qalqilya.
3. Other actions, such as threats and the mass detention of male civilians, also created situational pressures.
4. There were other, indirect reasons: the Palestinian villagers were ill-prepared to resist and cope with these situational pressures.
5. They were ill-informed and unfamiliar with the terrifying nature of the aerial attacks.
6. Some Palestinians were left to protect their family, particularly the honour of the women. To this we should add the organized 'transfer' operation (by buses) of Narkiss, Hertzog and Lahat. The extensive use of

loudspeakers in the main cities to encourage departure for Amman is also well documented.

7. The high population losses in some regions were the result of a 'psycho-logical legacy of pre-war events, a legacy of assorted fears', for instance, in the Hebron district and in the region surrounding the village of Qibya in the West Bank, where the Israeli army had carried out a large and infamous massacre in October 1953, in which 65 villagers (mostly women and children) were killed.

8. Another example was in the Latrun area where the over 6,000 residents of Yalu, 'Imwas, and Bayt Nuba were ordered to leave their villages by the Israeli army and the chain-reaction effect of their movement across the West Bank can be traced in the higher losses from other villages on the Latrun–Ramallah–Jerusalem highway.

EPILOGUE

There is a consensus among the Zionist parties in Israel – from Meretz on the left through the Labour and Likud Parties and on to the extreme right – against the Palestinian 'right of return' to the pre-1967 borders. Even liberal Israelis, such as Meron Benvenisti (deputy mayor of Jerusalem from 1971 to 1978) believe that the return of Palestinian refugees to their villages and lands is 'unrealistic'. Benvenisti calls for the right of return to be fulfilled only through 'compensation' and absorption of some refugees in the West Bank and Gaza.[105] In the final status negotiations the basic premises of the position of the Labour government are likely to be as follows: Israel will still refuse to recognize the 'right of return'; it will categorically reject any return of refugees based on UN Resolution 194 of 1948 or on any other international resolutions. Israel will also refuse to commit itself to admitting a fixed number or an annual quota of the 1948 refugees to the pre-1967 borders within a family reunion scheme. Israel will maintain that family reunion since 1948 has been a unilateral Israeli decision, based on purely humanitarian con-siderations, and that every application will be considered on its own merit. Even if Israel agrees to allow reunification of families based on humanitarian considerations, it will insist on being the only authority to decide who, how many, when and how they will be allowed to enter the country.

NOTES

1. A speech delivered at a meeting of the French Zionist Federation, Paris, 28 March 1914, in B. Litvinoff (ed.), *The Letters and Papers of Chaim Weizmann*, vol. 1, Series B (Jerusalem: Israel Universities Press, 1983), paper 24, pp. 115–16.

2. See protocol of Arthur Ruppin's statement at the Jewish Agency Executive's meeting, 20 May 1936, in Y. Heller, *Bamavak Lemedinah: Hamediniyut Hatziyonit Bashanim 1936–48* [The Struggle for the State: The Zionist Policy 1936–48] (Jerusalem: Zalmar Shazar Centre, 1984), p. 140.

3. Israel Zangwill, *The Voice of Jerusalem* (London: William Heinemann, 1920), p. 104.

4. (London, 1951), pp. 160–1.

5. David Ben-Gurion, *Zichronot* [Memoirs], vol. 4 (Tel Aviv: 'Am 'Oved, 1974), pp. 297–9.

6. Ibid.

7. Cited in Shabtai Teveth, *Ben-Gurion and the Palestinian Arabs* (Oxford: Oxford University Press, 1985), p. 189.

8. As reported in the *New Judea* (London), XIII, nos 11–12 (August–September 1937), p. 220.

9. Protocol of the Jewish Agency Executive meeting of 7 June 1938, in Jerusalem, confidential, vol. 28, no. 51, Central Zionist Archives, Jerusalem.

10. David Ben-Gurion, 'Lines for Zionist Policy', 15 October 1941.

11. Ibid.

12. Simha Flapan, *The Birth of Israel: Myths and Reality* (London: Croom Helm, 1987), p. 90.

13. David Ben-Gurion, *Yoman Hamilhamah* [War Diary], vol. 1, entry dated 6 February 1948, p. 211.

14. *Al Darchei Mediniyutenu: Mo'atzah 'Olamit Shel Ihud Po'ali Tzion (c.s.)-Din Vehesbon Male, 21 July–7 August* [1938] [A Full Report about the World Convention of Ihud Po'alei Tzion, C.S.] (Tel Aviv: Central Office of Hitahdut Po'alei Tzion Press, 1938).

15. Protocol of the Jewish Agency Executive meeting of 12 June 1938, vol. 28, no. 53, Central Zionist Archives, Jerusalem.

16. Cited in Yosef Gorny, *Zionism and the Arabs* (Oxford: Clarendon Press, 1987), p. 304. Katznelson's support for Arab transfer is also found in his writings. See Berl Katznelson, *Ketavim* [Writings] (Tel Aviv: Mapai Publications, 1949), vol. 12, pp. 241, 244. See also Anita Shapira, *Berl: The Biography of a Socialist Zionist* (Cambridge: Cambridge Univesity Press, 1984), p. 335.

17. Weitz Diary, A246/7, entry dated 20 December 1940, pp. 1090–1, Central Zionist Archives, Jerusalem.

18. Weitz Diary, A246/7, entry dated 17 July 1941, p. 1204, CZA.

19. Ibid., entry dated 20 March 1941, p. 1127.

20. Ibid., entry dated 18 April 1948, p. 2358, CZA.

21. Nur Masalha, *Expulsion of the Palestinians: The Concept of 'Transfer' in Zionist Political Thought, 1882–1948* (Washington, DC: Institute for Palestine Studies, 1992), pp. 30–8.

22. Ibid., pp. 93–9.

23. Aharon Cohen, memorandum entitled 'Our Arab Policy During the War', in Giva'at Haviva, Hashomer Hatza'ir Archives, 10 October 1995 (4).

24. Quoted in Benny Morris, *1948 and After* (Oxford: Clarendon Press, 1990), pp. 42–3.

25. Ibid.

26. Ibid., p. 2.

27. See Guy Erlich, in *Ha'ir*, 6 May 1992.

28. Quoted in ibid.

29. For further details, See Nur-eldeen Masalha, 'On Recent Hebrew and Israeli Sources for the Palestinian Exodus, 1947–49', *Journal of Palestine Studies* (Autumn 1988), pp. 122–3.

30. Ibid., pp. 127–30. See also two articles in *Hadashot*, 24, 26 August 1984; Benny Morris, *The Birth of the Palestinian Refugee Problem, 1947–1949* (Cambridge: Cambridge University Press, 1987), pp. 222–3.

31. Morris, *The Birth of the Palestinian Refugee Problem*, p. 230.

32. Ibid., p. 229.

33. Guy Erlich, in *Ha'ir*, 6 May 1992.

34. Ibid.

35. Ibid.

36. '*Al-Hamishmar*, 3 March 1978; *Jerusalem Post*, 28 February 1978.

37. Morris, *The Birth of the Palestinian Refugee Problem*, p. 71.

38. Ibid., p. 102; Netiva Ben-Yehuda, *Miba'ad La'avitut* [Through the Binding Ropes] (Jerusalem: Domino Press, 1985), pp. 243–8; Nafez Nazzal, *The Palestinian Exodus from Galilee, 1948* (Beirut, Institute for Palestine Studies, 1978), p. 36.

39. Ibid., p. 119.

40. Ibid., p. 120.

41. See 'Israeli Researcher Uncovers 1948 Bloodbath', to be found at <http://dailynews.yahoo.com/h/nm/20000/19/wl/mideast_massacre_1.htm>.

42. *Sefer Hapalmah*, vol. II, p. 565; Elhanan Orren, *Baderech El-Ha'ir, Mivtza' Dani* [On the Road to the City, Operation Dani] (Tel Aviv, Ma'arachot, 1976), p. 110; Michael Palumbo, *The Palestinian Catastrophe* (London: Faber and Faber, 1987), p. 137; Raja'i Buseilah, 'The Fall of Lydda: Impressions and Reminiscences', *Arab Studies Quarterly* 3, no. 2 (Spring 1981), pp. 123–51; Guy Erlich, in *Ha'ir*, 6 May 1992.

43. Erlich, in *Ha'ir*.

44. Ibid.

45. Ibid.

46. Ibid.

47. See *Masa al-Balad*, 24 March 1995, p. 25. Other documented atrocities in 1946–48 included: The King David Hotel bomb attack (carried out by the Irgun), 22 July 1946, which resulted in the death of about 90 British, Arab and Jewish men and women; Fajje, 20 May 1947, several Arab civilians were killed; 'Arab Sawarka, 21 May 1947; Abu Laban family, 15 July 1947; Damascus Gate, Jerusalem, a bomb attack by the Irgun, 13 December 1947, four Arab civilians were killed; Balad al-Shaykh, 11 December 1947 and 31 December–1 January 1948; 14 civilians, of whom ten were women and children, were killed; the second attack by the Haganah; Qazaza, 19 December 1947; five Arab children were killed in this Haganah attack; Jaffa Municipality and Welfare Centre, 4 January 1947; 17 Arab civilians were killed by attack by Lehi; Semiramis Hotel-Jerusalem, 5 January 1948: The Haganah blew up the hotel; 12 Arab civilians were killed, among them four women and five children; Khirbet 'Arab Sukrayr, 9 January 1948, five Arab were killed and five injured in a Haganah attack; Ramle, 20 February 1948, an attack by the Irgun, killing six Arab civilians and wounding 31. Among those killed were four children; Al-Husayniyya, 12 March and 16–17 March 1948. The Palmah 3rd Battalion twice attacked the village in Upper Galilee. In the first attack, 15 Arabs were killed, including ten women and children, and 20 seriously wounded. In the second raid more than 30 Arab civilians were killed.

48. Walid Khalidi (ed.), *All That Remains: The Palestinian Villages Occupied and Depopulated by Israel in 1948* (Washington, DC: Institute for Palestine Studies, 1992).

49. Morris, *The Birth of the Palestinian Refugee Problem*.

50. Salman Abu-Sitta, *Palestinian Right to Return: Sacred, Legal and Possible* (second edition, London: The Palestinian Return Centre, May 1999), p. 12.

51. Benny Morris, 'Yosef Weitz and the Transfer Committees, 1948–49', *Middle Eastern Studies* 22, no. 4 (October 1986), pp. 549–50.

52. Ezra Danin, *Tzioni Bekhol Tnai* [A Zionist in Every Condition], vol. 1 (Jerusalem: Kiddum, 1987), p. 317.

53. Ibid.

54. Yosef Weitz, *Yomani Veigrotai Labanim* [My Diary and Letters to the Children] (Tel Aviv: Massada, 1965), vol. 4, entry for 23 January 1949, p. 7.

55. Danin, *Tzioni Bekhol Tnai*, vol. 1, p. 319; Morris, *1948 and After*, p. 138, citing Danin's letter to Weitz from London dated 26 April 1949.

56. In the 1950s and the early 1960s there was a minority of left-wing and liberal Zionists, represented by the Mapam Party and the small group of Ihud, who were prepared to accept the absorption of a very limited number of refugees in Israel within the framework of an overall peace settlement of the Arab–Israeli conflict. See, for instance, *New Outlook* (December 1961), p. 9.

57. Morris, 'Yosef Weitz and the Transfer Committees', p. 556.

58. This and several other Israeli allegations have been examined and discredited as being part of an Israeli disinformation campaign. See *Spectator*, 12 May 1961; Morris, *The Birth of the Palestinian Refugee Problem*; Flapan, *The Birth of Israel: Myths and Reality*; Tom Segev, *1949: The First Israelis* (New York: The Free Press, 1986); Ilan Pappe, *The Making of the Arab–Israeli Conflict, 1947–1951* (London: I. B. Tauris, 1992); Masalha, *Expulsion of the Palestinians*, pp. 173–99.

59. According to the UN Technical Committee on Refugees, the number of Palestinian refugees in August 1949 was '711,000', comprising about half the total Palestinian population at that time (1.415 million). According to United Nations Relief and Works Agency, the number of Palestinian refugees in 1992 was some 2.7 million.

60. Shimon Peres, *The New Middle East* (London: Shaftesbury, Element Books, 1993), p. 198.

61. See Danin, *Tzioni Bekhol Tnai*, vol. 1, p. 317.

62. Benny Morris, *Israel's Border Wars, 1949–1956* (Oxford: Clarendon Press, 1993), n. 160, p. 164.

63. Cited in ibid.

64. Ibid.

65. Cited in Morris, *1948 and After*, p. 257.

66. Ibid., pp. 258–9; Yehuda Litani, in *Hadashot*, 7 December 1990.

67. See Morris, *1948 and After*, p. 134.

68. Ronald W. Zweig, 'Restitution of Property and Refugee Rehabilitation: Two Case Studies', *Journal of Refugee Studies* 6, no. 1 (1993), p. 61; Morris, *The Birth of the Palestinian Refugee Problem*, p. 259.

69. Zweig, 'Restitution of Property and Refugee Rehabilitation', p. 61.

70. Gazit, *The Palestinian Refugee Problem*, p. 11.

71. Zweig, 'Restitution of Property and Refugee Rehabilitation', pp. 59 and 62.

72. Ibid., pp. 61–2.

73. The estimate produced by Sami Hadawi and Atif Kubursi is £743 million, while Yusif Sayigh's estimate is £756.7 million. For further discussion, see Sami Hadawi, *Palestinian Rights and Losses in 1948: A Comprehensive Study* (London: Saqi Books, 1988), pp. 186–9; Yusif A. Sayigh, *The Israeli Economy* (Beirut: PLO Research Centre, 1966), pp. 92–133 (in Arabic).

74. Zweig, 'Restitution of Property and Refugee Rehabilitation', p. 62.

75. Gazit, *The Palestinian Refugee Problem*, p. 10.

76. On Arab refugee 'infiltration', see Morris, *Israel's Border Wars*, pp. 28–68; David McDowall, *The Palestinians: The Road to Nationhood* (London: Minority Rights Publications, 1994), pp. 35–6.

77. Segev, *1949: The First Israelis* (New York: The Free Press, 1986), p. 52.

78. Morris, *Israel's Border Wars*, pp. 135–7.

79. Livia Rokach, 'Israel State Terrorism: An Analysis of the Sharett Diaries', *Journal of Palestine Studies* 9, no. 3 (Spring 1980), p. 21.

80. Ibid., p. 154.

81. Ibid.

82. Ibid., p. 155.

83. Ibid., pp. 15–56.

84. Ibid., p. 157.

85. Ibid. W.W. Harris, *Taking Root: Israeli Settlement in the West Bank, the Golan and Gaza-Sinai 1967–1980* (Chichester: Research Studies Press, 1980), pp. 7 and 16–17.

86. Cited in Maddrell, *The Beduin of the Negev*, p. 6.

87. Cited in Christina Jones, *The Untempered Wind: Forty Years in Palestine* (London: Longman, 1975), p. 218.

88. Yitzhak Rabin, *Pinkas Sherut* (Service Notebook; memoirs written in collaboration with Dov Goldstein] (Tel Aviv: Sifriyat Ma'ariv, 1979), vol. 1, p. 97.

89. Eli Tabor in *Yedi'ot Aharonot*, 2 November 1982, p. 7.

90. Segev, *1949: The First Israelis*, p. 52.

91. Ibid.

92. Ibid.

93. Israeli State Archives (ISA), Foreign Ministry, 2401/19a.

94. Segev, *1949: The First Israelis*, p. 51.

95. Penny Maddrell, *The Beduin of the Negev* (London: The Minority Rights Group, Report No. 81, 1990), p. 7.

96. ISA, Foreign Ministry, 2401/21; ISA, Foreign Ministry, 2401/21b.

97. Segev, *1949*, p. 64.

98. Sabri Jiryis, *The Arabs in Israel* (New York: Monthly Review Press), p. 82.

99. Quoted in Morris, *Israel's Border Wars*, pp. 157–8. For further discussion of many incidents of expulsions during this period, see Nur Masalha, *A Land without a People: Israel, Transfer and the Palestinians, 1949–1996* (London: Faber and Faber, 1997), pp. 1–14.

100. Morris, *Israel's Border Wars* , p. 138.

101. Masalha, *A Land Without a People*, p. 135; Oren Yiftachel, *Planning a Mixed Region in Israel* (Aldershot: Avebury, 1992), appendix I, p. 313.

102. W. Harris, *Taking Root: Israeli Settlement in the West Bank, the Golan and Gaza-Sinai 1967–1980* (Chichester: Research Studies Press, 1980), pp. 7 and 16–17.

103. Israeli estimates range from 173,000 to 200,000 while Jordanian and Palestinian estimates range from 250,000 to 408,000 (from June 1967 until the end of 1968). Cited in Walid Salim, 'The [Palestinians] Displaced in 1967: The Problem of Definition and Figures', in *The Palestinians Displaced and the Peace Negotiations* (Ramallah, West Bank: Palestinian Diaspora and Refugee Centre, 1996), p. 21. The real figure is probably somewhere around 300,000 people.

104. Nur Masalha, 'The 1967 Palestinian Exodus', in Ghada Karmi and Eugene Cotran (eds), *The Palestinian Exodus, 1948–1998* (Reading: Ithaca Press, 1999), pp. 63–109.

105. Meron Benvenisti, *Sacred Landscape: The Buried History of the Holy Land since 1948* (Berkeley: University of California Press, 2000).

Part II

The Interests of the Major Actors

3 ISRAELI PERCEPTIONS OF THE REFUGEE QUESTION

Ilan Pappe

The current Israeli attitude towards and perception of the Palestinian refugee problem has to be analysed against their conduct in the 1948 Palestine war. The Zionist labour movement, at the time leading the Jewish community, wished to bridge the impossible gap between an ethnocentric nationalist ideology on the one hand, and a wish to belong to the community of liberal and democratic western states on the other. This movement, headed at the time by David Ben-Gurion, had declared in 1942 the whole of Palestine (including Transjordan) as the future Jewish state, but in 1946 had been content to revert to his 1936 tactical position – a Jewish commonwealth within Palestine – by transferring the indigenous population from areas in which Jews lived or from the vicinity in which they were living. By the time the British Mandate ended in 1948, the demographic composition and distribution in Palestine was such as to rule out any partition of the country into two homogeneous ethnic states. Even the UN General Assembly, in its famous partition plan of 29 November 1947, Resolution 181, recognized this complexity by dividing the land into an Arab state and a Jewish state, of which almost half the population was to be Arab.[1]

If the Jewish state was to remain bi-national and democratic, the Arab Palestinians could have had a decisive effect on the new state's identity and future. The Zionist labour movement rejected such a possibility out of hand.

This gap between a desire to be ethnically pure and preserve the principle of democracy could be bridged only by giving up the dream of a Zionist state or by cleansing the territory of the Jewish state of any substantial Palestinian presence. Nur Masalha and Benny Morris have both accumulated enough evidence to show how, from the beginning of the Zionist case, and at a much more intensive pace after 1936, the plan to transfer the Palestinians out of 'Jewish Palestine' became a major plank of Zionist thought and eventually a basic principle guiding the *Yishuv*'s policy in the 1948 war.[2] In the months leading to the war Israel prepared its ethnic-cleansing programme – a plan that included mass expulsions, sporadic massacres, campaign of terror and intimidation, and finally confiscation of land and assets.[3]

When the war ended every possible step was taken to prevent the repatriation of the refugees. The act of people returning to their homes after the winds of war subsided was regarded as an elementary and basic humanitarian development by the international community which, through the UN General Assembly, authorized it in Resolution 194.

International support for the unconditional repatriation of the Palestinian refugees was backed even by the US delegation to the United Nations. The Israeli government implemented a vigorous and callous policy of eradicating all that was left of the deserted Palestinian villages and neighbourhoods, establishing in their place new Jewish settlements or turning them into cultivated land.[4] This policy begun in August 1948 and ended only in 1954. By that time any demand for repatriation would necessitate uprooting Jewish settlers brought by the government to the new settlements or accommodated in the old Palestinian houses. During that time, some Israeli politicians and intellectuals put forward the idea of repatriating about 100,000 refugees, some, such as the Israeli Foreign Minister, Moshe Sharett, doing so in response to American pressure (which did not last for long); others, such as the Jewish philosopher Martin Buber, from a moral position. Sharett would later suggest transferring some of the money Israel received as compensation from the Germans to the refugees,[5] while Buber, in 1958, wrote to David Ben-Gurion, the prime minister, urging him to take the initiative and put forward an Israeli proposal for a solution.

In his memo to the prime minister, Buber went further than any Israeli politicians to this day. He pointed to the presence of internal refugees in Israel as well to the refugees in the camps. He wished the government to repatriate as far as possible the internal refugees as for those in camps:

In the case of the refugees living in the Arab states, it is possible for the Israeli government to change in a fundamental way their situation ... We suggest [the memo was written by the organization 'Ihud'] that the Israeli government would demand in the UN an immediate action and comprehensive action for solving the Palestinian refugee problem. Israel should declare its readiness to repatriate a certain number of refugees, provided that all the parties concerned would be willing to sit with Israel to discuss of how best this project can be implemented ... The Israeli government should invite experts to help devise a plan for resettlement both in Israel and in the Arab countries ... We do not suggest fixing a numbers right now, before a thorough examination of condition would be carried out ...[6]

What is missing here is Israel's moral responsibility for creating the refugee problem. But Buber had very clear notions about that. In correspondence with a former student, Gideon Fruedenberg, in December 1948, the ex-student was insulted by what he saw as Buber's doubt about Zionism's moral basis and justification given its conduct in the 1948 war. A few months before this correspondence, Buber had ridiculed the Zionist leadership's claim that their community had been the victim of the 1948 war and that the Palestinians had been the aggressors. Buber noted that Zionist policy from its very beginning had been an act of aggression against the Palestinians. Moreover, wrote Buber to his pupil, there are facts with regard to the war that refute your criticism, 'but I cannot explain it here, I am willing to do it in a conversation'.[7] The editor of Buber's letters, Paul Mendes-Flohr, wrote the following explanation for this ambiguous phrase: 'It is quite possible that Buber refers here to the clandestine actions of the Israeli Defence Forces which meant to encourage the flights of the Arabs from Israel. The insinuations employed here by Buber is the result of Buber's fear of the military censorship.'[8] Buber always believed that the wish to create a Jewish majority or exclusivity would end in the total 'moral bankruptcy' of the Zionist project, as it led to expulsion of the Palestinians in 1948. But Ben-Gurion rejected all these offers and led the anti-repatriation policy with full force.

He was fully supported by the intellectual and scholarly establishment. These political and academic forces, from 1954 until recently, excluded the refugees from the Israeli collective memory and replaced them in the consciousness of Israelis as well as in the Hebrew vocabulary with derogatory terms such as terrorists and saboteurs. There was no refugee problem on the agenda as far as the various Israeli governments were concerned; there was only Palestinian terror, which had to be dealt with military means.

At the end of the June 1967 war Israel created a new refugee problem. However, those expelled from the West Bank were acknowledged as refugees, since the public and the political systems were divided on the issue of the occupied territories. Since a large number of Israeli Jews were willing to withdraw from the West Bank and the Gaza Strip, the return of refugees to these territories seemed legitimate and did not involve any soul-searching on the part of the Israelis.

The Palestine question – for Israel and the world at large – was the fate of the Palestinian territories occupied by Israel in the 1967 war.[9] Israel conducted a quite successful campaign of excluding the refugee problem from the peace agenda. Ever since the first peace conference on post-1948 Palestine (the Lausanne meeting of April 1949), the refugee problem has been excluded from the peace talks and disassociated from the concept of 'the Palestine conflict'. In the wake of the June 1967 war, the world at large accepted Israel's claim that the conflict in Palestine revolves around the territories occupied by Israel in that war. Several Arab regimes have cooperated with this notion and have been ready to abandon the refugee problem as an issue in their bilateral peace negotiations with Israel. The issue of the refugees was kept alive and in the consciousness of people in the Middle East and in the world at large only by the PLO activity and policies. Outside the Middle East, it was the United Nations that mentioned in several of its resolutions the obligation of the international community to ensure the full and unconditional repatriation of the Palestinian refugees, a commitment first made in Resolution 194 from 11 December 1948.

The Oslo Accords are no different. Their architects, Americans, Israelis and Palestinians, have placed the refugee issue in a sub-clause, making it

almost invisible within the flood of words in the documents describing future
bridges, bypasses, garrisons and cantons. The Palestinian partners to the
Accords contributed to this obfuscation – probably out of oversight rather
than bad faith – but the result is all too clear. The refugee problem, the heart
of the Palestine conflict, a reality acknowledged by all the Palestinians
wherever they are and by anyone sympathizing with the Palestinian cause,
was marginalized in the Oslo documents. The structure built for implementing the accord accentuated the negotiators' disregard of, and almost
scornful attitude to, the refugee problem. A multilateral committee meant
to deal with the refugee problem was directed by the Israelis to deal only with
the 1967 West Bank refugees, but not the 1948 refugees.

The implementation of the documents was no better; it was in fact worse.
The rules of the Oslo game defined support by the Palestinian leadership for
the right of return as a violation of the game, similar to the building of a new
Jewish settlement in the occupied territories (not that new settlements were
not built in violation of the accord, but this is beside the point). Five years
after the bifurcation and cantonization of 'the Palestinian entity' and its
transformation into a Bantustan, the Palestinian leadership was given
permission to express its wish to deal with the refugee problem as part of the
negotiations over the permanent settlement of the Palestine question. The
Israeli discourse at this point distinguishes between the introduction of the
'refugee problem' as a negotiable issue on the agenda – a legitimate
Palestinian move – and the demand for the right of return, which is described
as a Palestinian provocation.

The victory of Ehud Barak in the 1999 Israeli general election was hailed
locally and internationally as the return of the Jewish state to the peace track.
A sigh of relief accompanied the defeat of Benjamin Netanyahu, and an air
of optimism surrounded the resumption of the peace negotiations. As the
international media were quick to note, the final stage in the long road begun
in Oslo was at hand.

This final stage was meant to be brought to completion in the Camp David
summit of July 2000. Barak declared before his departure that Israel would
never accept the right of return or Resolution 194. This was part of his list
of 'red lines', which were presented in Camp David, with the help of the
Americans, as a peace plan. Arafat was asked to show 'leadership', that is,
accept the Israeli map and vision of a final settlement. His refusal to do so
was condemned not only by the Israelis but also by President Clinton in his
final comments on the summit.

In a press conference given before his return to Israel, Barak gave a sound-
bite version of 1948, explaining why Israel did not bear any responsibility for
making the refugee problem. The Arab world had started the war, called upon
the population to leave and bears responsibility for keeping the refugees in
the camps. Leading Israeli essayists, in the centre and on the left, such as Dan
Margalit and the former Meretz Minister of Education, Amnon Rubinstein,
declared the demand for the right of return to be immoral and illegal.[10]

In a parallel move in July, legislation passed in the Knesset prohibiting any Israeli government from negotiating over the implementation of the right of return of Resolution 194 was speeded up (it had begun few months before).

The balance of power between the present Israeli government and the Palestinian Authority has ensured the exclusion of the refugees issue from the bilateral negotiations. The purpose of this last phase is to end the conflict so that permanent peace could be declared as being intact and valid.

The Camp David accord exposed very clearly how the superior side in the balance of power views the map and components of the post-conflict reality. Around 90 per cent of the West Bank and Gaza are under PA rule. In the remaining 10 per cent, two large blocs of Jewish settlements would be annexed to Israel (thus there is for the first time an Israeli agreement to evict 20 per cent of the settlers). Villages in the vicinity of Jerusalem could be made into *al-Quds* (literally, the Holy City) and a symbolic Palestinian presence would be recognized on Haram al-Sharif. A few thousand refuges could be united with their families, not as part of an overall settlement of the refugees problem, but rather as a 'humanitarian act'.

The failure of the summit was presented by the Barak government as a licence to perpetuate the present status quo – which includes settlement expansion, the takeover of Arab Jerusalem and disregard for any national Palestinian demands – until 'better conditions for peace' develop. The people in the occupied territories thought otherwise. Triggered by Ariel Sharon's provocative visit to Haram al-Sharif, they rebelled once again. However, unlike the *Intifada* of 1987, the October 2000 uprising is not just aimed against the occupation of the West Bank and Gaza Strip, it is also *Intifada al-Awda* (the uprising of the return) as it is the prelude to the uprising of the Palestinian minority in Israel. The refugees, and the Palestinians in Israel, are now joined again by the Palestinians under occupation, in a desperate move to refute the Israeli perception of what peace means and what the essence of a comprehensive settlement might be. The message was understood in many Jewish Israeli quarters. However, when faced with this clear message of what peace entails, the majority of the Jews, for the time being, prefer war and occupation. More people identified in the past with the peace camp. Now people such as Amos Oz, A.B. Yehushua and David Grossman have signed a petition against recognition of the right of return, thereby extending the local consensus against return. What is needed now is a campaign inside Israel, in the region and in the world at large to educate everyone interested or concerned about the essence of the conflict – the events of 1948 – and about the ways to solve it – by restitution, return and reconciliation. This should be argued for on a moral basis (the world has recently witnessed reconciliation efforts based on the recognition on the part of the victimizer of past evils) and at a practical level. Without such a move, the October 2000 uprising will be a prelude to a larger wave of violence engulfing everyone – Jews and Arabs in the land of Palestine.

NOTES

1. Ilan Pappe, 'Were They Expelled?: The History, Historiography and Relevance of the Palestinian Refugee Problem', in Ghada Karmi and Eugene Cotran, *The Palestinian Exodus, 1948–1988* (London: Ithaca Press, 1999), pp. 37–62.

2. Benny Morris, *The Birth of the Palestinian Refugee Problem* (Cambridge: Cambridge University Press, 1988); Nur Masalha, *Expulsion of the Palestinians* (Washington: Institute of Palestine Studies, 1992).

3. Pappe, 'Were They Expelled?'.

4. New information on how this had been done can be found in Meron Benvenisit, *Sacred Landscape* (Berkeley: University of California Press, 2000), pp. 11–54.

5. See Ilan Pappe, 'Moshe Sharett, David Ben-Gurion and the "Palestinian Option"', in *Studies in Zionism*, 7/1 (Spring 1986), pp. 77–95.

6. Martin Buber, *A Land of Two Peoples*, ed. with commentary by Paul R. Mendes-Flohr (Tel Aviv: Shocken House 1988), pp. 234–5.

7. Ibid., pp. 197–9.

8. Ibid., p. 199 n2.

9. See Ilan Pappe, 'Post-Zionist Critique on Israel and the Palestinians', Parts 1–3. *Journal of Palestinian Studies*, 26, no. 2 (Winter 1997), pp. 29–41; 26, no. 3 (Spring 1997), pp. 37–43; 26, no. 4 (Summer 1997), pp. 60–9.

10. These views appeared on a daily basis in *Ha'aretz* ever since the preparations for the Camp David summit began in earnest.

4   THE UNITED STATES AND THE REFUGEE QUESTION

Noam Chomsky

In this chapter, I shall concentrate on US policy. I would like to focus on one particular event – the signing of the Declaration of Principles and surrounding events in September 1993 in Washington, DC – and the way the processes have played themselves out since then, in a quite predictable fashion. I shall add a few words on how the situation evolved to that stage. I will have space to consider only a few highlights.

In September 1993, one issue was that of the Palestinian refugees. That didn't arise at the Washington meeting, but did a few months later, at the first meeting of the General Assembly, which took place after the Oslo Accords were signed in Washington, in December 1993. At that General Assembly meeting, the United States essentially settled the issue of the refugees, from its point of view, and, as Ilan Pappe points out (Chapter 3, this volume), the US point of view is decisive. It has overwhelming force, and though it does not determine everything, it has a huge impact on what happens in that region, and a nearly decisive impact. In effect, the Clinton administration at the United Nations rescinded Resolution 194 and voted against it for the first time. The preceding support for it had always been hypocritical, so in a way this was a welcome move – it resolved an element of hypocrisy. Nevertheless, the United States had voted against Resolution 194 for the first time. Two votes against it in that session, Israel and the United States. I should mention on the side that since the 1960s, since decolonization began to have an effect on the United Nations and it was no longer a completely pliable instrument of US policy, it has fallen out of favour, and the United States has been essentially trying to dismantle or marginalize it. That began in the 1960s; you can see that in many ways. For example, in Security Council vetoes, the United States is far in the lead, Britain second and France a distant third, contrary to standard propaganda. And it is on a whole range of issues, not just the Middle East, but all sorts of other issues. The same is true of General Assembly votes. UN agencies with a Third World orientation, such as UNESCO and UNCTAD, have been marginalized or, in some cases, destroyed, the organization starved of funds, and so on. So the rescinding of Resolution 194 fits into a more general pattern.

At the same General Assembly session, the United States called for 'restricting or terminating UN activity' with regard to Israel and Palestine, and eliminating all earlier UN resolutions as 'obsolete and anachronistic'. That included all calls for Palestinian rights, or all opposition to settlement in the territories. The US position was that it is 'unproductive to debate the legality of the issue'. Indeed, it was unproductive, because, from the US point of view, the issues had been settled. The United States was now proceeding to impose a settlement that it had been committed to in almost total inter-national isolation for more than two decades, but it was now being instituted. Rescinding Resolution 194 meant rescinding Article 13 of the Universal Declaration of Human Rights also. Resolution 194 was passed the day after the Declaration was passed unanimously, and it was essentially a spelling out of Article 13 – actually one half of Article 13; the other half is the best-known part of the Universal Declaration, the part that states: 'Everyone has the right to leave any country, including his own.' While the Cold War continued, every year in Boston and elsewhere there would be passionate denunciations of the Soviet Union for refusing to let our people go, and for their violation of Article 13 of the Universal Declaration, led by distinguished Harvard law professors and so on. I never once in all of those years saw a reference to the last few words of the same sentence: '... everyone has the right to leave any country, including his own, and to return to his country.' Never once did I see those words mentioned, and it is those words that were spelled out the next day, in Resolution 194. But by now, the first half of the resolution is irrelevant. You don't need it as a Cold War weapon any more and the second part is rescinded, so Article 13 is gone, and with it we have an end to hypocrisy, which, as they say, is a good thing.

The second main issue that arose at Oslo was the question of Palestinian rights, and they too were ignored. It is crucial to recall – and this is a big US victory – that the Declaration of Principles, in its reference to the permanent settlement (you know, what happens down the road) referred only to Resolution 242, and not to the other resolutions that call for Palestinian national rights alongside those of Israel. Resolution 242, of course, is completely rejectionist and says nothing about Palestinian rights; in fact, the word 'Palestinian' is not mentioned. There is a phrase about the just rights of refugees, but only in passing. So Resolution 242 is a totally rejectionist resolution, with nothing about Palestinians, and the fact that the permanent settlement is based on it is an important victory for the United States, one that was re-established in December 1993.

A third issue that arose is the right of resistance. Now, the international community has unanimously (except for the United States and Israel) agreed that people have the right of resistance to racist and colonialist regimes and foreign military occupations. That issue did arise, though it was not in the Declaration of Principles, but in a side part. Arafat was compelled to sign yet another statement – I don't know how many there have been, but this was another one – renouncing terrorism, but also pledging to suppress any resistance. So now the new Palestinian Authority is to become an agency of the United States and Israel in suppressing the right of resistance, which is accepted at least formally, and it is only formal, unanimously by the rest of the world. That has then been sharpened in subsequent agreements, at the Wye Accords[1] particularly, and so on.

This abrogation of the right of resistance is again, like the United Nations, not a specifically Israel–Palestine issue. It also applies elsewhere: obviously in Lebanon, where the Lebanese do not have the right of resistance to US-backed Israeli attacks, but also in other countries. So, for example, the Turkish army has carried out major sweeps in south-eastern Turkey in regions that have been virtually devastated in the some of the worst ethnic-cleansing operations and massive atrocities of the 1990s, with enormous US support. They have also invaded northern Iraq, and Kurds do not have the right of resistance to repression. This was vicious repression, supported by the Clinton administration, because the Kurds stand in the way of US policies. And it extends more generally. Nicaraguans didn't have the right of resistance, nor the right to defend their country, in fact. So this is general, but it was especially so in this case.

The fourth issue, which arose after refugees, Palestinian rights and the right of resistance were all eliminated, was the question of territorial settlement. Here the permanent settlement is supposed to be on the basis of Resolution 242, but it is important to bear in mind that there are two versions of Resolution 242. The initial version was approved, signed and initiated by the United States, and was the US position, and meant withdrawal to the pre-June 1967 borders, with minor and mutual territorial adjustments, so if some line was curved you could straighten it out. That was the world position, and the US position, and the interpretation of Resolution 242 until February 1971, when President Anwar Sadat of Egypt accepted the US version, in fact, an even more forthcoming version, leaving the United States in an odd position: it could either join Israel in rejecting Resolution 242, or it could maintain its own position, but support Egypt against Israel. It resulted in an internal bureaucratic battle, which was won by Henry Kissinger. That is one of his contributions to world peace. Perhaps that's one of the reasons he was the honorary guest of the International Chaplains' Association, at their humanitarian awards dinner. Kissinger won that internal struggle, and since then, since 1971, the US position has been that Resolution 242 does not call for Israeli withdrawal; it calls for withdrawal as determined by the United States and Israel, whatever that would be. And what it is, is some version of the Israeli Allon plan of 1968, which has changed a little over the years but is fundamentally the same. Effectively, Israel will maintain control over the usable territories and the resources of the West Bank and Gaza, but it doesn't want to administer Nablus or Gaza City, so these should be assigned to the Palestinian Authority to rule in the manner of other colonialist regimes, in the manner in which Indians ran India under the British empire, and Central American armies run Central America in the interests of the United States, or the black leadership of Transkei ran it in the interests of South Africa, and so on. These are traditional patterns. That was to be the territorial settlement. Again, a major victory for US rejectionism; in fact, if you look over the whole thing, it's a total victory, on every point. And this has been international isolation. It is worth remembering that the US unilateral interpretation of UN 242 has been unilateral; there is no notable support outside the United States. The same is true of other issues. In a now forgotten, but quite important, Security Council meeting of January 1976, there was a resolution, backed by essentially the entire world. The PLO seems to have forgotten it, but they publicly supported that resolution, and in fact, according to the Israeli UN ambassador, they actually prepared it, though I do not know if that is true. The resolution called for a two-state settlement, in accordance with Resolution 242, as it is understood elsewhere in the world. So, a settlement that incorporated all the wording of Resolution 242, but added that there should be a Palestinian state in the areas from which Israel would withdraw. Israel responded to the UN session by bombing Lebanon, killing about 50 people, a quasi-strike against the UN, yet supported by the United States so therefore legitimate. The United States reacted to the UN session by vetoing the resolution, and so, from that point on, the United States has been doubly isolated: once in rejecting Resolution 242, as understood by itself and the rest of the world, and again, in rejecting Palestinian national rights. Well, the General Assembly does not have the technical veto, but remember it is a veto: if there's a vote of 150 to 1, and the 1 happens to be the United States, or 150 to 2, or 3, or something like that, and that happens consistently on a whole range of issues – again, it's nothing specific to do with the Middle East – but it amounts to a veto: a veto of the resolution, and usually its vetoing from history, so they become forgotten. And the General Assembly did vote on this year after year, votes of 150 to 2, or thereabouts. The last vote, on December 1990, 144 to 2 on that occasion, called for essentially the same resolution. The date is important. Immediately after came the Gulf War. In the Gulf War, the United States made it transparently clear that it was going to run the region by force, and if anybody doesn't like it, they can get out of the way. That was the message. In fact, President Bush declared it succinctly when he announced the New World Order in four words: the New World Order means 'What we say goes', and if you don't like it, get out of the way. Well, that was understood, and that was the last UN resolution.

The Madrid meetings followed a couple of months later, in which the United States instituted its unilateral rejectionist settlement. We go on to Oslo, and to the implementation of the Oslo agreements. There shouldn't be anything particularly surprising about this. Anyone who pays attention to world affairs and who has been looking at what has been happening could have foretold step by step everything that was going to happen, and many people did. The world is ruled by force. The primary rule of international law is the rule of force. Now, of course, you appeal to the rule of law, and the way to do it, as the distinguished, respected elder statesman Dean Acheson pointed out 40 years ago, was to appeal to the rule of law in order 'to gild our positions' with moral posturing. But it is to be understood that the law does not apply to us. He happened to be addressing the American Society of International Law, and it was quite honest. That is the way the world runs, and it is the task of intellectuals to prettify and present it in some other fashion so that people do not see what is before their eyes. But it should be before their eyes. None of this is a law of nature, it can be changed, but I think it is rather clear that the most important changes will have to take place here. Unless they take place within the United States, it is not going to matter much what happens elsewhere.

EDITOR'S NOTE

1. Like all its predecessors since the Oslo agreement, the Middle East document, known as the Wye memorandum and signed at an official ceremony at the White House on 23 October 1998, is conceived, structured and nuanced by Israel to serve Israeli interests. It has surpassed all of them, however, in two respects. First, by holding the Palestinian Authority to a set of rigorous security commitments which, if carried out in full, would render decades of Palestinian struggles for liberation a mere exercise in random violence; and second, by binding the United States to pay for settlement-related projects. In addition there is an understanding which binds the United States to enhance 'Israel's defensive and deterrent capabilities' and upgrade their existing strategic alliance concluded during the Reagan period. (Naseer Aruri)

5   THE EUROPEAN UNION AND THE REFUGEE QUESTION

Alain Gresh

On hearing the title of my chapter, a friend of mine burst out laughing, 'But there is nothing to say. The European Union has never taken a clear stand on the right of return of refugees.' I was tempted to take him at his word after looking at the positions adopted by the European Union with the respect to the Middle East in recent years. The European Union certainly has taken a stand on the national rights of the Palestinians, on settlement policy, Jerusalem, the creation of a Palestinian state and Israel's right to security. But any references to refugees were vague and the term 'right of return' was never used.

I was on the point of giving up when I stumbled, almost by chance I must admit, on a text dated 1971 known as the 'Schumann document', named after Maurice Schumann, the French Foreign Minister at the time, under President Georges Pompidou.

It should be borne in mind that in those days the European Community had only six members: France, Germany, Italy, the Netherlands, Belgium and Luxembourg. Denmark, Ireland and the United Kingdom were preparing to join the organization in 1972. A year earlier, in 1970, the Community had launched European Political Cooperation, which provided for regular consultations on important foreign policy issues in order to 'strengthen their solidarity by favouring harmonization of points of view, concerted attitudes and, wherever possible and desirable, common actions'. This marked the very beginning of a process intended to make Europe a single entity that could have its say in international affairs and was keen to ensure that international crises did not jeopardize the European Community itself.

Obviously, in this context, the war in June 1967 and Israeli–Arab conflict represented a major topic for concern and intervention. Not only was the area involved geographically close to Europe, but also individual member-states were not in agreement, with France, under the leadership of De Gaulle, on one side, and Germany and the Netherlands, close to the Israeli position, on the other.

So, as the first steps towards political cooperation were being made, France persuaded its partners to adopt a joint text laying down the European proposals for solving the Israeli–Arab conflict. The Schumann document was unanimously approved on 13 May 1971 by the foreign ministers of the six member countries.

What are the main principles outlined in the document? Apart from points related to political mediation, and in particular support for the Jarring mission, the European Community confirmed its support for Security Council Resolution 242 and demanded specifically:

- an Israeli withdrawal to the lines occupied on 4 June 1967, with minor changes;
- the creation of demilitarized lines on both sides of the borders of Israel, with the presence of international forces not belonging to the four great powers;
- an international status for Jerusalem and continued suspension of any decision on the sovereignty of the old city;
- last of all, the right of return to their homes for Palestinian refugees or the option of being compensated.

To a large extent this plan was based on French proposals made on various occasions during the previous two years, and in particular by Maurice Schumann.

The publication of the document gave rise to a certain amount of disagreement amongst member-states. The German foreign minister, under pressure from Israel, even stated that the document had no practical value. But, setting aside these disagreements which reflected the European Community's difficulty in establishing a single position, a question remains. Why, after supporting the right of return of Palestinian refugees in 1971 – in keeping with support by European countries for Resolution 194 – did Europe then 'forget' this proposal? Why, despite the substantial increase in European involvement in the Middle East, is there not a single European Union text that mentions the right of return of refugees?

FROM THE RIGHTS OF REFUGEES TO THE RIGHT TO A STATE

To understand their silence we must place it in its context. After the end of the 1967 war, the Palestine Liberation Organization (PLO) and the *fedayeen* sought to win recognition for the national rights of the Palestinian people. The aim was to place the Palestinian problem in its political context and prevent it from being treated, as stipulated in Resolution 242, as nothing more than a problem of refugees. At a diplomatic level the PLO fought to obtain recognition for two principles:

- the PLO is the sole legitimate representative of the Palestinian people;
- the Palestinians are a nation and they are entitled to self-determination.

Under the circumstances it was almost to be expected that the refugee problem should be pushed into the background, at least at this stage.

Consider, for instance, the famous Venice declaration, which was adopted by the nine members of the European Community on 12 and 13 June 1980. It reads: 'A just solution must finally be found to the Palestinian problem, which is not simply a problem of refugees.' During the whole of the 1980s, the European position was just that: the Palestinian problem is *not* a problem of refugees. The declaration went on to state: 'The Palestinian people ... must be placed in a position ... to exercise fully its right to self-determination. The PLO will have to be associated with the negotiations.' Although the text mentions the question of Jerusalem and the settlements, it makes no mention of the right of return.

On 23 February 1987 at a meeting of the foreign ministers of the twelve member-states in Brussels the European Community opted for a solution based on the Venice declaration, by means of 'an international peace conference to be held under the auspices of the United Nations'. On 27 June 1987, at the Madrid summit meeting, the heads of state of the twelve came down in favour of 'upholding the right to security of all States in the region, including Israel, that is to say, to live within secure, recognized and guaranteed frontiers, and ... upholding justice for all the peoples of the region, which includes recognition of the legitimate rights of the Palestinian people, including their right to self-determination with all that this implies'. This was the first implicit reference to the right of the Palestinians to create a state.

This support for Palestinian national rights culminated in the Amsterdam European Council declaration, on 17 June 1997, which called on Israel to 'recognize the right of the Palestinians to exercise self-determination, without excluding the option of a State'. This was followed by the Berlin Declaration at the European Union summit meeting on 26 March 1999, which reaffirmed 'the Palestinians' permanent and unconditional right of self-determination including the State option'. It also stated that this right 'should not be subject to any veto' and Europe's 'readiness to consider the recognition of a Palestinian state in due course'.

In about 30 years Europe consequently came a long way towards recognizing the national rights of the Palestinian people and its right to an independent state. The 'perception' of Palestinians underwent a profound change in Europe. From being a simple refugee problem it became a problem of self-determination. However, we cannot avoid the fact that this was detrimental to the 'right of return'.

OSLO, REFUGEES AND THE 'RIGHT OF RETURN'

With the start of the Madrid process, in October 1991, and then the Oslo accords signed by the PLO and the Israeli government, in September 1993, European action entered a new phase.

On the one hand events confirmed that in political terms Europe had been sidelined. It played no significant role in the Madrid negotiations and was kept out of the secret Oslo talks. It was reduced to acting as a funding agency and, in the years that followed the accords, became a major source of funds for the Palestinian Authority (PA).

We need to understand the reasons for Europe's exclusion to be able to assess its chances of playing a part in a future settlement of the refugee problem:

- the European Union – and this is not restricted to the Middle East – has been slow to develop as a political power. Everyone sees it as 'an economic giant and a political dwarf'. Coordinating the policies of 15 states as politically diverse as the United Kingdom and France, Greece and the Netherlands, is not an easy task. Although the 1997 Treaty of Amsterdam included provisions 'relating to a common foreign and security policy' (CFSP) and appointed a Mr. CFSP, namely Javier Solana, we are still a long way from a straightforward decision-making process. Particularly as several member countries are convinced that Europe should leave the United States plenty of room for manoeuvre, as they are the only country capable of acting as an intermediary.
- The various parties involved in the negotiations – Arab states, Palestinians, Israel and the United States – do not take Europe seriously. This is easy enough to understand in the case of the Americans and Israelis, but the Palestinians and Arab states – who keep saying they want Europe to play an important part – do very little to support its participation in the field.

However, Europe's political role acquired new impetus when the government of Benjamin Netanyahu was in power, due to the latter's obstruction of the peace process. In 1996 this led to the appointment of Miguel Angel Moratinos as European Union representative for the Middle East, in addition to several political proposals to provide the various parties with guarantees, and a number of original ideas.

On the one hand, the European Union took part in the multilateral Refugee Working Group set up by the Madrid Conference, which started in October 1991. Canada is the gavel-holder for this group, and the United States, Japan and the European Union are co-organizers. The group organized seven sessions between May 1992 and December 1995. Although there is still little to show for the negotiations, they have forced the European Union to face up to the problem. However, it was above all the end of the interim period, in May 1999, and the start of the negotiations on final status that made everyone realise how important it was to find a solution to the Palestinian refugee problem.

At the European Council meeting in Luxembourg, on 12 and 13 December 1997, the European Union expressed its 'readiness to contribute to Permanent Status negotiations, by offering specific suggestions to the parties on related subjects, including possible Palestinian statehood, borders/security arrangements, settlements, refugees, Jerusalem and water issues'.

In April 1998, in line with this resolution, the COMEP decided to form an informal working group on refugees. It distanced itself from the multilateral peace process Refugee Working Group, setting the following objectives:

- to identify and develop topics on which information and thinking is inadequate;
- to foster contacts with and between the parties;
- to develop elements of reflection that would help the European Union to direct its policy in favour of a solution to the refugee question.

On 6 October 1998 the group approved a French proposal to prepare an internal memorandum on the guiding principles for a common European position on the refugee question. The group recommended that the terms of this document should not be too 'prescriptive', emphasizing that the solution could not be restricted to a bilateral issue and that it had a regional and international dimension that justified attempts to define a common European Union position on the subject. However, in the course of consultations no reference was apparently made to acceptance of Resolution 194 as a basis for discussion.

THE FRENCH POSITION

France is one of the few countries to continue to refer explicitly to the right of return. Addressing the Senate commission on foreign affairs, defence and the armed forces, on 24 November 1999, Hubert Védrines, the French minister of foreign affairs said:

Israel is clearly against the return of the 'first wave' of Palestinian refugees and is moving towards the idea of compensation. As far as France is concerned the basis in international law regarding this question is to be found in the various United Nations resolutions which affirmed the right of return of the refugees. Ultimately it is up to the interested parties to find a solution.

In other words, he clearly reaffirmed the refugees' right of return. This right was reiterated when Védrines visited Beirut in November 1999. In an interview with various Beirut radio stations on 12 November, he said, 'The Palestinian refugees in the Lebanon must be treated fairly and in keeping with international law. Resolution 194 speaks of the right of return. It is a principle to start from and we must try to move forward through negotiations and discussions.'

During this trip he also suggested that in due course 'international dialogue' should be initiated on Palestinian refugees. This should be based on the following principles:

- the problem of refugees and displaced persons is an important issue;
- it does not only concern Israel and the Palestinian Authority but also the so-called 'host' parties.

This proposal is still vague, but it could, if it were taken up by the various partners, in particular the Palestinians and Arab countries, gather substance, enabling the refugee problem to be formulated in a more positive fashion.

6   THE PALESTINIAN LIBERATION ORGANIZATION: FROM THE RIGHT OF RETURN TO BANTUSTAN

Jaber Suleiman

'My home, if we return, I vow to paint you with henna after whitewash.'
Palestinian folk song

Longing for home and to return is a sentiment that is deeply rooted in the very being of the Palestinian people, and Palestinians continue to express it in their songs, proverbs and folk tales. Indeed, the idea of return has been the primary force driving the contemporary Palestinian militant movement in the five decades since the *nakba* (Palestinian catastrophe), which began with covert action in the refugee camps of the 1950s and 1960s, continued amidst the armed struggle, and is now mired in the current negotiations. Return is the dream which has become a part of the collective memory of collective sorrow and suffering.

The meaning of return in the Palestinian collective consciousness is the very opposite of that of the *nakba*, of refuge and of exile. Return alone is supposed to be capable of dispelling the injustice that has afflicted the Palestinians ever since the *nakba* and its repercussions; it is sharply contrasted with assimilation and resettlement outside the homeland. The symbolic opposition between the notion of return and the reality of refuge has been manifest in Palestinian political discourse, to the extent that the first Palestinian National Council, which was held in Jerusalem in 1964, resolved to use the term 'returnee' in place of 'refugee' to describe those Palestinians who had been displaced from their homeland.[1]

Meanwhile, on the other side of the trenches, after a long period during which the return of the Palestinians had been a taboo subject in Israeli society, Israeli politicians have begun to mention it in quotation marks in their interviews and writings, and to identify it as a red line which cannot possibly be crossed. At best, it is considered an insoluble problem, to the point that one of Israel's prominent 'campaigners for peace', the former Knesset member Shulamit Aloni, has considered it to be 'not even a dream'. But no matter how it is viewed by Israelis of various political persuasions, the return

87

of Palestinians to their homes should not be considered a favour bestowed upon the Palestinians by Israel, but rather a right enshrined in international law and one of the principles accepted and recognized by civilized nations.

This chapter will discuss the various developments and changes in the position of the PLO regarding the issue of return, from its establishment in 1964 until its participation in the peace negotiations of Madrid (1991), Oslo (1993) and subsequent events. The position of the PLO will be examined against the background of the legal framework which has been established for the question of Palestine and Palestinian rights, with special reference to general international law and UN resolutions issued over the past five decades. In so doing, we will be tracking the evolution of the concept of return in Palestinian political thought since 1964.

The first section discusses the legal framework of the right of return, in terms of the sources of this right in international law, as well as its treatment in UN resolutions relating to the right of return of the Palestinian refugees. The second section examines the various changes in the PLO's position towards the issue of return, in both theory and practice. The main turning points are stressed and classified into distinct historical phases. The third and final section presents a number of conclusions and recommendations concerning the principled position towards the right of return and the various means that the Palestinians can deploy in order to achieve it.

THE LEGAL FRAMEWORK FOR THE RIGHT OF RETURN

The Sources of the Right of Return in International Law

John Quigley has specified two basic sources for the right of return in international law: human rights law and humanitarian law, in addition to the law on nationality.[2]

The Right of Return in International Human Rights Law

This right is enshrined in most international and regional legal documents which constitute that law:

- The Universal Declaration of Human Rights (1948), which is the cornerstone of international human rights law states: 'Everyone has the right to leave any country, and to return to his country' (Article 13, paragraph 2).
- The International Covenant on Civil and Political Rights (1966) states: 'no one shall be arbitrarily deprived of the right to enter his own country' (Article 12, paragraph 4).
- The International Convention on the Elimination of All Forms of Racial Discrimination states that a state may not deny, on racial or ethnic grounds, the opportunity 'to return to one's country' (Article 5 (d) (11)).
- Protocol no. 4 to the European Convention for the Protection of Human Rights and Fundamental Freedoms states: 'no one shall be

deprived of the right to enter the territory of the state of which he is a national' (Article 3, paragraph 2).

- The American Convention on Human Rights states: 'no one can be expelled from the territory of the state of which he is a national or be deprived of the right to enter it' (Article 2, paragraph 5).
- The African Charter on Human and People's Rights states that every individual is entitled 'to return to his country' (Article 12, paragraph 2).

The Right of Return in Humanitarian Law

Humanitarian law deals with families that have been displaced as a result of hostilities, but not those that have been displaced after the occurrence of the belligerent occupation. This body of law guarantees a group of rights for those living in occupied territories, including the right of return. In this regard, Quigley relies on Article 43 of The Hague Regulations on the Law of War and the 1949 Geneva Civilians Convention.

The Palestinian Right of Return in United Nations Resolutions

Resolution 194, which was issued by the UN General Assembly during its third session on 11 December 1948, is the primary source concerning the right of return among all UN resolutions on the question of Palestine. This resolution provides the legal basis for the right of return, despite its ambiguous status. Resolution 194 (III) states that the General Assembly

resolves that the refugees wishing to return to their homes and live at peace with their neighbours should be permitted to do so at the earliest practicable date, and that compensation should be paid for the property of those choosing not to return and for loss of or damage to property which, under principles of international law or equity, should be made good by the governments or authorities responsible. (paragraph 11)

This resolution has never been implemented, despite strenuous efforts by the United Nations Conciliation Commission for Palestine (UNCCP), especially during the first three years of its formation, from late 1948 onwards. The General Assembly has reaffirmed Resolution 194 regularly during each session, with the exception of 1951; it has also expressed regret over its non-implementation.

Resolution 194 is therefore not the only one that deals with the right of return. Other important resolutions issued by the General Assembly have reaffirmed the right of return as it is specified in paragraph 11 of Resolution 194 and have explicitly linked it to the right of self-determination of the Palestinian people. The General Assembly has adopted approximately 49 resolutions which, in one form or another, have referred to Resolution 194, including the following:

- Resolution 2535 (XXIV), of 10 December 1969, states: 'Recognizing that the problem of the Palestinian Arab Refugees has arisen from the denial of their inalienable rights under the Charter of the United Nations and the Universal Declaration of Human Rights ...'.

- Resolution 2649 (XXV), of 30 November 1970, states that the General Assembly 'condemns those governments that deny the right to self-determination of peoples recognized as being entitled to it, especially of the peoples of southern Africa and Palestine' (paragraph 5).
- Resolution 2672 A, B, C, D (XXV) of 8 December 1970, states: 'The General Assembly...
  1. (c) Recognizes that the people of Palestine are entitled to equal rights and self-determination, in accordance with the Charter of the United Nations...
  2. (c) Declares that the full respect for the inalienable rights of the people of Palestine is an indispensable element in the establishment of a just and lasting peace in the Middle East.'
- Resolution 3089 A, B, C, D, E (XXVIII), of 7 December 1973, states that the General Assembly 'declares that the full respect for and realization of the inalienable rights of the people of Palestine, particularly its right to self-determination, are indispensable for the establishment of a just and lasting peace in the Middle East, [and that] the enjoyment by Palestine Arab refugees of their right to return to their homes and property, recognized by the GA in resolution 194 (III) of 11 December 1948 ... is indispensable for the achievements of a just settlement of the refugee and for the exercise by the people of Palestine of its right to self-determination' (paragraph D).
- Resolution 3236 (XXIX) of 22 November 1974 reads as follows: 'The General Assembly:
  1. Reaffirming the inalienable right of the Palestinian people in Palestine including:
     (a) The right to self-determination without external interference.
     (b) The right to national independence and sovereignty;
  2. Reaffirms also the inalienable right of the Palestinians to return to their homes and property from which they have been displaced and uprooted, and calls for their return ...'. This resolution has attracted the attention of a number of international legal scholars, including Tadmor (1994), who notes that the resolution does not distinguish between the refugees of 1948 and those of 1967, and considers the right of return to apply to a single group.[3] Cassese (1993) considers that the decisive contribution of the resolution is that it shifts the debate from the level of a personal right of return to the level of the Palestinian people's right to self-determination. In addition, the resolution uses the expression 'Palestinian people' instead of 'Palestinian refugees.'[4] Moreover, Weiss (1978) goes further by describing Resolution 3236 as 'a bill of rights for the Palestinian people'.[5]

- Resolution 3376 (session 30), issued on 10 November 1975, established the Committee for the Exercise of the Inalienable Rights of the Palestinian People. In its first report, the committee reaffirmed the link between the right of return and the national rights of the Palestinian people. The same report outlines a number of recommendations concerning the implementation of the right of return, which were adopted by the General Assembly at its next session (session XXXI).
- Resolution 31/20 of 24 November 1976, clearly links the right of return to the right of self-determination, since the introduction to the resolution reaffirmed 'that a just and lasting peace in the Middle East cannot be established without the achievement, *inter alia*, of a just solution of the problem of Palestine on the basis of the attainment of the inalienable rights of the Palestinian people, including the right of return and the right to national independence and sovereignty in Palestine, in accordance with the Charter of the United Nations'; while paragraph (2) of the resolution clearly adopted the recommendations of the Committee for the Exercise of the Inalienable Rights of the Palestinian People. It reads: '[The General Assembly] takes note of the report of the Committee and endorses the recommendations contained therein, as a basis for the solution of the question of Palestine.'

Thus it is clear that the resolutions of the General Assembly of the United Nations, beginning with Resolution 2535 (December 1969), and especially since the passage of Resolution 3089 (December 1973) and Resolution 3236 (November 1974), have not only reaffirmed the right of the Palestinian people to self-determination, but have also linked this right incontrovertibly to the right of return, making the latter a necessary condition of the former.

Summary

The international community, represented by the United Nations, recognizes the existence of the Palestinian people, and international law recognizes the right of the Palestinian people to exercise sovereignty over their territory as defined by the partition resolution, Resolution 181 (II) of 29 November 1947.

It also holds that the occupation or annexation of this territory, or the implementation of a mandate over it by different states over the past several decades, does not change its legal system and does not give another state the right to control it.

The Palestinian people have not yet managed to exercise their right to self-determination, which is considered binding according to international law, because of the absence of a necessary precondition: the presence of the Palestinian people on their territory. This condition cannot, in turn, be satisfied without the implementation of the right of return.

The situation of the Palestinian people is distinctive from the point of view of international law because of the disparity between their geographical

dispersal and juridical unity. This disparity cannot be eliminated except by
unifying the people and the land, by way of the implementation of the right
of return as a national right.[6]

THE PLO AND THE ISSUE OF RETURN

The PLO's position on the issue of return has witnessed some decisive developments since the convening of the first Palestine National Council (PNC)
in Jerusalem in 1964. As a result of these developments, the centrality of the
concept of return in the contemporary Palestinian struggle has been called
into question. This has occurred as a result of the PLO's attempt to come to
terms with the balance of power and the conditions laid down by Arab and
international actors concerning the Palestinian cause. These developments
have taken place gradually and in stages, in such a way that each step has
paved the way for each subsequent step.

From the Establishment of the PLO to the Provisional Political Programme

The issue of return was never detached from the goal of liberating the entire
territory of Palestine until the twelfth session of the Palestine National
Council (1–8 June 1974). At that session the PNC adopted what was
variously known as the 'Provisional Political Programme', the 'Ten-Point
Programme' or the 'National Authority Programme'. The programme has
been considered a turning point in Palestinian political thinking, as we shall
see. Until then, return was considered the natural outcome of total liberation.
This fact was reflected in the main slogan of the PLO at that time: 'National
Unity – National Mobilization – Liberation'. It was also reflected in a
fundamental manner in the text of the Palestine National Charter, as revised
by the 'armed elements', that is, the armed factions which deposed PLO
Chairman Ahmad Shuqairi and seized control of the PLO following the defeat
of June 1967. That text affirms that Palestine is the homeland of the
Palestinian Arab people, and that it 'has the right to its homeland Palestine
within its mandatory borders'. The revised Article 9 of the Charter states that
'armed struggle is the only way to liberate Palestine', and that the aims of
struggle are 'the liberation of the homeland, the return to it, and self-determination in and sovereignty over Palestine'.

The PLO did not change this position – that return would be achieved by
means of total liberation – and continued to affirm it in successive resolutions
of the PNC from its establishment in 1964 until the eleventh session. This
can be illustrated by examining the resolutions of the tenth extraordinary
session of the PNC, which was held in Cairo on 6–12 April 1972. The session
was convened as a result of the announcement on 5 March 1972 by King
Hussein of Jordan of the establishment of the United Arab Kingdom. The
session was held in parallel with the Palestinian Popular Conference, to give
a greater impact to the resolutions issued to confront the Jordanian move.

The political programme proposed by the Popular Conference states:

the PLO is the sole legitimate representative of the Palestinian people ... and no one is permitted to make decisions concerning the people and territory of Palestine except the Palestinian people represented by the PLO, in accordance with its Charter and its commitment to the total liberation of the territory of Palestine.

The Popular Conference declared its total rejection of the plan for a United Arab Kingdom, 'in accordance with the total and continued rejection of any plan which aims at liquidating the Palestinian cause, the abandonment of any part of Palestinian territory, and the surrendering of any right pertaining to the Palestinian people ...' The political programme states: 'The right of self-determination for the Palestinian people means the complete liberation of the territory of the homeland and the establishment of the Palestinian national state there.'

The last cited text shows that the right of self-determination is linked to liberation; meanwhile, return is considered an implicit by-product of the act of liberation or the actual equivalent of liberation.

Rashid Khalidi has stated that the 'idea of return was generally subsumed under the idea of the total liberation of Palestine' until 1968.[7] However, we regard this to have remained in place until the convening of the twelfth session of the PNC in 1974, a claim that is implicitly confirmed by Khalidi, since he writes that: 'By 1974, however, PLO thinking underwent a major shift, and the question of the return was re-evaluated.'[8] In the same context, he explains that the Palestinians did not countenance any compromises or diplomatic solutions during this historical phase. Therefore, he concludes that 'the specificities of the return presumably did not seem particularly important or pressing from the Provisional Political Program to the Declaration of Independence'.[9]

In conformity with Arab and international conditions following the Arab-Israeli war of October 1973 and subsequent developments, the PLO adopted the Provisional Political Programme of 1974. This constitutes a decisive turning point in Palestinian political thinking, with regard to the relationship between the strategic goals of the Palestinian national movement and its interim tactical goals, as well as with regard to the conduct of the conflict with Israel and the Zionist movement. Whereas it had earlier been held that the total liberation of Palestinian territory (including the territory occupied in 1948) was a precondition for the establishment of a Palestinian state, this programme called for the establishment of an independent Palestinian state on any liberated territory. At the time, this was thought to be a realistic goal within the realm of the possible, given prevailing Arab and international conditions. We believe that the dominant thinking among the PLO mainstream, which pushed for the adoption of the Provisional Political Programme, was not so much the possibility of liberation in phases, but the possibility of Israeli withdrawal from the West Bank and Gaza Strip as a result of an international settlement of the Arab-Israeli conflict. This would, in turn, enable the establishment of a Palestinian state in these territories.

As for the issue of return, the expression 'right of return' makes its first appearance in the preamble to the Ten-Point Programme, after having been absent from the resolutions of previous PNC meetings. This was also the first time that 'return' was discussed separately from 'liberation'. The Programme affirmed that the right of return was one of the 'foremost and primary' rights of the Palestinian people, but made no reference to Resolution 194, nor to any of the other relevant UN resolutions. As stated above, the Provisional Political Programme seems to have been proposed in an effort to conform to Arab and international conditions. In this regard, one must not lose sight of the Arab League resolution, passed at the Rabat summit in 1974, which considered the PLO to be the sole legitimate representative of the Palestinian people. This gave the PLO Arab legitimacy in its struggle with the Jordanian regime over the representation of the Palestinian people, including that portion of the Palestinian people living in the West Bank. It also gave the PLO a licence to struggle for the establishment of a future Palestinian entity in the territory of the West Bank and Gaza Strip, which had been occupied in 1967. The adoption of the Provisional Political Programme must also be seen in the context of the UN General Assembly resolutions issued between 1969 and 1974, which affirmed the legitimate and inalienable national rights of the Palestinian people, including the right of return, and the rights of self-determination, independence and national sovereignty. These resolutions – especially Resolution 3236 of 22 November 1974 (see above) – considered the Palestinians to be a 'people' rather than a mere group of 'refugees'.

The Provisional Political Programme rejected UN Security Council Resolution 242 on different grounds from those previously cited for rejecting the resolution. Formerly, the PLO rejected Resolution 242 on the grounds that it rested on the principle of 'land for peace' and the recognition of Israel's secure borders. However, the Interim Programme rejected the resolution on the grounds that it ignored the national rights of the Palestinian people and treated their cause as a refugee issue. The PLO's rejection of Resolution 242 was expressed in categorical terms, since it ruled that 'dealing with this resolution is rejected at all levels'.

Despite the opposition to the Provisional Political Programme by those organizations that described themselves as the 'Rejection Front', the PLO mainstream pursued a policy of conformity to international legitimacy, with the aim of achieving a peaceful resolution of the Arab-Israeli conflict. Thus, the PLO attached great importance to diplomatic activity on the international scene, and this activity was rewarded by the granting of observer status to the PLO mission at the United Nations, as well as by the invitation extended to Yasir Arafat to address the UN General Assembly on behalf of the PLO, the sole legitimate representative of the Palestinian people. These moves were accompanied by the formation of the Committee for the Exercise of the Inalienable Rights of the Palestinian People by the General Assembly of the United Nations, in accordance with Resolution 3376 of 10 November 1975. The policy of the PLO mainstream reached its natural conclusion with the convening of the nineteenth session of the PNC in Algiers in 1988, in an atmosphere influenced by the previous *Intifada* – the uprising which erupted in Palestine in late 1987. This meeting marked the apex of the effort to establish a 'national authority' or 'independent state' in the West Bank and Gaza Strip as a result of a regional settlement of the conflict.

The meeting issued two documents: the political statement and the declaration of independence. Both documents reaffirmed the right of return and the resolution of the refugee issue within the context of UN resolutions. This was especially clear in the declaration of independence, which explicitly linked the right of return to the national rights of the Palestinian people, such as the right to independence and sovereignty on its territory. In addition, the declaration of independence reiterated the Palestinian people's right to establish an independent state based on Resolution 181 (II) of 1974. It held that this resolution continued to provide 'international legitimacy to right of the Palestinian people to sovereignty and national independence'. Until then, the PLO had rejected that resolution.

Meanwhile, neither document referred in any way to Resolution 194 as a legal basis for the right of return. According to Khalidi, the position concerning the right of return implicit in these two documents constitutes an important break with the position taken at the eighteenth session of the PNC (Algiers, April 1987), which mentioned the right of return without referring to UN resolutions.[10]

Summary

The political discourse of the PLO, including the discourse concerning the right of return, underwent a substantial transformation over a period of almost a quarter of a century (1964–88). This period began with the convening of the Jerusalem PNC, which passed the Palestinian National Charter, and ended with the nineteenth PNC in Algiers, which passed the declaration of independence. In between these two sessions, the twelfth PNC adopted the Provisional Political Programme. In this discourse, the PLO was transformed from the 'national liberation movement' of the Palestinian people, which aimed at the liberation of Palestine, the overthrow of the ideological basis of the state of Israel and the establishment of a democratic state on the whole territory of Palestine, to a 'national independence movement' exerting efforts to secure a 'statelet' or a Palestinian entity alongside Israel. In the process, it came to accept UN resolutions as a basis for the right of return and as a framework for resolving the refugee issue.

This transformation in political thought and practice prepared the PLO to join the ongoing peace negotiations which were launched in Madrid.

From Madrid to Oslo and Beyond (1991–present)

As we have seen, there were clear precedents to the PLO's joining the peace negotiations launched in Madrid. The PLO mainstream had resolved since the nineteenth PNC to capitalize on the *Intifada* to achieve the goal of freedom and independence. This step was taken in the conviction that the *Intifada* had shifted the centre of gravity of Palestinian struggle from outside to inside Palestine, and provided the impetus to implement the provisional political position which would lead to the establishment of an independent Palestinian state.

Among the precedents which paved the way for Madrid were a number of unofficial meetings in Europe and North America, which were encouraged if not sponsored by the PLO. These meetings brought together Palestinian academics and politicians with their Israeli counterparts from the so-called 'peace camp', and were considered 'confidence-building measures'. According to Elia Zureik they played an important role in pushing the PLO towards concessions and mutual recognition. One of the tangible results of these meetings was a series of secret meetings between Israeli and Palestinian academics in the early 1990s, which constituted the precedent for the Oslo agreement, formally known as 'The Declaration of Principles on Interim Self-Government Arrangements', and which was later signed in Washington on 13 March 1993.[11]

What is of primary concern here is the PLO position with respect to the right of return in the course of the negotiating process from Madrid to Oslo and beyond. This will be analysed as it is revealed in the contents of basic documents (the letters of mutual recognition, and the Declaration of Principles), in statements made by PLO negotiators and other officials, as well as in the practical results of the negotiations.

THE MADRID CONFERENCE

The Madrid Conference was convened on 31 October 1991 on the basis of UN Security Council Resolutions 242 and 338, which deal with the results of the Arab-Israeli wars of 1967 and 1973, respectively. Resolution 242 calls for a just resolution of the refugee issue, but without specifying the precise nature of the refugees. This led to the possibility of varying interpretations of this resolution. The Israeli interpretation considered it to refer merely to the refugees of 1967, while the Arab interpretation covered the refugees of both 1948 and 1967. These two resolutions do not discuss the legitimate national rights of the Palestinian people. Hence, the PLO joined the negotiations on a basis which excluded legitimate international resolutions which recognized the Palestinian people's right to self-determination and to independent statehood, including UN General Assembly Resolution 181 (1947), which the PLO had relied upon in its Declaration of Independence. This resolution also provides the sole international legal basis for the establishment of the state of Israel, according to former Israeli Foreign Minister Abba Eban.

Meanwhile, the head of the Palestinian delegation to the Madrid Conference spoke at the opening session about the distortion of the Palestinian version of history and about Palestinian displacement. He also affirmed the central place of the right of return in the contemporary Palestinian struggle, calling for the return of the refugees. He stated: '... despite the fact that the international community has affirmed their right to return in the form of Resolution 194, this fact continues to be intentionally ignored and obstructed ... We Palestinians do not want anything less than justice.'

As a result of the Madrid Conference, a working group to address the issue of refugees was formed within the framework of the multilateral negotiations. The agenda of the Refugee Working Group (RWG), headed by Canada, was set by a Steering Committee which met in Moscow in January 1992. The RWG held its first meeting in Ottawa on 12 May 1992, in the absence of Israel, which boycotted the meeting on the grounds that the head of the Palestinian delegation Dr Elias Sanbar was a refugee from the Palestinian diaspora. Resolution 194 was adopted as the basis for discussing the refugee issue. The head of the Palestinian delegation said in his statement at the meeting that 'the refugee issue is the political core of the question of Palestine'. He added that, in the absence of official recognition of the right of return of the refugees, the lives of Palestinians and the conditions of the refugee would not return to normal. At the second meeting of the RWG, which was also held in Ottawa, on 11 November 1992, the Palestinian delegation was headed by Dr Muhammad Hallaj, who reiterated the principle that Resolution 194 was the legal framework for resolving the refugee issue. Israel rejected the idea of considering Resolution 194 as the legal reference for discussing the refugee issue, and insisted that the proceedings of the RWG be restricted to humanitarian and technical matters. This remained the practice in all subsequent meetings. The Palestinian delegation continued to make reference to Resolution 194 in the closing statements of the RWG meetings, wherein all decisions are taken unanimously, but the reference to the resolution was a mere formality.

THE LETTERS OF MUTUAL RECOGNITION AND THE DECLARATION OF PRINCIPLES

The letters of mutual recognition were signed by Yasir Arafat and Yitzhak Rabin on 9 September 1993, a mere four days before the signing of the Declaration of Principles (DOP). Thus, the DOP was signed in the wake of the letters, which gives the letters the status of the main document while the DOP remains the subsidiary document, a circumstance that serves Israeli interests.

In Arafat's letter to Rabin, the PLO accepted UN Security Council Resolutions 242 and 338 and the right of the state of Israel to live in peace and security. Over the course of five decades of Arab-Zionist conflict, Israel had long sought a recognition of its legitimacy from its victims. This would lend the necessary support to international recognition of its legitimacy, which was based on facts imposed by force rather than on principles of justice. Arafat's letter to Rabin did not mention the Palestinian people's right to self-determination, including the right of return, and effectively postponed the discussion of final status issues, including the refugee issue, on the grounds that it would be resolved on the basis of negotiation.

The recognition of the PLO contained in Rabin's letter to Arafat was conditional upon the commitments contained in Arafat's letter, most critically the commitment to consider that the articles of the Palestinian National Charter which conflict with the commitments in the letter to be (not to become) 'ineffectual and invalid'. In this context, discussion centred on Articles 2, 9, 10, 19, 20, 12 and 22 of the Charter. Article 9 affirms that the Palestinian people are determined to continue the armed struggle 'for the liberation of their country and their return to it ... and to exercise their right to self-determination and sovereignty over it'.

The Declaration of Principles was arrived at as a result of secret negotiations in which the Palestinian party to the negotiations accepted terms that had formerly been rejected during the Washington negotiations launched by the Madrid Conference. Article 1 of the DOP, which concerns the aims of the negotiations, states that the interim arrangements are an inseparable part of the whole peace process, and it affirms that 'final status talks will lead to the implementation of Security Council Resolutions 242 and 338'. The DOP thereby ignores the sources of the national rights of the Palestinian people found in international law and in UN resolutions, particularly the right of return, which is based on the exercise of the right of self-determination. Article 5, paragraph 3 (5/3) of the DOP relegates the solution of the refugee issue to the final status talks, without linking the issue to any legal reference. Moreover, the DOP distinguishes two types of refugee: the refugees of 1948 and those of 1967. The latter are referred to in the terminology of the negotiations as 'displaced persons', which reflects the Israeli interpretation of Resolution 242. Article 12 of the DOP calls for cooperation between Israel and the Palestinian representatives on the one hand, and the governments of Jordan and Egypt on the other, in order to establish the Quadripartite Committee to discuss the means of returning the displaced people of 1967 to the West Bank and Gaza Strip. According to the DOP, the return of each displaced person is conditional upon Israeli approval and is subject to Israel's security considerations, on the pretext of 'preventing chaos and disorder'. This condition is confirmed by the DOP's endorsement of Israel's right to have joint sovereignty over all crossing points, by land, air and sea.

The Quadripartite Committee resolved, according to the closing statement issued after its first session held in Amman on 7 March 1995, to consider the DOP, its annexes, the articles concerning displaced persons in the Jordanian–Israeli treaty, and the Camp David agreement, as the basis for the committee's deliberations. Given the vagueness inherent in both the

DOP and the Jordanian-Israeli treaty when it comes to the definition of a 'refugee', it is not surprising that the committee continues to debate the definition of a 'refugee'.

OFFICIAL AND QUASI-OFFICIAL STATEMENTS

Because of the limitations of Resolution 194 and the complexities it introduces to the right of return, as well as the wide gap between the Palestinian and Israeli positions concerning the implementation of this right, some official and quasi-official Palestinian statements have been made in recent years which advocate interpreting the right of return in such a way that a distinction is made between the principle and its implementation. These interpretations call for distancing the right of return from the concept of 'absolute justice'. Among these statements are those by Nabil Sha'th and Faysal al-Husayni which deliberately refrain from identifying the destination to which the refugees should return.[12] This vagueness militates for an interpretation of the official Palestinian position as restricting the right of return to the territories controlled by the Palestinian Authority and the projected Palestinian entity, rather than to their actual homes, as mandated clearly and unambiguously by Resolution 194. Palestinian Legislative Council member Ziad Abu Zayyad expressed this view unequivocally by saying: 'One must distinguish between, on the one hand, the "right of return" as a principle, and on the other hand, exercising that right by literally returning to Palestine as a national homeland and to that same home ...'[13]

According to Rashid Khalidi, despite the fact that the PLO has not taken an official stand which explicitly puts such restrictions on the right of return, such statements by Palestinian officials indicate the general line of thought among the Palestinian leadership in this regard. In his view: 'This is potentially the most significant modification of the traditional Palestinian understanding of the right of return.'[14]

A noteworthy stance has been taken in this regard by As'ad Abdul Rahman, the Palestinian minister responsible for refugee affairs, who has said that he would not rule out the possibility that Yasir Arafat and Mahmoud Abbas might strike a deal with Israel without his knowledge, according to an Israeli press report.[15] One week before making this statement, Abdul Rahman contributed a column to the Lebanese daily *al-Safir* in which he accused certain unnamed Palestinian ministry employees of failing to adhere to the guidelines adopted by the PLO Executive Committee concerning the refugee issue, including a commitment to Resolution 194. Abdul Rahman accused these officials of crossing certain 'red lines' and of relying on 'alternative sources of authority to that of international legality', which constitutes in his view a 'free Palestinian concession'.[16]

One could also mention, under the category of statements which put restrictions on the right of return, those statements by certain Palestinian officials which speak of the right of Palestinians in the diaspora to hold passports issued by the future Palestinian state, so that they would be considered emigrant communities. If this were to transpire, the legal status of Palestinian refugees would be altered and it would undermine their right to return. The same could be said about overt and covert negotiations, with the participation of Palestinian officials, concerning compensation.

In a similar vein are those calls by a number of Palestinian officials for the establishment of a confederation between the future Palestinian state and Jordan, in accordance with resolutions issued by the Palestine National Council since its sixteenth session. Such a confederation would lead to the assimilation of 1.25 million Palestinian refugees and their absorption in their current places of residence on the East Bank of the River Jordan. This would ultimately deprive them of exercising their right of return to their original villages and homes.

Summary

The Declaration of Principles and its four annexes, as well as the letters of mutual recognition, are very clear when it comes to Israeli interests, but are vague and ambiguous when it comes to the rights of the Palestinian people. Such ambiguities are ultimately favourable to the stronger party, since the stronger party can force an interpretation of the documents which serves its interests. These documents have given Israel certain prerogatives which conflict with international legality, since according to international law, Israel is still considered an occupant. While these documents have also attempted to pre-empt the Palestinian people's rights of return, self-determination and sovereignty and to deprive the Palestinian struggle of its international legitimacy, they have by no means revoked the legal basis for the Palestinian right of return (Resolution 194) or the right to sovereignty (Resolution 181). They have attempted to make the negotiations the reference point for Palestinian rights, rather than vice versa.

According to Elia Zureik, the Palestinian position towards the right of return can be characterized as follows: 'It responds to crises and initiatives from the outside, but it lacks an articulated agenda and a clear position on the refugee issue.'[17]

FROM RIGHT OF RETURN TO BANTUSTAN

The PLO position on the right of return, as expressed in practice since Oslo has tampered with the legal framework of Palestinian rights as found in international law and the resolutions of the United Nations. It has also contravened the National Charter, which affirms the unity of the Palestinian people and the unity of its historic national aspirations regarding its ancestral homeland. Some Israeli and US positions may serve to convey the grave damage that has been done to the Palestinian national struggle. Former Israeli Prime Minister Shimon Peres has described the amendment of the Palestinian National Charter as the most important ideological shift during the current century. Similarly, former US Secretary of State Madeleine

Albright stated in September 1994 that UN resolutions concerning the question of Palestine were contentious, irrelevant and obsolete.

The consequences of the negotiations on the Palestinian track and the expectations from the negotiations on other Arab tracks all point towards bypassing the right of return and prolonging Palestinian displacement. They also presage the undermining of the right of self-determination by the creation of a mere 'Palestinian entity' which resembles a Bantustan more than it does a fully sovereign independent state.

It is one of the ironies of history that the racist regime in South Africa, which is a throwback to the heyday of imperialism, has been dismantled at a time when Israel continues to impose a resolution of the question of Palestine which consolidates a kind of racist apartheid in Palestine, with the full backing of the United States. Moreover, this is taking place at the start of the twenty-first century, which is supposed to be the century of democracy and human rights.

Some Palestinian scholars have compared the nascent Palestinian autonomy to Transkei in South Africa, the autonomous region set up by the racist South African regime for blacks in 1963, which was declared an independent state despite the fact that it gained recognition only from the apartheid regime itself.[18]

Other Palestinian scholars have noted that the reality which Israel is currently putting into effect on the land of Palestine is drawn from three sources. The first is the apartheid system imposed by white South Africans on blacks. The second is the system of reservations which was imposed by the United States and Canada on the indigenous inhabitants of North America. And the third is the system of segregation which was adopted in the United States up to the early 1960s to isolate American blacks from whites in their places of residence, work, public services, and so on.[19] In so doing, Israel takes its cue from the notion of racial or ethnic purity found in Zionist ideology, and implements this in confiscating and annexing Palestinian land with the smallest proportion possible of Palestinian inhabitants, according to a statement once made by former Israeli Prime Minister Yitzhak Rabin.

After the signing of the final status accords, the Palestinian people will probably find themselves split between insiders and outsiders, with half the population living in exile, in isolation from the other half which will live in the projected Palestinian entity, deprived of its legitimate rights to return and self-determination in its homeland. In order to avoid such a bleak fate, the Palestinian people everywhere must reiterate their insistence on the unity of the land and the people. In particular, the Palestinians of the diaspora must form a historic coalition to express a resolute position on the right of return and self-determination, and to reject resettlement or restitution instead of return. May return remain a legitimate dream which will be implemented in practice.

NOTES

1. Rashid Hamid (ed.), *Muqarrarat al-majlis al-watani al-filastini 1964–1974* [Resolutions of the Palestinian National Council 1964–1974] (Beirut: Palestine Research Centre, 1975), p. 46.
2. John Quigley, 'Displaced Palestinians and the Right of Return', *Harvard International Law Journal*, vol. 39, no. 1 (1998), pp. 193–8.
3. Elia Zureik, *Palestinian Refugees and the Peace Process* (Beirut: Insitute for Palestine Studies, 1996), p. 110.
4. Ibid.
5. Ramadane Babadji et al., *Haq al-'awdah lil sha'b al-filastini wa mabadi' tatbiqih* [The Right of Return of the Palestinian People] (Beirut: Institute for Palestine Studies, 1996), p. 106.
6. Ibid., pp. 111–13.
7. Rashid Khalidi, 'Observations on the Right of Return', vol. XXI, no. 2 (Winter 1992), p. 33.
8. Ibid., p. 34.
9. Ibid.
10. Ibid., p. 35.
11. Zureik, *Palestinian Refugees and the Peace Process*, p. 90.
12. Khalidi, 'Observations', p. 36.
13. Ziad Abu Zayyad, 'The Palestinian Right of Return: A Realistic Approach', *Palestine-Israel Journal of Politics, Economics, and Culture*, no. 2 (Spring 1994), p. 77.
14. Khalidi, 'Observations', p. 36.
15. *Jerusalem Post*, 28 January 2000.
16. *Al-Safir*, 21 January 2000.
17. Zureik, *Palestinian Refugees and the Peace Process*, p. 94.
18. Hisham Sharabi, *al-Hayat*, 19 May 1996.
19. Burhan al-Dajani, *Mufawadat al-salam: al-masar wa al-khiyarat wa al-ihtimalat* [Middle East Peace Talks: Course, Options and Prospects] (Beirut: Institute for Palestine Studies, 1994), pp. 165–6.

Part III

Return or Permanent Exile

7   RETURN OR PERMANENT EXILE?
Joseph Massad

Before the 'peace process' that began in Madrid in 1991 and continued with the inauguration of the Oslo process in 1993, all representatives of the Palestinians inside and outside the Palestine Liberation Organization (PLO) agreed that the varied interests of the Palestinian people were inherently compatible. The 'peace process', however, has altered this equation radically. Following the various agreements signed with Israel by the PLO and subsequently by the Palestinian Authority (PA), the interests of the different sections of the Palestinian people effectively were separated and made incompatible if not outright contradictory. Israeli Palestinians, through their elected leadership, are challenging Israel to shed its Jewish character and become a state of *all* its citizens, while West Bank and Gaza Palestinians, through their elected leadership, seem to be preparing for the fantasy of a sovereign, independent Palestinian state. To realize this fantasy, the leadership of the West Bank and Gaza Palestinians is heeding 'pragmatic' and 'realist' advice on the necessity to concede the rights of refugee and diaspora Palestinians to return and/or be compensated. In turn, diaspora and refugee Palestinians, since the Oslo process began, have been bereft of leadership and have no identifiable goals. Such a development makes it essential to chart briefly the course that led to this outcome and assess the recent positions and proposals advanced by official and non-official Palestinians and Israelis on how to resolve the refugee question.

THE ROAD TO OSLO

The prerequisite to this situation was the 1988 Declaration of Independence proclaimed by the Palestine National Council at a meeting in Algiers. Until that time, the PLO, at least officially, had sought to create a secular, democratic Palestinian state in all of pre-1948 Palestine, a state wherein all Palestinian refugees would be repatriated, the Israeli occupation of the West Bank and Gaza would end, and the situation of Israeli apartheid, under whose yoke Israeli Palestinians live, would be terminated. Unofficially, however, the change occurred much earlier. Whereas between 1964 and 1974 the PLO had tilted more towards the diaspora in its programme for liberation, beginning in the mid-1970s, pressure from the emerging pro-PLO

Palestinian elite in the West Bank and Gaza to accept a two-state solution was bearing fruit. (The PLO has always ignored Palestinians living in Israel.) The two-state solution, which became more acceptable as early as 1974, was officially understood to be a prelude to the ultimate unification of Palestine, and that the establishment of a West Bank and Gaza mini-state would not be at the expense of the diaspora and the refugees. Although most groups within the PLO, including leftist groups, had informally accepted that repatriation would be impossible in the context of a two-state solution, officially they all stuck to the position that achieving one did not preclude the achievement of the other.

In those years, the Palestinian leadership rested with the diaspora, which built, nourished and sustained it. The 1982 defeat of the diaspora leadership in Beirut and its exile to Tunis not only weakened the PLO but also diaspora Palestinians, who had sustained the hope that the PLO would be able to realize their dreams. The West Bank and Gaza *Intifada*, which erupted in December 1987, jolted the Palestinian people everywhere. Terrified of an independent Palestinian leadership in the Occupied Territories, the increasingly corrupt PLO sought to undermine it by hijacking the *Intifada* financially and organizationally. But the *Intifada* strengthened the West Bank and Gaza Palestinians' push for an official unequivocal acceptance of the two-state solution. In that context, the Palestine National Council declared an independent Palestinian state in 1988 in the West Bank and Gaza Strip as an expression of the will of the Palestinian people's revolt against their Israeli oppressors. The declaration itself finally constituted the PLO's official stamp on the two-state solution, with no mention of the rights of the diaspora or Israeli Palestinians, except in the statement that the independent state shall be the 'state of Palestinians wherever they may be'.[1]

Until that moment, the PLO did not refer to the 1948 UN General Assembly Resolution 194, which affirmed that Palestinian refugees 'wishing to return to their homes and live at peace with their neighbours should be permitted to do so at the earliest practicable date, and that compensation should be paid for the property of those choosing not to return and for loss of or damage to property, which, under principles of international law or in equity, should be made good by the governments or authorities responsible'.[2] The 1988 declaration marked the first time in its history that the PNC reaffirmed the Palestinian people's right of return based on UN resolutions; previously, that right was always affirmed with no reference to such resolutions.[3] As Rashid Khalidi explains:

in explicitly accepting the terms of resolution 194 of 1948, the PLO has accepted certain crucial limitations on a putative absolute right of return. The first is that Palestinians who were made refugees in 1948 are offered an option whereby those 'choosing not to return' become eligible for compensation for their property ... Acceptance of the fait accompli of Israel's creation in 1948 at the expense of the Palestinians has now in effect been legitimized by the PLO ... the politically impossible demand that all Palestinians made refugees in 1948 be allowed to return is dropped, without dropping the principle that such people have certain rights in the context of a negotiated settlement, and without abandoning the reading of history which is the basis of this principle. This also makes the demand of implementation of the right of return a slightly more realistic one, without the PLO appearing to make a concession.[4]

Moreover, although neither the PLO nor the PA has specified officially the destinations of returning refugees, individuals associated with both have done so. As early as 1989, Nabil Sha'th and Faysal Husayni made statements to the effect that such destinations would be primarily confined to the Palestinian state-to-be.[5] The subsequent peregrinations of Yasir Arafat to satisfy US conditions for speaking to the PLO were exemplified by his pathetic renunciation of armed resistance, coded 'terrorism' in Zionist-speak, and his declaration that the now infamous PLO charter was '*caduc*' (obsolete).[6] Even these humiliating concessions achieved only a short-term dialogue soon to be terminated by the Americans.

Following the Gulf War, and the American plan to convene an international conference in Madrid, the Palestinians were not even allowed to participate in an independent delegation. At Israeli insistence, only West Bank (but not East Jerusalem) and Gaza Palestinians were allowed to participate as part of the Jordanian delegation. As for the PLO, for fear of a competing leadership, it sought to undermine the Palestinians negotiating within the Madrid process by conducting its own secret talks with the Israelis. Its subsequent signing of the Declaration of Principles (DOP) was premised on its transformation from a diaspora leadership to a West Bank and Gaza leadership which would be willing to forsake the rights of the diaspora and the refugees altogether. It was within the confines of the DOP that the PLO leadership was transformed into the Palestinian Authority and the Palestinian refugees were relegated to one of the many issues to be discussed during the 'final status talks' whenever they materialize.

By separating the interests of the inside (native West Bank and Gaza Palestinians) and the outside (diaspora and refugee Palestinians) and forcing the PLO to accept that separation officially, Israel effectively laid the groundwork for the Oslo process. It was in Madrid that the issue of refugees was separated from the bilateral tracks and relegated to what was called the 'multilateral track', which set up a 'Refugee Working Group' (RWG) chaired by Canada. The purpose of the RWG is not to negotiate over the status of the refugees, but rather to improve the living conditions of the Palestinian refugees, particularly those outside the West Bank and Gaza. The only political issue that was discussed at the RWG besides Palestinian representation was the question of family reunification wherein the Israelis agreed to increase the pre-existing annual quota of 1,000 to 2,000, it being understood that Israel had never fulfilled the earlier or later quota anyway.[7]

As for the DOP, its declared aim was to reach a 'permanent settlement based on Security Council Resolution 242 and 338'.[8] Resolution 242, as is commonly known, calls, as an aside, for a 'just settlement of the refugee problem'.[9] The DOP asserts that only in the permanent status negotiations between representatives of the Palestinian people and the Israeli government will the remaining issues, including that of the 'refugees,' be covered.[10] Moreover the DOP called for inviting the governments of Jordan and Egypt to participate in establishing 'cooperation arrangements', which will include the 'constitution of a Continuing Committee that will decide by agreement on the modalities of admission of persons displaced from the West Bank and Gaza Strip in 1967' (Article XII). So far, neither committee has produced anything that is remotely connected to resolving the status of Palestinian refugees. Moreover, the so-called peace process remains frozen on issues pertinent to non-refugee issues which themselves are being compromised.

PROTECTING ISRAELI INTERESTS AS PRAGMATISM

In anticipation of the final status negotiations, much literature has appeared on the question of the refugees. Those proposals that express semi-official positions most likely will be used as a reference for the negotiations – should these ever take place – and thus merit careful scrutiny. Before proceeding to review these different proposals, a presentation of the human dimension of this question is in order, namely the numbers of refugees from 1948 and 1967. In 1995, according to the figures of the United Nations Relief and Works Agency (UNRWA), the 1948 refugees (and their descendants) living in the West Bank, Gaza, Jordan, Lebanon and Syria numbered 3,093,174 people. As for 1948 refugees who remained in Israel proper (and are referred to by the Israeli government as 'present absentees'), they number between 120,000 and 150,000.[11] In 1994, the number of 1967 refugees (termed displaced persons) numbered 1,132,326 people, half of whom also were 1948 refugees, that is, those who had been displaced for the second time.[12] These numbers do not include Palestinian refugees in Egypt, Iraq, North Africa and the Gulf Arab countries, nor do they include Palestinian Bedouins who were no longer allowed to return to their grazing lands within Israel, nor the middle-class Palestinian refugees who did not register with UNRWA, nor the children of Palestinian women who married non-refugee Palestinians or non-Palestinians, as UNRWA no longer considers these as refugees. Those belonging to these four categories number around 300,000 people. [13]

What is striking about most of the proposals advancing solutions to the refugee question is the discourse of 'pragmatism' and 'realism' they deploy. The definition of pragmatism in this discourse is one wherein everything Israel rejects is 'not pragmatic', while everything it accepts is 'pragmatic'. What this means is that the Palestinians are the only party being asked to be 'pragmatic', as Israeli positions function as base referents and are therefore deployed as 'pragmatic' *a priori*.[14] Examples of the deployment of this discourse are found in the two most recent projects that have been advanced to resolve the refugee problem: Donna Arzt's *Refugees into Citizens, Palestini-*

ans and the End of the Arab-Israeli Conflict,[15] and the proposal advanced by Harvard University's Program on International Conflict Analysis and Resolution, which was debated by a group of Palestinians and Israelis and written by Khalil Shikaki and Joseph Alpher (in addition to Shikaki, the Palestinian group included other Palestinian pragmatists, namely Ghassan Khatib, Ibrahim Dakkak, Yezid Sayigh, Nadim Rouhana and Nabeel Kassis).[16] Both are important as they are being touted as starting points for the most likely scenario for refugee negotiations.

Arzt's proposal, considered 'objective' by mainstream Western, Israeli and some PA-supported circles, foresees the settlement of Palestinian refugees mostly in neighbouring Arab countries and in the West Bank with the multi-conditioned possibility of returning a mere 75,000 refugees to Israel. The premise of the book is that no one can establish who was responsible for the Palestinian exodus in 1948 and therefore everyone must share in the responsibility of resolving the plight of the refugees – not only in terms of resettlement but also in terms of compensation. Some of the possible explanations for the exodus that Arzt lists include Israeli expulsion as well as the now discredited Israeli propagandistic claim that Arab leaders called on the Palestinians to leave in order to clear the way for the descending Arab armies. Even if one were to accept Arzt's claim that it is impossible to establish who was responsible for the exodus of *every* Palestinian in 1948 and 1967, one nevertheless can easily prove with extant *Israeli* evidence that Palestinians living in Lydda and Ramle were expelled by Israeli army units led by none other than Yitzhak Rabin, that thousands more were expelled from the Galilee area, and that 12,500 Palestinians were deported individually by the Israeli government between 1967 and 1994.[17] Despite Arzt's interest in verifying responsibility, she never investigates from within her conceptual framework whether those whose expulsion is supported by Israeli government records should be allowed to return to Israel and be compensated by it, while the rest be the responsibility of multiple parties, including Israel. Moreover, even if one agreed with Arzt's and the Israeli government's propaganda that Israel should not compensate the refugees because it did not expel them, then should not the compensation for stolen property be the responsibility of those who expropriated it? It is an uncontested fact that Israeli Jews and the Israeli government are the parties that took over the abandoned property of Palestinians in 1948 and refuse to return it to its rightful owners. However, Arzt is concerned only that Israel be spared the financial responsibilities, not to mention the demographic 'threat' that Palestinians are said to constitute to its existence. She soberly states that the Palestinian refugee question should be resolved with minimal Israeli paybacks in order to calm 'Israelis who will need assurance that a Palestinian will not someday show up on their children's doorstep demanding title to the property and/or with a multi-million dollar compensation claim'.[18] Arzt suggests that Israel's 'contribution to the compensation pool could, appropriately, come from the "rents" it collected in the 1940s and early 1950s from the Jewish users of "absentee" Arab property'.[19] As for returning refugees, Israel could take 75,000 refugees whom it should have the right to carefully screen for a variety of sins and crimes. Arzt is careful to add that such a returning group will most likely be restricted to non-reproductive Palestinians: 'A population subgroup very likely to seek return ... would be ... the oldest living generation of Palestinians, the ones who retain personal memories of life before 1948.'[20] The implicit concern here seems to be that a young population of 75,000 refugees might reproduce in ways detrimental to maintaining Jewish demographic supremacy in Israel!

The Harvard group study proposes four solutions: two 'traditional' Palestinian and Israeli solutions and two 'compromise' solutions, one Palestinian and one Israeli. A conclusion includes commonalities between the Palestinian and the Israeli compromise solutions. Whereas Arzt's solution is legitimated by a 'Foreword' written for her by a Palestinian Jordanian, Rami Khouri, the Harvard paper expresses the views of a committee of Palestinians and Israelis. The Palestinian compromise position 'seeks to provide an acceptable, honorable – though not necessarily just – resolution of the refugee issue while accommodating the realities on the ground and Israeli security concerns'.[21] Whereas this solution calls on Israel to 'fully acknowledge' the 'individual moral right of Palestinian refugees to return to their homes and property in Palestine', the proposal writers insist that '[n]o return *en masse* of the Palestinian refugees is envisaged ... [rather] a return of only a limited number is seen as feasible'.[22] The writers assert that most refugees will opt for compensation and concede to Israel the right 'to have a say to the number of refugees allowed to return'.[23] However, they do assert that Palestinians who want to return should have the right to return to a Palestinian state-to-be with Israel having no say in that matter. The compromise is stated succinctly by the authors: 'In this final settlement, the Palestinians make a strategic trade-off. They demand a return to the 1967 border, in order to absorb the largest possible number of refugees, in return for forgoing the full exercise of the right of return.'[24] The remaining refugees should be settled in host countries. Israel should be responsible to find the funds and to pay individual compensation as well as collective compensation, the latter to be paid to the Palestinian state-to-be. This solution, the authors tell us, 'provides *realistic* and *reasonable* justice by granting a moral/political right while acknowledging realities on the ground' (emphases added).[25]

Whereas the Israeli government has officially refused to make the 1948 refugees part of the negotiation agenda and consistently makes statements that only few of the 1967 refugees will be allowed to return, some Israelis are advancing informed proposals about what the Israeli government might be agreeable to in the future. While, on the one hand, Rabin insisted after the DOP that Israel would not allow more than a few thousand 1967 refugees to return, adding that if the PLO 'expect[s] tens of thousands [of refugees to return] they live in a dream, an illusion',[26] on the other hand, the Israeli compromise position, as the Harvard group of Israeli politicians and pundits see it, insists that Israel can share 'practical (but not moral) responsibility, together with the other parties to the process that culminated in the 1948 war, for the plight [but not the flight] and suffering of the refugees'.[27] Furthermore, the fact that half the 1948 Palestinian refugees 'left' Palestine before 14 May 1948, is not relevant to the exegetical eye of these authors. These Israelis assert that in their compromise 'Israel also accepts the right of return to the Palestinian State, but not to Israel proper. Israel also may accept repatriation of "tens of thousands" of Palestinian refugees as part of its family reunification program'.[28] On the question of compensation, Israel would compensate Palestinians on a 'collective basis' in tandem with the 'relevant Arab countries creat[ing] a similar mechanism for Arab collective compensation of Jewish refugees'[29] – a reference to Arab Jews who immigrated to Israel between 1949 and 1953. Also, the Palestinian state must limit the number of returning Palestinians to its own territory, otherwise the Israelis will curtail their obligations of compensation.[30] The combined authors believe that the ultimate solution would be somewhere in between their two compromise solutions, it being understood that these solutions will not apply to Israeli Palestinian internal refugees.[31] Israel's possible payment of compensation to refugees

might generate parallel demands by Israeli Arabs who also abandoned lands or were removed from them, even though they remained in Israel. This could have far-reaching implications for Jewish–Arab relations with Israel. Hence the Israeli-Palestinian agreement on refugees must, from the Israeli standpoint, clearly define the PLO role as representing only Palestinians outside of Israel, while the government of Israel is responsible for all Israeli citizens, including Arabs.[32]

Actually, the compromise position presented by the Harvard group of Israelis does not differ much from a proposal presented in 1994 by Shlomo Gazit, a retired Israeli army general with military intelligence background and a close friend of Rabin. Gazit also became an adviser to the Israeli multilateral negotiating teams, with special reference to refugee issues.[33] Gazit, like the Harvard group of Israelis, is clear that 'the option of "return" should never be given to the Palestinians'.[34] If Israel does decide to return some refugees on a humanitarian basis, and second only to its security and national concerns, the Palestinians should have no say in the number of those returning.[35]

In addition to these proposals, a number of semi-official Palestinian proposals and positions also have been circulating.[36] One such position is articulated by Salim Tamari, who is a member of the Refugee Working Group (RWG) created by the Madrid Process. Tamari begins by situating the refugee question in the 'peace process'. He states:

solving the refugee problem is fast becoming part of the new dichotomy within Palestinian politics between the contingencies of state-building on the one hand and the demands of the diaspora for representation and repatriation on the other.[37]

It was at Palestinian insistence on including refugees as a final status element that the RWG was born in the first place. This move was engineered to 'send a signal to Palestinian refugees in Jordan, Syria and Lebanon that they had not been forgotten in the protracted interim negotiations. This in turn would lend much-needed legitimacy to the impending signing of an Israeli-Palestinian accord, which was bound to be seen as too conciliatory by diaspora Palestinians without a refugee component.'[38] However, as already mentioned, the RWG was not designed to *resolve* the refugee problem, but rather to *dissolve* it through resettlement and amelioration of standards of living.[39] Tamari concludes by asserting:

As final status negotiations loom on the horizon, immense diplomatic pressure will start building on the Palestinians to abandon their insistence on the right of return. The Israelis have made it clear that they will not support any categorical 'right of return' for the Palestinians – either to Israel itself or to the West Bank and Gaza.[40]

Whereas it took the Palestinians four decades to accept finally the concessions enshrined in Resolution 194, Tamari surmises that Palestinians will have to forget that resolution altogether. He firmly states that 'repeated reference to UN resolutions on Palestinian refugees, particularly General Assembly Resolution 194 (1948) and Security Council Resolution 237 (1967), is futile even though they do constitute the proper international legal framework in which these issues should be addressed'.[41] He asserts that 'Palestinian negotiators ... operate under constraints that dictate that issues of principle and ideological predisposition be tempered by what is *realizable* and *obtainable*' (emphases added).[42] Tamari also recommends that in

return for Arab and Palestinian acceptance to absorb the bulk of Palestinian refugees in the West Bank, Gaza and Arab host countries, Israel should absorb a limited number of refugees. Proper compensation should be paid to all refugees who choose to return as well as to those who choose to be naturalized in their host countries.[43]

Tamari is not alone in his recommendations. The Palestinian intellectual Sari Nusseibeh (along with the Israeli Mark Heller), in a proposal to deal with the refugee question in the context of a two-state solution, does not require Israel to repatriate the refugees. All he requires is that 'Israel should be prepared to entertain applications on a case-by-case basis on humanitarian grounds'.[44] Indeed, the pragmatism of these proposals revolves around finding a face-saving formula with minimal costs for Israel, not the Palestinians. Israel is not expected to repatriate the Palestinians it expelled, but were it to ever consider to repatriate a few, this would be considered a 'humanitarian' act on its part.

PRAGMATISM AND REFUGEE INTERESTS

This discourse of pragmatism is not only prevalent among the group of Palestinian *comprador* intellectuals associated with the Palestinian Authority, it has also influenced many Palestinian intellectuals who are committed to their people's struggle for justice, but who see no way out for the refugees in the face of continued Israeli intransigence and American support of it. In a tentative proposal, Rashid Khalidi wants to offer a solution that he calls 'attainable justice, or justice within the realm of the possible'.[45] Khalidi, one of the few Palestinians involved in the Madrid process who opted out soon after the PLO's deal at Oslo, asserts that 'the refugee issue cannot be addressed as many other issues have been dealt with in the Israeli-Palestinian negotiations to date ... [wherein] history has been tossed out the window ... as if there were no past which had to be accounted for and dealt with'.[46] He says:

[o]n the refugee issue, there can be no such cavalier treatment of history ... it is because this issue is so central to the national narrative and the self-view of the Palestinian people that any approach which tries to sweep history under the rug will fail utterly. The Palestinians might put up with humiliating and unequal agreements based on ignoring history in the economic sphere, in the area of security, and in other domains. But it is hard to visualize them standing for an attempt to pretend that the refugee issue does not have specific historic roots, and can be resolved accordingly.[47]

Khalidi's call is a genuine one for a realizable solution. In the light of current and projected Israeli intransigence, he affirms that 'to argue seriously for Israeli acceptance of unlimited liability ... means to argue against the possibility of any real solution to this issue'.[48] Whereas Khalidi's pessimism is understandable, arguing seriously for unlimited Israeli liability does not mean that this is the only thing Palestinians would accept; it simply means that this should be the Palestinian opening position in any negotiations, as it is based on historical facts and on historical and national rights. Giving up these UN-sanctioned rights before the negotiations begin will surely snowball into numerous concessions. Khalidi's conclusion that 'it is inconceivable that most refugees will be allowed to exercise their right of return to their original homes in what is now Israel for the foreseeable future, or perhaps ever' unfortunately has been taken up by pro-Israeli US academics (such as the Harvard Group led by Leonard Hausman) who quote Khalidi to add legitimacy to their recommendations, which amount to liquidating the refugee issue.[49]

Khalidi asserts the legal right of Palestinians to return in principle. He likens their situation to 'people forced to flee their homes by a flood which has permanently inundated their original communities, and who have a right to return which they simply cannot exercise by reason of *force majeure*'.[50] The only difference, he hastens to add, is that 'unlike the flood, the state of Israel is not a state of nature – although it sometimes may have seemed like one to those unfortunate enough to find themselves in its path.

And because it is not a force of nature, it can and must be held responsible for its actions.'[51] Khalidi calls on the Israeli government to pay reparations rather than compensation, wherein the former designates its responsibility.

Khalidi's solution includes Israeli recognition of the hurt it inflicted on the Palestinian people, an acceptance that all Palestinian refugees and their descendants have a right to return to their homes in principle, although most will not be able to exercise that right as a result of Israel's refusal and/or because their homes and villages no longer exist. He suggests that 'a few thousand or tens of thousands of people' whose villages still exist or who have family in Israel should be allowed to return.[52] A third element of Khalidi's solution is the payment of reparations for all those not allowed to return and compensation for those who lost property in 1948. These sums for property losses alone (not to mention reparations) range from $92 billion to $147 billion at 1984 prices. In addition to the compensation, Khalidi comes up with a reparation figure of $20,000 per person for an arbitrarily chosen figure of 2 million refugees totalling $40 billion, which amounts to little more than a decade's worth of US aid to Israel (Atif Kubursi's calculations in 1994 prices reach the figure of $253 billion in reparations and compensation).[53] It is important to note that Israeli colonial settlers who had to vacate Israeli colonies in the Sinai before it was returned to Egypt were paid $250,000 per household.[54] The fourth element of Khalidi's solution is the right of Palestinian refugees to live in the state of Palestine-to-be, which will be circumscribed only by its absorptive capacity, and finally a resolution to Palestinian refugees in Lebanon and Jordan.[55]

IS RETURN PRAGMATIC?

Salman Abu-Sitta is the only Palestinian intellectual to date who is not awed by what is 'realistic,' 'pragmatic' or 'reasonable' within the confines of the Madrid and Oslo process. Unlike most proposals dealing with refugees, which look at what is practical from the viewpoint of Israeli leaders and which aim to resolve the Israeli part of this problem at the expense of Palestinians, Abu-Sitta proposes what he simply calls 'The Feasibility of the Right of Return'. He begins by affirming that:

One of the persistent myths is the 'impracticality' of the return of the refugees, on the assumption that the country is full of immigrants, the villages are destroyed and it is impossible to find old property boundaries. This view is advanced by the Israelis and by well-meaning people who agree that the Right of Return is perfectly legal but cannot be implemented on physical grounds.[56]

Abu-Sitta counters these claims by demonstrating that the 'return of the refugees is practically feasible, and even desirable for permanent peace to prevail'.[57] The elements of Abu-Sitta's proposal are as follows. The majority of refugees whether they live inside or outside Palestine are within a 100-mile radius of their former homes. Although most of their houses are destroyed, 'a return would be to the same land, most frequently the same site, with reconstruction of villages and repairing long-neglected Palestinian cities. With the exception of the Central District, relatively few village sites are occupied by modern construction. Most Kibbutz and prefab units are installed away from old village remains.'[58]

Also, 'it is claimed that boundaries have disappeared and are impossible to determine. Available Palestine and Israel maps, assisted by modern technology, now used by Israel to lease refugee's land, are sufficient to determine old and new boundaries. It can be demonstrated that all boundaries and ownerships are well recorded. Not only the villages are kept [*sic*] in the memory of the refugees and their children, but their images are kept for posterity through the British aerial survey of 1945–46.'[59]

To the ostensible horror of Israelis, Abu-Sitta dares to divide Israel into Areas A, B, and C. Area A includes 8 per cent of the land in Israel and is occupied by 68 per cent of the Israeli Jewish population. Area B encompasses 7 per cent of the land and is inhabited by 10 per cent of the Jewish population. Thus 78 per cent of Jews in Israel live on 15 per cent of the land. Area C encompassing 85 per cent of the land area in Israel 'is remarkably similar, but not exactly identical, to the Palestinian land from which they were driven'. The inhabitants of Area C include 800,000 urban Jews living in urban centres, 154,000 rural Jews and 465,000 Israeli Palestinians. 'Thus 154,000 Jews cultivate the land of 4,476,000 refugees who are prevented from returning to it.'[60] Since most of the rural Jews are leasing the land, once the lease expires, the land can be given back to the Palestinians. Even with the return of the refugees, overall population density in Israel would be 482 persons/sq. km, instead of the present 261. 'The new overall density of 482 persons/sq. km, is a far cry from the congested miserable conditions which the refugees have to endure while their land is the playground of the privileged Kibbutz.'

If his plan is implemented, Abu-Sitta states that Area A will remain largely Jewish (76 per cent Jews), Area B will be mixed and Area C will be largely Palestinian (81 per cent Palestinian). Since Area A would be congested, Palestinians from that area (900,000) can relocate to Areas B and C, while the rural Jews of Area C numbering 154,000 can relocate to Area A should they not want to live with Palestinians.[61] Abu-Sitta concludes by asserting that his 'proposed plan represents the most congested (worst) case, i.e. all refugees return and all Jews stay'.[62] Since many refugees might not take that option, reality would be even less congested than this maximalist proposal. Abu-Sitta adds that 'even in the most congested case, only 154,000 Jews may choose to relocate elsewhere in Israel to allow 4, 476,000 refugees to return to their homes and end half a century of destitution and suffering. This is a very cheap price [which] Israel should pay for what it inflicted upon the Palestinians and still cheaper price to pay for a secure future for both peoples.'[63]

Abu-Sitta states that 'the Palestinians have no obligation, moral or legal, to accommodate the Israelis at their expense. By any standards, the Israelis have such an obligation – to correct a monumental injustice they have committed. Nevertheless, the refugees' return has nothing to do with Israel's sovereignty. It has nothing to do with whether [the] Oslo agreements succeed or fail. It has nothing to do with settlements, boundaries, or even Jerusalem. Let all these issues take their natural course.'[64]

What Abu-Sitta's proposal offers is a challenge to the pervasive discourse of pragmatism and realism. Proposing a feasible solution, he challenges the capitulationist stance of the PA and its apologist intellectuals. In fact, in their overzeal for pragmatism, these *comprador* intellectuals are going beyond what even the PA and the PLO think is acceptable. As'ad Abdul Rahman, a member of the PLO executive committee and the PLO appointee responsible for the refugee portfolio, implored these intellectuals to 'save us from your harmful interest'. He added that the involvement of Palestinian intellectuals in discussions with Israelis on how to resolve the refugee issue would have been fine had they had the 'national interest' as a priority and had they 'pursued the realization' of the national interest. Abdul Rahman affirmed that any scenario or proposal that veers away from international legality with regards to the refugees' right of return constitutes a 'free concession' even if it were presented in an unofficial capacity. He concluded by asserting the refugees' right to return and by affirming that it is not the 'mission of Arab intellectuals, especially the Palestinians among them, to give up a basic human right, that of living in one's home, nor should their goal be to find solutions to Israeli problems by intensifying problems for the Palestinians, nor to present free concessions before even reaching the stage of refugee negotiations'.[65]

Elia Zureik, a member of the RWG, provides an accurate summary of the official Palestinian position in the context of the Madrid process:

In succumbing to the dictates of the Madrid Conference, Palestinians have been framing the debate, implicitly if not explicitly, over the issue of the right of return *not* as one of whether the refugees should return to their 1948 homes, but rather as a debate over (1) whether there should be unhampered right of return for all refugees and displaced Palestinians to an independent state in the West Bank and Gaza; (2) how to compensate the refugees and normalize the civil and human rights of non-returnees in neighboring countries; (3) whether to grant Palestinian passports to all refugees remaining in their places of refuge; and (4) how to get Israel to allow a symbolic return of some refugees from the 1948 war to Israel proper and to recognize that a historical injustice was done to the Palestinian people.[66]

Indeed, rumours circulating since 1996 and reported by the Israeli newspaper *Ha'aretz*, claim that secret talks between the PA and Shimon Peres resulted in an agreement, wherein the Israeli government would help resettle the refugees outside its borders, in neighbouring countries.[67]

SEPARATING PALESTINIAN POLITICAL INTERESTS

Native West Bank and Gaza Palestinians are reaping the benefits of a phantasmatic state-to-be by forsaking refugee rights, just as Zionists who never included the rescue of European Jews as a priority in their political programme, received the financial and political benefits for the murder of these Jews by Nazi Germany.[68] The premise that diaspora and refugee Palestinians are part of the final settlement of the 'peace process' presupposes that they are at one with native West Bank and Gaza Palestinians. Yet all proposed resolutions by PA elements and its coterie of *comprador* intellectuals sacrifice most of their rights in favour of separating them from native West Bank and Gaza Palestinians who are the ultimate beneficiaries of whatever Israeli largesse the PA and its cronies are able to extract. Palestinian refugees living in the West Bank and Gaza (numbering upwards of 1.2 million people) have been disproportionately impoverished by the dismal economic performance of the PA.[69] They are also increasingly denigrated on the bases of status and class by native West Bankers and Gazans, as the refugees' role as canon fodder during the *Intifada* is no longer needed and has been rendered *démodé* by the PA–Israeli peace process. Despite their increasingly difficult situation since the PA came to power, West Bank and Gaza refugees have mobilized themselves through convening a number of popular refugee conferences, organized by the refugee camps' Union of Youth Centre, as early as December 1995 in Far'a (the site of a former Israeli prison). This was followed by conferences in the Deheishe refugee camp for the Bethlehem area refugees in 1996, as well as other popular conferences in Gaza.[70] Recommendations were issued, especially at the 1996 conference in Deheishe;[71] however, due to the diversity of opinions among refugees regarding relations with the PA and the PLO, the conference programme and recommendations were not implemented; as a result, refugees have not been able to elect their own leadership. Salah Abed Rabbo states that the obstacles facing West Bank and Gaza refugees include: the hostile attitude of the PA and some PLO factions to any independent refugee leadership, which they regard as a threatening alternative leadership to themselves; the PA and other factions' view that the right of return has been rendered 'obsolete'; the belief by the Palestinian opposition that a refugee leadership could easily be coopted by the PA; and the fact that refugees in the diaspora (in Jordan, Lebanon and Syria) have not joined the refugee conferences nor held their own.[72] Despite the lack of progress, a number of organizations (like Badil) have emerged in the West Bank and Gaza to defend refugee rights, a situation that is unmatched among diaspora refugees.

But if the Palestinian diaspora, which is composed of a majority of refugees, is not the beneficiary of this 'peace process', why must it acquiesce in it by conceding all its rights? To ask the diaspora and the refugees to sacrifice their rights, hopes and dreams so that some meagre political benefits can accrue to native West Bank and Gaza Palestinians is to ask the diaspora and refugees more generally, to commit national suicide. Since those who are now conceding Palestinian diaspora and refugee rights have never been elected to their positions nor have they ever been given a mandate by diaspora and refugee Palestinians to concede their rights, then they perforce have no authority to negotiate on behalf of the diaspora and the refugees. Faced with a similar situation wherein their interests have been ignored by the PA, Israeli Palestinians, who have their own elected leadership, have been pursuing their own goals and interests separate from the peace process – their main goal being the transformation of Israel from an apartheid state of world Jewry to a state of its own Israeli citizens, Jews and Arabs. Moreover, Israeli Palestinian internal refugees, numbering between 120,000 and 150,000 people and constituting one fifth of Israeli Palestinians, are also seeking compensation on their own from the Israeli government. In March 1995, the Committee for the Defence of the Rights of Refugees in Israel convened a conference to register refugee grievances. The conference was attended by 300 delegates from 40 uprooted villages within Israel proper.[73] The Committee was founded in 1992 after the Madrid conference, as according to one its founders 'the convening of the Madrid Conference convinced us beyond the shadow of a doubt that the PLO and Arab countries had abandoned the Arabs of '48. Therefore, we decided to take matters into our own hands.'[74]

Since Israel agreed to negotiate with West Bank and Gaza Palestinians only in Madrid and with the PLO only in so far as the latter transformed itself into the PA and ceased to represent the diaspora, no official body representing diaspora Palestinians has been a party to the Madrid or Oslo processes This situation makes it imperative, as many Palestinians have recommended in recent years, that free elections must be held in the diaspora to elect a new representative leadership that can negotiate with Israel and the international community on behalf of diaspora Palestinians. The diaspora and the refugees must extricate themselves completely from the West Bank and Gaza leadership, effectively seceding from it and from a 'peace process' that addresses only native West Bank and Gaza Palestinians, as they have nothing to gain from it and everything to lose.[75]

Israel has succeeded in destroying the political unity of the Palestinian people, a goal whose achievement was finally formalized in Madrid and has since been further solidified by the Oslo process. Diaspora and refugee Palestinians must harbour no illusions about the intentions of the PA, which has separated *de facto* the interests of the refugees and the diaspora from those of native West Bankers and Gazans (and this is aside from the actual and *real* separation between West Bankers and Gazans themselves to the detriment of the latter). Diaspora and refugee Palestinians must seek to separate their interests *de jure* from native West Bank and Gaza Palestinians and pull the rug from under the PA. The refugees' and the diaspora's conflict with Israel is different from that of the PA and its supporters. Although the Palestinian people remain one spiritually, their material interests are different. The 'peace process' from Madrid to the present has not only deepened the differences between these material interests, it has also rendered them contradictory in an Israeli-dictated and PA-accepted zero-sum game, wherein so-called gains for native West Bank and Gaza Palestinians must be attained at the expense of real losses on the part of the refugees and the diaspora.

ACKNOWLEDGEMENT

The author would like to thank As'ad Abu-Khalil and Neville Hoad for reading an earlier version of this chapter.

NOTES

1. Palestinian Declaration of Independence, 15 November 1988, Algiers, reproduced in the *Journal of Palestine Studies*, no. 70 (Winter 1989), p. 215.
2. United Nations General Assembly Resolution 194 (III), 11 December 1948, Article 11. Reproduced in George J. Tomeh (ed.), *United Nations Resolutions on Palestine and the Arab-Israeli Conflict, Volume One 1947–1974* (Washington, DC: Institute for Palestine Studies, 1975), p. 16.
3. See Rashid Khalidi, 'Observations on the Right of Return', *Journal of Palestine Studies*, no. 82 (Winter 1992), p. 35.
4. Ibid., p. 36.
5. See 'Interview with Faysal Husayni', in the *Journal of Palestine Studies*, no. 72 (Summer 1989), pp. 11–12. Sha'th's and Husayni's views are cited in Khalidi, 'Observations', p. 36.
6. Statement made by Arafat at a press conference on 14 December 1988, Geneva, reproduced in the *Journal of Palestine Studies*, no. 71 (Spring 1989), p. 181.
7. Salim Tamari, *Palestinian Refugee Negotiations, From Madrid to Oslo II*, A Final Status Issues paper (Washington DC: Institute for Palestine Studies, 1996), pp. 7, 9–13.
8. *Israeli–PLO Declaration of Principles, December 13, 1993 (Article I)*, reproduced in the *Journal of Palestine Studies*, no. 89 (Autumn 1993), p. 115.
9. United Nations Security Council 242, 1967, Article 2B, reproduced in Tomeh, *United Nations*, p. 143.
10. *Israeli–PLO Declaration of Principles*, 13 December 1993 (Article V-3), reproduced in *the Journal of Palestine Studies*, no. 89 (Autumn 1993), p. 117.
11. See Elia Zureik, *Palestinians Refugees and the Peace Process* (Washington, DC: Institute for Palestine Studies, 1996), pp. 18–19.
12. Ibid., p. 23.
13. Ibid., p. 19.
14. On the discourse of 'pragmatism' and 'realism', see Joseph Massad, 'Political Realists or Comprador Intelligentsia: Palestinian Intellectuals and the National Struggle', in *Critique* (Autumn 1997), pp. 21–35.
15. Donna Arzt, *Refugees into Citizens: Palestinians and the End of the Arab–Israeli Conflict* (New York: Council on Foreign Relations, 1997).
16. Joseph Alpher and Khalil Shikaki, 'The Palestinian Refugee Problem and the Right of Return', Working Paper Series, Paper No. 98–7, Weatherhead Center for International Affairs, Harvard University, May 1998. Of the Palestinian group, only Kassis did not partake of the final drafting of the report (see p. x). Israeli and US Jewish participants included Joseph Alpher, Gabriel Ben-Dor, Yossi Katz, Moshe Ma'oz, Ze'ev Schiff, Shimon Shamir and Herbert Kelman.

17. On Lydda and Ramle and other expulsions, see Benny Morris, *The Birth of the Palestinian Refugee Problem, 1947–1949* (Cambridge: Cambridge University Press, 1988), on the Galilee expulsions, see Benny Morris, 'Operation Hiram Revisited: A Correction', *Journal of Palestine Studies*, no. 110 (Winter 1999), pp. 68–76.
18. Arzt, *Refugees into Citizens*, p. 99.
19. Ibid., p. 98.
20. Ibid., p. 91.
21. Alpher and Shikaki, *The Palestinian Refugee Problem*, p. 17.
22. Ibid.
23. Ibid., p. 18.
24. Ibid.
25. Ibid., pp. 18–19.
26. *New York Times*, 27 October 1993, p. A 3.
27. Alpher and Shikaki, *The Palestinian Refugee Problem*, p. 20.
28. Ibid.
29. Ibid.
30. Ibid., p. 21.
31. Ibid., p. 23.
32. Ibid., p. 26.
33. See Zureik, *Palestinian*, p. 73. For Gazit's propoal, see Shlomo Gazit, *The Palestinian Refugee Problem* (Tel Aviv: Jaffee Center for Strategic Studies, 1994).
34. Gazit, *The Palestinian*, p. 12.
35. Ibid., p. 14.
36. See, for example, Ziad Abu Zayyad, 'The Palestinian Right of Return: A Realistic Approach', *Palestine–Israel Journal of Politics, Economics and Culture*, no. 2 (Spring 1994), pp. 74–8. Abu Zayyad is a member of the Palestinian Legislative Council.
37. Salim Tamari, *Palestinian Refugee Negotiation, From Madrid to Oslo II* (Washington, DC: Institute for Palestine Studies, 1996), p. 2.
38. Ibid., p. 3.
39. Tamari is clear that 'The debate over compensation versus return is a false dichotomy that is often raised in the negotiations. It is clear from a 1961 UNCCP Report that two modes of compensation were being considered: one for returning refugees and one for nonreturning refugees.' See ibid., p. 44.
40. Ibid., p. 45.
41. Ibid., p. 51. UNSC Resolution 237 to which Tamari refers 'calls upon the Government of Israel ... to facilitate the return of those inhabitants who have fled the areas since the outbreak of hostilities', Article 1 of Security Council Resolution No. 237 of 14 June 1967, reproduced in Tomeh, *United Nations*, p. 142.
42. Ibid.
43. Ibid., p. 53.
44. See Mark Heller and Sari Nusseibeh, *No Trumpets, No Drums, A Two-State Settlement of the Isareli–Palestinian Conflict* (New York: Hill and Wang, 1991), p. 95.
45. Rashid Khalidi, 'Toward a Solution', in *Palestinian Refugees: Their Problem and Future*, A Special Report (Washington, DC: Center for Policy Analysis on Palestine, October 1994), p. 21.
46. Ibid.

47. Ibid., p. 22.
48. Ibid.
49. See George Borjas, Leonard Hausman and Dani Rodrik, 'The Harvard Project on Palestinian Refugees', paper presented to the United Nations Department of Political Affairs, International NGO Meeting, European NGO Symposium on the Question of Palestine, Palais des Nations, Geneva, Switzerland on 2 September 1996, p. 7.
50. Khalidi, 'Toward a Solution', p. 23.
51. Ibid.
52. Ibid., p. 24.
53. See Atif Kubursi, *Palestinian Losses in 1948: The Quest for Precision*, Information Paper No. 6 (Washington, DC: Center for Policy Analysis on Palestine, August, 1996), p. 5. See also Sami Hadawi and Atif Kubursi, *Palestinian Rights and Losses in 1948, A Comprehensive Study* (London: Saqi Books, 1988).
54. Cited by Zureik, *Palestinians*, p. 122.
55. Khalidi, 'Toward a Solution', pp. 24–5.
56. Salman H. Abu-Sitta, 'The Feasibility of the Right of Return', ICJ and CIMEL paper, June 1997, p. 1. The paper is available on the internet at <www.arts.mcgill.ca/mepp/prrn/papers>.
57. Ibid.
58. Ibid., p. 2.
59. Ibid.
60. Ibid., p. 4.
61. Ibid., p. 5.
62. Ibid., p. 6.
63. Ibid.
64. Ibid., p. 9.
65. Cited in 'Tahdhir Filastini min al-Mubadarat al-Fardiyyah Lil-Bahth fi Qadiyyat al-Laji'in ma' al-Isra'iliyyin' (A Palestinian Warning against Individual Initiatives to Look into the Refugee Issue with the Israelis), in *Al-Hayat*, 3 March 1999, p. 5.
66. Zureik, *Palestinians*, p. 119.
67. Ze'ev Schiff, *Ha'aretz*, 22 February 1996, cited by Zureik, *Palestinians*, pp. 117–18.
68. On Zionism's policies towards the rescue of Euroepan Jews from the Nazis, see Lenni Brenner, *Zionism in the Age of the Dictators* (Westport: Lawrence Hill, 1983).
69. Sara Roy, 'Dedevelopment Revisited: Palestinian Society and Economy Since Oslo', *Journal of Palestine Studies*, no. 111 (Spring 1999).
70. For information about the refugee conferences, see 'The Voice of Palestinian Refugees in Palestine', in *Article 74*, Issue 15, April 1996; 'First Refugee Conference – Bethlehem', in *Article 74*, Issue 17, September 1996.
71. See 'Recommendations and Decisions Issued by the First Popular Refugee Conference in Deheishe Refugee Camp/Bethlehem', in *Article 74*, Issue 17, September 1996.
72. See Salah Abed Rabbo, 'A Unified Strategy Against All Odds: The Popular Refugee Movement', in *Article 74*, Issue 22, December 1997.
73. See Ahmad Ashkar, 'Internal Refugees: Their Inalienable Right to Return', *News From Within*, vol. XI, no. 8 (August 1995), pp. 14–17.

74. Ibid., p. 17. On internal refugees in Israel, see also Ahmad Ashkar, '1948 Palestinian Refugees: "We'll Return to the Village Alive or Dead"', *News From Within*, vol. XI, no. 9 (September 1995), pp. 21–4.

75. Hamid Shaqqura makes the important suggestion that West Bank and Gaza refugees are related to the Palestinian authority not as 'citizens' but as refugees from another country. Therefore the PA cannot speak for them or simply treat them as citizens. See Hamid Shaqqura, 'Refugees and the Palestinian Authority', *News from Within*, vol. XI, no. 8 (August 1995), pp. 18–20.

8 THE OBLIGATIONS OF HOST COUNTRIES TO REFUGEES UNDER INTERNATIONAL LAW: THE CASE OF LEBANON

Wadie Said

For the past 53 years, Palestinian refugees in Lebanon have been living in refugee camps and other temporary shelters, victims of the Arab–Israeli wars and internal upheaval and conflict in Lebanon. Displaced in 1948 from areas currently within the boundaries of the state of Israel, the Palestinian refugees now number approximately 350,000 and represent 12 per cent of the entire population of Lebanon.[1] Yet there still exists no solution or formula for their repatriation. Recent agreements signed by the Israeli government and the Palestine Liberation Organization (PLO) have further marginalized the refugees and demonstrate that a permanent solution based on their right of return is as remote as ever. Meanwhile, the refugees continue to live in miserable conditions of poverty, suffering from, on the one hand, the neglect and cruelty of the Lebanese government, and on the other, the staunch refusal of Israel to repatriate them. They represent the poorest sector in all of Lebanese society and the poorest grouping of Palestinian refugees in any Arab country. Nevertheless, most discourse in the Middle East centres on the Palestinian–Israeli peace process. The Palestinians in Lebanon are thus neglected by the PLO, Israel and Lebanon, and overlooked in intellectual circles.

A survey of the Lebanese laws relating to Palestinian refugees demonstrates the plight of the refugees. Lebanese law designates Lebanon's Palestinian refugees as 'foreigners' who must obtain work permits if they are to work in most industries. The refugees enjoy no special refugee or resident status that would allow them to circumvent the work permit requirement, despite the fact that they have lived in Lebanon for 50 years and will remain there for the foreseeable future. Even if they do obtain work permits, refugees are categorically excluded from certain professions. While legally residing in Lebanon, they have suffered through periods when their right to travel to and from Lebanon has been impeded. Medical care and social security coverage are denied to them.

Lebanon has continued to deny civil rights to its Palestinian population in the belief that such a step would signal Lebanon's willingness to nationalize and absorb its Palestinian refugees. Lebanon's position that civil rights are the first step to settling the refugees permanently in Lebanon is insufficient. Lebanon must afford better and more humane treatment to its Palestinian refugee population, while realizing that such a step does not necessarily indicate its willingness to assume permanent responsibility for absorbing the refugees into Lebanese society. Affording the refugees a form of legally recognized residence, which guarantees certain basic rights such as the right to work and to unimpeded travel, would be an adequate interim measure before reaching a final settlement of the plight of the Palestinian refugees.

Lebanon has its share of problems – social, political and otherwise – which have affected all residents of Lebanon. But these problems do not explain the Palestinian refugee situation, since the Palestinian refugees in Lebanon do not enjoy the same rights, *de facto* and *de jure*, as Lebanese citizens. This arrangement contradicts the will and letter of international law, which upholds and guarantees certain inalienable rights to all persons generally, and refugees specifically. The Palestinians' uneasy predicament in Lebanon can be attributed to a number of factors, most notably the weakness of the Lebanese central government due to the presence of foreign powers on its soil (who are, in effect, in a constant state of violating Lebanese sovereignty). Although in May 2000 Israel almost completely withdrew from a strip of territory in the south it had occupied for 18 years, Syria continues to station approximately 40,000 troops in the rest of the country. Granting certain inalienable rights to the Palestinians should not, however, represent an infringement of Lebanese sovereignty or citizenship. However, Lebanon has never afforded its Palestinian population proper legal status or protection under its laws, except when the Palestinian military presence there has dictated otherwise. The Palestinian refugees in Lebanon represent the forgotten victims of the Arab–Israeli conflict.

In this chapter, I will analyse what I consider to be the most politically charged and controversial area of Lebanese legislation dealing with Palestinians – those concerned with the right of the Palestinians to work, residence, travel, social security and health benefits. My analysis is not intended to be comprehensive and thus will not cover such issues as the Palestinians' right to Lebanese citizenship (or lack thereof), the laws governing property ownership and the right to education. Rather, I intend to demonstrate how Lebanese legal impediments on the Palestinians' rights constitute violations of at least two international instruments to which Lebanon has acceded – the International Covenant on Economic, Social and Cultural Rights and the International Convention on the Elimination of All Forms of Racial Discrimination[2] – and contravene the international standards, such as the Convention Relating to the Status of Refugees, that govern the treatment of refugees.

In closing, I will discuss the impact of the Oslo agreements signed by the PLO and Israel in 1993 and 1995, and how they affect the Palestinian refugees in Lebanon and their right of return, a right guaranteed by the United Nations. I shall argue that the Palestinian refugees in Lebanon should not have to give up their right to repatriation, regardless of what the Oslo agreements and *realpolitik* dictate. They deserve to hold on to that right, as well as to receive from the Lebanese government treatment befitting all human beings. I offer no solutions to the refugee problem in the Middle East, other than to say that as long as international law recognizes the Palestinians' right of return, no agreement between Israel and the PLO can nullify it without consulting the refugees themselves, who have a right to decide their own fate.

In section 1 I will examine the history of the Palestinians in Lebanon. In section 2, I will discuss the Palestinian refugees' right of return under international law. Finally, in section 3, I will look briefly at the Oslo agreements and their impact on the predicament of the Palestinian refugees in Lebanon.

1 HISTORY

Following the defeat of the Ottoman Empire in the First World War, the British government established a Mandate in the former Ottoman province of Palestine. Increased Jewish migration to Palestine in the decades before the Second World War coincided with open rebellion by the native Palestinian Arab population to British rule, most notably in 1936–39. Tension between the Jewish settler community, the *Yishuv*, and the Palestinian Arabs developed as the Zionist doctrine behind Jewish settlement in Palestine called for the establishment of an independent Jewish state in the Holy Land.

The end of the British Mandate in 1948 saw the outbreak of hostilities between the Arab and Jewish communities. Enmity was high because of the United Nations' decision, as expressed in General Assembly Resolution 181 of 29 November 1947, to partition Palestine into two states, one Arab, the other Jewish.[3] The British decision to withdraw in May 1948 led to widespread fighting throughout Palestine and to the creation of the state of Israel on 15 May 1948. The fledgling state occupied 77 per cent of the area of Mandate Palestine. Throughout and following the conflict, the Zionist army, the Haganah (the precursor to the Israeli army before statehood), pursued a policy of extirpating the Arab population from the areas it had occupied.[4] The goal of the Haganah was to 'cleanse' the areas of the new Jewish state of as many Arabs as possible. As a result, 750,000 out of an estimated 900,000 Palestinians in Mandate Palestine were uprooted from their homes and became refugees;[5] 110,000 of them, mostly from the Galilee and the coastal areas, emigrated to Lebanon.[6] They settled in refugee camps scattered all over the country, with the majority near or in the coastal cities of Beirut, Tripoli, Sidon and Tyre. The remaining 640,000 fled to Syria, Jordan, Egypt and other Arab nations, as well as to refugee camps within the

West Bank and Gaza Strip, controlled at that time by Jordan and Egypt, respectively.[7]

Unlike Jordan, which offered nationality to those refugees which it assimilated, and Syria, which offered civil and political rights, Lebanon has always refused to give the Palestinians even the most basic of rights. Lebanon is a highly sectarian country, divided between its various Christian and Muslim communities. The majority of Christians are Maronite, but there exist within Lebanon substantial minorities of Greek Orthodox and Greek Catholics, Armenian Orthodox, Protestants, Chaldeans and Syriac Christians.[8] Lebanese Muslims are divided principally between Shiite and Sunni Muslim, although the Druze make up a significant percentage of the Lebanese population. Lebanon is governed by a tripartite power-sharing agreement known as the National Pact of 1943.[9] Under the terms of the Pact, a Maronite Christian must be President, a Sunni Muslim Prime Minister, and a Shiite Muslim Speaker of Parliament. This tenuous alliance has, since 1948, been threatened by the spectre of the Palestinians, who are overwhelmingly Sunni Muslim. Hence, there exists a perennial fear within Lebanon that any step towards naturalization of the refugees will upset the delicate sectarian balance. This has governed official Lebanese policy towards the refugees since their arrival in the country.[10]

The Palestinian refugees were generally confined to the camps and received assistance from the UN Relief Works Agency for Palestine Refugees (UNRWA), which was created to provide the Palestinian refugees with emergency relief. They were subject to the repressive practices of the Deuxième Bureau, the Lebanese internal security service, until 1969 when the PLO began to play a larger role in Lebanese affairs generally.[11] The PLO provided the refugees with the organizational structure and financial support, among other things, to organize and liberate the camps from the yoke of the Deuxième Bureau.

In 1970, the main armed elements of the PLO were defeated in their war with Jordan, causing their mass relocation to Lebanon. The PLO quickly became a major force in Lebanese politics and served as a catalyst for the Lebanese civil war.[12] By bankrolling and militarily supporting elements of the Lebanese left, as well as arming and organizing the refugees to take part in armed struggle with Israel, the PLO quickly invoked the ire of the Lebanese government and right-wing parties, which were dominated by Maronite Christian leaders. PLO attacks on Israel drew heavy retaliation and increased the tension between Palestinians and certain sectors of the Lebanese population, who were unsympathetic to the Palestinians' plight. The right-wing Lebanese Christian groups blamed the 'foreign' Palestinian presence for instigating a 17-year civil war. The PLO did in fact play a role in breaking down the confessional structure, through which Christians enjoyed the bulk of power and wealth while many Muslims (especially Shiites) lived in conditions of abject poverty.[13] However, the potential for civil strife was great, independent of PLO activities, because of the economic and social inequality between certain sectors and confessions within the population.

During the hostilities of 1975–76, the refugee camps became the focus of the Lebanese right wing's ire. Several were destroyed in the fighting, the most notable being Tel el-Za'atar, which was besieged for 51 days by right-wing Lebanese forces, who massacred all the inhabitants upon their surrender.[14] Lebanon descended into a period of uneasy truce from 1976 to 1982, during which time the Israeli army occupied a strip of southern Lebanon in 1978 in order to administer a local client army to fight the PLO and its allies. The truce was broken by the Israeli invasion of 1982, the primary purpose of which was to drive the PLO from Lebanon. After a two-month siege of Beirut, the PLO finally agreed to withdraw permanently from Lebanon, leaving the residents of the camps vulnerable to the attack of their Lebanese enemies.

Over three days in September 1982, gunmen of the Lebanese forces entered the Beirut refugee camps of Sabra and Shatila and massacred the inhabitants, killing an estimated 2,000 refugees.[15] Several years later, the Beirut camps were again under attack, this time from the Shiite militia, Amal.[16] Palestinian–Shiite tensions ran high because the PLO had abused the residents of the South – who were overwhelmingly Shiite – during its stay in Lebanon, and made them subject to Israeli reprisals for attacks launched from Shiite territory. The battle in the camps lasted

Lebanon's inability and unwillingness to provide sufficient means of support to its refugee population has been alleviated somewhat by the efforts of UNRWA. UNRWA was created by UN General Assembly Resolution 302 of 8 December 1949. Its task is to 'prevent conditions of starvation and distress among [the Palestinian Refugees] and to further conditions of peace and stability, and that constructive measures should be undertaken at an early date with a view to the termination of international assistance for relief'.[17] As of March 1996, there were 349,773 Palestinians refugees registered with UNRWA currently residing in Lebanon – a substantial increase from the figure of 127,600 recorded in 1950 – with over half living in twelve UNRWA-registered refugee camps, geographically dispersed across the whole of Lebanon. UNRWA continues to provide 'essential education, health, relief and social services to Palestine Refugees in Lebanon, Syria, Jordan, the West Bank, and the Gaza Strip'. Its mandate is extended periodically, because of the lack of a lasting solution to the refugee problem in the region. The role of UNRWA as an all-purpose relief agency is crucial to ensuring basic social relief to the Palestinian refugees in the face of official Lebanese neglect. However, UNRWA remains an under-resourced relief agency, which cannot overcome the obstacles placed in the path of the refugees by Lebanese law.[18]

Forty thousand refugees live in camps not recognized by UNRWA, and an estimated 35,000, displaced in the Lebanese civil war, are currently housed in makeshift shelters.[19] Approximately one-third of the refugee population live in Lebanese towns and cities and experience different levels of economic status, ranging from homeless squatters to those who own or rent their own residences. Camp-dwellers are forbidden from building vertically and are severely restricted in the types of materials they can use to construct their dwellings, so as to reflect the temporary nature of their homes. Further, some of the reconstruction projects planned by the Lebanese government threaten to eliminate several of the Palestinian camps, and so far no alternative housing policy for these refugees has been put forward by the government.

Because of the rent-free nature of the dwellings in UNRWA camps, generally high rents in Lebanon and the high real estate tax required of foreigners (16.5 per cent for Palestinians versus 6.5 per cent for Lebanese), few Palestinians choose to leave the camps. The average Palestinian residence in a camp consists of 2.2 rooms, with an average of 2.6 individuals living in a single room. In accordance with Lebanese official restrictions on building in the camps, the residences are poorly constructed; as a result approximately 20 per cent of Palestinian dwellings provide inadequate shelter and protection from the elements. Access to proper sewage systems, running water and electricity remains insufficient, as camp dwellers are forced to obtain these utilities through expensive private contractors. The Lebanese government has done very little, if anything, to alleviate this situation.

Unemployment is extremely high among the Palestinians in Lebanon, who are legally permitted to work in very few industries in Lebanon without a work permit, which is rarely granted. Over three-quarters of the Palestinian refugees in Lebanon are affected by some form of poverty, preventable diseases are endemic and infant mortality rates are alarmingly high. Palestinians are denied access to Lebanese public health services, and rely on UNRWA, the Palestinian Red Crescent Society (the PLO's medical relief service) and non-governmental organizations (NGOs) for health care. In addition to the often inadequate level of medical care available, the patient/doctor ratio for Palestinians in Lebanon is 1166:1, as compared with a ratio of 318:1 for Lebanese citizens. The patient/hospital bed ratio reflects a similar disproportion.[20]

In the periods immediately prior to and following the end of the Lebanese civil war in 1990, Palestinians received no support from the Lebanese government in its efforts to rebuild its devastated country. The government's attitude has become even more defiant and unhelpful towards the refugees after the announcement of the signing of the Oslo agreements between Israel and the PLO. The Palestinians continue to enjoy few rights, while the PLO, Israelis and Lebanese refuse to help them. A permanent solution for the Palestinians in Lebanon, which allows them the right to repatriation, is as unlikely today as in 1948.

2 THE PALESTINIANS UNDER LEBANESE LAW: AN OVERVIEW

History of the Laws Governing Palestinian Refugees in Lebanon

Lebanon is not a signatory to either the Convention Relating to the Status of Refugees of 1951 or the 1967 Protocol Relating to the Status of Refugees, so the safeguards and guarantees of these documents are not legally binding on Lebanon with regard to its Palestinian population. In any event, the Convention would not apply to the Palestinian refugees because they 'are at present receiving from organs or agencies of the United Nations other than the United Nations High Commissioner for Refugees protection or assistance'.[21] The exclusion of Palestinians derives from the fact that their predicament differs from that of other refugees who are covered by the Convention – the Palestinians are striving to be repatriated to their homeland, not to be assimilated into the country in which they currently reside. The status of most refugees is that they are fleeing their country to gain asylum, and subsequently absorption, into another country. The status of the Palestinian refugees is quite the opposite.[22]

The history of the legal apparatus of governance of the Palestinians in Lebanon is fairly straightforward. In 1950, the Lebanese government created a special committee – the Central Committee for Refugee Affairs – to administer the Palestinian presence in Lebanon. Pursuant to Legislative Decrees No. 42 and No. 927 of 31 March 1959 (published simultaneously), the Department of Affairs of the Palestinian Refugees in Lebanon, an office of the Ministry of the Interior, was created and its tasks delineated.[23] They are as follows:

Article One: The Department of Affairs for the Palestinian Refugees shall undertake the following tasks specifically:

1. Contacting the International Relief Agency[24] in Lebanon to ensure relief, shelter, education and health and social services for the refugees.
2. Receiving applications for passports for departure from Lebanon, the study of these applications, submission of comments and subsequent transfer to the relevant departments of the Public Security.
3. Registering personal documents relating to birth, marriage, divorce, marriage annulment, change of residence, and change of sect or religion, following confirmation of validity as per the relevant stipulations in Articles 2, 3, 4, 7, 9, 13, 14, 15, 17, 22, 23, 27, 28, 30, 31, 41, and 42 of the Law Governing Registration of Personal Documents, dated 7 December 1951.
4. Approving applications for the reunion of dispersed families as per the texts and directives of the Arab League and after consultation with the Armistice Commission.
5. Approving, in the case of incoming persons from Palestine for purposes of family reunification, as per the stipulations of the previous item, exemption from customs duties on their personal or household belongings.
6. Designating the localities of the camps and undertaking transactions for lease or ownership of properties required for them.

7. Allocating permits allowing transfer of residence from one camp to another where circumstances so dictate in the estimation of the Department.

8. Transferring residency of refugees from one camp to another where security considerations so require.

9. Approving applications for marriage submitted by any male or female refugee residing in Lebanon seeking marriage with a refugee from another Arab country.

10. Approving transfer of frozen or incoming funds to beneficiary refugees by way of the Bank of Syria and Lebanon.

11. Rectifying errors that inadvertently occur in personal identification cards regarding names, identities and ages of the refugees.

Article Two: The Ministries of the State shall provide the Department of Affairs of the Palestinian Refugees in Lebanon with technical and administrative assistance falling within their specialization to facilitate the Department's exercise of its powers.

Article Three: This Decree shall be published and announced when and where required.[25]

This Decree is considered to be the first piece of legislation relating to the Palestinians in Lebanon. It is notable because it gives the Department of Affairs of the Palestinian Refugees in Lebanon control over the Palestinians' personal affairs by dint of its bureaucratic function. The Decree provides the legal framework for administering the Palestinian presence in Lebanon, and gives the Department the right to designate the area occupied by each refugee camp, to have a record of everyone who lives in that camp and to document each refugee's movements. Most Palestinian social and sociological activities, including births, marriage and change of residence, are to be run and administered by the Department. The Decree gives the Department the right to issue passports to the refugees, and assigns it the task of making sure that the information contained in each Palestinian's personal identification card remains correct and updated. Finally, the Decree allows the Department to approve or deny financial aid to the refugees, which is transferred to the refugees from abroad through the Bank of Syria and Lebanon.

While the Decree seems somewhat innocuous, detailing a mere bureaucratic function, it in fact serves a more sinister purpose. By entrusting the Department of Affairs for the Palestinian Refugees in Lebanon with these functions, the Decree ensures that the Lebanese state has an accurate profile of each refugee and can thus assess the security risk that he/she presents. For example, by approving when a particular Palestinian refugee may transfer residence to another camp, the Department is given the right to deny a move based on factors relating to Lebanese internal security. In other words, if the Lebanese government believes that a Palestinian might instigate social or political unrest if allowed to move, the Department is allowed to prevent such a move. However, security concerns do not necessarily dictate a dedication to humanitarian concerns. Accordingly, the Department pledges merely to 'contact' UNRWA to 'ensure' that basic social services are being provided. The Decree does not require the Lebanese government or the

Department to provide such services, and therefore ensure that the needs of the refugees in this regard are met. This responsibility is left to UNRWA.

Lebanese legislation is similarly non-committal and vague regarding the status of Palestinian refugees in Lebanon. Article 1 of the Law Pertaining to the Entry into, Residence in and Exit from Lebanon, dated 10 July 1962, states that '[a]ny natural person holding other than Lebanese nationality shall, for the purposes hereof, be deemed a foreigner'.[26] Since the Palestinians are refugees and do not hold Lebanese nationality, they are by default deemed foreigners. Their special status as resident refugees does not entitle them to anything other than the designation 'foreigner'. Similar provisions of this law confirm this and allow no room for interpretation. Article 19 states:

The Director of Public Security may, in the following two cases, grant foreigners not holding any travel document a laisser passer to the countries to which they are destined:

(a) If the foreigner is a refugee or of an undetermined nationality;
(b) If the foreigner holds the nationality of a state having no representative in Lebanon.[27]

Since the Lebanese state does in fact grant laisser passer travel documents to the Palestinian refugees, the implication here is that they are foreigners. They qualify as such under both clauses a) and b) of Article 19 of the Law Pertaining to the Entry into, Residence in and Exit from Lebanon.[28]

The Right of Palestinian Refugees to Employment in Lebanon

In their capacity as foreigners, Palestinian refugees in Lebanon may not work unless they have received official permission to do so from the government. Article 25 states that '[a] foreigner, other than an artist, is prohibited from carrying on in Lebanon any work or occupation unless permitted to do so by the Ministry of Labour and Social Affairs under the valid laws and regulations'.[29]

A glimpse at the Refugee Convention of 1951 may be useful at this stage. While the Convention does not apply to the Palestinian refugees in Lebanon, for reasons stated above, it provides insight into the international norms on the refugee's right to work. Article 17, Wage-Earning Employment, is as follows:

1. The Contracting States shall accord to refugees lawfully staying in their territory the most favourable treatment accorded to nationals of a foreign country in the same circumstances, as regards the right to engage in wage-earning employment.
2. In any case, restrictive measures imposed on aliens or the employment of aliens for the protection of the national labour market, shall not be applied to a refugee who was already exempt from them at the date of entry into force of this Convention for the Contracting State concerned, or who fulfils one of the following conditions:
    (a) He has completed three years' residence in the country ...

3. The Contracting States shall give sympathetic consideration to assimilating the
   rights of all refugees with regard to wage–earning employment to those of
   nationals ...[30]

Under the Convention, refugees have an unrestricted right to work and
should be treated as well as any foreign worker might be in their host
country. Additionally, it holds that any restrictions imposed on refugees who
have been residents for over three years should be lifted and that those
refugees have rights equal to those of a citizen in the 'national labour
market'. Therefore, at the very least, the government of Lebanon should be
striving to afford Palestinians the same rights as those of Lebanese in the
workplace. The heavy restrictions placed on Palestinian labour in Lebanon
attest to a total disregard of international law under the Refugee Convention.

Lebanon did, however, accede to both the ICESCR and CERD in 1972.[31]
While certainly not as specific and detailed on the issue of the refugees' right
to work, the former does recognize 'the right to work, which includes the
right of everyone to gain his living by work which he freely chooses or
accepts, and [the States Parties to the Present Covenant] will take appropriate
steps to safeguard this right'.[32] The latter guarantees the rights to 'work ...
[and] form and join trade unions'.[33] The international community has
voiced its opinion on the issue of work and employment, and, by virtue of its
accession, Lebanon has a duty, if not a legal obligation, to preserve and afford
the right of employment to 'everyone', refugees included.

The distinction between international law norms for refugees and those
stipulated in Lebanese law is striking. There is no provision granting any
sort of preferred status to foreigners who have resided in Lebanon for more
than three years. Moreover, Lebanese law does not afford a separate legal
status to them or even define the term 'refugee'.[34] The closest statutory
language of this nature is contained in Article 19 of the Law Pertaining to
the Entry into, Residence in and Exit from Lebanon of 1962, which gives the
Director of Public Security the right to issue travel documents (laisser-passer)
to those 'foreigners' who are refugees. Since Lebanese law does not define
the term 'refugee', it cannot begin to take steps necessary to remedy its
refugee population's suffering. The most the government of Lebanon is
willing to do is 'contact' UNRWA to 'ensure' that the Palestinians are
obtaining adequate relief.

Foreign labour in Lebanon was not always so regulated. Indeed, before
1962 there was no labour law in Lebanon at all regarding foreigners.[35] In
1969 the PLO and the Lebanese government signed the Cairo Agreement.
This agreement has been remembered primarily as a military accord that
permitted the PLO to operate militarily in the strategic border zone with
Israel, to police the refugee camps and to establish training camps for its
cadres.[36] However, the more far-reaching and socio-economically important
part of the accord dealt with the right of Palestinians to employment. It states:
'It was agreed [between the Commander of the Lebanese Army, General

Emile Bustani, and the Chairman of the PLO, Yasir Arafat] to re-establish the Palestinian presence in Lebanon on the basis of ... [t]he right of Palestinians presently in Lebanon to work, reside, and move freely ...' [37] Due to the imposing and undeniable military strength of the PLO in Lebanon, Palestinians were granted more rights and freedoms – especially within the context of employment – than ever before. The Palestinian military presence allowed the refugee community to 'free itself from the shackles of the Lebanese security apparatus ... organise its affairs, particularly in the Palestinian settlements (euphemistically referred to as refugee camps) and to initiate programs of social, economic, and cultural action that would sustain and develop it'.[38]

Following the 1982 Israeli invasion and PLO evacuation of Lebanon, however, the situation changed. In 1987, the Lebanese Parliament – during the regime of President Amin Gemayel, and operating in a time of mass official, confessional and popular hostility against the Palestinians – declared all provisions the Cairo Agreement null and void.[39] Thereafter, a Palestinian refugee in Lebanon would have to receive an official work permit, like any other foreigner, as a condition of being employed in Lebanon. The only exceptions to this rule are employment within the camps and with UNRWA.

The requirements surrounding the award of work permits are stringent. They are awarded by the Director-General of the Ministry of Labour and Social Affairs, and are valid for a maximum period of two years.[40] Additionally, the law spells out a clear preference for Lebanese nationals. Article 17 of No. 17561 Regulating Foreigner Work states:

The work permit shall be cancelled, at any time, if it is revealed that any document is incorrect or as may be required in the interests of Lebanese labour, particularly in the following cases:

1. If the enterprise dismisses a Lebanese wage-earner, under Article 50 of the Lebanese Labour Law, and retains a foreign wage earner of equal proficiency and service conditions;
2. If the enterprise refuses to give priority of work to a Lebanese satisfying the conditions of the required job;
3. If the enterprise fails to perform its obligations in training a
4. Lebanese national to replace the foreigner;
5. If the foreigner violates the terms of the Prior Approval and the work permit;
6. If he is convicted for any defamatory crime or offence.[41]

Under this article, if a company fires a Lebanese worker and hires a foreign worker of equal capacity in his stead, that foreign worker's work permit will be revoked. At all times in the hiring process, if Lebanese applicants do not receive preferential treatment over foreigners, the foreigners' work permits may be cancelled. It is assumed that Lebanese will be trained to take over the positions occupied by foreign workers, at the risk of the revocation of their work permits. Finally, violating the conditions of the work permits or breaking the law in Lebanon results in cancellation of the work permit.

While other nations may have similar labour laws regarding foreign workers – the United States being a perfect example[42] – and differing views exist as to their effectiveness and fairness to the foreign worker in general, it is reasonable to state that such laws impose a heavy and insurmountable burden on the Palestinian refugees resident in Lebanon. They do not hold any form of citizenship and have no other country in which they can legally seek employment. The fact that Palestinians have been present in Lebanon since 1948 has not influenced the Lebanese government's perception of the their right to work. Only force of arms allowed Palestinians the right to employment and residency for a brief period from 1968 to 1987, and since the majority of that time coincided with the Lebanese civil war, they have scarcely known favourable conditions in which to look for work in peacetime.

The work permit requirement does not merely impose an onerous burden on the Palestinian refugee; it effectively rules out his/her prospects for employment, except within the narrow sphere of employment permissible without a work permit. Legally, Palestinians can only work within UNRWA, the Palestinian Red Crescent Society, NGOs and in fields not requiring official permission ('such as agriculture, animal husbandry, or small enterprises within the camps').[43] In 1994, 4.86 per cent of a potential workforce of 218,173 worked in these fields. A mere 0.14 per cent of the workforce – an estimated 350 workers – obtained work permits in the same year. The remaining 95 per cent were unemployed or temporarily engaged in work in the informal sector, which is characterized by uncertain, low-paying, dangerous and non-regulated work in fields such as construction and seasonal agriculture.

As stated above, Palestinians receive work permits from the Lebanese government in markedly small numbers. Yet even the grant of such permits does not ensure Palestinians the right to work in certain trades, nor does it allow Palestinians to benefit from the Lebanese social security system. For example, for a person to be admitted to the Lebanese Bar, he or she must have been a Lebanese citizen for at least ten years.[44] The same condition applies for anyone seeking employment with any state or governmental agency.[45] Despite having to make social security payments, a Palestinian with a work permit cannot reap any benefits that such payments normally entail. Paragraph 4 of Article 9 of the Lebanese Social Security Law states:

Foreign labourers working on Lebanese soil are not subject to the provisions of this law, and therefore not entitled to the benefits of any and all sections of Social Security, except if the country of their origin affords its Lebanese residents the same treatment as its own citizens with regard to Social Security.[46]

Since the Palestinian refugees are stateless, it is impossible for them to fulfil such a requirement. The denial of social security and other social services violates both Article 5 of the CERD and Article 9 of the ICESCR, which guarantee those rights, and to which Lebanon has acceded.[47] This same condition exists as a prerequisite for those Palestinians wishing to practise medicine, engineering or pharmacology in Lebanon outside the context of UNRWA and the refugee camps.[48] Finally, Palestinians with work permits who are 18 years of age and over and who do not have a criminal record may join a trade union, but cannot vote or be elected to any office. They may only elect a representative who is allowed to defend their interests to the union board.[49]

The inability to work because of their status as 'foreigners' has reduced the Palestinian refugees in Lebanon to abject poverty. One scholar has estimated that 80 per cent of the refugee population is thus affected.[50] The two other main factors contributing to the downward trend in the material conditions of the Palestinian refugees in Lebanon are the elimination of the Gulf countries as a potential place of employment following the 1991 Gulf War, and the cessation of PLO aid following the Oslo I accord of 1993. Before the 1990s, Palestinians who lived and worked in Kuwait and other Gulf countries had contributed substantially to the income of Palestinians all over the Middle East. However, following the Gulf War, Palestinians were expelled from Kuwait and other Gulf countries because of the PLO's perceived stance of siding with Iraq. Additionally, the PLO has cut off most forms of aid to Palestinian refugees outside the West Bank and Gaza, preferring to direct its spending to its self-rule areas.[51] Simply stated, the inability to work has devastated the Palestinians in Lebanon.

Palestinians are not allowed to use Lebanese government hospitals or other government-related health services.[52] This policy violates the CERD.[53] Palestinian refugees no longer receive the same amount of aid from the Palestinian Red Crescent Society, because PLO financial assistance to the refugees in Lebanon has been drastically reduced.[54] In essence, Palestinians are 'entirely dependent on UNRWA health services'.[55] In addition, Lebanon has been receiving proportionally less aid from UNRWA than the West Bank and the Gaza Strip, in the aftermath of the Oslo accords.[56] UNRWA can no longer meet the medical needs of a growing number of impoverished refugees. Certain expensive treatments are not covered in the UNRWA aid scheme, and the refugees are left to bear the costs, which are often insurmountable.[57] A recent ABC News report highlighted the problem of inadequate health care for Palestinians in Lebanon, who now succumb even to treatable illnesses because they cannot afford to pay the high costs of medical care.[58]

The Residency and Travel Rights of the Palestinian Refugees in Lebanon

While Lebanese legislators have failed to distinguish between foreigners and Palestinian refugees who reside in Lebanon with respect to labour laws, they have managed to allow most Palestinians to reside legally in their country. Ordinance No. 319 of 2 August 1962, issued by the Minister of the Interior, states:

It is upon those non-Lebanese currently present in Lebanon to rectify their situation regarding residence if they fall in the following ... categor[y]:

...

3. Foreigners who do not carry documentation from their countries of origin, and reside in Lebanon on the basis of resident cards issued by the Directorate of Public Security, or identity cards issued by the General Directorate of the Department of Affairs of the Palestinian Refugees in Lebanon.[59]

Article 4 of the same Ordinance provides for the issuance of special Palestinian refugee identity cards which provide the holder with permanent or temporary residence. The vast majority of Palestinians in Lebanon hold these cards and reside there legally. Additionally, refugees living outside the camps can move wherever they wish, provided they inform the Department of Affairs of Palestinian Refugees in Lebanon; camp dwellers may move to other camps in Lebanon, pending security clearance from the same department.[60] These regulations are consistent with the laws binding on foreign residents in Lebanon, and the principles articulated in the Convention Relating to the Status of Refugees.[61]

Until January 1999, Palestinians were not so free or fortunate in their travel to and from Lebanon. Currently, the only country to which they may go without travel documents is Syria.[62] They had been previously subject to stringent visa requirements each time they left Lebanon and wished to return, conditions not imposed on Lebanese citizens. This policy was revealing politically, as it has its origins in a somewhat surreal and rather depressing episode that took place in Libya in 1995. In September of that year, in a move designed as a protest against the Palestinian–Israeli peace process, President Qadhafi of Libya decided to deport all foreigners then working in Libya. The only people who were unable to return to their country of origin were the Palestinians. His goal was to highlight the powerlessness of Chairman Arafat to deal with his people's residency rights and to demonstrate that the refugee problem remained unsolved. His action set off a regional crisis, where the Arab countries, Lebanon chief among them, refused to allow those who were expelled to enter. Lebanon, which faced an influx of over 15,000 refugees, did not want to be regarded as the country to which Palestinians would take refuge every time there was a regional crisis concerning the Palestinian predicament.

Lebanon responded to the crisis by forbidding all ships originating from the Libyan port of Benghazi from landing in Lebanon. The Lebanese Minister of the Interior then issued Order No. 478 of 22 September 1995. Article 2 of that Order states: '[t]hose Palestinians outside Lebanese territory will have to obtain an entry visa to Lebanon through the Lebanese missions in the countries where they are; the visa is given after approval by the General Directorate of Public Security via the Ministry of Foreign Affairs'.[63] This decision caused a great deal of controversy and suffering. Many refugees were trapped along the Libyan–Egyptian border, unable to move, dependent on emergency relief aid and held in the most inhumane of situations –

homeless and stateless. The issuance of Order No. 478 also had the effect of forcibly denying entry to an estimated 100,000 refugees residing abroad but possessing residency rights in Lebanon.[64] The Order stipulated that any Palestinian residing outside Lebanon must apply for a return visa from the Lebanese consulate of the country in which he was currently living.[65] In fact, Lebanese consulates issued very few return visas, thereby denying those 100,000 Palestinians living outside of Lebanon the right to return to the only country in which they enjoy full residency status. Order No. 478 represented a clear violation of Article 9 of the Universal Declaration of Human Rights, which states that '[n]o one shall be subjected to arbitrary arrest, detention, or exile'.[66] The denial of a re-entry permit *de facto* forces Palestinian refugees who reside abroad into 'arbitrary exile' from Lebanon. While Lebanon is not their country of citizenship, the Palestinians reside there legally and any attempt to deny them their right of residency without due process of law is 'arbitrary exile' for the purposes of the Universal Declaration of Human Rights. When the government of Lebanon refuses to give re-entry visas to those Palestinians who legally reside in its country, despite the fact that they have followed all the stipulated application procedures, it certainly is acting in an 'arbitrary' manner.

Article 32 of the Convention Relating to the Status of Refugees of 1951 is also informative for these purposes. While not binding on Lebanon or applicable to its Palestinian refugees, Article 32 forbids the arbitrary expulsion of a refugee without due process of law, and then only 'where compelling reasons of national security otherwise require'.[67] Likewise, the International Covenant on Civil and Political Rights states that '[n]o one shall be arbitrarily deprived of the right to enter his own country';[68] and the CERD has a similar provision.[69] Clearly, international law regards refugee status as protected from arbitrary expulsion. The legal applicability of these international instruments on Lebanon, however, is suspect. Since the Palestinian refugees' own country is not, technically speaking, Lebanon, and the Convention Relating to the Status of Refugees is not legally binding in this case, their right to enter is not safeguarded by international law, despite the fact that their travel documents are Lebanese. Nevertheless, the international community has articulated standards that apply to the treatment of refugees and the type of legal residence they enjoy. Palestinians in Lebanon should be afforded similar rights based on those standards.

However, certain aspects of Lebanese law bolster the Lebanese government's position. Article 2 of the Law Pertaining to the Entry into, Residence in and Exit from Lebanon reads as follows: 'Notwithstanding the provisions of International Conventions or of any specific law, foreigners shall be subject to the provisions hereof as regards their entry into, exit from and residence in Lebanon.'[70] Accordingly, Article 21 states that '[a] laisser passer shall not vest in the holder a right to return to Lebanon unless it contains a return visa'. While the Minister of the Interior's Order may be consistent with some provisions of Lebanese law, it remains inconsistent with others. First, the

Order appears to have been issued in violation of correct procedure. Lebanese law requires that all new legislation be published in the Official Gazette of Lebanese Legislation for it to be considered valid. Order No. 478 was published in the Lebanese newspapers and did not appear in the Official Gazette, and may therefore have been void on procedural grounds.[71] Second, the Order contradicted both the letter and spirit of the Palestinian laisser passer travel document issued by the Lebanese government. Page 2 of the official laisser passer for Palestinian refugees reads: 'It is requested of all employees of the government of the Lebanese Republic, its representatives abroad, and the concerned foreign authorities, to allow the holder of this document freedom of movement, and to provide all that he requires by way of aid and guidance.'[72] Additionally, the last page of the laisser passer states: 'This document is good for a return to Lebanon for as long as it remains valid.'[73] No mention is made of the need to obtain a re-entry visa in order to return to Lebanon. Thus, Lebanese law seems inconclusive and contradictory when dealing with a Palestinian refugee's right to enter Lebanon.

The legality of the Lebanese Minister of the Interior's actions, measured by both domestic Lebanese and binding international standards, should not be the main issue. The notion that some 100,000 refugees can be stripped of their legal residency and denied the right to visit their homes and families most certainly should. Non-binding international law, in the form of the Convention Relating to the Status of Refugees, articulates the protected type of residency to which a refugee is entitled. The inconsistent nature of Lebanese law on the issue of allowing Palestinians unimpeded entry into and exit from Lebanon cannot be ignored. The denial of the right of entry could also constitute 'cruel, inhuman, or degrading treatment' in this case, which is forbidden by the Universal Declaration of Human Rights.[74] Certainly, those Palestinian refugees resident in Lebanon, who were held on the Libyan–Egyptian border in makeshift shelters without adequate food and water, were subject to such inhuman treatment, in part by Lebanon, because it refused to allow them in.

There have however been several welcome developments on the issue of the travel rights of Palestinians resident in Lebanon. In January 1999, the Lebanese government announced that it would no longer require Palestinians travelling on a Lebanese-issued travel document to obtain a return visa.[75] Additionally, Lebanon and the PLO have formed a joint ministerial committee designed primarily to strengthen relations between the two entities, improve the living conditions of Palestinian refugees in Lebanon and call for the implementation of UN General Assembly Resolution 194.[76] While these developments are encouraging and promise better bilateral relations between Lebanon and the PLO, as well as enhancing the quantity and quality of rights enjoyed by Palestinians in Lebanon, they do not guarantee a situation in which the Palestinians will always enjoy such rights. Since 1948, the Palestinians have been subject to numerous displacements by both Israel and the Arab countries, in all areas of the Middle East. The volatility of the political situation, as evidenced by the Libyan fiasco, means that such episodes may be repeated with relative frequency. The Lebanese government is to be commended for its recent initiative with respect to the plight of its Palestinian population, yet the very recent nature of the events triggered by the expulsions from Libya makes it almost impossible to predict if such an initiative signals a principled shift in Lebanon's position or is merely a political ploy.

Lebanese Attitudes towards the Palestinian Refugees

Finally, the issue of Lebanese attitudes towards the Palestinian presence needs to be addressed, both on the governmental and, to a lesser extent, the popular level. Prime Minister Rafiq Al-Hariri summarized Lebanon's official position on its Palestinian refugees by stating that the refugees were solely the responsibility of Israel. He added: 'We cannot give them Lebanese nationality. We cannot do so because they are not and if we did so, we feel that we are implementing the plan of Israel.'[77] The prime minister made no attempt to offer a rational response to why the Lebanese government has not been willing to alleviate the refugees' suffering, but merely stated that Lebanon would not naturalize them. In fact, the Lebanese government acknowledges only three possible solutions to the Palestinian refugee issue: naturalization in Lebanon, a return to Palestine/Israel, or a settlement featuring a combination of the above two solutions. No alternative method of analysis exists in the Lebanese government's handling of the situation. One writer has suggested that the Palestinian Authority (PA) grant the refugees in Lebanon official Palestinian documents and proof of citizenship, as per the 1988 Palestinian Declaration of Independence in Algiers, and then permit Lebanon to give them some form of residency, similar to a permanent resident alien status in the United States.[78] This position would serve the dual purpose of legally documenting the Palestinians in Lebanon and according them certain inalienable rights, while allowing the Lebanese and Palestinian peoples jointly to resist resettlement schemes that are not in their interest. Other scholars have proposed more elaborate and all-encompassing resettlement schemes that articulate a total solution to the entire Palestinian refugee problem, which reflect the current balance of power in the Middle East to varying degrees.[79] Unfortunately, a refusal to implement any change continues to operate as the Lebanese government's blanket excuse for its treatment of its own Palestinian refugee population. It perceives any effort in granting the Palestinians greater rights as a step towards total absorption.

Government opprobrium and invective, legally personified by the denial of the rights to employment and residency, often take the more direct form of threatening words or actions. One minister, reacting to the expulsions in Libya and the possibility of those deported being allowed entry into Lebanon, proclaimed that Lebanon would not become a 'dumping ground for human waste'.[80] He stated that the Palestinians would inevitably have to leave Lebanon.[81] Indeed, an attempt, in August 1994, by the Minister of State for the Displaced to implement a scheme to rehouse 4,000 of the 6,000 Palestinian families displaced in the Lebanese civil war proved unsuccessful on two occasions and provoked dissent within the ruling Lebanese cabinet.

The first attempt to rehouse these refugees on the site of the original camps (now destroyed) in which they lived was rejected by the Maronite Church, the custodian of the lands in question. The Church felt that allowing the refugees to return and the camps to be rebuilt would foment ethnic tension while Lebanon was trying to reconstruct itself from the ashes of civil war. The camps in question – Tel el-Za'atar, Dbayyeh, Jisr al-Basha and Nabatiyyeh – were the sites of particularly brutal fighting involving the PLO forces and its Lebanese allies, engaged in combat with the Maronite Christian-led right-wing Lebanese forces militia. The Lebanese forces massacred and then drove out the survivors of the siege of Tel el-Za'atar in August 1976.[82] The Minister for the Displaced then tried to implement a rehousing scheme in the Iqlim al-Kharroub region. The permanent nature of the dwellings and the large area allotted for the scheme[83] aroused suspicions that the Palestinians were being permanently settled in Lebanon. There was a fear that this would both upset the sectarian balance and solve the refugee issue at Lebanon's expense. Ministers threatened to resign in order to bring down the prime minister's cabinet. They suspected that Lebanon was to receive a sort of settlement payment to absorb the Palestinian refugees, and the Minister of the Displaced was acting on that. The Palestinians themselves were also against the plan because they too feared that they were being permanently settled, and would consequently have no hope of returning to their homeland. Finally, Lebanese officials and citizens were outraged at the notion of resettling Palestinians displaced during the civil war before resettling displaced Lebanese citizens. The project was never implemented.

According to a survey conducted by *al-Safir*, a leading Lebanese daily, Lebanese popular opinion is against the naturalization and absorption of the Palestinian refugees.[84] The chief sentiments expressed by those surveyed, who included a cross-section of individuals from different areas of the country and different sects, were twofold. First, there was concern that the Palestinians, if naturalized, would further complicate Lebanese confessional problems. In addition, citizens felt that Lebanon was too small to absorb such a large number of refugees.[85] No discussion was given in the survey to the granting of more civil rights to the Palestinians, as the survey seemed incapable, like the government, of distinguishing between awarding civil rights and out and out resettlement.

Conclusion

Lebanese law places severe restrictions on the Palestinian refugees' rights to work, residency and travel. It provides few safeguards from arbitrary measures, as the Palestinian are officially designated as foreigners and are therefore not entitled to the protections and benefits of citizenship, or even those of permanent residents. The refugees are denied social security and access to public hospitals, and have in the past been denied the right to return to Lebanon if they decided to travel abroad. These restrictions violate Lebanon's duty, under the ICESCR and CERD, to the Palestinian refugees, as well as the spirit of the Convention Relating to the Status of Refugees. Lebanese official and popular attitudes exacerbate the problem. Both the government and, to a lesser extent, the public regard any attempt to grant more civil rights and freedoms to Palestinians as a ruse for forcing Lebanon to naturalize the Palestinians, and thereby to solve the refugee issue at Lebanon's expense. The legal and political status of the Palestinians in Lebanon is therefore precarious under Lebanese law.

3 THE CURRENT PREDICAMENT OF THE REFUGEES: THE OSLO ACCORDS AND BEYOND

The Right of Return

Central to any discussion of the current predicament of Palestinian refugees is the right of return. The principle of a 'right of return' for the Palestinians made refugees in 1948 is premised on the notion that those refugees should be allowed to return to their areas of origin, even if such areas are currently within the state of Israel. This is among the most controversial issues in the ongoing Arab-Israeli conflict. The primary piece of international law on this issue is UN General Assembly Resolution 194, ratified on 11 December 1948. Vis-à-vis the situation in Palestine, the General Assembly declared:

the refugees wishing to return to their homes and live at peace with their neighbours should be permitted to do so at the earliest practicable date, and that compensation should be paid for the property of those choosing not to return and for the loss of or damage to property which, under the principles of international law or in equity, should be made good by the Governments or authorities responsible.[86]

This Resolution has been affirmed by the General Assembly over 40 times and represents the strongest claim, under international law, for the inalienable right of repatriation available to the Palestinian refugees. Indeed, one scholar has remarked that Article 11 was 'written on the assumption that the principle of right of return was not in issue and that the central task of was achieving practical implementation of repatriation'.[87] Its language is clear and exacting, yet its goal remains as far from realization as the day the resolution was passed.

This position remains at odds with the official Israeli stance on the Palestinian refugees' right of return. Israel disputes the legality of the Palestinian claim based on UN General Assembly Resolution 194, because, were it to accept such a right, it would have to assume responsibility for repatriating refugees whom it blames the Arab states for creating. The official Israeli position, according to most mainstream scholars, is that the Arab states are responsible for creating the Palestinian refugees, because they ordered the refugees to flee so that Arab armies could liberate Palestine from the Zionists.[88] Further, Israel could never accept the Palestinian right of return because it would alter the character of the Jewish state, making the Jews a minority, where they previously were not. With the new wave of Israeli 'revisionist' historians uncovering more material on the war of 1948 and the origins of the Palestinian refugee problem, it has become clearer that the mass flight of Palestinian civilians from the area of Mandate Palestine was a strategic goal of the founders of Israel.[89] The myth of Arab responsibility for the evacuation of the Palestinians has been debunked, yet Israeli mainstream scholars and the government still adhere steadfastly to this position and refuse to allow the Palestinian refugees to return.

The right of return is a crucial issue to the Palestinian refugees in Lebanon. The overwhelming majority of Palestinians in Lebanon are from Galilee and the coastal areas of historic Palestine – areas that are currently within the state of Israel. While no thorough research or documentation exists on this point, and Palestinian positions on the right of return have been poorly articulated, it is presumed that Palestinians in Lebanon are seeking to return to their areas of origin within Israel. Their ties to the West Bank and Gaza are weak and a move to those areas is unfeasible, for both the refugees and the Palestinians currently resident there. They have strong family and cultural ties to the areas of their origin and have little or no connection or direct experience with the areas of the West Bank and Gaza Strip. They could probably not afford to move to the West Bank and Gaza Strip, where unemployment is high and the economy is in ruins.[90] Thus, the option of resettlement in the Occupied Territories or areas administered by the Palestinian Authority is not an appealing one. They lost any legal status they might have claimed in Israel in 1952, when the Knesset passed the Nationality Law, which stipulated that non-Jews were entitled to citizenship only if they were Palestinian citizens before the creation of Israel and were registered as living there in March 1952.[91] As refugees residing in Lebanon since 1948, they have been officially excluded from Israel by virtue of the Nationality Law. Additionally, they are barred from entering the West Bank and Gaza Strip, as Israel has retained the right to control who enters and who leaves territories under its dominion, as stated in its official agreements with the PLO.[92]

The Oslo Accords

The principles articulated by the international community on the Palestinian refugees' right to return in Resolution 194 have been theoretically suspended, based on the language of the Oslo I and II peace agreements signed by the Government of Israel and the PLO, in its capacity as the 'sole legitimate representative of the Palestinian people'.[93] The Declaration of Principles on Interim Self-Government Arrangements (Oslo I), signed on 13 September 1993 by Israel and the PLO, declares the intent of both parties to reach a permanent settlement on the basis of UN Security Council

Resolutions 242 and 338.[94] Resolution 242 calls on Israel to withdraw from the territories it occupied in the 1967 war, as well as for a fair settlement for the Palestinian refugees.[95] Resolution 338 merely calls for the implementation of Resolution 242 in the wake of the cease-fire that brought the hostilities of the 1973 Arab-Israeli war to a close.[96] The Declaration of Principles also states that finding a solution for 'persons displaced from the West Bank and Gaza Strip in 1967' will be addressed in talks conducted by a 'Continuing Committee', made up of Israel, the PLO, Jordan and Egypt.[97] Refugees, not defined or distinguished from 'displaced persons', will be dealt with in the final status negotiations.[98] The government of Jordan agreed to similar principles vis-à-vis displaced persons in its peace treaty with Israel,[99] while stating that the issue of refugees will be worked out in the 'framework of the Multilateral Group on Refugees'.[100] The multilateral Refugee Working Group (RWG) was established in January 1992 with the purpose of facilitating the arrival of a comprehensive solution to the refugee problem and easing the refugees' current suffering. In addition to the 'core' group of Egypt, Jordan, Israel and the PLO, the RWG features a whole host of participants, ranging from Russia and the United States (the sponsors of the Middle East peace process) to numerous Arab, European, Asian and African states. The RWG meets periodically, but Lebanon and Syria have yet to participate in any of its meetings. Little progress has been made in finding a solution to the refugee question. Finally, the Israeli–Palestinian Interim Agreement on the West Bank and the Gaza Strip (Oslo II), signed on 28 September 1995, reaffirmed the principles laid out in Oslo I and, subsequently, the Israeli–Jordanian peace accord, and identified the date, 4 May 1996, on which final status talks would begin.[101]

No mention was made of UN General Assembly Resolution 194, affirming the right of the Palestinian refugees to return to their homes, in either the Oslo I or Oslo II agreements. These accords were negotiated on the presumption that a solution would be reached based on Security Council Resolutions 242 and 338, which cover territory occupied by Israel in 1967. The accords explicitly left out General Assembly Resolution 194. The PLO has effectively given away the Palestinian refugees' right of return to the areas occupied by Israel in 1948. The right of return will potentially be applied only to whatever Palestinian entity eventually exists in the West Bank and Gaza, and not to areas within Israel. In any event, the purpose of the Oslo accords was not to reach a lasting and durable solution to the refugee problem, but rather to cement Israeli control. According to former Israeli prime minister Shimon Peres, the Oslo accords allow Israel to keep 73 per cent of the land of the West Bank and Gaza Strip, be responsible for 97 per cent of the security of those areas, and control 80 per cent of the water supply.

Additionally, not only has the right of return to Israel been eliminated, but progress on the issue of the refugees has ceased. The most recent Palestinian–Israeli peace talks, conducted in Taba, Egypt, in January 2001,

failed to yield any results on the issue of the right of return. The election of
Ariel Sharon as Israeli prime minister does not bode well for the advancement
of the right of return in the near future. While violence continues to rage in
Palestine, the Israelis, people and government, remain insistent in their
refusal to recognize the suffering of the Palestinians made stateless by them
in 1948.

The purpose of this cursory examination of the most pertinent standards
of international law with respect to the 1948 Palestinian refugees' right of
return serves to demonstrate that such a right still exists, despite the
language of the Oslo accords, insufficient as they are in this regard, and
despite the position of the current Israeli government. While the PLO has
been deemed the 'sole legitimate representative' of the Palestinian people,
most notably by the Arab League in 1974,[102] its once solid popularity
among the refugees in Lebanon is now declining.[103] Given the PLO's
abandonment of these refugees in its negotiations with Israel – a high-
ranking Palestinian Authority official even remarked that the Palestinians
in Lebanon are the responsibility of UNRWA[104] – its legitimacy to safeguard
and uphold their claims seems doubtful. The Palestinians in Lebanon should
be free to seek their right to repatriation, regardless of what the PLO
acquiesces to, so long as UN General Assembly Resolution 194 remains in
force. If they are truly an independent body of refugees, they can assert their
rights in that capacity, or at least in conjunction with Palestinian refugees
from other Arab countries. Their right to return should not simply be
discarded because their former representative in the international political
arena, the PLO, has relieved itself of its duty. International law, one would
hope, does not operate in such a manner.

CONCLUSION

The near future will not offer many answers for the Palestinian refugees in
Lebanon, and there are no simple solutions to their many and very
complicated problems. While solutions have been proposed which divide the
responsibility for the Palestinians' repatriation between Israel, Jordan,
Lebanon and Syria, it is imprudent to speculate on what may or should
happen, especially since international law, as embodied in Resolution 194,
seems clear in this regard. Unfortunately, *realpolitik* has kept the refugees'
repatriation from occurring.

It is clear, however, that the Palestinians in Lebanon are entitled to certain
basic rights under international law, and, in order to survive, they need to be
granted those rights. The International Covenant on Economic, Social and
Cultural Rights and the International Convention on the Elimination of All
Forms of Racial Discrimination, to which Lebanon has acceded, both uphold
the right of the individual to work. Additionally, the Refugee Convention
recognizes that after three years of residency in the host country, refugees
should be treated as citizens with respect to the right to work. Continuing to
treat Palestinian refugees as 'foreigners' and *de facto* to deny them work

authorization is a violation of international law and legal principles, and Lebanon must take the appropriate measures to remedy this situation.

Despite the fact that the Refugee Convention is not applicable to Lebanon and its Palestinian refugee population, and the language of the Universal Declaration of Human Rights language is more exhortatory than legally binding, these documents serve as a strong reminder as to the opinion of the international community and international law on the right of refugees to residency. Palestinians in Lebanon should enjoy full residency rights and be allowed to travel to and from Lebanon unimpeded, without risking the loss of these rights each time they travel abroad. International law is clear on this issue. Recent developments have been encouraging on this front, and the Lebanese government is to be commended for lifting the return visa requirement and forming a joint ministerial committee with the PLO. However, it is too early to know if these developments will herald a new era of cooperation and change between Lebanon and its refugees. Lebanon's position of denying Palestinians civil rights has been based on the misconception that every right granted to the Palestinians is a step in the direction of settling the refugee issue at its expense. Civil rights do not, and should not, imply a willingness on the part of Lebanon to settle the Palestinians. Such rights are necessary, however, to alleviate the suffering and deprivation of a long neglected sector of the Palestinian refugee population, and are protected by international law. Again, Lebanon needs to reassess its position on this issue, in order to bring its policy in line with current international legal standards and norms.

While Palestinian refugees in Lebanon are entitled to certain fundamental rights, they also have a right to return to the areas of their origin, which are now part of the state of Israel. UN General Assembly Resolution 194 upholds this right, and to this day that document remains the most direct and relevant article of international law which speaks to the Palestinian refugees' right to return. The Universal Declaration of Human Rights and the International Covenant on Civil and Political Rights contain provisions which reflect the principle articulated in Resolution 194. The Fourth Geneva Convention condemns the forced mass transfer of populations, language that covers what befell the Palestinians in 1948. The Palestinian refugees' right to return to areas within Israel is obviously a contentious issue, and the likelihood of such a right ever being recognized is poor at best. Perhaps even to argue that it is still applicable, based on Resolution 194, is futile and unhelpful for finding a lasting solution to the Palestinian refugee problem.

In my view, Resolution 194 and the right to return are crucial to those Palestinians in Lebanon who wish one day to enjoy a durable solution to their status as refugees. Israel has been extremely stubborn, to the point of intransigence, when dealing with the issue of the Palestinians it made refugees in 1948 and their right to return to areas within Israel. It has offered no alternative solutions as to how to best deal with the problem, and continues to absolve itself of any responsibility for their current plight, preferring instead to blame the Arab states for their flight from their homes. I believe it is best to deal with what the international community, through the organ of the United Nations, has articulated vis-à-vis the right to return for the Palestinian refugees. Leaving refugees in a state of legal, social and political helplessness cannot help ensure a stable or peaceful Middle East, and both Israel and the Palestinians themselves have to understand what support they may or may not draw from the international community. Whether or not Israel will ever adhere to Resolution 194 is immaterial.

The Oslo agreements do not even deal with the issue of the Palestinian refugees of 1948, as their intention is to find a solution based on UN Security Council Resolutions 242 and 338, which deal with territory occupied by Israel in 1967, and expressly do not mention General Assembly Resolution 194. With the PA–PLO ostensibly giving up responsibility for the Palestinian refugees in Lebanon (the joint Lebanon–PLO ministerial committee being a small exception to this general rule) and Israel failing to offer any type of solution for their predicament, I have tried to state the case for their ultimate repatriation, based on principles and positions articulated in international law. I do consider this a worthwhile exercise, the balance of power in the Middle East notwithstanding.

In this chapter I have tried to demonstrate how the suffering of the Palestinians in Lebanon from both official Lebanese and Israeli intransigence remains one of the many obstacles to a true and just peace in the Middle East. Realistically, I would suggest that it is of the utmost urgency for Lebanon to afford the Palestinians the right to work, residency, travel and to receive various social benefits services in order to meet the standards enunciated by international law. This seems to me to be of great importance for humanitarian as well as political reasons. As long as Palestinian refugees are mistreated and abused by Arab and Israeli governments, there will be no lasting peace in the Middle East. There numbers are too large, especially in Lebanon, to be ignored and have their rights violated, without the stability of the region being affected. Obviously, their repatriation is the ultimate goal, and I believe that this chapter has shown that their right of return is still recognized by international law. In the meantime, I believe that the Palestinians in Lebanon must be afforded some of the most basic rights, such as work and residency, before we can begin to discuss peace in the region and their repatriation.

NOTES

This chapter is a revised and abridged version of a paper first published as 'The Palestinians in Lebanon: The Rights of the Victims of the Palestinian-Israeli Peace Process', *Columbia Human Rights Law Review* (Spring 1999).

1. Farid El Khazen, 'Permanent Settlement of Palestinians in Lebanon Recipe for Conflict', 10 *Journal of Refugee Studies* 275 (1997), pp. 280–1.
2. International Covenant on Economic, Social and Cultural Rights (ICESCR), opened for signature 16 December 1966, UNTS 2 (entered into

force 3 January 1976); International Convention on the Elimination of All Forms of Racial Discrimination (CERD), opened for signature 7 March 1966, 660 UNTS 195 (entered into force 4 January 1969).

3. See Ilan Pappe, *The Making of the Arab-Israeli Conflict* (1992), pp. 41–6.

4. See Norman G. Finkelstein, *Image and Reality of the Israel–Palestine Conflict* (1994), pp. 51–87.

5. Nur Masalha, *A Land without a People: Israel, Transfer and the Palestinians, 1949–96* (1997), p. xi.

6. Rosemary Sayigh, *Too Many Enemies: The Palestinian Experience in Lebanon* (1994), p. 17.

7. See Samih K. Farsoun and Christine E. Zacharia, *Palestine and the Palestinians* (1997), pp. 123–7.

8. See National Emergency Committee on Lebanon, 'Lebanon, the Palestinians and the PLO: A Profile', 24 *Race & Class* (1983), pp. 327, 328.

9. See Kamal Salibi, *A House of Many Mansions: The History of Lebanon Reconsidered* (1988), pp. 185–6.

10. See Sayigh, *Too Many Enemies*, pp. 206–8.

11. Ibid., pp. 29–30.

12. See Michael Hudson, 'Palestinians and Lebanon: The Common Story', 10 *Journal of Refugee Studies* (1998), pp. 243, 251–5.

13. See Jonathan C. Randal, *Going All the Way: Christian Warlords, Israeli Adventurers and the War in Lebanon* (1983), pp. 54–5. See also Sayigh, *Too Many Enemies*, pp. 161–70.

14. Charles Glass, *Tribes with Flags: A Journey Curtailed* (1990), pp. 379–80.

15. See Amnon Kapeliouk, *Sabra and Shatila: Inquiry into a Massacre* (1982) (Khalil Jahshan trans., AAUG Press, 1983).

16. See, for example, Sayigh, *Too Many Enemies*, pp. 125–227.

17. GA Res. 302, UN GAOR, 4th sess., UN Doc. A/1251 (1949).

18. See Yves Besson, 'UNRWA and its Role in Lebanon', 10 *Journal of Refugee Studies* (1997), pp. 335, 336.

19. See Mahmoud Abbas, 'The Socio-Economic Conditions of the Palestinians in Lebanon: The Housing Situation of the Palestinians in Lebanon', 10 *Journal of Refugee Studies* (1997), pp. 379, 380–1.

20. See Ali Hassan, 'The Socio-economic Conditions of the Palestinians in Lebanon: Health amongst the Palestinians', 10 *Journal of Refugee Studies* (1997), pp. 392, 393–5.

21. Convention Relating to the Status of Refugees, 28 July 1951, art. 1(D), 189 UNTS 150, 137.

22. Elia Zureik, 'Palestinian Refugees and Peace', *Journal of Palestine Studies* (Autumn 1994), pp. 5, 8.

23. Souheil Al-Natour, 'The Legal Status of the Palestinians in Lebanon', pp. 5–6 (on file with author). An abridged version of this paper appears in 10 *Journal of Refugee Studies* 360 (1997).

24. This must mean UNRWA, since UNRWA was the primary international relief agency operating in the region with respect to the Palestinian refugees at the time.

25. Al-Marsoum Al-Ishtirai' [Legislative Decree] No. 42 (1959) (Leb.); Legislative Decree No. 927 (1959) (Leb.), *quoted in* Al-Natour, 'The Legal Status of the Palestinians in Lebanon', pp. 6–7. In consultation with the Arabic text, I took some liberties in changing the translation to make it, in my opinion, less cumbersome.

26. Law Pertaining to the Entry into, Residence in and Exit from Lebanon, art. 1 at 2 (1962) (Leb.).

27. Ibid., art. 19, at 4.

28. Ibid.

29. Ibid., art. 25, at 5.

30. Convention Relating to the Status of Refugees, art. 17.

31. ICESCR; CERD.

32. ICESCR, art. 6, para. 1.

33. CERD, art. 5, paras (e)(i), (iv).

34. Despite the fact that Decree No. 927 refers specifically to 'Palestinian refugees', Lebanese law makes no attempt to distinguish them from 'foreigners,' and hence they are considered as such by the Lebanese authorities.

35. See Souheil Al-Natour, *awDa' ash-Sha'b al-Filastini fi Lubnan* [The Predicament of the Palestinian People in Lebanon] (1993), p. 111.

36. See Randal, *Going All the Way*, pp. 163–4.

37. The Cairo Agreement, 3 November 1969, reprinted in Istvan Pogany, *The Arab League and Peacekeeping in Lebanon* (1987), p. 198.

38. See Ibrahim Abu-Lughod, 'The Meaning of Beirut, 1982', 24 *Race and Class* (1983), pp. 345, 350.

39. Lebanese Law No. 87/25, art. 1 §2, 6/18/1987.

40. Decree No. 17561 Regulating Foreigner Work, art. 11–14 at 22–23 (Leb.).

41. Ibid., art. 17.

42. See, for example, Immigration and Naturalization Act (INA) §§ 203 (b), 212 (a).

43. Hussein Shaaban, 'Unemployment and its Impact on the Palestinian Refugees in Lebanon', 10 *Journal of Refugee Studies* (1997), pp. 384, 386.

44. See Al-Natour, *The Predicament of the Palestinian People in Lebanon*, p. 125.

45. Legislative Decree No. 112 (1959), in 6 *Majmu'at at-Tashri' al-Lubnani* [Anthology of Lebanese Legislation] 1 (Hon. Salim Abi-Nader, ed., 1962).

46. Social Security Law, art. 9, para. 4, in *Qanun al-Daman al-Ijtimai' wa Qanun Tasheel al-Iskan fi-Lubnan* [The Social Security Law and the Housing Facilitation Law in Lebanon], pp. 13–14 (compiled and edited by Iskandar Saqr) (author's translation).

47. CERD, art. 5., para. (e)(iv); ICESCR, art. 9.

48. See Al-Natour, *The Predicament of the Palestinian People in Lebanon*, pp. 125–6.

49. *Qanun al-'Amal al-Lubnani* [Lebanese Labour Law], arts. 91, 92, reprinted in *Anthology of Lebanese Legislation* (Hon. Salim Abi-Nader Lubnani, ed., 1962).

50. Shaaban, *Unemployment and its Impact*, p. 387.

51. See Rosemary Sayigh, 'Palestinians in Lebanon: Harsh Present, Uncertain Future', *Journal of Palestine Studies* (Autumn 1995), pp. 37, 39.

52. See ibid., p. 44. See also Besson, 'UNRWA and its Role in Lebanon', p. 339.

53. CERD, art. 5, para. (e)(iv).

54. See Besson, 'UNRWA and its Role in Lebanon', p. 339.

55. Ibid.

56. See Sayigh, 'Palestinians in Lebanon', p. 39.

57. See Besson, 'UNRWA and its Role in Lebanon', p. 339.

58. See *ABC News Nightline* (ABC television broadcast, 19 January 1998).

59. Qarar raqm [Order Number] 319, 2 August 1962, reprinted in Al-Natour, *The Predicament of the Palestinian People in Lebanon*, p. 106 (author's translation).

60. See Al-Natour, *The Predicament of the Palestinian People in Lebanon*.

61. Convention Relating to the Status of Refugees, art. 26.

62. Law Pertaining to the Entry into, Residence in and Exit from Lebanon, art. 28, para. 1.

63. Order No. 478, Relating to Control of the Entry and Exit of Palestinians from Lebanon, 22 September 1995, art. 2.

64. See Al-Natour, *The Predicament of the Palestinian People in Lebanon*, p. 15.

65. Order No. 478, art. 2.

66. Universal Declaration of Human Rights, art. 9, GA Res. 217A, UN GAOR, 3rd sess., UN Doc. A/810 (1948).

67. Convention Relating to the Status of Refugees, art. 32.

68. International Covenant on Civil and Political Rights (ICCPR), art. 12(4), GA Res. 2200A, UN GAOR, 21st sess., Supp. No. 16, at 52, UN Doc. A/6316 (1966).

69. CERD, art. 5(d)(ii).

70. Law Pertaining to the Entry into, Residence in and Exit from Lebanon, art. 2.

71. Miri' Nasser, 'Qarar al-Ta-sheerah Mukhalif lil-Qawanin wa lil-Ittifaqiyat wa al-Muahadat al-'Arabiyah wa ad-Dawliyyah' [Visa Order Violates International and Arab Laws, Agreements, and Covenants], *al-Safir* newspaper, 28 May 1997.

72. Ibid. (author's translation).

73. Ibid. (author's translation).

74. Universal Declaration of Human Rights, art. 5.

75. See Ben Lynfield, 'PA Welcomes Lebanese Refugee Travel Decision', *Jerusalem Post*, 17 January 1999, p. 2.

76. 'Al-Lajna al-Wizariyya al-Filastiniyya al-Lubnaniyya al-Mushtarika Tajtami' fi Bayrut al-Youm', Al-Ayyam (visited 7 April 1999) <http://www.al–ayyam.com/today/ pl10.html>.

77. *ABC News Nightline*.

78. See Nawaf Salam, 'Palestinians in Lebanon', *Journal of Palestine Studies* (Autumn 1994), pp. 18, 24–5.

79. See, for example, Donna E. Arzt, *Refugees into Citizens: Palestinians and the End of the Arab–Israeli Conflict* (1996); Rex Brynen, 'Imagining a Solution: Final Status Arrangements and Palestinian Refugees in Lebanon', *Journal of Palestine Studies* (Winter 1997), pp. 53–6.

80. Nasrallah, 'Lebanese Perceptions', p. 356. The minister's comment was intended to show the similarity between the issue of the Palestinian expulsions from Libya and that of illegal toxic waste dumping by certain right-wing militias that occurred during the Lebanese civil war, which was a *cause célèbre* in the Lebanese press at roughly the same time. Perhaps he wanted to link popular outrage at the toxic waste dumping to his so-called 'human waste dumping'. The phrases in Arabic for toxic waste (*nifayat samma*) and human waste (*nifayat bashariyya*), respectively, were employed to demonstrate that Lebanon had been dumped on enough.

81. Lebanese Foreign Minister Faris Buwayz, remarks on Palestinians in Lebanon, *Journal of Palestine Studies* (18 April 1994), pp. 130–1.

82. See, for example, Robert Fisk, *Pity the Nation: Lebanon at War* (1990) (providing for a full account of these events).

83. A secret administrative order, issued by Lebanese Public Security, forbids increasing the size of any refugee camp, stipulates that houses in the camps must have walls of stone and roofs of aluminum, and forbids building additional storeys on top of one's dwelling. See Al-Natour, *The Predicament of the Palestinian People in Lebanon*, 108.

84. The Arabic word for the naturalization and absorption of the refugees is *tawTeen* and has been translated as 'implantation'.

85. See 'Salbiyyat at-Tawteen Kama Yaraha al-Lubnaniyun wa Muqarana ma' Dirasa Ukhra hawla Mawqif al-Filastiniyiin' [The Negative Aspects of Naturalization as Seen by the Lebanese and a Comparison with another Study on the Position of Palestinians], *al-Safir* newspaper, 20 February 1993.

86. GA Res. 194, UN GAOR 3rd sess. UN Doc. A/810, at 24 (1948).

87. Thomas Mallison and Sally V. Mallison, *The Palestine Problem in International Law and World Order* (1986), p. 179.

88. See Benny Morris, *The Birth of the Palestinian Refugee Problem, 1947–1949* (1987), p. 1.

89. See, for example, Finkelstein, *Image and Reality*; Simha Flapan, *The Birth of Israel: Myths and Realities* (1987); Morris, *The Birth of the Palestinian Refugee Problem*; *New Perspectives on Israeli History: The Early Years of the State* (Laurence J. Silberstein, ed., 1991); Pappe, *The Making of the Arab-Israeli Conflict, 1947–1951*.

90. Israel is much better situated to absorb a high number of returning refugees. It has a strong economy and absorbed some 700,000 new immigrants from the former Soviet Union over the years 1989–96. See Benny Morris, 'Israel's Elections and their Implications', *Journal of Palestine Studies* (Autumn 1996), pp. 70, 74.

91. See David J. Goldberg, *To the Promised Land: A History of Zionist Thought* (1996), p. 236.

92. See Raja Shehadeh, *From Occupation to Interim Accords: Israel and the Palestinian Territories* (1997), pp. 95–6.

93. Mark Tessler, *A History of the Israeli–Palestinian Conflict* (1994), p. 484.

94. Excerpts: Declaration of Principles on Interim Self-Government Arrangements (hereinafter DOP), arts. I & V, reprinted in Arzt, *Refugees into Citizens*, pp. 213–15.

95. SC Res. 242, UN SCOR, 22nd sess., 1382nd mtg. at 5–6, UN Doc. S/INF/22/Rev.2 (1967). Incidentally, the text of the Resolution does not use the word 'Palestinian' when referring to the refugees and does not elaborate on what exactly a 'just settlement' for those refugees might be.

96. SC Res. 338, 28 UN SCOR, 1747th mtg. at 10, UN Doc. S/INF/29 (1973).

97. DOP, art. XII, reprinted in Arzt, *Refugees into Citizens*, pp. 213–15.

98. Ibid., p. 214.

99. Excerpts: Treaty of Peace between the State of Israel and the Hashemite Kingdom of Jordan, art. 8(2)(b)(i), reprinted in Artz, ibid., pp. 215–17.

100. Andrew Robinson, 'The Refugee Working Group, the Middle East Peace Process, and Lebanon', 10 *Journal of Refugee Studies* (1997), pp. 314, 315–16. See also Joel Peters, 'The Multilateral Arab–Israel Peace Talks and the Refugee Working Group', 10 *Journal of Refugee Studies* (1997), 320, 332–3.

101. See 'The Israeli–Palestinian Interim Agreement on the West Bank and the Gaza Strip', <http://www.arc.org.tw/USIA/www.usia.gov/regional/nea/peace/interim.htm#annex>.
102. Edward W. Said, *The Question of Palestine* (1992), p. 25.
103. See Abbas Shiblak, 'Palestinians in Lebanon and the PLO', 10 *Journal of Refugee Studies* (1997), pp. 261, 270–1.
104. See Sayigh, 'Palestinians in Lebanon', p. 41 ('At UNRWA's emergency meeting last March [1995], PA delegate Nabil Shaath stated emphatically that Palestinians in Lebanon were not the PA's responsibility but UNRWA's').

9 MEETING THE NEEDS OF PALESTINIAN REFUGEES IN LEBANON

Nahla Ghandour

Meeting the needs of Palestinian refugees in Lebanon is an ambitious title for my chapter. As this subject is highly complex, I shall describe my personal experience in meeting the needs of 'some' Palestinian refugees in Lebanon.

What do I do? I direct a rehabilitation pre-school in Mar Elias camp for Lebanese and Palestinian children with multiple disabilities. I also work in the Ghassan Kanafani Cultural Foundation executive committee, where I collaborate closely with other NGOs (non-governmental organizations) working for the Palestinian and Lebanese communities.

I will start by sketching the life of the Palestinians in the camps, and also introduce the organizations active in them. Then I will elaborate upon issues of disability and its many manifestations. This will allow me to conclude with some personal reflections on the development of the Palestinian identity as a politicized, social entity in Lebanon, which contributes to the continuity of Palestinian culture in exile. This broad plan also prompts me to qualify myself, forcing me to ask the following question: Can I adequately describe – much less meet the complicated physical needs of – Palestinian refugees in Lebanon?

PALESTINIANS IN THE LEBANESE CAMPS

Lebanon hosts more than 368,000 Palestinian refugees[1] residing in 13 official Palestinian camps. UNRWA (United Nations Relief and Works Agency for Palestinian Refugees) is responsible for providing cleaning and maintenance services in the camps. Due to UNRWA's limited budget as well as political pressure, the physical conditions in the camps are rapidly deteriorating, and the water and sewage infrastructure is in a state of collapse. This situation is aggravated because of the restrictions imposed by the Lebanese government on any maintenance, or are exacerbated by another appalling aspect of the problem: the construction work in some of the camps, regardless of how minor these works are. In these dire circumstances Palestinian families displaced from demolished camps, such as Tel el-Za'atar, Jesr al Basha and Nabatieh, and residing outside the camp boundaries, receive no social services at all.

The conditions of the camps in Lebanon are not separate from the history of Palestinians in Lebanon. Rather, they are a direct consequence of that history, especially in the active and major role they played in the Lebanese civil war before 1982 (that is, the year of the Israeli invasion) and afterwards, in the passive but important role they played as a key component in the unfolding peace process during the 1990s. The experience of the Palestinians in Lebanon is unparalleled in any other of the various Arab countries. They have been subjected to social, economical and political restrictions, not to mention violence and repression during their almost 50 years of exile. Their rights and obligations have been kept ambiguous.[2] Born in exile, they have also been displaced from one camp to another, the consequence being the almost total fragmentation of a once large and politically powerful community.[3]

These circumstances have created appalling social conditions for the Palestinian refugees, some of which have been revealed in a 1992 UNRWA survey. The most significant of these though is this: 60 per cent of this community live below the poverty line and 36 per cent subsist without a regular income. Another survey done by Hussein Shaaban in 1995 shows that unemployment among the Palestinian population has reached 40 per cent.[4] What is more, Palestinians in Lebanon do not have the right to work and therefore are denied access to health care and other social services. The opportunity to work in Lebanon for the Palestinians – as indeed for all of us – is becoming ever slighter in the last decade, not least because many of the Palestinian NGOs have been forced to cease operations.[5] Here is a community that is legally prevented from entering the formal Lebanese workforce, an enforced exclusion obliging Palestinians to become construction workers or agricultural labourers. In other words, Palestinians are forced to resort to low-paying jobs earning below the normal Lebanese rates, a situation that severely limits their chances of economic and social development and material improvement.

In the past 50 years the Palestinian communities in Lebanon have contributed in a very dynamic and varied history. However, in recent years (since 1982), theirs has been a condition of social (and economic) stagnation. This has resulted in regressive and undesirable social practices among the young, such as early marriage, invariably accompanied by a high and early birth rate, low levels of educational achievement and low rates of employment (specifically, an 80–92 per cent unemployment rate according to UNRWA estimates).[6] Furthermore, a lack of work opportunities has driven Palestinians in Lebanon to migrate in search of work, better education and security. Shafiq Al Hout, a former PLO (Palestinian Liberation Organization) representative, has estimated that 75,000 Palestinians have left Lebanon in the past ten years.[7] Many families are scattered over several countries, resulting in further fragmentation of community/familial structures and the widespread neglect of the elderly left who are behind. Lastly, it should be noted that Palestinian refugees in Lebanon feel betrayed and abandoned by PLO, and effectively excluded from the peace process:

In Lebanon marginalization takes many forms. It is spatial near-confinement due to the continuous threat of violence towards demarcated and controlled camps; institutional (the exclusion from public institutions of social life); and economic (the extremely restrictive categories of employment available to Palestinians). The generic Palestinian refugee is cast as a troublemaker and cause of Lebanon's woes, a fearsome oddity to be managed, quarantined and moved at will.[8]

ACTIVE ORGANIZATIONS IN THE CAMPS

Within this situation of social and political marginalization and despite the difficult working environment, some 16 NGOs work with the Palestinian community. NGOs have targeted their services to meet refugee needs that are not addressed by UNRWA providing mainly educational and health services such as vocational training, pre-school education,[9] special needs education, rehabilitation/habilitation, illiteracy classes, and home economics for young girls. In addition to their services, these organizations have become important sources of employment for the Palestinian community. UNRWA, however, remains the main provider of services even though their availability has been declining since 1988. Other than infrastructure works, UNRWA currently operates 73 schools in Lebanon with an enrolment of around 38,400 students (grades 1–10). UNRWA also funds two secondary schools – one in Bourj al Barajinah-Beirut, and the other in Ain Al Helwe in Sidon –which accommodate 650 students. Despite their high profile in Palestinian communities, UNRWA school facilities are commonly in poor condition, and their institutional standards are varied, heavily dependent on individual incentives. Half the schools operate morning and afternoon shifts to accommodate heavy enrolment demands. While NGOs try to cover vocational training, higher education remains the main problem for the majority of Palestinians, who cannot afford secondary school and university education.

As far as health services are concerned, UNRWA operates 24 clinics and one mother-and-child centre in Lebanon. It has also established agreements with 13 Lebanese hospitals to provide health and medical services for Palestinian refugees. Expenses are part-funded by UNRWA, although their future availability remains uncertain given the organization's current budget reductions.[10] In addition to UNRWA, the HCS (Health Care Society) and the PRCS (Palestinian Red Crescent Society) provide health services. The HCS works to part-fund hospitalization, surgery, treatment of chronic illnesses, and emergency and hardship cases.[11] PRCS has four hospitals and nine primary health care facilities. The clinics deliver services to Palestinian patients at a lower cost.[12] Yet these services remain inaccessible to a substantial number of Palestinians as some may require token or partial payments which are unaffordable given the current economic situation and work status of the Palestinian refugees.

Disability is my field of work and scope of interest; I will try to give a fair account of services provided for Palestinian refugees with disabilities. The Ministry of Social Affairs provides care for Lebanese with disability; its services include hospitalization, rehabilitation, orthotic and prosthetic management and education. With regard to Palestinians specifically, PRCS and UNRWA used to provide hospitalization expenses and orthotic and prosthetic care prior to the civil war. Then, Palestinians with disabilities were considered individuals with health needs and were not treated as a particular medical problem or as distinct social entity. In the early 1980s, however, attention was first directed to the issue of disability in Lebanon. In fact, the camps were one of the initial sites providing rehabilitation, especially for war casualities. This specifically war-related initiative paved the way for the establishment of yet more treatment centres providing a broader range of therapies in other camps. Despite the opportunities for physical rehabilita- tion, children and adolescents with disabilities had negligible chances of receiving a proper education, as the educational facilities were unable to meet the special needs of these students.[13]

Some pre-school and vocational education projects cater specifically to Palestinians with disabilities, and an attempt was undertaken in September 1997 to issue them with disability cards. Before that, services were scattered and unorganized. It was also determined at that time to minimize wasted effort and cost by engaging in a more thorough study of needs, to organize services avoiding potential duplication and to channel donations to the most needy. A computer network was established to exchange medical and social data. Finally, each camp was equipped with at least two centres for regis- tration of the disabled and for card disbursement. By the end of 1999, 85–90 per cent of people with disabilities had been registered. What the survey revealed was a stark reality: that around 1 per cent of the Palestinian population of Lebanon are disabled.[14]

During the Disability Card project a forum[15] was established including all NGOs together with UNRWA and PRCS. Although efforts have now been combined and streamlined, some aspects of this work is still lacking.[16] For instance, a study I conducted in spring 1999 of 20 children with multiple disabilities in Ain Al Helwe camp revealed that the majority of the children (85 per cent) had had no access to any type of intervention. Consequently, their untreated disabilities will only get worse. What is more, the living conditions of these children will decline in quality for both them and their families. Although an attempt was made to resolve this issue by establish- ing a habilitation pre-school, the dual needs of economic and technical support far exceeded the supply available from the Palestinian community. The pre-school never materialized.

Palestinian children with disabilities are the most neglected group within the Palestinian community, lacking proper education, habilitation or training (of any sort). They are particularly at high risk of emotional neglect, physical discipline and sexual abuse. They become scapegoats for their families' sufferings, the unwitting victims of their families' private social despair.[17] Tragically, these children spend most of their lives within the confines of their homes; their solitary lives interrupted by only a few encounters with their health practitioners.

In 1986 the Ghassan Kanafani Cultural Foundation started a pilot project in Mar Elias camp in Beirut: a habilitation pre-school for children with multiple disabilities. It includes early intervention, pre-school habilitation and education.[18] Our pre-school is unique in the services it offers. Just how different is perhaps best evidenced by the fact that it offers group therapy services, training and awareness.[19] We also have a specialized library[20] as well as a carpentry workshop.[21]

In the Palestinian camps there is only one pre-school for children with mental retardation[22] (with a capacity of 16 children) in Ain Al Helwe camp. A few children with visual impairment are mainstreamed in UNRWA's Ain Al Helwe elementary school.[23] In Tyre a centre for children with visual impairments has been established. In the north of Lebanon CBR, a community-based rehabilitation project in Bidawi, and another in Naher Al Barid, are functioning. In Bikaa services are nonexistent.

Hence, education for children with disabilities is limited to the pre-school level. Palestinian children with disabilities grow up as unskilled, illiterate, financially dependent adults. Nevertheless it is amazing to witness the quality of care provided by some caregivers to children with severe disabilities, even if with the minimum life resources.[24]

Living conditions in the camps are bad enough for people with no disabilities. There is no doubt, however, that the situation becomes far worse when life is coupled with a disability, a circumstance that magnifies the severity of even a minor impairment and increases the physical, economic and emotional burdens on the person and his family as well.

Another major problem is the exclusion of the Palestinians with disabilities from the workforce. Their lack of access to work makes it virtually impossible for even the educated minority to be employed. These and many other problems have proved a continuous worry for Palestinians with disabilities as well as for the NGOs providing them with services.

Due to these problems various NGOs active in the Palestinian communities in Lebanon met in September 1997 and established a forum for all organizations working in the disability field. The main objectives of the forum, aside from the Disability Card project, are as follows:

1. Organize and coordinate services for Palestinians with disabilities.
2. Gather statistics on real need in the field of disability in the Palestinian community.
3. Advocate and lobby for local and foreign NGOs to work in the disability field.

Let me, at this point, shift my focus and share with you some personal thoughts as a way of concluding this chapter.

Apart from the matter of the institutionalized treatment of the Palestinian disabled population, what particularly concerns me is the way the living conditions of Palestinian refugees contribute to the formation of the Palestinian future adult. I believe that the two most critical aspects that affect the development of the Palestinian child in Lebanon are: the inevitable sense of a transitory and unstable life; theirs/ours is a future which is (as it has been) always unpredictable and we seem to have no control over it. The second is the impossibility for the parents to build a career or have a long-term job that minimizes their control on the future of their families, on both the economic and social fronts. Parents are constantly struggling for financial stability. Rather than providing security for their young, uncertainty governs their lives. Thus are sown the first grains of a profound inter-generational mistrust. Our children are forced to resolve all these dilemmas on their own. Their parents are mostly preoccupied with the never-ending search for employment and battling with the private demons of their familial inadequacy. Can Palestinian children come to trust their environment? Can they learn to trust their parents and be certain that they will be protected and accept themselves and believe in their own abilities? Continuous worry about how to secure a steady income creates insecurity and instability and thus dis-ability for planning of the future. Their continuous involvement in day-to-day issues deprives them of the most basic human needs, to explore and develop. Hobbies, leisure or recreational activities have no place in their lives.

Using the Adult Development model first proposed by Erick Erickson and then modified by George E. Vaillant, I want to speculate on the future of the Palestinian generations in Lebanon. The Palestinian children, as a consequence of their parents' and their own adverse experiences, acquire the most negative elements of the tasks of Adult Development. First mistrust, then shame, which moves on to guilt, inferiority and identity diffusion (that is, sustained separation from social, residential, economic and ideological dependency on family of origin).[25]

Palestinian children have to deal with ambivalent life situations at a very early age; they reach adulthood with no residual, enduring coping strategies. They are constantly wondering if there will be there food today. Can they play in this dirty environment without becoming ill? Are they free to roam without being the target of abuse? Are they free to make friends? Are they safe enough to sleep soundly at night and dream of sunshine, greenery and beautiful houses?

How can a Palestinian child become a Palestinian? From where can he or she acquire a strong belief in continuity? What will he or she believe in – poverty, abuse, trauma, and insecurity? Who serves as his or her role model – an unemployed father, an exhausted mother, an unjust rule, or a hostile neighbour? Barring such identification, shame and guilt seep easily into the formulation of Palestinian self-identity!

Following a childhood like this, the adolescent can only sustain previous negative experiences making it difficult to pass through adulthood without falling by the wayside. They are faced with poor educational standards, limited and scarce opportunities for higher education in addition to most being excluded from enjoying the benefits of a steady and secure job.

The adult will be obsessed with meeting basic survival needs, which will gradually allow rigidity and then despair to take over. Such a situation will prevent the Palestinian future adult from being a 'Keeper of Meaning', as defined by George Vaillant;[26] that is preserving his culture which involves developing a social radius that extends beyond the immediate community. For that role to be assumed by the future adult, food, water, education, health and work should be available without humiliation, degradation or inferiority.

A questionnaire was conducted for the purpose of this chapter, in which three questions were put to 132 Palestinians residing in different camps in the Lebanese territories. The cohort included people aged from 11 to 62 years, and covered different community sectors: women, men, students, employed and unemployed residents. A summary of responses is as follows:

Question 1: *What do you think about the agreements between the United States, Israel and the Palestinian National Authority?*
Ninety-one per cent were against the agreements, which were described as: a lie, a failure, unjust (the rule of the powerful), a conspiracy, abandonment by the Arabs, degrading, shameful, a betrayal. Almost all shared the belief and opinion that the agreements do not include the right of return for Palestinians in the diaspora. The agreements are the element dividing the Palestinians and diffusing their cause.

Question 2: *Do you think that the agreements will affect the Palestinian refugees of Lebanon?*
Eight-nine per cent said that it will have a negative effect on the Palestinians in Lebanon, mainly by disregarding them. They have no human rights of any sort, no right to work, no rights to adequate health care and to education. They all refused the *tawteen* (resettlement) and they aspire to return to their homeland.

Question 3: *Do you think that the agreements will affect services provided for Palestinians in Lebanon?*
Eighty-eight per cent stated that services would be reduced. They all agreed that already existing services, such as they are, are negligible. This is keenly felt through the policy of UNRWA and PLO through the last years.

One resilient fact surpasses all these data: the enduring sense of the importance of the homeland as a sole concern that resists falling into the stage of despair, and the return to the homeland is the only future certainty in the daily life of Palestinians. Thus, it is the only concept from which cultural, social and human identity is evolving. The strongest belief shared by all Palestinians, employed or not, young or old, men or women, is the hope and insistence on their right to return to their beloved homeland. This belief strengthens their endurance in such degrading and difficult living conditions and, most importantly, it preserves their cultural identity and humanity.

I will end with the words of Jihan, a widow with five children from Haifa residing in Shatilla camp. She said in response to our questions:

The 'peace' agreements will affect us because if we stayed in Lebanon, nothing will change, we will remain as we are, having no will, carrying burdens that outweigh us. And our forced immigration is another burden that has stopped us from living a normal social, just life or having rights of possession, insurance, residence, or any other services. We need to decide our own fate/faith and rejoice in our right of return, in order to have an honorable land unspoiled by any Israeli hand. Neither Israel, nor the rich/affluent, or any other has the right to think for us or talk on our behalf. I, as a widow and a mother of five, have no one to care for my family or consider our needs, down to the tiniest of them. Who will look to me? The state here does not care for us, we are Palestinians! UNRWA promises, Israel threatens, and America supports, and we are as is, no health security, no medication, hungry with no food, cold with no decent shelter, our houses in Shatilla have waterfalls in them among other things. How can we stay? We will not stay and we want the right to return.

ACKNOWLEDGEMENTS

I would like to thank Wafa al-Yaseer and Kasem al-Sabah who provided me with background material and reports about the Palestinians in Lebanon. I also thank Richard Becherer for his editorial comments. My deepest appreciation goes to Laila Ouayda and Marwan Ghandour for helping out throughout the writing of this chapter.

NOTES

1. These included 364,551 Palestinian refugees registered with UNRWA and a further 3,684 refugees registered with UNHCR as well as 42,000 unregistered Palestinians in Lebanon (1998 statistics). The estimated numbers of Palestinians in Lebanon, as of 1997–98, are approximately 364,551.
2. Steven Edminster, *Trapped on All Sides* (Washington, DC: US Committee for Refugees, June 1999).
3. Worldwide Refugee Information (Washington, DC: US Committee for Refugees, January 1999).
4. Palestinians in Lebanon Conference, Centre for Lebanese Studies, Oxford 1996. Dr. Hussein Shaaban, 'Unemployment and its Impact on Palestinian Refugees in Lebanon' (data from this study are not yet complete):

    in 1992 the salary of a doctor working in PRCS was 250,000 Lebanese pounds;
    in 1994 only 350 work permits were issued to Palestinians;
    in 1995 unemployment reached 40 per cent of the Palestinian population;

0.16 per cent of the Palestinian labour force had the right to work;
1.10 per cent worked for UNRWA;
1.5 per cent who worked did not need a work permit (for agricultural labour).

5. Edminster, *Trapped on All Sides*.
6. Lack of social awareness, the financial burden of bringing up girls, in addition to the belief in the necessity of having a large family resulted in early marriages, which lacked all the properties of a successful one – mental preparedness, a home, an income, similar age. According to UNRWA and other estimates, Palestinian women form the bulk of the unemployed, their unemployment rates ranging from 80 to 92 per cent. The critical health among Palestinian women in Lebanon is as follows:

    (a) continuing high and early fertility;
    (b) rapid childbirth;
    (c) frequent miscarriages;
    (d) absence or misuse of birth control methods;
    (e) high child mortality;
    (f) lack of knowledge and information about women's health.

7. Rosemary Sayigh, *Palestinians in Lebanon: Harsh Present, Uncertain Future* (1995).
8. *Worldwide Refugee Information* (Washington, DC: US Committee for Refugees, January 1999).
9. The number of pre-schools in the refugee camps are as follows: South Lebanon (7 in Rachidieh, 11 in Ain el Helwe); Beirut (3 in Mar Elias, none in Shatilla, 9 in Bourj Al Barajneh); North Lebanon (8 in Beddawi, 18 in Nahr el Bared).
10. UNRWA covers only one third of hospital fees excluding doctors' fees, laboratory tests, X-rays and emergency admissions. Patients suffering from chronic illnesses, women in labour, emergency cases and the disabled are not provided with any financial assistance.
11. The Health Care Society covers 10–15 per cent of medical costs, those not supported by UNRWA are granted 15 per cent of an amount not exceeding US$1,250, HCS's budget comes from two sources: external funding and monthly contributions from employed Palestinians in the NGOs.
12. Depending on the yearly budget, services by HCS are not consistent. In 1998 all services were cut (including the monthly $50 for psychiatric cases) due to a zero budget.
13. Continuous funding for monthly wages is not sustainable, affecting in turn the quality of service.
14. A couple of year ago some Lebanese institutions had a special agreement with UNRWA to cover fees for Palestinian children with disabilities. Due to UNRWA's budget cuts these organizations decreased in number, giving rise to the few and often unprofessional centres that cater for Palestinian children with disabilities.
15. The total number of Palestinian refugees with disabilities reached approximately 2,859 that is around 1 per cent of the estimated population of Palestinians in Lebanon. This figure does not include people on kidney dialysis, with cancer or with old age disabilities such as Parkinson's or Alzheimer's disease, or with back pain, fractures, post-surgery treatment,

and disc problems. The distribution of disabilities of Palestinians in Lebanon is as follows:

Area	% of Total
Tyre and surrounding area	22.02
Sidon and surrounding area	32.97
Bekaa Valley	11.34
Beirut and Suburbs	11.77
North (Bidawi and Naher Al Barid)	21.90

As a consequence of the above mentioned problems the 14 NGOs working with Palestinians with disabilities established a Forum, through the initiation of Mrs. Wafa Al Yaseer, the local representative of NPA in Lebanon.

16. Therapy services in the Palestinian community

Service	No. of Centres	People in Need
Physiotherapy	5 (1 for children)	400
Occupational therapy	4 (1 for children)	300
Speech therapy	2 (1 for children)	200
Vocational Training	2	250
Special education	4 (2 for children)	300

17. It was impossible for us on one occasion to remove a girl aged 8 with mild disability from her family after she had been subjected to chronic sexual abuse. This girl, in addition to suffering severe psychological problems, has acute inflammation of the urinary tract which has become chronic.

18. Daily kindergarten programme:

> children attend 5 days a week 4 hours a day;
> ages range 3–8 years;
> children receive to two programmes: educational and rehabilitation;
> outreach programme: children undergo assessment (applying standardized and specially developed tests), an individual treatment plan is then taught to parents to implement at home.

19. The family programme includes: 1) educational assemblies, 2) family counselling, 3) information booklets, 4) family training, 5) support groups.

20. The specialist library includes texts, references, periodicals and audiovisual material.

21. The carpentry workshop covers design and execution of special aids, adaptations and educational toys for children with disabilities.

22. One of the Ghassan Kanafani Cultural Foundation kindergartens.

23. At present, mainstreaming is not a solution for these children, they complain of boredom and alienation, while those responsible for them lack awareness and knowledge of the means to integrate the children.

24. A study performed on 20 children with multiple disabilities in Ein Al Hilwe camp, Spring 1999.

25. George E. Vaillant, *The Wisdom of the Ego* (3rd edition, Cambridge, Mass.: Harvard University Press, 1997).

26. Ibid.

Part IV

Refugee Claims and the Search for a Just Solution

10 REINTERPRETING PALESTINIAN REFUGEE RIGHTS UNDER INTERNATIONAL LAW

Susan M. Akram

Palestinian refugees have a status that is unique under international law. Unlike any other group or category of refugees in the world, Palestinians are singled out for exceptional treatment in the major international legal instruments governing the rights and obligations of states towards refugees and stateless persons. Almost all states and international entities have interpreted the relevant provisions in these instruments as severely restricting the rights of Palestinian refugees in comparison to the rights guaranteed every other refugee group. As a result, Palestinian refugees have been treated as ineligible for the most basic protection rights international law provides to refugees and stateless persons in general, further eroding the precarious international legal guarantees that international human rights and humanitarian law currently extend to this population.

A number of consequences flow from this unique application of refugee law to the Palestinian refugee situation. First, it affects the type of protection afforded Palestinians under international refugee law, as opposed to the assistance they receive as refugees. Second, it affects the extent to which Palestinian refugees/stateless persons can assert guarantees of international human rights[1] and whether there are fora available for them to assert such rights. Third, it implicates the issue of what entity or agency has the authority to represent the interests of Palestinian refugees, whether in international bodies such as the United Nations, before other international or domestic legal/political fora, or in negotiations with states such as Israel. Fourth, it raises the complex issue of whether individual human rights recognized under international law can be protected and promoted in the Palestinian refugee case when such rights collide with collective rights under international law – in this case, the right to self-determination.

It is the contention of this author that interpreting refugee law principles and instruments as requiring a special but exceptionally weak international human rights regime for Palestinian refugees is an incorrect interpretation of the law. Palestinian refugees are entitled not to reduced protection, but to a heightened protection regime. These conclusions are based on an exhaustive review of the plain language of the relevant provisions, the intentions of the drafters of the instruments, and the purpose and scope of coverage of the instruments themselves.[2] Reinterpreting the instruments in this way dramatically changes the conclusions one draws on each of the issues listed above. This chapter addresses in summary form the four issues listed, examines their application under the reinterpreted instruments and discusses some of their implications for establishing durable solutions for Palestinian refugees.

INTERNATIONAL LAW PRINCIPLES AND INSTRUMENTS APPLICABLE TO PALESTINIAN REFUGEES

A number of international instruments affect the status of Palestinians as refugees and as stateless persons: the 1951 Geneva Convention Relating to the Status of Refugees (Refugee Convention)[3] and its 1967 Protocol (Refugee Protocol);[4] the 1954 Convention Relating to the Status of Stateless Persons;[5] and the 1961 Convention on the Elimination or Reduction of Statelessness.[6] There are also three international organizations whose activities affect the international legal rights of Palestinian refugees: the United Nations Conciliation Commission on Palestine (UNCCP);[7] the United Nations High Commissioner for Refugees (UNHCR);[8] and the United Nations Relief and Works Agency for Palestine Refugees in the Near East (UNRWA).[9] Because of the unique circumstances of the original and continued expulsion of Palestinians from their homes and lands,[10] Palestinians in the diaspora may be stateless persons, refugees or both. (The legal definitions of these terms, as well as the manner in which they are applied to Palestinians, will be discussed below.) As such, they should be entitled to the internationally guaranteed rights offered other stateless persons or refugees in the world.[11]

The 1951 Convention Relating to the Status of Refugees[12] is the most important treaty affecting Palestinian human rights in most of the areas of the world where they find themselves. It is also the primary international instrument governing the rights of refugees and the obligations of states towards them. This Convention, and its 1967 Protocol, incorporate the most widely accepted and applied definition of refugee,[13] and establish minimum guarantees of protection towards such refugees by state parties. The Refugee Convention and Protocol incorporate two essential state obligations: the application of the now universally accepted definition of 'refugee' which appears in Article 1A(2) of the Convention, and the obligatory norm of *non-refoulement*, which appears in Article 33.1 of the Convention.[14] The principle of *non-refoulement* requires that a state not return a refugee to a place where his/her life or freedom would be threatened. It is important to note that nowhere in the Refugee Convention or Protocol, nor in any other international human rights instrument, is there an obligation on any state to grant the status of political asylum or any more permanent status than *non-refoulement*.

The simple recognition that an individual meets the criteria of a 'refugee' as defined in the Convention, however, triggers significant state obligations towards them, not the least of which is the obligation of *non-refoulement*. The Convention requires states to grant refugees a number of rights which Palestinians are often denied, including: identity papers (Article 27); travel documents (Article 28); freedom from unnecessary restrictions on movement (Article 26); freedom from restrictions on employment (Articles. 17 and 18); basic housing (Article 21), welfare (Article 23), education (Article 22), labour and social security rights (Article 24); and freedom of religion (Article 4). It also makes them eligible for more permanent forms of relief such as residence and citizenship, subject to the discretion of the granting state.

The Convention and Protocol define a 'refugee' as:

[a person who], owing to a well-founded fear of being persecuted for reasons of race, religion, nationality, membership of a particular social group or political opinion, is outside the country of his nationality and is unable or, owing to such fear, is unwilling to avail himself of the protection of that country; or who, not having a nationality and being outside the country of his former habitual residence as a result of such events, is unable or, owing to such fear, is unwilling to return to it.[15]

This author contends that the Convention Article 1A(2) definition was never intended to, and does not, apply to Palestinians, for several critical reasons. First, as UN delegates involved with drafting the Refugee Convention pointed out: '[T]he obstacle to their repatriation was not dissatisfaction with their homeland, but the fact that a Member of the United Nations was preventing their return.'[16] Second, the Palestinians as an entire group had already suffered persecution by virtue of their massive expulsion from their homeland for one or more of the grounds enumerated in the definition. Thus, they were given special recognition as a group, or category, and not subject to the individualized refugee definition. Third, the delegates dealt with Palestinians as *de facto* refugees, referring in a general way to those who were defined by the relief agencies at the time (UNRPR and later UNRWA), but not limiting the term 'refugee' to those Palestinians who were in need of relief. Although they did not specifically define them as such, the delegates were referring to Palestinian refugees as persons normally residing in Palestine before 15 May 1948, who lost their homes or livelihood as a result of the 1948 conflict. For these and other reasons (discussed below), the delegates drafted a separate provision – Article 1D – in the Refugee Convention that applies solely to Palestinian refugees.

Refugee Convention Article 1D states:[17]

This Convention shall not apply to persons who are at present receiving from organs or agencies of the United Nations other than the United Nations High Commissioner for Refugees protection or assistance.

When such protection or assistance has ceased for any reason, without the position of such persons being definitively settled in accordance with the relevant resolutions adopted by the General Assembly of the United Nations, these persons shall *ipso facto* be entitled to the benefits of this Convention.

Although Palestinian refugees are not specifically mentioned in this provision, it is evident both from the drafting history and the interrelationship of Article 1D with three other instruments that Palestinians are the only group to which the Article applies.[18] The most important reasons for drawing this conclusion are that, first, the drafting history of the provisions clearly reflects that the only refugee population discussed in relation to Article 1D was the Palestinians. Second, one of the paramount concerns of the drafters of the Refugee Convention was that they wished to determine the precise groups of refugees to which the Convention would apply, so they could decide the extent to which the signatory states could accept the refugee burden. There is no indication that Article 1D was drafted with any different intention – that is, with an open-ended reference to other groups of refugees not contemplated by the United Nations at the time. (The universal application of the Refugee Convention definition is a later development with the entry into force of the Refugee Protocol.) Third, there was only one group of refugees considered to be in need of international protection at the time of drafting Article 1D that was receiving 'from other organs or agencies of the United Nations other than the United Nations High Commissioner for Refugees protection or assistance', and that was the Palestinians. Fourth, the interrelationship of the mandates of the United Nations agencies relevant to the needs of Palestinian refugees indicates that these are the agencies referred to by the language of Article 1D. These mandates are reflected in the Statute of the UNHCR, the Regulations governing UNRWA, and UN Resolution 194 establishing the United Nations Conciliation Commission for Palestine (UNCCP).[19]

The UNHCR Statute, paragraph 7(c) provides that 'the competence of the High Commissioner ... shall not extend to a person ... who continues to receive from other organs or agencies of the United Nations protection or assistance'. The 'other agencies of the United Nations' originally referred to both UNRWA and the UNCCP. The significance of the language in these provisions lies primarily in the distinction between 'protection' and 'assistance', which are substantially different concepts in refugee law. UNRWA's mandate is solely one of providing assistance to refugees' basic daily needs by way of food, clothing and shelter.[20] In contrast, UNHCR's mandate, in tandem with the provisions of the 1951 Refugee Convention, establishes a far more comprehensive scheme of protection for refugees qualifying under the Refugee Convention.[21] This regime guarantees to refugees the rights embodied in international human rights conventions, and mandates the UNHCR to represent refugees, including intervening with states on their behalf, to ensure such protections to them. Aside from the distinction between the mandates of UNRWA and UNHCR, the refugee definition applicable to Palestinians is different from and far narrower under

UNRWA Regulations than the Refugee Convention definition. Consistent with its assistance mandate, UNRWA applies a refugee definition that relates solely to persons from Palestine meeting certain criteria who are 'in need' of such assistance.[22]

In December 1948, the UN General Assembly created a separate 'protection' agency, established for the primary purpose of resolving the Palestinian refugee crisis and seeking a solution for the Palestinian-Israeli problem in line with the Partition recommendation.[23] This agency was the United Nations Conciliation Commission for Palestine (UNCCP). The composition and terms of reference of the UNCCP were set out in UNGA Resolution 194.[24] The resolution provided for the UNCCP to comprise three states members of the United Nations, who were to continue the efforts of the United Nations Mediator on Palestine and begin conciliation efforts immediately.[25] The UNCCP was further instructed to 'take steps to assist the Governments and authorities concerned to achieve a final settlement of all questions outstanding between them'[26] – specifically, according to UNGA Resolution 194(III), paragraph 11, to ensure repatriation and compensation.[27]

UNGA Resolution 194(III), paragraph 11:

Resolves that the refugees wishing to return to their homes and live at peace with their neighbours should be permitted to do so at the earliest practicable date, and that compensation should be paid for the property of those choosing not to return and for loss of or damage to property which, under principles of international law or in equity, should be made good by the Governments or authorities responsible; *Instructs* the Conciliation Commission to facilitate the repatriation, resettlement and economic and social rehabilitation of the refugees and the payment of compensation and to maintain close relations with the Director of the United Nations Relief for Palestine Refugees and, through him, with the appropriate organs and agencies of the United Nations.

Thus, the UNCCP was entrusted with the essential protection functions normally assigned to the UNHCR,[28] but with a very specific mandate concerning the requirements of a just resolution of the Palestinian refugee problem. The recommendations to the UN and UN Resolutions concerning the Palestinians drafted when UNCCP, UNHCR and UNRWA were created, affirm that the consensus of the world body was that resolution of the Palestinian problem had to involve realizing the refugees' right of return to their homes and to appropriate compensation for their losses,[29] in line with binding legal principles on the right of the refugees to return, and in accordance with their wishes.[30] The UNCCP struggled to fulfil its mandate. Its efforts were handicapped by a complete stalemate: the Arab states and the Palestinians demanded full repatriation, while Israel refused to accept any repatriation of the refugees.[31] By 1952, the UNCCP had ceased all protection functions towards the refugees and confined its operations to collecting records and documenting refugee properties in Israel – operations that have continued until now.[32] Thus, within four years of its formation, the

UNCCP devolved from an agency charged with the 'protection of the rights, property and interests of the refugees' to little more than a symbol of UN concern for the unresolved Arab-Israeli conflict.[33]

INTERNATIONAL LAW PRINCIPLES OF STATELESSNESS APPLICABLE TO PALESTINIANS

Aside from the Refugee Convention, the individual human rights of Palestinians are also affected – although to a lesser extent – by instruments governing their rights as stateless persons. The issue of what international legal status defines Palestinians is extremely complicated and, of course, determines which rights are to be afforded them. In brief, under the British Mandate, Palestinians had recognized legal status as either nationals or citizens of Palestine, or both.[34] The status of Palestinian nationals/citizens after the establishment of the state of Israel is determined by principles of state succession,[35] human rights[36] and humanitarian law.[37] There is considerable debate over whether the declaration and recognition of the state of Israel terminated the citizenship status of Palestinians as a matter of international law.[38] The net effect of the establishment of Israel and the passage of Israeli nationality law was that the vast majority of Palestinians expelled from their homes and lands became stateless, whether *de jure* or *de facto* – as a matter of law or in practical effect.

Thus, in addition to the Refugee Convention and Protocol, two international law instruments affect the status of Palestinians in a number of European countries: the 1954 Convention Relating to the Status of Stateless Persons[39] and the 1961 Convention on the Reduction of Statelessness.[40] These two Conventions are relevant to Palestinians who are refugees and stateless,[41] but who are unable to obtain the benefits of the 1951 Refugee Convention, and to Palestinians who are not refugees but remain stateless.[42] Although these Conventions are significant in terms of the legal rights they afford stateless persons and the obligations required of state signatories, they have limited reach, as they have been ratified by very few states.[43] In order to obtain the benefits of these Conventions, a person must be determined to be 'stateless', that is 'a person who is not considered a national by any State under the operation of its law'.[44] The 1961 Convention adopts the same definition of stateless persons, but also recommends that 'persons who are stateless *de facto* should as far as possible be treated as stateless *de jure* to enable them to acquire an effective nationality'.[45] Despite the limited accessions to these two Conventions, their basic definition of 'stateless persons' is now considered customary international law, and therefore binding even on states that are not party to one or other of these Conventions.[46]

The focus of the 1954 Convention is to improve the status of stateless persons and to grant them the widest possible guarantees of fundamental human rights.[47] The 1961 Convention was drafted to address the gaps left by the 1954 Convention and to reduce as much as possible, or eliminate entirely, the phenomenon of statelessness.[48] The 1961 Convention requires states to grant nationality to persons born in their territories who would otherwise be stateless (Article 1). It also prohibits – with a number of exceptions – depriving someone of their nationality (Article 8). It categorically prohibits denial of nationality on grounds of race, religion or political opinion (Article 9). By far the most important aspect of the 1961 Convention for Palestinians is the recommendation for an expanded 'stateless' definition, and Article 11, which provides for the establishment of an agency with authority to protect and assist stateless persons claiming the benefit of that Convention. In 1974, the UN General Assembly entrusted the UNHCR with the mandate to protect and assist stateless persons as required by Article 11.[49] The UNHCR has never exercised this mandate under the 1961 Convention.[50] Thus, Palestinians have been without an agency that could seek enforcement of the rights guaranteed by that Convention.

The 1954 Stateless Convention has a clause similar to the Refugee Convention and UNHCR Statute, stipulating that the Convention

shall not apply to persons who are at present receiving from organs or agencies of the United Nations other than the United Nations High Commissioner for Refugees protection or assistance so long as they are receiving such protection or assistance.[51]

It is undisputed that this provision applies, as well, only to Palestinians. The explicit omission of Palestinians in one and the lack of obligation to apply the expanded stateless definition in the other have a substantial impact on rights afforded Palestinians residing in European states which have signed one or both of them.[52] As a single example, Germany, which is party to both the 1954 and 1961 Conventions, takes the position that Palestinians 'originating' from Lebanon are not stateless, but have 'indeterminate' or 'unsettled' status, and therefore are not eligible for the guarantees of the 1961 Convention.[53] However, the vast majority of Palestinians coming from many of the Arab states are *de facto* stateless. By not recognizing them as such, Germany denies them such rights guaranteed under the 1961 Convention as obtaining documents for travel, employment authorization and granting nationality to their children born in Germany. Aside from being denied such benefits as obtaining travel documents, regularizing a period of stay or residence, obtaining authorization to work and obtaining fundamental human rights guarantees, Palestinians have also not received the benefit of UNHCR's protection mandate under the 1961 Convention. Thus, with the interplay of the various 'Palestinian exclusion clauses', the vast majority of Palestinian refugees and stateless persons find themselves without international legal protection – despite the widespread guarantees of the 1951 Refugee Convention, the 1954 Statelessness Convention, the 1961 Reduction of Statelessness Convention and the various mandates of the relevant United Nations organs.

A REINTERPRETATION OF THE REGIME APPLICABLE TO PALESTINIAN REFUGEES, AND THE IMPACT OF REINTERPRETATION OF THE SEARCH FOR DURABLE REFUGEE SOLUTIONS

According to the widespread interpretation of these instruments and the mandate of these agencies, Palestinian refugees are entitled to nothing more than assistance for their basic quotidian needs through the offices of UNRWA. For the most part, they are left outside the protection mandate of UNHCR,[54] the Refugee and Statelessness Conventions. Moreover, with UNCCP's protection mandate emasculated, they are left without protection mechanisms or guarantees to which all other refugees in the world are entitled.[55] Certain consequences flow from this standard interpretation of the Palestinian refugee regime. These include that no agency (since none has a viable protection mandate) is recognized as having the authority to intervene on behalf of Palestinian refugees to represent their interests in any international fora,[56] or to protect their human rights against infringement by states,[57] or to negotiate on their behalf to demand a just solution to their refugee situation.[58] In addition, since this interpretation assumes Palestinians are left outside the Refugee Convention regime as long as UNRWA continues to provide assistance, they are not eligible for the guarantees of that Convention in Arab states, including eligibility for absorption and legal residence.[59]

Since UNHCR claims not to have a mandate over Palestinians in areas where UNRWA assistance is offered, UNHCR also does not intervene to protect Palestinians through negotiated agreements with Arab states that are not Refugee Convention signatories. UNHCR has entered into scores of such 'memoranda of understanding' or 'memoranda of agreement' with non-Refugee Convention states to protect the rights of refugees and displaced persons and promote human rights guarantees in many areas of the world.[60] In non-Arab states (mostly European and North America), under the most prevalent interpretations of Article 1D, the majority of Palestinians who apply are not granted the basic rights required for Convention refugees, nor are they granted the right to remain, legally reside or permanently resettle as refugees or asylum seekers.[61] These states also fail to apply to Palestinians the protections of the two statelessness Conventions, such as travel documents, or nationality for Palestinian children born in their territories.

A final consequence of this application of the Palestinian refugee regime is that there is neither a representative authorized to take Palestinian refugee/stateless claims to international fora, nor is there a forum with jurisdiction over their claims of repatriation, compensation or restitution.[62]

There is now substantial evidence that the prevalent interpretation of these instruments and relevant agency mandates is incorrect. As this author has argued in more detail elsewhere, the history and purpose of Article 1D in the context of the creation of the Palestinian refugee problem indicates that the *ipso facto* language was intended to provide Palestinian refugees with continuity of protection under various organizations and instrumentalities.[63] Rather than interpreting Article 1D as an exclusion clause, it is more accurate to interpret it as a contingent *inclusion* clause,[64] or a provision that would include Palestinians under the Convention regime if certain contingencies occurred. Those contingencies were the cessation of either protection or assistance provided by the two UN agencies entrusted with those functions. This interpretation is the most consistent with the plain language, drafting history and applicable canons of treaty construction of the relevant provisions referred to above.[65]

Not all the issues raised by the language of the provision on its face can be addressed here. However, there are two main issues of note. First, the two sentences of Article 1D are inconsistent in their language. The first sentence excludes all Palestinians receiving 'protection or assistance'. The second sentence then includes Palestinians for whom such 'protection or assistance has ceased'. Thus, the language itself raises the question: Must Palestinians be receiving either protection or assistance from a UN agency, or must they be receiving neither of those benefits to be included under the Convention? In order to clarify this critical ambiguity, one must consult the drafting history of the provision and the purpose for which it was designed. Second, each word of the *ipso facto* clause of the second sentence has special meaning, particularly in relation to language used in other provisions of the Refugee Convention. The combination of the reference to 'persons' with the *ipso facto* phrase makes it clear that Palestinians, unlike other putative refugees, need not qualify as 'refugees' under the Convention definition to be eligible for its benefits.

The drafting history and purpose of Article 1D provide significant evidence of how that provision – and the related ones – should be interpreted. The *travaux préparatoires* of the Refugee Convention lead to two main conclusions: the United Nations was to guarantee a heightened regime of international protection and assistance to the Palestinians, and was to provide such a regime until it implemented the durable solution of their choice, which was return and compensation. Such an interpretation is grounded on two main factors discussed at length by the UN delegates concerned with the issue. First, the UN body recognized that it bore a large part of the responsibility for creating the refugee situation in the first place by way of General Assembly Resolution 181 (II) of November 1947, recommending partition of Palestine.[66] Second, the Palestinian refugee problem was to be resolved on the basis of a special formula, that of repatriation and compensation – on which there was complete consensus by all states but Israel[67] – rather than the formula commonly accepted for refugees at the time, which was third-state resettlement.[68] The consensus of the world body, as is evident from the drafting history of the Refugee Convention and related instruments, was that the Palestinian refugee situation required special attention because of the unique responsibility of the UN in creating it, and was of such urgency that it should not be subsumed under the existing refugee regime, but required a *heightened protection regime*.[69] The discussions in the drafting history of the 1951 Refugee Convention, the UNHCR Statute, and the Committee and Conference that drafted the 1954 Convention Relating to the Status of Stateless Persons provide ample evidence for such a conclusion.[70]

Viewing the instruments in this way completely alters the conclusions one draws to the questions raised here at the outset. As to the first question, that of what type of protection Palestinians are guaranteed under international law, as opposed to the assistance they receive as refugees, Article 1D in the context of a regime of heightened protection requires that they receive at a minimum the full panoply of protection rights as all other refugees in the world.[71] Appropriately analysed, the heightened regime set up two agencies with immediate mandates over the Palestinian refugees: UNRWA, which was to be the assistance agency, and UNCCP, which was to be the protection agency. Article 1D's function was to ensure that if for some reason either of these agencies failed to exercise its role before a final resolution of the refugee situation, that agency's function was to be transferred to the UNHCR, and the Refugee Convention would fully and immediately apply without preconditions to the Palestinian refugees.[72] That is what the 'protection *or* assistance' and the *ipso facto* language of Article 1D requires. The ramifications of this are quite clear: first, if UNCCP has failed to fulfil its protection mandate, that function must be fulfilled by UNHCR. UNHCR has for quite some time expanded its protection mandate over Palestinian refugees in some situations, in *de facto* if not explicit recognition of this requirement.[73] The protective duties of UNHCR spelled out in its Statute thus applicable to Palestinian refugees include:

1. promoting the conclusion and ratification of international conventions for the protection of refugees, supervising their application and proposing amendments thereto ...
2. assisting governmental and private efforts to promote voluntary repatriation or assimilation within new national communities;
3. promoting the admission of refugees, not excluding those in the most destitute categories, to territories of states;
4. endeavouring to obtain permission to transfer their assets and especially those necessary for resettlement.

Thus, UNHCR is fully empowered to oversee and implement the appropriate Conventions and Resolutions relating to the rights and enforcement of solutions for the Palestinian refugees.[74] Second, if the UNCCP ceases to function (as it has), triggering the alternative regime under Article 1D, then the Refugee Convention and all its guarantees towards refugees become fully applicable to the Palestinian refugees as well. These guarantees include rights to freedom of movement, access to courts, administrative assistance, rights in movable and immovable property, freedom of religion and housing rights, among many others.[75]

The second question flows logically from the first, that is, what is the extent to which Palestinian refugees can assert guarantees of *international human rights* protections? The answers to question one begin to answer this question as well: at an absolute minimum, all international human rights protections available to other refugees are equally available to Palestinian refugees. Although in theory all human rights protections are available to Palestinian refugees, without the appropriate representation to assert those rights, and a forum where such rights can be raised, such rights can simply not be enforced for this population.[76] In addition to general human rights protections, refugee law principles applicable to other refugee situations are applicable to the Palestinians as well. These principles include the guarantee that the options for permanent solutions available to refugees will be guided by each refugee's voluntary choice in determining which of the three main durable solutions s/he wishes to exercise for her/himself.[77] In fact, in delineating durable solutions, UNHCR describes them as voluntary repatriation, host country absorption, or third country resettlement.[78] Refugee law principles and precedents also include the right to claim restitution of property, and/or compensation for losses caused by the refugee-producing state.[79] In the last 20 years the principles on refugee return, restitution and compensation have been greatly strengthened by provisions in numerous negotiated settlements, such as the Comprehensive Plan of Action in the Indochinese refugee situation; the Bosnia-Serbia settlements in the Dayton Peace Accords; and the peace agreements on Guatemala and El Salvador.[80]

But the heightened refugee regime for Palestinians requires the application of an additional body of declaratory principles, that of the numerous UN Resolutions which are to be implemented in any final resolution of the refugee problem. The legal effect of these Resolutions, which include on the refugee issue UNGA Resolution 194 and UNGA Resolution 181, has been discussed at length elsewhere, but is relevant to the body of rights and principles applicable to the Palestinians as refugees.[81] The Resolutions establish a body of legal authority reflecting the consensus of the world community that in addition to standard refugee law and rights, the Palestinian case is to be resolved in accordance with a particular agreed upon solution coinciding with the desires of the refugees themselves, that of repatriation and compensation. Article 1D's language, 'without the position of such persons being definitively settled in accordance with the relevant resolutions adopted by the General Assembly of the United Nations ...' emphasizes that Palestinian refugees continue to be entitled to Refugee Convention benefits under the special scheme because their situation is not resolved unless the solution is consistent with the UN Resolutions. This also means that if Palestinian refugees obtain residence in host or resettlement states, their right to exercise the choice of repatriation or compensation is not necessarily compromised because their position has not been 'definitively settled in accordance with the relevant resolutions'.[82] The fact that UNGA Resolution 194 has been reaffirmed over 100 times is strong evidence of its authority as customary international law on the Palestinian refugee question.[83]

As to the third question, that of which entity or agency has the authority to represent the interests of Palestinian refugees, one must first recognize that the special regime requires that a separate agency be empowered with the capacity to stand in the shoes of the Palestinian refugees.[84] With that premise, if the UNCCP is not capable of carrying out such a mandate, the obvious choice – effectuating Article 1D – is the UNHCR. Indeed, UNHCR has a clear mandate to represent refugees in most international fora, in negotiations over durable solutions for refugees, and in bilateral or multilateral committees or task forces. The UNHCR does, in fact, play such a role in addition to the state or non-state representatives that are negotiating over conflicts in which substantial refugee populations are concerned. In the Palestinian case, the UNHCR should be involved along with the PLO in representing the refugees' interests. Moreover, the UNHCR could also take up the Palestinian refugees claims and rights to the United Nations General Assembly, to ECOSOC and to the International Court of Justice (ICJ). The ICJ has recognized in its Advisory Opinion on *Reparations for Injuries Suffered in the Service of the United Nations* that the United Nations has the capacity to bring an international claim against a state with a view to obtaining reparation for damage caused to its agent or to the 'interests of which it is the guardian'.[85] Under the theory of this Advisory Opinion, UNHCR, as a UN subsidiary body, has the right to represent the interests of refugees before that body. If the theory of the Reparations case is sound, the UNHCR should be authorized to raise at the World Court issues directly within its competence, as specified in its Statute. These include promoting voluntary repatriation and transferring the assets of the refugees. Article 38 of the Refugee Convention also provides that disputes over issues arising under the Convention may be taken to the ICJ. Until such time as a Palestinian government comes into being that represents a state, the UNHCR, under the strength of the *Reparations* opinion, should be authorized to take such claims on behalf of Palestinian refugees to the ICJ. State signatories to the Refugee Convention that have Palestinian residents in their territories may also take claims against Israel to the ICJ under Article 38, however none has taken such action to date.

A second option would be to expand UNRWA's role to include certain aspects of international refugee protection, such as acting as a representative of the refugees' interests in international negotiations. Such efforts have been made from time to time. For example, UNRWA has been present in an observer capacity in the committees established by the multilateral negotiations under the Madrid agreement.[86] However, Israel has vehemently protested any expansion of UNRWA's role,[87] and UNRWA currently does not have the capacity to represent the refugees by the terms of its own

Regulations.[88] UNRWA, moreover, cannot substitute for UNHCR's many years of rich experience in international refugee protection in all parts of the globe. One solution, which would combine the strengths of both agencies for the full benefit of Palestinian refugees would be for UNHCR to assume the protection functions under its Statute, and for UNRWA to continue its assistance function. That would be most consistent with the original regime of heightened refugee protection. Although General Assembly action may be necessary to effect such a regime, the UNHCR Statute and UNHCR practice already provide for such an option. Under Chapter II, para. 10 of the UNHCR Statute, the Agency may delegate and coordinate refugee assistance with other 'private and public' agencies. UNHCR coordinates assistance at a practical level with numerous agencies and organizations all over the world.

A final possibility for representing the refugees is to create separate bodies directly authorized by the refugees to carry out their wishes. Examples are the various Jewish groups that negotiated for restitution and compensation with Germany after the Second World War.[89] Another example is the World Organization of Jews from Arab Countries, which represents the interests of those individuals in their claims for restitution and compensation against the Arab states.[90]

The issue of representation of the Palestinian refugees is critical and urgent vis-à-vis the final status talks. The PLO, which is conducting the negotiations on behalf of Palestinians, represents the interests of all the stakeholders on the Palestinian side. Thus, in the Palestinian case individual refugee interests may be diametrically opposed to the collective rights of the Palestinians and to other stakeholders in the process. Under refugee law principles, the interests of refugees should be represented separately by a competent protection agency, along with the PLO, in the negotiations involving their long-term solutions. Under the heightened protection regime established for Palestinian refugees, the representation issue must immediately be resolved by way of one of the options suggested here.

As to the last issue, whether individual human rights recognized under international law can be protected and promoted in the Palestinian refugee case when such rights collide with collective rights, the Palestinian case appears unique in this regard. It is unique in that in no other refugee situation has the entire population been deprived of nationality as well as access to the entire territory comprising their former state. The UN Resolutions on the Palestine question follow two different tracks: initially, they focused on individual rights; and then, in the 1970s, the Resolutions called for a solution focusing on the collective right of self-determination of the Palestinian people.[91] Based on the premise that Palestinian refugees are entitled to benefit from the precedents established in other refugee situations, one can apply the formulae used in similar cases where both individual and collective rights are involved. In each such situation – Bosnia and Kosovo are prime examples – the collective rights to an independent entity or statehood were preserved, along with a mechanism for individual refugees to assert their claims to repatriate and obtain restitution and/or compensation.[92] Each of these situations involved the establishment of claims commissions as part of a negotiated settlement, but the right of the individual to assert his/her claim was preserved independently of the outcome of the self-determination issue.[93]

CONCLUSION

Interpreting Article 1D of the Refugee Convention and the provisions related to it in the UNHCR Statute, UNCCP Resolution and UNRWA Regulations accurately compels the conclusion that a heightened protection regime was intended – and indeed established – for Palestinian refugees. Although it is not possible to do more than summarize the bases for the conclusions drawn here, and their consequences for the Palestinian-Israeli final status talks on the issue of refugees, it is critical to assess the overall refugee law framework in which a final resolution of the Palestinian refugee question must be found. There is no evidence that a weakened protection system was ever envisaged for Palestinian refugees by the drafters of the relevant instruments. Moreover, there is no legal justification for denying Palestinian refugees the benefits of the existing refugee regime governing the rights of all other refugees worldwide. To be consistent with international refugee law principles and precedents, certain immediate issues must be addressed:

1. An agency or entity fully competent to represent the interests and further the claims of the refugees must be immediately empowered to do so, both in the context of the negotiations themselves and before international and other fora.

2. The alternative scheme of Article 1D must be recognized as affording Palestinian refugees full benefits under the Refugee Convention, including access to the right of temporary protection,[94] asylum and residence in whatever state they find themselves until they can exercise their rights of return, compensation and restitution, in accordance with the relevant UN Resolutions.

3. UNHCR, as the appropriately mandated agency, must immediately intervene with Israel and with other state signatories to the Refugee Convention and the two Statelessness Conventions in which Palestinian refugees are found to demand their protection as refugees and/or stateless persons. Such intervention is necessary to prevent further erosion of the refugees' human rights pending a final resolution of their status. This may include the agency utilizing the ICJ's advisory opinion to make claims before that body until there is a fully sovereign entity empowered to raise such claims on the refugees' behalf.

4. UNHCR or the agency chosen to represent the refugees should draft its own framework for durable solutions based on the appropriate UN

Resolutions on the question, and make clear to all stakeholders that an agreement not based on these Resolutions embodying the consensus of repatriation, restitution and compensation will not be acceptable to the refugees.

Refugee communities themselves need to become aware of the legal framework available to them in order to accurately assess options and possibilities for raising their own claims within and outside the context of negotiations. Only with such a framework can a just and durable solution to the Palestinian refugee situation be found.

NOTES

1. International human rights law applies to every individual human being, regardless of place and circumstance. The primary international human rights instruments developed after the Second World War comprise the Universal Declaration of Human Rights (UDHR) GA Resolution 217(A), UN GAOR, 3rd sess., UN Doc. A/810(1948); the International Covenant on Civil and Political Rights (ICCPR), opened for signature 19 December 1966, 999 UNTS 171 (entered into force 23 March 1976, adopted by the United States 8 September 1992); the International Covenant on Economic, Social and Cultural Rights (ICESCR), opened for signature 19 December 1966, 993 UNTS 3 (entered into force 3 January 1976), 6 ILM 360 (1967). The provisions of these instruments, as well as others, apply to Palestinian refugees and Palestinians in general as individuals. Whether the provisions of the instruments are binding against a state in any particular situation depends on a number of complex factors, which cannot be addressed here.

2. Under the treaty analysis set out in the 1969 Vienna Convention on the Law of Treaties, Article 31(1), 'A treaty shall be interpreted in good faith in accordance with the ordinary meaning to be given to the terms of the treaty in their context and in light of its object and purpose.' Vienna Convention on the Law of Treaties, 22 May 1969, Article 31(1), 1155 UNTS 331, 8 ILM 679. For a detailed treaty interpretation of the provisions affecting Palestinian refugees discussed here, see Susan M. Akram and Guy Goodwin-Gill, 'US Department of Justice, Executive Office for Immigration Review, *Brief Amicus Curiae*', in 11 *Palestine Yearbook of International Law*, pp. 45–81.

3. Convention Relating to the Status of Refugees (Refugee Convention), 28 July 1951, 189 UNTS 137.

4. Protocol Relating to the Status of Refugees (Refugee Protocol), 31 January 1967, 606 UNTS 267.

5. Convention Relating to the Status of Stateless Persons (1954 Statelessness Convention), 28 September 1954, 360 UNTS 117.

6. Convention on the Reduction of Statelessness (1961 Statelessness Convention), 30 August 1961, 989 UNTS 175 (entered into force 13 December 1975).

7. The UNCCP was created by GA Resolution 194(III), UN Doc. A/810(1948).

8. GA Resolution 428(V), Annex: Statute of the Office of the United Nations High Commissioner for Refugees, 5 UN GAOR Supp. No. 20, UN Doc. A/1775 (1950).

9. GA Resolution 302(IV) of 8 December 1949 established the UNRWA under Article 22 of the UN Charter, which authorizes the General Assembly to establish subsidiary organs to carry out its functions.

10. The origins of the Palestinian refugee problem can be traced to the Zionist programme of creating a 'homeland' for Jews in Palestine primarily through expulsion and transfer of the native Palestinian population. See Nur Masalha, *Expulsion of the Palestinians: The Concept of 'Transfer' in Zionist Political Thought, 1882–1948* (Washington, DC: Institute of Palestine Studies, 1992); and Nur Masalha, *A Land without a People: Israel, Transfer and the Palestinians 1949–96* (London: Faber and Faber, 1997). The Zionist programme was ostensibly legitimized by the UN recommendation to partition historic Palestine into two states, one Jewish and one Arab. GA Resolution 181, UN GAOR, 1st sess, UN Doc. A/64 (1946). The Jewish state was to be established in 56 per cent of the territory, for a Jewish population comprising less than one third of the population and owning no more than 7 per cent of the land in Palestine. The Arab state, which was to receive 44 per cent of the land, was to be the homeland of the Palestinians who represented more than 80 per cent of the indigenous population of Palestine, and owned more than 93 per cent of the land. Edward W. Said, *The Question of Palestine* (2nd edition, New York: Vintage Books, 1992). On land ownership, see Walter Lehn, *The Jewish National Fund* (London: Kegan Paul International, 1988); *A Survey of Palestine* (London: Her Majesty's Stationery Office, Prepared in December 1945 and January 1946) reprinted by Institute of Palestine Studies (Washington, DC, 1991). When war broke out between the Arab and Jewish communities, the disorganized and primarily unarmed Palestinian Arab population was expelled in huge numbers by the Zionist militias through a combination of terror tactics, a series of massacres and forced expulsion at gunpoint. See Masalha, *A Land without a People*, and Ilan Pappe, *The Making of The Arab–Israeli Conflict, 1947–51* (London: I.B. Taurus, 1992). Although the exact numbers of Palestinians who became refugees due to the conflict in 1948 is disputed, the best-documented figures are between 750,000 and 800,000 refugees. See Janet Abu-Lughod, 'The Demographic Transformation of Palestine', in Ibrahim Abu-Lughod (ed.), *The Transformation of Palestine 1953–61* (Evanston, Ill: Northwestern University Press, 1971). In order to ensure that the refugees would not be able to return, the Zionists razed completely or partially destroyed approximately 530 Palestinian villages, dynamiting homes (at times with occupants still inside), destroying crops and declaring Palestinian towns and villages 'closed military areas' to justify shooting any Palestinians who sought to return. On depopulated villages, see Salman Abu-Sitta, *The Palestinian Nakba 1948, Register of the Depopulated Localities in Palestine* (London: The Palestinian Return Centre, 1998). See also Walid Khalidi (ed.), *All That Remains, The Palestinian Villages Occupied and Depopulated by Israel in 1948* (Washington, DC: Institute of Palestine Studies, 1992). On Israel's 'shoot to kill' policies to prevent return, see Benny Morris, *Israel's Border Wars, 1949–56* (Oxford: Clarendon Press, 1997).

11. Palestinian citizens of Israel may also be displaced persons with distinct protection needs similar to those of other internally displaced people, and which are of concern to the international community. The legal issues related to internally displaced Palestinian who are citizens of Israel cannot be addressed in detail in this chapter.

12. The Refugee Convention and Protocol are among the most widely adopted of all international human rights instruments. As of December 1999, there are 134 state parties to one or the other. Due to the broad reach of the Refugee Convention and Protocol, Palestinian refugees are particularly affected by whether the Convention and Protocol apply to them or exclude them from those instruments' benefits. Despite the widespread acceptance of the Refugee Convention and Protocol, few Arab states are signatories to one or the other. Only Algeria, Egypt, Morocco, Sudan, Tunisia and Yemen are parties to the Convention and Protocol. Israel is a party to both, but has never passed implementing legislation in its domestic law. Jordan, Lebanon and Syria – the countries with the largest Palestinian refugee populations – are parties to neither the Convention nor Protocol. 1 Multilateral Treaties Deposited with the Secretary-General 259–60, 283–84, UN Doc. ST/LEG/SER.E/18 (2000).

13. It is important to note that, although the Refugee Convention definition has the most widespread acceptance among states, there are two other refugee definitions which have increasing relevance to the protection of refugees. Both the Organization of African Unity (OAU) 1969 Convention and the 1984 Cartagena Declaration on Refugees have much broader definitions of 'refugee' than the Refugee Convention and Protocol. Organization of African Unity, Convention on the Specific Aspects of Refugee Problems in Africa, opened for signature 10 September 1969, 1000 UNTS 46 (entered into force 20 June 1974); 1984 Cartagena Declaration on Refugees, 22 November 1984, reprinted in Annual Report of the Inter-American Commission on Human Rights, OAS Doc. OEA/Ser.L/V/II.66/doc.10, rev. 1 (1984–85). The UNHCR also has an expanded mandate for non-Convention refugees, including those covered by the broader African and Latin American definitions, under successive General Assembly Resolutions.

14. Refugee Convention Article 33.1 states: 'No Contracting State shall expel or return (*"refouler"*) a refugee in any manner whatsoever to the frontiers of territories where his life or freedom would be threatened on account of his race religion, nationality, membership of a particular social group or political opinion.' There is much debate about the parameters of the obligation of *non-refoulement* towards persons fleeing situations not covered by the Refugee Convention definition, for example, persons fleeing armed conflict, widespread violations of human rights, or other grave emergencies. Despite the debate about its reach, *non-refoulement* is the most fundamental principle of refugee law and practice, and is remarkably widely respected by states. Guy Goodwin-Gill, *The Refugee in International Law* (2nd edition, 1996), pp. 167–71; Deborah Perluss and Joan F. Hartman, 'Temporary Refuge: Emergence of a Customary Norm', 26 *Virginia Journal of International Law* (1986), p. 551. The UNHCR observed in its 1985 report to the General Assembly that the principle of *non-refoulement* had become a peremptory norm of international law. *Report of the UNHCR*, paras. 22–3, UN Doc. E/1985/62 (1985).

15. There are two separate analyses required by the Refugee Convention's Article 1A(2) definition, one applying to persons having a nationality, and a separate one applying to stateless persons. Persons who have a nationality must prove a well-founded fear from the state of which they are a national; for persons who are stateless, the well-founded fear must be from the state of 'former habitual residence'. This has particular significance for Pales-

tinians, for if the Article 1A(2) definition is applied to them, they must prove a well-founded fear from the state of last residence, which is far more difficult than showing an 'inability' to return to their original homes due to ongoing or past persecution by Israel. The manner in which most Refugee Convention states apply this analysis to Palestinians results in the majority being denied recognition as refugees.

16. Comments of the Representative of Lebanon, UN GAOR 5th sess., 3rd comm., 328th mtg., para. 47.

17. Refugee Convention, at Article 1(D).

18. For the drafting history of Article 1D and the related provisions, and the intentions of the drafters in drawing them up, see Alex Takkenberg and Christopher L. Tahbaz (eds), *The Collected Travaux Préparatoires of the 1951 Geneva Convention Relating to the Status of Refugees*, 3 vols (Amsterdam: Dutch Refugee Council, under the auspices of the European Legal Network on Asylum, 1989). See also, Atle Grahl-Madsen, *The Status of Refugees in International Law* (Leiden: Sijthoff, 1966); and Paul Weis (ed.), *The Refugee Convention, 1951* (Cambridge: Cambridge University Press 1995).

19. GA Resolution 194(III).

20. See UNRWA's purposes, described in its founding resolution, GA Resolution 302(IV), UN Doc. A/1251 at 23 (1949). For its record of providing assistance to Palestine refugees, see *A Brief History of UNRWA, 1950–1962*, Information Paper No. I (Beirut, 1962); UNRWA, *A Brief History, 1950–1982* (Vienna, 1983); UNRWA, *UNRWA: Past, Present and Future* (Vienna, 1986); UNRWA, *UNRWA 1950–1990: Serving Palestine Refugees* (Vienna, 1990); UNRWA, *The Long Journey: Palestine Refugees and UNRWA* (Vienna, 1995).

21. The UNHCR's functions of protection are detailed in its Statute, GA Resolution 428(V), UN GAOR, 5th sess., para. 8, UN Doc. A/1775(1950).

22. The only legal definition of 'Palestine refugee' is that included in the UNRWA Regulations. The working definition of 'Palestine refugee' which operated from 1952 until 1993 was: 'A Palestine refugee is a person whose normal residence was Palestine for a minimum period of two years preceding the outbreak of the conflict in 1948 and who, as a result of this conflict, has lost both his home and his means of livelihood ... and who is in need.' Operational Instruction No. 104, 18 February 1952. In 1993, this definition was amended in the Consolidated Registration Instructions, 1 January 1993, para. 2.13: '[Palestine refugee] shall mean any person whose normal place of residence was Palestine during the period 1 June 1946 to 15 May 1948 and who lost both home and means of livelihood as a result of the 1948 conflict.' It is important to note that the UNRWA definition relates directly to UNRWA's mandate of providing material assistance – food, clothing, shelter – to the refugees. Although reference to 'Palestinian refugees' by the UN bodies concerned with the problem was to the relief definition, it was never formally adopted as a general legal definition of a Palestine refugee for purposes of international protection.

23. GA Resolution 181(II), UN GAOR, 2nd sess., UN Doc. A/519(1947).

24. GA Resolution 194(III), UN Doc. A/810, at 21(1948). The resolution was adopted with 35 votes in favour, 10 abstentions and 15 against, including Egypt, Iraq, Lebanon, Saudi Arabia, Syria and Yemen. GA Resolution 194(III) states, in relevant part: 'The General Assembly ... 2. *Establishes* a Conciliation Commission consisting of three States Members of the United

Nations which shall have the following functions: a) To assume ... the functions given to the United Nations Mediator on Palestine by resolution 186(S-2) of the General Assembly of 14 May 1948; b) To carry out the specific functions and directives given to it by the present resolution and such additional functions and directives as may be given to it by the General Assembly or by the Security Council; c) To undertake, upon the request of the Security Council, any of the functions now assigned to the United Nations Mediator on Palestine or to the United Nations Truce Commission by resolutions of the Security Council ...' Among the functions assigned to the UN Mediator on Palestine, Count Folk Bernadotte, was implementation of the 'right of repatriation' of the refugees, as stated in paragraph 11 of Resolution 194(II).

25. Ibid., paras. 2–4.
26. Ibid., para. 6.
27. Ibid., para. 11.
28. At the most basic level, international refugee protection provided by UNHCR is two-fold: the direct protection of refugees' human rights on a day-to-day basis, and the search and implementation of durable solutions for refugees from the available choices of voluntary repatriation, resettlement or host country absorption. See Goodwin-Gill, *The Refugee in International Law*, pp. 212ff. The UNCCP likewise was to 'facilitate the repatriation, resettlement and economic and social rehabilitation of the refugees and the payment of compensation' and, through UNGA Resolution 394(V), to 'continue consultations with the parties concerned regarding measures for the protection of the rights, property and interests of the refugees'. In short, the UNCCP was given both the direct protection functions (protecting the refugees' rights and interests) and the function for implementing durable solutions ('facilitate repatriation, resettlement and ... rehabilitation'). For the discussions in the General Assembly of the functions of the UNCCP and the consensus on the protections it would provide, see the records of the Third Session of the General Assembly, UN GAOR, 1st Comm., 3rd sess., 142nd–236th mtg. at 768–933, UN Doc. A/C.1/SR.142–236 (1948). Even the delegate of the 'Provisional Government of Israel' understood that the Conciliation Commission 'would be the instrument of the United Nations in the settlement of the political dispute in Palestine.' Ibid., 142nd–236th mtg. at 827.
29. See GA Resolution 186, UN GAOR, 2nd sess., Supp. no. 2. UN Doc. A/555 (1948) (authorizing the functions of the United Nations Mediator on Palestine); GA Resolution 212(III) of 19 November 1949 (establishing the United Nations Relief for Palestine Refugees); GA Resolution 194(III), UN Doc. A/810 (1948)(establishing the UNCCP); GA Resolution 302(IV), UN Doc. A/1251 (1949) (establishing UNRWA 'without prejudice to the provisions of paragraph 11 of General Assembly Resolution 194(III) ...').
30. Although the UN Resolutions on the subject reflect a consensus on the appropriate durable solution to be implemented for this refugee population, the Resolutions themselves simply embody international legal principles which were already binding on states that required persons to be able to return to their places of origin, and which prohibited mass expulsion of persons, particularly on religious, national, ethnic or political opinion grounds. For detailed discussions supporting the internationally grounded right of return of Palestinian refugees to their 'places of origin', see W.T. Mallison and S. Mallison, 'The Right of Return', 9 *Journal of Palestine Studies*

(1980) p. 125; John Quigley, 'Family Reunion and the Right to Return to Occupied Territory', 6 *Georgetown Immigration Law Journal* (1992), p. 223; *The Right of Return of the Palestinian People*, UN Doc. ST/SG/SER.F/2 (1978); Kathleen Lawand, 'The Right to Return of Palestinians under International Law', 8 *International Journal of Refugee Law* (1996), p. 533. For commentators refuting that Palestinians have a right of return to their places of origin, see Kurt Rene Radley, 'The Palestinian Refugees: The Right to Return in International Law', 72 *American Journal of International Law* (1978), pp. 586, 590–5; Ruth Lapidoth, 'The Right of Return in International Law, with Special Reference to the Palestinian Refugees', 16 *Israel Yearbook of Human Rights* (1986). p. 103; Paul Weis, 'The Middle East', in K. Vasak and S. Liskofsky (eds), *The Right to Leave and to Return*, Papers and Recommendations of the International Colloquium Held in Uppsala, Sweden, 19–20 June 1972 (Ann Arbor: The American Jewish Committee, 1976).

31.   For Israel's position refusing the repatriation of Palestinian refugees in the period following the 1948 conflict, see David P. Forsythe, *United Nations Peacemaking: the Conciliation Commission for Palestine* (Baltimore: Johns Hopkins University Press, 1972), pp. 70–83; see also Benny Morris, *The Birth of the Palestinian Refugee Problem* (Cambridge: Cambridge University Press, 1987), pp. 132–96; Sami Hadawi, *Bitter Harvest: A Modern History of Palestine* (fourth edition, New York: Olive Branch Press, 1991), pp. 127–33.

32.   In its fifth session in 1950, the General Assembly passed Resolution 394(V) concerning the functions of the UNCCP. The relevant portions of that Resolution acknowledge 'that the repatriation, resettlement, economic and social rehabilitation of the refugees and the payment of compensation have not been effected' and that the UNCCP should focus on 'such arrangements as it may consider necessary for the assessment and payment of compensation in pursuance of paragraph 11 of [GA Resolution 194(III)] ...; (b) Work out such arrangements as may be practical for the implementation of the other objectives of paragraph 11 ... (c) Continue consultations with the parties concerned regarding measures for the protection of the rights, property and interests of the refugees.' There is some disagreement concerning whether UNGA Resolution 394(V) reduced or augmented UNCCP's existing mandate. The issue is irrelevant to the applicability of Article 1D, as the critical language of the first sentence of 1D refers to 'persons who are at present receiving ... protection or assistance', and the language of the second sentence refers to 'when such protection or assistance has ceased for any reason'. Thus, it is the UNCCP's failure to provide protection to Palestinian refugees for any reason that triggers the application of that provision. In light of Resolution 394, the UNCCP itself took the position that it was no longer required to apply the 'principled basis used up to that time' to solve the refugee problem, but that it was to concentrate on practicalities, specifically documenting and collecting property records. UN Doc. A/AC.25/W.82/Rev. 1 at 21 (1951). See Forsythe, *United Nations Peacemaking*, p. 84.

33.   In the sixth session of the General Assembly, a significantly reduced budget was passed for the UNCCP. The budget simply reflected the UNCCP's new phase as an office for record collection, and incorporated sufficient funds for the UNCCP's operations in New York with no major expenditures to sustain the broader protection activities vis-à-vis the refugees. UN GAOR, 6th sess., Annex, Agenda Item 24(a) at 1, UN Doc. A/2072 (1952).

34. The legislation of Great Britain – as Mandatory power in Palestine under League of Nations' auspices – regulated Palestinian nationality/citizenship status. The Palestine Citizenship Order of 1925–41 conferred 'Palestinian citizenship', and the British-administered government of Palestine issued passports stamped 'Palestinian citizen under Article One or Three of the Palestinian Citizenship Order, 1925–41'. Palestinian Citizenship Order in Council, 1925, S.R.& O., no. 25. See Anis Kassim, 'Legal Systems and Developments in Palestine', 1 *Palestine Yearbook of International Law* (1984), p. 19 (concerning laws under British occupation of Palestine).

35. As far as Israeli legislation concerning nationality, there was none until 1952. The 1952 Nationality Law retroactively repealed the Palestine Citizenship Orders, and provided: 1) that every Jewish immigrant was automatically entitled to Israeli nationality [under the Law of Return]; and 2) former Palestinians of Arab origin were eligible for Israeli nationality under a series of restrictive conditions. 1952 Nationality Law, 5712/1952, 93 *Official Gazette* 22 (1952). The conditions were such that few Palestinians were eligible for citizenship. The vast majority of Palestinians who fled or were forced from their homes and lands became stateless both *de jure* and *de facto*. On the effect of state succession to this population, see note 38 below.

36. Under human rights law principles, a state's actions in stripping a particular category of inhabitants of their nationality on the basis of race, religion or political opinion is unequivocally prohibited. On the prohibition of expulsion of individuals and groups, see generally, J. M. Henckaerts, *Mass Expulsion in Modern International Law and Practice* (The Hague: Martinus Nijhoff Publishers, 1995); Alfred de Zayas, 'The Right to One's Homeland, Ethnic Cleansing, and the International Criminal Tribunal for the Former Yugoslavia', 6 *Criminal Law Forum* (1995), p. 257; Alfred de Zayas, 'The Illegality of Population Transfers and the Application of Emerging International Norms in the Palestinian Context', 7 *Palestine Yearbook of International Law* (1990/91), p. 17; Alfred de Zayas, 'Population, Expulsion and Transfer', in Rudolf Bernhardt (ed.), 8 *Encyclopedia of Public International Law* (Amsterdam: Elsevier Science Publishers B.V., 1985); V.R. Krishna Iyer, 'Mass Expulsion as Violation of Human Rights', 13 *Indian Journal of International Law* (1973), p. 169.

37. The four Geneva Conventions of 1949, and particularly the Fourth Convention, have explicit provisions affirming the right of repatriation to persons forced from their homes by hostilities. Geneva Conventions of 1949, 6 UST 3114, TIAS No. 3362, 75 UNTS 31; 6 UST 3217, TIAS No. 3363, 75 UNTS 85; 6 UST 3316, TIAS No. 3364, 75 UNTS 135; 6 UST 3516, TIAS No. 3365, 75 UNTS 287. The Fourth Geneva Convention also strictly prohibits 'forcible transfers as well as deportations of protected persons from occupied territory'. Geneva Convention Relative to the Protection of Civilian Persons in Time of War, 12 August 1949, Article 49(1), 75 UNTS 287.

38. The weight of international opinion finds a presumption that 'the population follows the change of sovereignty in matters of nationality'. See Ian Brownlie, *Principles of Public International Law* (fourth edition, Oxford: Clarendon Press, 1990), p. 661. Consistent with this presumption, General Assembly Resolution A/RES/55/153 provides: 'persons concerned [nationals of predecessor state] having their habitual residence in the territory affected by the succession of States are presumed to acquire the nationality of the successor state on the date of such succession'. (General Assembly Resolution A/RES/55/153, 12 December 2000, adopting

'Articles on Nationality of Natural Persons in Relation to the Succession of States, Article 5.)

39. The 1954 Statelessness Convention.

40. The International Law Commission (ILC) initially drew up a Draft Convention on the Elimination of Future Statelessness and a Draft Convention on the Reduction of Future Statelessness, which were considered by a UN Conference of Plenipotentiaries in Geneva. The Conference adopted a Convention on the Reduction of Statelessness on 28 August 1961. 1961 Statelessness Convention.

41. Stateless persons who are also refugees are covered by the Refugee Convention, and the Article 1A(2) definition has a separate analysis for refugees who are stateless. However, as described in this chapter, most Palestinians are excluded from the benefits of the Refugee Convention, or the Article 1A(2) analysis for stateless refugee is applied to them rather than the second sentence of Article 1D, which results in widespread loss or denial of legal protection. Thus, Palestinians may not be recognized as 'refugees' either under Article 1D or under Article 1A(2), but they would be so recognized if the appropriate definition were applied, as argued in this chapter.

42. Palestinian residents of the West Bank and Gaza who have remained in their places of origin are not refugees, whether in the sense of the Refugee Convention, or in the *de facto* sense used by the drafters of Article 1D. Unless they have taken Israeli citizenship – as many East Jerusalemites have done – they are not 'nationals of any state', as there is no recognized state of Palestine to date. They are thus stateless, but not refugees. In addition, Palestinians who are recognized by the government of a country in which they reside as having the rights and obligations of a national may be excluded from consideration as refugees under the Refugee Convention. Refugee Convention, see note 3, at Article 1E. Such persons may not be refugees, but remain stateless. Palestinians who have acquired both a new nationality and the protection of the new state are no longer considered refugees, and are also not stateless under the terms of the two statelessness Conventions. Refugee Convention, see note 3, at Article 1C(3); 1954 Statelessness Convention, at Article 1. However, whether Palestinians who are Jordanian citizens have both a new nationality and protection is not a simple question in light of the many actions Jordan has taken to strip Palestinians of their passports, to issue them temporary passports and to deny groups or categories of Palestinians fundamental human rights and freedoms. It is important to note that whether or not a Palestinian remains a refugee or stateless person does not necessarily affect his/her right to return to his place of origin or to obtain restitution and compensation of his refugee property within the 1948 borders.

43. As of December 1999, 42 states are party to the 1954 Statelessness Convention. Of the Arab states, only Algeria, Libya and Tunisia are parties. Israel is a party to the Convention. See note 12, at 274. Moreover, as of December 1999, only 19 states have ratified the 1961 Convention on Statelessness; of those only one is an Arab state – Libya. Israel is a signatory, but has not ratified the Convention. See note 12, at 281.

44. Statelessness Convention, see note 5, at Article 1.

45. Statelessness Convention, see note 6, at Article 1.

46. See Goodwin-Gill, *The Refugee in International Law*, pp. 243–6.

47. The 1954 Statelessness Convention provides benefits very similar to those guaranteed under the Refugee Convention. It also requires state parties to grant travel documents to stateless persons. Unlike the Refugee Convention, however, the 1954 Statelessness Convention does not give states discretion to penalize persons covered by its terms for entering or staying unlawfully in their territories. Nor does it set up an international body, such as the UNHCR, to protect stateless persons or to monitor compliance with its terms.

48. Preamble, 1961 Statelessness Convention, see note 6.

49. GA Resolution 3274, UN GAOR, 29th sess., Agenda Item 99, UN Doc. A/RES/3274 (XXIX) (1975). This mandate was extended indefinitely by GA Resolution 31/36, UN GAOR, 31st Sess., Agenda item 78, UN Doc. A/RES/31/36 (1976).

50. Batchelor, 'Stateless Persons: Some Gaps in International Protection', 7 *International Journal of Refugee Law* (1995), pp. 232, 235.

51. Statelessness Convention, see note 5, at Article 1, para. 2(i).

52. As of December 1999, European state parties to the 1954 Statelessness Convention are Belgium, Bosnia and Herzegovina, Croatia, Denmark, Finland, France, Macedonia, Germany, Greece, Holy See, Ireland, Italy, Liechtenstein, Luxembourg, the Netherlands, Norway, Sweden, Switzerland, the United Kingdom and Yugoslavia. European state parties to the 1961 Statelessness Convention are Austria, Bosnia and Herzegovina, Denmark, France, Germany, Ireland, Latvia, the Netherlands, Norway, Sweden and the United Kingdom. See note 12, at p. 274.

53. Lex Takkenberg, *The Status of Palestinian Refugees in International Law* (Oxford: Clarendon Press, 1998), p. 181; also discussed in Akram and Goodwin-Gill, 'US Department of Justice'.

54. UNHCR's position concerning whether it has a protection mandate over Palestinian refugees has been inconsistent. The Agency's official position is found in the Office of the United Nations High Commissioner for Refugees, *Handbook on Procedures and Criteria for Determining Refugee Status* (Geneva, 1992), paras 142–3 (1992), in which it claims that it does not have a protection mandate over Palestinian refugees in the areas where UNRWA's assistance is provided. Thus, UNHCR does not officially offer protection to Palestinians in the Arab states where UNRWA operates: Lebanon, Syria, Jordan, the West Bank, Gaza and Egypt. Of course, it is in these states where the lack of legal protection has had the most severe consequences for Palestinian refugees. UNHCR's interpretation of its limited protection mandate is flawed on a number of grounds, not only on the basis of this author's arguments that Palestinian refugees were intended to receive both protection and assistance at all times. Other commentators criticize aspects of UNHCR's official position. See Atle Grahl-Madsen, *The Status of Refugees in International Law* (1966); James Hathaway, *The Law of Refugee Status* (Toronto: Butterworths, 1991), p. 208; and Takkenberg, *The Status of Palestinian Refugees*, p. 101. Even with regard to countries outside UNRWA's areas of operations, in which UNHCR claims to have a protection mandate over Palestinian refugees, its protection activities and interpretation of its role towards Palestinian refugees has been inconsistent. This inconsistent role is only partly explained by the differing state interpretations of Article 1D and Article 1A (2) of the Refugee Convention with respect to Palestinian refugees. For a brief description of UNHCR's differing

interpretations and applications of its authority towards Palestinians, *see* Takkenberg, *The Status of Palestinian Refugees*, pp. 304–9.

55.   Palestinians have not only been without the basic protection mechanisms and activities engaged in by UNHCR, but they have also been precluded from the benefits of the expanded role taken on by UNHCR pursuant to evolving concepts of international protection. For example, UNHCR has continuously expanded its mandate over persons who are not strictly considered Convention refugees: displaced persons; returnees; persons who fall within the broader refugee definitions of the OAU Convention and Cartagena Declaration. Beginning in 1957, the UNGA has authorized the UNHCR to assist refugees who did not fall under the statutory definition, but were 'of concern to the international community'. See GA Resolution 1167 (XII), 12 UN GAOR Supp. (No. 18), UN Doc. A/3805 (1957); GA Resolution 1286(XIII)(1958); GA Resolution 1389(XVI)(1959), GA Resolution 1500(XV)(1960). The UNGA then developed the concept of 'good offices' and finally, 'refugees of concern' as a general term to extend UNHCR's mandate over other non-Convention refugees, without the necessity of a UN resolution addressing a specific refugee situation. Since the mid-1970s the UNGA has referred to and commended the UNHCR's activities towards 'refugees and displaced persons of concern' to the Agency. ECOSOC and the General Assembly have passed a number of resolutions authorizing UNHCR to extend its 'good offices' towards displaced persons and others 'of concern'. See, for example, ECOSOC Resolutions 1655(LII), 1 June 1972; 1705(LII), 27 July 1972; 1741(LIV), 4 May 1973; 1799(LV), 30 July 1973; 1877(LVII), 16 July 1974. See GA Resolutions 2958(XXVII), 12 December 1972; 3271(XXIX), 10 December 1974; 3454(XXX), 9 December 1975. Moreover, refugees have benefited from the expanded concepts of human rights embodied in more recent international conventions, and in mechanisms to enforce those rights.

56.   UNHCR has a designated 'international personality'. It is a subsidiary of the UN General Assembly, and thus has distinct international rights and duties, as well as recognition as a player in the international arena. UNHCR has been entrusted with the express function of providing international protection to refugees. 'The "effective discharge" of this function evidently requires capacity to assert claims on behalf of individuals and groups falling within the competence of the Office'. Goodwin-Gill, *The Refugee in International Law*, p. 217, citing the *Reparations Case*, 1949 ICJ 174 at 180. The UNHCR has never raised a claim to the ICJ under this authority, but its ability to intervene on refugees' behalf in directly negotiating with states for their welfare and in the search for durable solutions has possibly brought more practical results. Palestinian refugees have not benefited from either strategy.

57.   One of UNHCR's major activities is direct intervention with states to protect the day-to-day rights of refugees. UNHCR and UNRWA have periodically sought to intervene with governments concerned in situations where Palestinian refugees' lives and fundamental rights have been violated. These efforts have had negligible results due to the perceived limitations on the respective mandates of the agencies. For a good review of UNHCR and UNRWA's efforts towards protecting Palestinian refugees, see Takkenberg, *The Status of Palestinian Refugees in International Law*, pp. 278–309.

58.   UNHCR has played a major role in numerous negotiated resolutions of mass refugee crises, including the Comprehensive Plan of Action (CPA)

concerning Indochinese refugees; the Declaration and Comprehensive Plan of Action in Favour of Central American Refugees, Returnees and Displaced Persons (CIREFCA); and the Dayton Peace Agreement concerning Bosnia-Herzegovina. On the CPA, see United Nations High Commissioner for Refugees, *The State of the World's Refugees: The Challenge of Protection* (Harmondsworth: Penguin Books, 1993), pp. 26–9, 117–20; see also 'Focus on the Comprehensive Plan of Action', 5 *International Journal of Refugee Law* (1993), p. 507. On CIREFCA, see United Nations High Commissioner for Refugees, 'Consolidating Peace in Central America through an Inter-Agency Approach to Longer-Term Needs of the Uprooted'. *Report on the Conclusion of the CIREFCA Process*, UN Doc. A/AC.96/831 (31 August 1994); see also Hector Gros Espiell et al., 'Principles and Criteria for the Protection of and Assistance to Central American Refugees, Returnees, and Displaced Persons in Central America', 2 *International Journal of Refugee Law* (1990), p. 83. On the Dayton Agreement, see United Nations High Commissioner for Refugees, *The State of the World's Refugees 1997–1998: A Humanitarian Agenda* (New York: Oxford University Press, 1997–98), pp. 170–1.

59. In the Arab states there has been a long-standing consensus that the solution to the Palestinian refugee problem is repatriation to their homes and lands. As such, a series of agreements and resolutions bound Arab host countries to give Palestinian refugees the right to remain in their territories with only temporary status. For the relevant resolutions of the Arab states, see LASC Resolution 424, 13 September 1952; LASC Resolution 524, 9 April 1953; LASC Resolution 714, 27 January 1954. One of the most important documents on the consensus of the Arab states towards Palestinian refugees is the 'Casablanca Protocol' – the Protocol on the Treatment of Palestinians in the Arab States, 11 September 1965. Aside from the Arab states' consensus that Palestinians were not to be granted permanent status, the more critical focus is on the refugees themselves, who have persistently declared their desire and right to repatriate to their homes and lands. See ESM Report, UN Doc. A/AC.25/6 (1949); Bernadotte report, UN SCOR, 3rd sess., Supp., at 146–7, UN Doc. S/955 (1948). This author has argued that in light of repatriation being the appropriate durable solution for Palestinian refugees, an interim measure that would provide Palestinian refugees with adequate legal protection yet not compromise their desired solution is the status of *temporary protection*. See Susan M. Akram, Badil, Brief No. 4, *Temporary Protection and its Applicability to the Palestinian Refugee* Case (Bethlehem, West Bank, June 2000).

60. See generally, United Nations High Commissioner for Refugees, *The State of the World's Refugees* (1995).

61. There are many differing interpretations of the applicability of Article 1D and/or Article 1A(2) to Palestinian refugees in the jurisprudence of state parties to the Refugee Convention. This author and her students examined the jurisprudence of 11 states concerning their application of the Refugee Convention towards Palestinians. Although the jurisprudence cannot be reviewed in detail here, some general observations can be made. A number of states have not incorporated Article 1D into their domestic refugee legislation at all, and hence consider requests for determination of refugee status by Palestinians exclusively under Article 1A(2). Canada, the United States, Austria and Switzerland are in this category. Another group of states, while acknowledging the applicability of Article 1D, interpret it to

refer back to Article 1A(2) for determining a Palestinian's qualification for refugee status. The Federal Republic of Germany and the Netherlands apply such an analysis. Among and even within those states that apply or discuss Article 1D, there are discrepancies. Some interpret it as meaning that any Palestinian refugee outside the UNRWA areas is eligible for consideration under Article 1A; others interpret it as meaning that even if a Palestinian finds himself outside UNRWA jurisdiction, as long as he can theoretically avail himself of UNRWA assistance, he is precluded from Convention coverage. For a detailed discussion of the jurisprudence examined by this author, see Akram and Goodwin-Gill. 'US Department of Justice'.

62. Israel's domestic laws preclude Palestinian claims for return and restitution. Moreover, Israel has, through a series of legal mechanisms, effectively insulated itself from such claims in most international fora. Although Palestinians may make claims for compensation for Israel's expropriation of Palestinian refugee property, such claims are limited by Israeli law to no more than 1950 value. For a short description of Israel's legal insulation from Palestinian restitution and compensation claims, see Susan M. Akram, *Palestinian Refugee Rights: Part I, Failure under International Law*, Information Brief No. 40 (Washington, DC: The Center for Policy Analysis on Palestine, 28 July 2000) and *Palestinian Refugee Rights: Part II, Israel's Legal Maneuvers*, Information Brief No. 41 (Washington, DC: The Center for Policy Analysis on Palestine, 2000).

63. Goodwin-Gill and Akram, 'US Department of Justice'.

64. Goodwin-Gill, *The Refugee in International Law*, p. 93. Remarks of the French delegate at the 1951 Statelessness Conference, UN Doc. A/CONF.2/SR.19, at 11–12, and the Egyptian and Iraqi delegates, at 16–17.

65. See Goodwin-Gill and Akram, 'US Department of Justice', for the application of this analysis to Article 1D of the Refugee Convention and the related provisions.

66. See W.T. Mallison and S. Mallison, *An International Law Analysis of the Major United Nations Resolutions Concerning the Palestine Question*, UN Doc. ST/SG/SER.F/4 (1979) on the international legal status of GA Resolution 181.

67. See R. I. Khalidi, 'Observations on the Right of Return', 21 *Journal of Palestine Studies* (1992), pp. 29, 33. The GA has reaffirmed Resolution 194(III) every single year, with virtually every UN member state including the United States (but not Israel) voting in favour. In 1993, for the first time, the United States abstained from voting on the resolution. It is noteworthy that the United States' abstention in 1993 came on the heels of the Oslo agreement. George F. Kossaifi, *The Palestinian Refugees and the Right of Return*, Information Paper No. 7 (Washington, DC: The Center for Policy Analysis on Palestine 1996).

68. For a review of international responses to refugee flows prior to the drafting of the Refugee Convention, and the move from early arrangements for repatriation and assistance of refugees (1922–1938) to resettlement in the arrangements leading up to and embodied in the Refugee Convention (1938–1951), see *A Study of Statelessness* 34–38, UN Doc. E/1112 (1949). See generally, Goodwin-Gill, *The Refugee in International Law*. Although it is true that the international consensus at the time the Refugee Convention was drafted was for third-country resettlement, and that states should grant asylum in their discretion, this consensus was simply a reflection of the attitude towards the categories of refugees who were the main UN concern

at the time: post-Second World War European refugees and displaced persons. The international consensus towards refugee solutions has changed over time, and the current consensus for the last 20 years has quite consistently been to seek solutions focusing on refugee repatriation to place of origin.

69. For the complete discussion of the reasons for proposing Article 1D and establishing a separate regime of protection for Palestinian refugees, see the reports of the *Ad Hoc Committee on Statelessness and Related Problems*, the record of the Third Committee of the General Assembly, and the July 1951 debate of the Conference of Plenipotentiaries which finalized the drafting of the Refugee Convention in 3 *Collected Travaux Préparatoires*.

70. The Egyptian, Saudi Arabian and Lebanese UN delegations proposed the two amendments that became Article 1D. In proposing the first amendment, the Lebanese representative stated: 'The delegations concerned were thinking of the Palestine refugees, who differed from all other refugees. In all other cases, persons had become refugees as a result of action taken contrary to the principles of the United Nations and the obligation of the Organization toward them was a moral one only. The existence of Palestine refugees, on the other hand, was the direct result of a decision taken by the United Nations itself, with full knowledge of the consequences. The Palestine refugees were therefore a direct responsibility on the part of the United Nations and could not be placed in the general category of refugees without betrayal of that responsibility. Furthermore, the obstacle to their repatriation was not dissatisfaction with their homeland, but the fact that a Member of the United Nations was preventing their return.' The Saudi representative added: 'If the General Assembly were to include the Palestine refugees in a general definition of refugees, they would become submerged and would be relegated to a position of minor importance. The Arab states desired that those refugees should be aided pending their repatriation, repatriation being the only real solution to their problem. To accept a general definition without the clause proposed by the delegations of Egypt and Lebanon, as well as his own, would be to renounce the insistence on repatriation ... Pending a proper settlement of [the Arab–Israeli conflict], the Palestine refugees should continue to be granted a separate and special status.' Ibid., paras 52, 55.

71. See notes 69, 70.

72. The second sentence of Article 1D (the *ipso facto* sentence) was proposed as an amendment to the draft Refugee Convention Article 1 in the Conference of Plenipotentiaries. The amendment was offered by the Egyptian delegate, who stated that it was necessary to amend the clause 'to make sure that Arab refugees from Palestine, who were still refugees when the organs or agencies of the United Nations at present providing them with protection or assistance ceased to function, would automatically come within the scope of the Convention'. Summary Record of the Twenty-Ninth Meeting, UN GAOR, UN Doc. A/Conf.2/SR.29 reprinted in 3 *Collected Travaux Préparatoires*, at 488. The Iraqi representative added that 'the amendment represented an agreed proposal on the part of all the Arab States ... It was obvious that, if the Egyptian amendment was rejected, the refugees it was designed to protect might eventually find themselves deprived of any status whatsoever.' Ibid., at 489. The discrepancy between the two sentences of Article 1D was not addressed primarily because the second amendment (second sentence) was introduced so late in the process that there was no

time to reconcile the language. A number of participants, however, recognized the dichotomy between the language and intended effect of the provision. See, for example, the amendment proposed to the Conference of Plenipotentiaries at the final stage of the drafting process by the Commission of Churches on International Affairs. Concerning Article 1D, second sentence (then numbered Article 1C), the Commission noted: '(iii) Material assistance is not in itself a guarantee of protection and the Commission suggests that, if this clause is to stand, it should be amended to read "assistance *and* protection" rather than assistance or protection.' The Conference of Plenipotentiaries on the Status of Refugees and Stateless Persons (Geneva, 2–25 July 1951), Commission of the Churches on International Affairs Observations Concerning Article 1: A/CONF.2/NGO/10 p.2. 3 *Collected Travaux Préparatoires*, p. 633.

73. See note 57.
74. See note 28.
75. See p. 167.
76. For example, if there were an entity authorized to represent Palestinian refugee claims, whether a state or non-state representative, Palestinian refugee claims might be raised in any of the regional human rights organs: the African Commission which binds the states-members of the African Charter and Organization of African Unity; the Inter-American Commission and Court that bind the states-members of the American human rights system; the European Court of Human Rights, binding the European state members of the Council of Europe and signatories of the European Convention on Human Rights. Moreover, Palestinian refugees might make claims or seek reports/advisory opinions from the following bodies: the UN Human Rights Commission; the Human Rights Committee (responsible for monitoring compliance with the ICCPR 1966); the Committee on Economic, Cultural and Social Rights (responsible for the ICESCR, 1966); the Committee Against Torture (responsible for the 1984 Convention Against Torture); the Committee Against Racial Discrimination (concerning the Convention on the Elimination of all Forms of Racial Discrimination); the Committee on the Rights of the Child (responsible for the 1989 Convention on the Rights of the Child); the International Labor Organization (monitoring a number of ILO Conventions including Convention No. 118 on Equality of Treatment of Nationals and Non-Nationals in Social Security, 1962; and Convention No. 97, on Migration for Employment, 1949). Only recently has there been an effort to raise Palestinian refugee claims to any of these bodies. The efforts have been made by non-governmental organizations. See, for example, *Concluding Observations of the Human Rights Committee*, 63rd sess., UN Doc. CCPR/C/79/Add.93 (1998); *Report of the Committee on Economic, Social and Cultural Rights, Summary Record of the 31st Meeting*, 19th sess., UN Doc. E/C.12/1998/SR.31 (1998); *Concluding Observations of the Committee on the Elimination of All Forms of Racial Discrimination: Israel*, 52nd sess., UN Doc. CERD C/304/Add.45 (1998); *Resolutions of the Human Rights Commission, 2000: Resolution on the Situation in Occupied Palestine*, 35th meeeting, UN Doc. E/CN.4/RES/2000/4 (7 April 2000); *Resolution on the Question of the Violation of Human Rights in the Occupied Arab Territories, including Palestine*, 52 nd meeting, UN Doc. E/CN.4/RES/2000/6 (17 April 2000); *Resolution S-5/1 of the Fifth Special Session of the Commission on Human Rights on Grave*

and Massive Violations of the Human Rights of the Palestinian People by Israel, UN Doc. E/CN.4/RES/S-5/1 (27 October 2000).

77. The international consensus of what the appropriate implementation efforts of states should be in any particular refugee situation does not negate the fundamental principle of refugee choice. The UNHCR is prohibited from implementing a solution that does not reflect the voluntary choice of the refugee him/herself. At the same time, the right of any person to return to his/her place of origin has been a fundamental principle of international law since at least the time of the Magna Carta. For an authoritative review of the Palestinian right of return under international law, see note 66. There is no such fundamental right for any person to resettle elsewhere – that is within the sole discretion of a receiving state, with few limitations. It is important to emphasize that there is no internationally recognized right to obtain or to grant political asylum, residence or citizenship. Neither the Refugee Convention nor any other international instrument imposes such an obligation on any state. The only obligation imposed on states by the Refugee Convention is to respect the principle of *non-refoulement*, and, if the state does grant political asylum or other status to refugees, then it must respect additional rights provisions in the Convention.

78. See United Nations High Commissioner for Refugees, Executive Committee (Excomm) Conclusion No. 15 (Xxx), Refugees without an Asylum Country (1979); United Nations High Commissioner for Refugees, Excomm Conclusion No. 18 (Xxxi), Voluntary Repatriation (1980); United Nations High Commissioner for Refugees, Excomm Conclusion No. 40 (Xxxvi) Voluntary Repatriation (1985); United Nations High Commissioner for Refugees, Excomm Conclusion No. 67 (XLII) Resettlement as an Instrument Of Protection (1991).

79. On war claims, reparations and restitution, see Nicholas Balabkins, *West German Reparations to Israel* (New Brunswick: Rutgers University Press, 1971); Norman De Mattos Bentwich, *International Aspects of Restitution and Compensation for Victims of the Nazis* (Oxford: Oxford University Press, 1956); Institute of Jewish Affairs, *Compensation to Victims of Nazi Persecution for Property Losses in Expulsion and Similar Areas* (New York, 1957); Richard B. Lillich and Burns H. Weston, *International Claims: Their Settlement by Lump Sum Agreements*, Part I: *The Commentary* and Part II: *The Agreements* (Charlottesville: University Press of Virginia, 1975). On specific refugee restitution and compensation claims, see Maren Zerriffi, Palestinian Refugee Research Net, Inter-University Consortium for Arab Studies, *Refugee Compensation: Selected Cases and Source Materials* (Montreal: McGill University, July 1999, prepared for the International Development Research Centre).

80. On the Bosnia-Serbia agreements, see Annex 7 to the Dayton Peace Accords, 35 *International Law Materials* 136 (1996); and Commission for Real Property Claims of Displaced Persons and Refugees, Book of Regulations on the Conditions and Decision-Making Procedure for Claims for Return of Real Property of Displaced Persons and Refugees (Sarajevo, 4 March 1999), <http://www.crpc.org.ba/english/text/info/general/crpcrules.htm>. See also John Scheib, 'Threshold of Lasting Peace: The Bosnian Property Commission, Multi-ethnic Bosnia and Foreign Policy', 24 *Syracuse Journal of International Law* (1997), p. 119; and United Nations High Commissioner for Refugees and Commission for Real Property Claims of Displaced Persons and Refugees, Discussion Paper, *Return, Relocation, and Property Rights* (December 1997). On Guatemala, see Andrew Painter,

'Property Rights of Returning Displaced Persons: The Guatemalan Experience', 9 *Harvard Human Rights Journal* (1996), pp. 145–83.

81. See in particular, Mallison and Mallison, *International Law Analysis*.
82. See note 59.
83. See note 67.
84. See notes 54–7.
85. Reparation for Injuries Suffered in the Service of the United Nations, 1949 ICJ 174, 178–9 (11 April).
86. A UN delegation that included UNRWA representatives was included in the Refugee Working Group set up under the multilateral negotiations established in 1991 by the Madrid Peace Conference. Muhammad Hallaj, The Center for Policy Analysis on Palestine, 'The Refugee Question and the Peace Process', *Palestinian Refugees: Their Problem and Future* (Washington, DC: The Center for Policy Analysis on Palestine, 1994), p. 11. See also Salim Tamari, *Palestinian Refugee Negotiations: From Madrid to Oslo II* (Washington, DC: Institute for Palestine Studies, 1996); *The Third Generation: UN Aid to Palestinians* (Syracuse, NY: Syracuse University Press, 1995), p. 251; see also Takkenberg, *The Status of Palestinian Refugees in International Law*, pp. 280–303.
87. Benjamin Schiff, *Refugees unto The Third Generation: UN Aid to Palestinians* 251 (1995); see also Takkenberg, *The Status of Palestinian Refugees in International Law*, at 280–303.
88. See United Nations, Joint Inspection Unit, Report On UNRWA, UN Doc. Jiu/Rep/83/8, A/38/143,42 (1983).
89. See Historical Precedents for Restitution of Property or Payment of Compensation to Refugees (Working Paper by the United Nations Secretariat, Geneva, 1950), UN Doc. A/AC.25/W.81/Rev.2. Reprinted in Sami Hadawi, *Palestinian Rights and Losses in 1948: A Comprehensive Study*, App. II (London: Saqi Books, 988).
90. See Don Peretz, The Center for Policy Analysis on Palestine, 'The Question of Compensation', in *Palestinian Refugees: Their Problem and Future* (Washington, DC: The Center for Policy Analysis on Palestine, 1994), pp. 15, 18.
91. Contrast, for example, the language of GA Resolutions 181(II), 194(III), 273(III) and 302(IV), which focus on individual and human rights of Palestinians with GA Resolutions 2535 B(XXIV) and 3236(XXIX), referring to the 'inalienable rights of the Palestinian people in Palestine'. Kossaifi, *The Palestinian Refugees and the Right of Return*, pp. 10–12; Mallison and Mallison, *International Law Analysis*, pp. 35–6. John Quigley argues that United Nations Security Council Resolutions 242 and 338 incorporate GA Resolution 194, as the latter is the internationally accepted standard for the 'just settlement of the refugee problem' required by 242. John Quigley, 'Displaced Palestinians and a Right of Return', 39 *Harvard International Law Journal* (1998), pp. 171, 192. Thus, inclusion of these two Security Council Resolutions as the framework for all the Arab-Israeli peace negotiations also includes the standards of GA Resolution 194. This may be an accurate legal interpretation, however, the parties to the negotiations have not acted as though 194 were within their terms of reference. See Kossaifi, *The Palestinian Refugees and the Right of Return*, p. 17.
92. See note 80.
93. Ibid.
94. See note 59.

11   THE RIGHT OF RETURN:
SACRED, LEGAL AND POSSIBLE

Salman Abu-Sitta

The departing twentieth century witnessed the downfall of Nazism and fascism, the collapse of communism, the fading away of colonialism and the dismantling of the apartheid system. It was a momentous century. Many millions of people in many countries broke free of these evils, except in Palestine. Palestine is the only country in the world still subject to the sustained and powerful grip of many of these evils. Almost since its foundation, the United Nations has been occupied with the task of ridding the Palestinians from these evils. Hundreds of resolutions have been passed affirming their rights, offering assistance and condemning violations of human rights. Nevertheless these resolutions lacked the will and enforcement of major powers as was done in many other cases.

The victims of these evils are 5 million refugees, 3.7 million registered with UNRWA and 1.3 million unregistered refugees.[1] They constitute two-thirds of the 8 million Palestinians and represent the largest, oldest and most politically important group of refugees in the world.

The refugees come from 531 towns and villages shown in Figure 11.1 together with existing villages today. They were 85 per cent of the inhabitants of the land that became Israel. Their land is 92 per cent of Israel's area. By any standards, this is the largest, most carefully planned and continuous ethnic-cleansing operation in modern history (Figure 11.1).

For all Palestinians the right of return is sacred. It is built into their psyche. It moved an astonished Israeli writer to note: 'every people in the world lives in a place, except the Palestinians. The place lives in them.'[2]

Statistics support this contention. Today 86 per cent of the refugees live in historical Palestine and within a 100-mile radius around it. This proximity to their homes is indicative of the bond they have to their places of origin. That is also why over three dozen schemes of their resettlement, anywhere in the world except their homes, have failed.

The pattern of the refugees' movement when expelled in 1948 confirms the bond to the place of origin. When expelled, the refugees hovered around their villages, then moved to the next safe village, and so on. None moved straight to their final place of refuge, except those who took the sea route.

AL NAKBA 1948

- • Depopulated Village in 1948
- • Existing Village Today
- —— Partition Plan
- —— Armistice Line 1949

Figure 11.1 The Distribution of Depopulated and Existing Villages in Israel

All this indicates that the social fabric of the Palestinian society remains largely intact after the *nakba*. Today the children are registered in schools according to their village of origin, not according to their camp address. Here is a society that defied geographical genocide and remained intact.

The right of return is legal. The subject is long and well documented by the United Nations.[3] We only have to remember that Resolution 194 is not an invention. It is the embodiment and restatement of international law. There is no equal to this resolution in the UN history, neither in the length of upholding it, nor in its unique application to the Palestinian people. It enjoys sustained, universal and overwhelming consensus, more than 100 times in the last 52 years. Contrary to common misconception, it is not a single resolution. It is three in one: first, it affirms the right of refugees to return home, that is, to their place of origin; second, it provides welfare to the refugees until they return; and third, it creates a mechanism to effect that return: a UN organ named the Conciliation Commission of Palestine.

Because Resolution 194 is so basic, it survived the passage of Resolution 242, which is meant to eliminate the consequences of the 1967 war; it survived the ill-fated Oslo process, because it does not address the core problem of the refugees and it will survive the tribulations of Palestinian statehood because statehood addresses political matters of sovereignty which does not supersede the right to return home. Much to the displeasure of the Palestinians' adversaries, Resolution 194 is still alive and well. If we examine UN records as recently as December 1999, we find that Resolution 194 is still being affirmed by the international community with the exception of Israel and, more recently, the United States. Moreover Resolution 54/74 of the same month affirms the entitlement of the refugees to their properties and their revenues since 1948.

Now I will come to the issue that is the subject of many myths and misinformation. It is often said by well-intentioned people that refugees have the *right* to return, but it is impossible for them to do so: the country is full; there is no space left and so on.[4] Nothing is further from the truth. Of course, even if that were true, the right of return is not diminished. If an occupier expels an owner at gunpoint, he is not entitled to keep the house simply because he fills it with his family and friends.

Let us examine Israel's demography.[5] Israel divided the West Bank into A, B, C areas. Let us now divide Israel into A, B, C areas (Figure 11.2).

Area A has a population of 3,013,000 Jews (end of 1997) and its area is 1,628 sq. km, which is the same area and largely in the same location as the land which the Jews purchased or acquired in 1948. Its area is 8 per cent of Israel. This is the total extent of Jewish ownership in Israel. Clearly 92 per cent of Israel is Palestinian (or 94 per cent of Palestine). In this 8 per cent two-thirds of the Jews live. Here is the heaviest Jewish concentration. Most Jews still live in the same old neighbourhood of 1948.

Area B has a mixed population. Its area, which is 6 per cent of Israel, is just less than the land of Palestinians who remained in Israel. A further 10

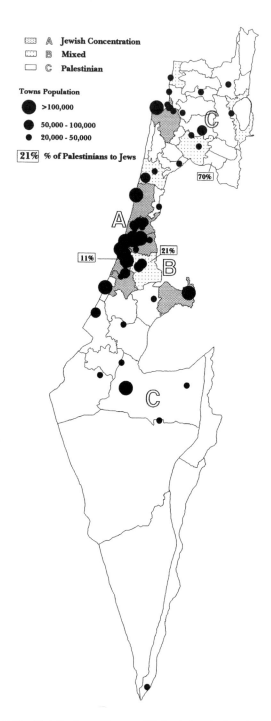

Figure 11.2 The Distribution of Jews and Palestinians in Israel

per cent of the Jews live there. Thus, in a nutshell, 78 per cent of the Jews live in 14 per cent of Israel.[6]

That leaves Area C, which is 86 per cent of Israel. This is largely the land and the home of the Palestinian refugees. Who lives there today? Apart from the remaining Palestinians, the majority of the Jews who now live there live in a few towns (shown circles according to size).

860,000 urban Jews live either in originally Palestinian towns or newly established towns. The average size of a new town in Area C is comparable to the size of a refugee camp. In fact, Jabaliya camp in Gaza is larger than two new towns in C north or larger than three new towns in C south. If Jabaliya camp were a town in Israel, its order would be in the top 8 per cent of Israeli urban centres.

Who, then, controls the vast Palestinian land in area C? Only 200,000 rural Jews exploit the home and heritage of 5 million refugees packed in refugee camps and denied the right to return.

The refugees in Gaza are crammed at the ratio of 4,200 persons/sq. km. If you were one of those refugees and you looked across the barbed wire to your land in Israel, and you saw it was almost empty, at five persons/sq. km (almost 1,000 times less density than Gaza) what would be your feeling? Peaceful? This striking contrast is the root of all evil, which will not be eliminated without the return of the refugees. These 200,000 rural Jews, holding 5 million refugees hostage, are obstructing all prospects of a just peace.

What do these people do? We were told they cultivate the (Palestinian) land and produce wonderful agriculture. We were not told that three-quarters of the kibbutzim are economically bankrupt and that only 26 per cent of them produce most of the agriculture. We are not told that the kibbutzim are ideologically bankrupt; there is constant desertion, and not many new recruits. Irrigation takes up about 75 per cent of the water in Israel, two-thirds of it is stolen Arab water. Agriculture in the south alone uses 500 million cubic metres of water per year. This is equal to the entire water resources of the West Bank now confiscated by Israel. This is equal to the entire resources of upper Jordan including Lake Tiberias for which Israel is obstructing the peace with Syria. This irrigation water, a very likely cause of war with the Syrians, Palestinians and Jordanians, produces agricultural products worth only 1.8 per cent of Israel's GDP. Such waste, such extravagance and such disregard for the suffering of the refugees and denial of their rights is exercised by this small minority of kibbutzniks.[7] Yet their small number is comparable to the Jewish settlers who drifted to the West Bank, excluding Jerusalem due to be evacuated in a new peace deal, or to about three of the 60 refugee camps scattered in the Middle East.

Let us consider two scenarios, which if applied are likely to diffuse much of the tension in the Middle East. Let us imagine that the registered refugees in Lebanon (362,000) are allowed to return to their homes in Galilee. Even today, Galilee is still largely Arab. Palestinians there outnumber the Jews one and a half times. If the Lebanon refugees return to their homes, the Jewish concentration in area A will hardly feel the difference, and the Jews will remain a majority in all areas, even when they are least in number, like area C.[8]

Furthermore, if 760,000 registered refugees in Gaza are allowed to return to their homes in the south, now largely empty, they can return to their same original villages while the percentage of the Jewish majority in the centre (area A) will drop by only 6 per cent. It is a sad sign of the miscarriage of justice to note that the number of these rural Jews who may be directly affected by the return of the suffering Gaza refugees to their homes in the south does not exceed 78,000 or the size of a single refugee camp.

One of the manifestations of such injustice is that the Russian immigrants, mostly economic and largely non-Jews, are freely admitted to live on Palestinian land because they claim to be Jews. The striking fact is that their number is almost the same as that of Lebanon and Gaza refugees combined. In other words, if those refugees returned, Israel will not be more densely populated than it is today and surely the prospects of peace will be greatly improved.

So much for the claim of the physical 'impossibility' of the return. The vacancy of Palestinian land is so problematic to Israel that it is trying to find people to live on this land. None other than Sharon and Eitan, both hardline Zionists, started a scheme in 1997 to sell the refugees' land to builders to build apartments so that an American or Australian Jew can buy an apartment without being an Israeli. A portion of the land rented by the kibbutzim was sold at exorbitant prices (up to $1,000 per square metre in the centre). Kibbutz farmers who rented this land from the Custodian of Absentee (i.e. refugee) Property received 'compensation' of up to 25 per cent of its sale value. This made the bankrupt farmers rich overnight. City dwellers who did not share this wealth went into uproar and the Ronen Committee was formed to submit a moderating proposal to limit this sudden wealth.[9]

This illegal activity, selling a land in custody, prompted the United Nations to issue resolutions affirming the entitlement of the refugees to receive any income of their property for the last 50 years and calling on all states to present all documents and information they may have on the refugees' property. In September 1998, the Arab League passed a resolution to call on the United Nations to send a fact-finding mission to report on the status of the refugees' land and appoint a Custodian to protect their property.

With their land being sold, we see persistent efforts to scatter the refugees around the world.[10] Since 1948, there have been more than three dozen schemes to resettle the refugees anywhere in the world except their homes, all devised by pro-Israelis, all failed. Why? Because the refugees refuse to be treated like cattle carted away in trains or planes away from their homes. There are hideous parallels from the Second World War. These plans are nothing less than ethnic-cleansing plans, punishable if effected by international law.

Consider the proposal by Donna Arzt[11] (Table 11.1). Analysis of the figures shows that over 1,500,000 have to be carted away in yet another

Table 11.1 Analysis of Arzt's Transfer Plan

RESETTLEMENT = ETHNIC CLEANSING

Place of Refuge	Arzt Estimate 1995	Arzt Final Solution 2005	Transfer from	Transfer to West Bank	Transfer to Arab countries	Transfer to the World	Resettlement in Present Exile
Israel	840,000	1,075,000	-14,087	14,087			1,075,000
Gaza Strip	880,000	450,000	-690,948	690,948			450,000
West Bank	1,200,000	2,400,000					1,555,838
Jordan	1,832,000	2,000,000	-375,246	139,128	141,671	94,447	2,000,000
Lebanon	372,000	75,000	-407,310		215,874	191,436	75,000
Syria	352,100	400,000	-56,509		28,254	28,254	400,000
Other Arab Countries	446,600	965,000					579,031
Non-Arab Countries	452,000	900,000					586,032
TOTAL	6,374,700	8,265,000	-1,544,099	844,162	385,799	314,137	6,720,901
Transferred Population						1,544,099	6,720,901
Missing Population							1,129,610
Total Palestinians							9,394,610

Notes: Arzt estimated Palestinians in 1995 before transfer and in 2005 after transfer. This jump in time and place is analysed separately for each of the two and compared with the population had they not been transferred. The result is Transfer and Resettlement columns. Missing population is the figure not accounted for by Arzt due to errors and underestimation of 1995 figures.

ethnic-cleansing operation and the rest have to remain in exile. Such ideas will never materialize. It is a shame that we still have to witness proposals of this kind.

Compensation is often mentioned as a solution. That is to say, offering paltry sums to be advanced by the United States and Europe to pay the refugees off, so that Israel ends up with a legal title for a huge real estate and its water free of charge. Compensation is a not accepted for homes and land – these are not for sale but for restitution.[12] Compensation is due for material and non-material damages and losses which the refugees have incurred for 50 years, and reparations for war crimes. It is much cheaper to pay for the rehabilitation of the refugees in their homes. It is even cheaper to pay off those economic Russian immigrants who come to occupy the refugees' homes.

Now it is often said that Israel opposes the return of the refugees on the basis that this will change the Jewish character of the state. In the words of a noted Jurist: 'The Jewish character is really a euphemism for the Zionist discriminatory statutes of the State of Israel which violate the human rights provisions ... The UN is under no more of legal obligation to maintain Zionism in Israel than it is to maintain *apartheid* in the Republic of South Africa.' Not only is this immoral, it is also illegal under the enlightened human rights law and is abhorrent to the civilized world. Most recently, the reports of treaty-based bodies, such as the Human Rights Committee, the Committee on the Elimination of Racial Discrimination, the Committee on Economic, Social and Cultural Rights and the Committee against Torture, have all condemned Israeli practices and characterized for the first time so clearly the exclusive structure of the Israeli state as the root cause of all those violations of international law. How, then, can the international community accept the premise of a 'Jewish character' as a basis for the denial of the right to return home?

Socially, the idea of the Jewish character is a misnomer. Would anyone believe there is much in common between a Brooklyn Jew and an Ethiopian Jew? Or between a Russian claiming to be a Jew and a Moroccan Jew? The gulf between the Ashkenazi and the Haredim will never be bridged. The Sephardim (Mizrahim) are allocated the lower rungs of the social ladder. Jerusalem and Tel Aviv are being polarized on sectarian lines. Israel has long given up on the idea of a melting pot. Israel remains and will continue to be a segregated society.

In this chequered mosaic live the Palestinians who remained in their homes. They now represent 26 per cent of all Jewish Israelis. They are everywhere (Figure 11.3). In area A (the highest concentration of the Jews), they are 11 per cent of the population. In the mixed area B, they are 21 per cent of the population. In area C they are 70 per cent of the population on average, but they are double the number of Jews in the Little Triangle and 1.5 times the number of the Jews in Galilee. How could Israel ignore their presence? Will Israel plan another massive ethnic-cleansing operation? Very unlikely, or there will be a sea of blood. They are there to stay, and will

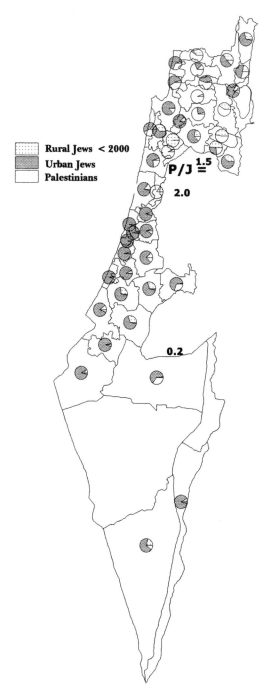

Figure 11.3 Percentage of Urban and Rural Jews and Palestinians by Natural Region in Israel

increase. In the year 2010, Palestinians in Israel will be 35 per cent of the population and they will be equal to the number of Jews in 2050 or much earlier when immigration dries up. So what is the value of chasing an elusive target while innocent people continue to suffer? (Figure 11.3.)

In Palestine today (Israel, West Bank and Gaza) – that is from the river to the sea – Palestinians are already 47 per cent of the whole population. They will be equal in number to the Jews in four years' time. In the year 2050, the Jews in Israel will number 11 million assuming that very few Jews remain in the United States and Europe. But by this time, present Palestinians within historical Palestine will number 32 million, and there will be another 32 million waiting outside Palestine if they have not already returned.

The Israeli notion of numerical superiority is therefore impractical and shortsighted. As is the notion of an exclusive and homogeneous Jewish society. Neither has any chance of success. On the contrary, maintaining those racist policies will alienate most of the world (as it does today) and will accumulate a great deal of anger that may explode one day with disastrous results.

I have tried to show that the right of return is sacred in the eyes of the Palestinians, and that they have not the slightest intention of abandoning it. A new movement among refugees in all Arab and foreign countries to reaffirm their right of return is developing rapidly. If only 1 per cent of them assert their rights forcefully, this means 50,000 angry people, or 10,000 in each of the five UNRWA areas. It will be foolish to ignore this. The right of return is also legal, as demonstrated consistently by the international community, and it is also possible and feasible, contrary to Israeli claims. There is enough space to accommodate the returning refugees with minimum dislocation of Jews. The oft-repeated Israeli notions of retaining an exclusive and superior Jewish society are immoral, illegal and simply untenable in the long run.

This leads us to conclude that the current Israeli policies of denying the refugees the right to return are doomed to failure. It would be wise for the Israelis to invest in the future by building bridges of goodwill, instead of building arsenals of weapons of mass destruction.

It also leads us to conclude that the return of the refugees is the most important stabilizing factor, without which there can be no permanent peace in the Middle East. The return of the refugees to their land and to their agricultural pursuit will take up the slack in Israel's GDP and will put to proper use the wasted water in the vast, unutilized, currently confiscated refugees' land. If more water is needed in the future, it can be obtained by friendly regional agreements, not by a new war and conquest of new land.

The Palestinians are dynamic and intelligent people. If left in peace, which they deserve, in their homes, to which they are entitled, they are likely not only to support themselves but also to produce a considerable surplus. Witness their contribution to the development of Jordan, Lebanon, Kuwait and the Gulf at a time when they have emerged from a harrowing experience, the *nakba*.

The international community supported by diplomacy the right of return in Tajikstan, Abkhazia, Namibia and Cyprus. Why not in Palestine?

The international community implemented UN resolutions by military force in Kuwait, Bosnia, Kosovo and East Timor. Why not in Palestine?

The return of the refugees is the realistic solution. It is not realistic to condemn 5 million people to oblivion.

It is a dangerous illusion to think that peace can prevail in the Middle East without the implementation of the right of return to the largest, oldest and most politically important refugees in the world.

What do the Palestinians have to do? They have shown over and over again that, in spite of many catastrophic setbacks, they still survive. They are capable of surprises; witness the *Intifida* and the unexpected lesson they gave Jospin. But that is not enough.

They must keep hammering at the racist colossus of Israel, and chipping it piece by piece. Already the land claimed to be 'for the Jewish people for ever' is being sold. Already the Palestinian Qa'dan family have won the right of any citizen in Israel to own a house, just as a Russian immigrant could do upon arrival. Already Mahmoud Darwish poems are introduced to teach Israeli children that, after all, Palestinians are human beings, who belong to the land of Palestine.

Again that is not enough. Palestinians must build an efficient network of an enlightenment campaign, assisted by the irresistible force of fast communication. They must never allow a return to those days in 1948 when their destruction and geographical genocide was hailed in the West as a divine intervention and a victory for civilization.

In the final analysis, there is no substitute for the voice of the rightful owners of the home and land. Palestinian society is a monolithic structure and the refugees from 531 towns and villages, who were expelled by the Israelis, are no exception. They survived all adversity and ravages of war. Today a grandchild of a 1948 refugee says she/he comes from her/his original village, not from her/his present camp address. Israelis may have destroyed his village on the ground, but not from his mind. That is what counts.

NOTES

1. For details of the Palestinian refugees, per village, both registered and unregistered, see S.H. Abu-Sitta, *The Palestinian Nakba 1948: The Register of Depopulated Localities in Palestine* (2nd edition, London: PRC, May 2000). Also at <www.prc.org.uk>. See also the map of Palestine 1948 showing the location of 531 villages and other data, published by PRC.

2. Danny Rubinstein, *The People of Nowhere, the Palestinian Vision of Home* (New York: Times Books, Random House, 1991), p. 7. Writing sympathetically, he is astonished at the Palestinians' tenacity and attachment to their homes. Home to them, he notes, is not only Palestine, but their

ancestral village, not even another one 2 kilometres away (ibid., p. 90). He marvels at their emphasis on and compilation of their heritage (ibid., p. 120). While this is to the Palestinians a natural affinity, it is not so to a Jewish immigrant whose wealth and heritage lies in his brain and suitcase, both are mobile.

3. For a representative legal opinion of Palestinian Rights, see 'The Palestine Question', Seminar of Arab Jurists on Palestine (Algiers, 22–27 July 1967); G.J. Tomeh, Symposium on the Middle East Crisis, Law and Contemporary Problems, Duke University School of Law, Durham, NC, Winter 1968); idem., 'Legal Status of Arab Refugees', Monogram 20, Institute for Palestine Studies, Beirut, 1969; Muhammad Farah, 'Legal Status of Israel and the Occupied Territories', Association of Arab-American University Graduates Inc., Information Paper No. 15, April 1975; John Quigley, *Palestine and Israel: A Challenge to Justice* (North Carolina: Duke University Press, 1990); Ramadane Babadji and Monique Chemillier-Gendrean, *The Right of Return for the Palestinian People* (in Arabic) (Beirut: The Institute of Palestine Studies, 1996); and Henry Cattan, *Palestine and International Law* (London: Longman, 1973). For a comprehensive review of the Right of Return as per the UN resolutions, see W.T. Mallison and S.V. Mallison, 'The Right of Return', *Journal of Palestine Studies* (Spring 1980), pp. 125–36 (extracted from the full text: UN publication: ST/SG/SER.F/4, entitled: 'An International Law Analysis of the Major United Nations Resolutions Concerning the Palestinian Question', New York, 1979). Frank L. M. Van de Craen ('The Territorial Title of the State of Israel to Palestine: An Appraisal of International Law', *Revue Belge de Droit International*, vol. 14 (2) [1978–79], pp. 500–38), in a careful review noted that 'the right to self-determination of the Palestine People is in that sense unique in that it is probably the only case of a well-established recognition of a right to sovereignty and independence of a people who live for the greater part outside their national homeland' (p. 534).

4. See, for example, Don Peretz, *Palestinians, Refugees and the Middle East Process* (Washington, DC: US Institute of Peace Press, 1993), who argues that the return is 'neither feasible nor practical' (p. 72) and that 'conditions have so changed' (p. 73), so as not to permit return. See also the comments by Elie Sanbar, the Chief Palestinian delegate in the multilateral talks on refugees. After refusing to forfeit the right of return, the Palestinian delegation was given 'the practical difficulties' as a pretext for no return. (See his interview in *al Hayat* daily (London), 18, 19 December 1996, p. 18.) See also Don Peretz, 'Palestine Arab Refugee Compensation', undated, based on his book, *Israel and the Palestine Arab*s (Washington, DC: The Middle East Institute, 1956); Elias Sanbar, *Palestine 1948* (Arabic trans.) (Beirut: Arab Society for Studies and Publishing, 1987). This is, unfortunately, the view of a tiny minority of Palestinian writers, see Ahmed S. Khalidi,*International Herald Tribune* (12 February 1997) and Rashid Khalidi's frequent writings, for example, 'Truth, Justice and Reconciliation', in *The Palestinian Exodus, 1948–1998*, ed. G. Karmi and E. Cotran (London: Ithaca Press, 1999).

5. For an earlier version of this study, see S.H. Abu-Sitta, 'The Feasibility of the Right of Return', <http://www.arts.mcgill.ca/mepp/prrn/paper/abusitta.html>. Also in *The Palestinian* Exodus, ed. Karmi and Cotran (London: Ithaca Press, 1999), pp. 171–96.

6. These figures are compiled from *CBS Israel Statistical Abstracts*, No. 49, 1998; and *Israel Yearbook and Almanac, 1998*, Vol. 52.

7. For the demise of the Kibbutz, see Eliezer Ben Rafael, *Crisis and Transformation: The Kibbutz at Century's End* (New York: SUNY Press, 1997); and Yair Aharoni, *The Israeli Economy: Dreams and Realities* (London: Routledge, 1991), pp. 20, 134, 208–13. See also numerous articles in *Ha'aretz*, particularly June and July 2000.

8. Refugee numbers are extracted from UNRWA records. For the distribution of the returning refugees, density of population and Jews percentages in the return scenarios, see Table 10, p. 47 in *Palestine Right to Return: Sacred, Legal and Possible* (2nd edition, London: PRC, May 2000); also at <www.prc.org.uk>.

9. For sale of refugees' land, see S.H. Abu-Sitta, 'The Great Israel Land Grab', *Jordan Times* (2 March 1998), p. 6, *Opinion and Analysis* and *Ha'aretz*: Hannah Kim, 'A Liquidation Sale of Public Lands' (20 June 2000); and Yair Sheleg, 'The Big Sellout' (23 June 2000).

10. There is a plethora of pro-Israeli papers suggesting resettlement of refugees as the only alternative to their return. There are no Arab and only a few neutral opinions suggesting the same course of action. For the first group, see Howard Adelman, *Palestinian Refugees: Defining the Humanitarian Problem* (New York: World Refugee Survey, 1983). Adelman sees the solution in providing aid and protection to the refugees, which they lack, and nothing else. See also Mark A. Heller, *A Palestinian State: The Implications for Israel* (Cambridge, Mass: Harvard University Press, 1983), p. 83, who proposes resettlement and limited return (750,000 out of eligible 2,700,000 (1980)) to a teethless state in the West Bank and Gaza, not to their homes. Similar proposals but more detailed are advanced by Donna E. Arzt and Karen Zughaib, 'Return to the Negotiated Lands: The Likelihood and Legality of a Population Transfer between Israel and Future Palestinian State', *New York Journal of Law and Politics*, vol. 24 (1992), pp. 1399–1511. Peretz, who wrote frequently on the subject, endorses solutions which allow a limited return to a new state, not to their homes. He also considers limited compensation for lost property less than the amount claimed by Jews who left Arab countries after 1948 to take up residence in Israel (see *Palestinians, Refugees, and the Middle East Process*). All these ideas are more forceful and frequent variations on resettlement schemes proposed immediately after 1948, but before 1967, by western sources, with the hope that UNRWA would be the instrument for implementation. All these schemes have failed. For early schemes suggesting resettlement in Iraq or Syria, see Sibylla Gratiana Thicknesse, *Arab Refugees: A Survey of Resettlement Possibilities* (London and New York: Royal Institute of International Affairs, 1949), VIII, 68 pp.

11. Donna Arzt, *Refugees to Citizens* (New York: Council on Foreign Relations, 1997).

12. See S.H. Abu-Sitta, 'The Trap of the Refugees Compensation', *Al-Hayat* (London) (25 August 1999), p. 14, and *Al Ayyam* (Jerusalem) (26 August 1999); S.H. Abu-Sitta, 'Who Demands Compensation and Why?', *Al-Hayat* (London), Opinion (11 July 2000) p. 9.

12 DECONSTRUCTING THE LINK: PALESTINIAN REFUGEES AND JEWISH IMMIGRANTS FROM ARAB COUNTRIES

Jan Abu Shakrah

From the renewal of final status negotiations on Palestinian refugees in September 1999 through the Camp David II summit and beyond, the demand that Arab countries compensate 'Jewish refugees' for properties left during the 1950s has been revived. The concept of Jewish refugees from Arab countries rests on a central myth perpetuated by Israeli officials and writers that a 'population exchange' occurred as a result of the 1948 war. Palestinians in this scenario abandoned their properties while 'fleeing' to surrounding Arab countries, which in retaliation expelled their Jewish citizens and confiscated their properties. The 'refugee problem' can thus be resolved by permanently resettling Palestinians outside Palestine and effectively cancelling Palestinian compensation claims through counter-claims of even greater losses by Jews immigrating to Israel. Is there a link between the Palestinian refugees and the immigration of Jews from Arab countries to Israel? Do the posited counter-claims rest on valid legal or moral grounds? Does the myth hold up to scrutiny?

THE CREATION OF THE 'POPULATION EXCHANGE' MYTH

As a result of the 1948 war, some 750,000 Palestinian refugees were forced to abandon their properties comprising over 80 per cent of what became Israel's total land area, along with whole cities, towns and buildings. Under the Emergency Ordinance of 15 November 1948, farm properties seized from the refugees were leased by the Custodian of Absentee Properties to thousands of new Jewish immigrants, many from Arab countries, and thousands of new immigrants moved into 'abandoned' Arab dwellings and sublet shops, offices and stores. In 1950, the tasks of the Custodian were institutionalized in an absentee property law that authorized the Custodian to sell lands to a state development authority (the Israeli Land Authority – ILA) at prices not less than 80 per cent of the official value. The ILA, technically an independent agency, leased the properties to Jews only.[1]

From the beginning, Israel maintained a consistent position that it bears no responsibility for the creation of the Palestinian refugee problem. A half-century later, many Israeli historians, including those of the Israeli army (IDF) itself, conservatively estimate that the dispossession of at least 70 per cent of the Palestinian refugees was due to Israeli war-related efforts and an orchestrated terror campaign.[2] Hundreds of villages were razed, and their lands, including the lands of Palestinians who remained in the country, were taken over by the Custodian of Absentee Properties. Refugees who tried to gain access to their homes and fields were killed or forcibly driven out and prohibited from returning. The 'infiltration' problem was a constant source of concern and debate within the Israeli government throughout the period.[3]

Israel came under intense international pressure – during its first years at least – to compensate the refugees for their property. Israel's admission to the United Nations depended on its acceptance of General Assembly Resolution 194, which resolved 'that the refugees wishing to return to their homes and live at peace with their neighbours should be permitted to do so at the earliest practicable date, and that compensation should be paid for the property of those choosing not to return and for loss of or damage to property ...'.[4]

Israel showed no signs of complying with the resolution or of arranging for property compensation. Israeli officials did, however, declare Israel's intent to pay compensation for 'abandoned' lands, but only under certain conditions.

The refugees' rights to repatriation and restitution were totally ignored. Israel demanded to set the terms for any compensation payment, which would be based not simply on the value of the property, but on factors such as Israel's ability to pay, considering the impact of the Arab boycott, Israel's need to maintain a big defence budget, and the costs of absorbing immigrants. Israeli loss of life and damages for a war that had been thrust upon it would also have to be considered. On these terms, Israel would contribute its fair share to an international fund as a collective payment to be used to resettle the refugees in Arab countries. Such payment and resettlement would end Israel's obligations and preclude any individual refugee claims or demands for repatriation.

A significant component of this position was added in 1951. In a speech before the Knesset on 4 November 1951, Foreign Minister Moshe Sharett added the following point to Israel's position: 'an appropriate amount from any compensation which Israel undertook to pay would be deducted for Jewish assets frozen in Iraq'.[5] Coincidentally, unofficial estimates by Iraqi Jewish leaders who immigrated to Israel placed a value on the Jewish property left in Iraq at 156 million Israeli pounds, roughly the value of abandoned Palestinian property estimated by the United Nations Conciliation Commission on Palestine (UNCCP).[6] Since the United Nations, including the United States, Britain and Arab states, all rejected Israel's conditions, including the linkage to Jewish properties in Arab countries, the issue of compensation, together with repatriation, reached a dead end.

To understand how Jewish properties in Arab countries were injected into the Palestinian refugee issue, it is necessary to examine the circumstances under which Arab Jews, particularly Iraqi Jews immigrated to Israel.

THE CASE OF THE IRAQI JEWS

While the population exchange myth rests on the supposed balance of 750,000 Palestinian refugees being replaced by approximately 700,000 Jews who left Arab countries (500,000 of them to Israel), the Israeli position on compensation has focused almost exclusively on the properties of Iraqi Jews.

Before 1948, Jews in Iraq generally enjoyed complete freedom and equal status as citizens, in addition to a flourishing cultural, political and economic life fully integrated into Iraqi society.

The 1948 war brought political unrest and economic instability, as well as the imposition of martial law, which affected all Iraqis. No specifically anti-Jewish laws were passed, but the position of Iraqi Jews began to deteriorate.[7] Large numbers of Jews were dismissed from public service, restrictions on travel abroad and disposal of property were instituted, and Jewish banks were deprived of licences to deal with foreign exchange, presumably because of attempts to channel funds abroad illegally. Martial law, which was lifted at the end of 1949, mainly targeted Communists, with a secondary focus on Zionist activity.[8] At the same time, the international Zionist campaign, accompanied by a Zionist movement inside Iraq, gained ground.

Shiblak cites two factors as crucial to mass Jewish emigration from Iraq. The first was pressure, primarily from Britain and the United States, for a transfer or population exchange proposal to resettle 100,000 Palestinians in Iraq in exchange for 100,000 Iraqi Jews to be resettled in Israel. Britain in particular urged Iraq to accept a deal whereby Israel would compensate Iraqi Jews for their lost property in Iraq, a move Britain viewed as justified on the basis for Israel's refusal to compensate Palestinian refugees. Iraq's pro-western government none the less viewed the proposal as impractical, and probably expected or hoped that the Palestinian refugee problem would be successfully resolved by the UNCCP. In any case, Israel never agreed to compensate the Iraqi Jews.

The second factor that facilitated the Iraqi Jewish exodus was the enactment of Law 1/1950, known as the denaturalization law, and its annex, 'Ordinance for the Cancellation of Iraqi Nationality' (Law 62/1933). The annex empowered the Council of Ministers 'to divest any Iraqi who wished, of his own free will and choice, to leave Iraq for good, of his Iraqi nationality'.[9]

The law, enacted under pressure from Britain and the United States and welcomed by Israel, was designed to respond to the rising rate of illegal Jewish emigration, estimated at 3,000 before the law was enacted. According to Shiblak, Iraqi officials expected no more than 7,000–10,000 to leave under the 1950 law, and they believed that it would undermine Zionist propaganda against the Iraqi government. The law placed no restrictions on property, despite the urging of Britain and some Iraqis that such restrictions would be appropriate retaliation for the seizure of Palestinian properties.

In the event, some 40,000 Jews emigrated in the year the law was in effect, transferring some 10 million Iraqi dinars, in addition to a 50 Iraqi dinar limit set after the law came into effect for each emigrant.

Apparently in response to the unexpected drain on Iraq's economy, Law 5/1951 and Regulation 3/1951, enacted on the expiration of Law 1/1950, froze the assets of Jews who applied to relinquish their Iraqi nationality. In the following year, another 80,000 Jews left for Israel via Cyprus.

Before 1950, Iraqi Jews were highly unlikely to go to Israel. 'Operation Ali Baba' changed that. This organized campaign to bring Iraqi Jews to Israel relied on extensive propaganda internationally and in Iraq's Jewish community, as well as two other programmes. The first was an evacuation plan negotiated by Shlomo Hillel (an Iraqi-born Mossad agent who later served as a minister in several Labour governments as well as Speaker of the Israeli Knesset) with Iraqi Prime Minister al-Suwaidi. Through Near East Air Transport, Inc., a US company owned by the Jewish Agency, Hillel transported over 100,000 Jews via Cyprus to Israel, facilitating the scheme through payoffs to Iraqi officials, financial assistance from the United States, and the acquiescence of the British.[10]

The second crucial component of 'Operation Ali Baba' was a series of five bomb attacks on Jewish targets from April 1950 through June 1951. Only 14 months into the bombing campaign did Iraqi officials finally uncover the spy ring responsible for the attacks and make the first arrests, which included an Israeli officer and a British subject who was also a Mossad agent. Explosives, papers and plans uncovered at the time confirmed the intent of the ring to terrorize Jews and to force them to immigrate to Israel. In November 1951 an Iraqi court found 15 out of 21 defendants guilty. A local Zionist commander, Mordechai Ben-Porat, later a member of the Israeli Knesset and president of the World Organization for Jews from Arab Countries (WOJAC), was identified by several Israeli sources as the ring-leader of the bombing campaign. As noted by Shiblak and confirmed by other sources, the bombing campaign could have been carried out only with decisions taken at a high level in Tel Aviv and with the personal knowledge of Yigal Allon (in charge of external Mossad operations) and the prime minister, David Ben-Gurion.[11]

Several features of the 1951 law and the circumstances of the mass Jewish exodus from Iraq should be noted. First, departure under the law was voluntary. Approximately 5,000 Jews, among the most well established and highly integrated members of the Jewish community stayed in Iraq and administered communal Jewish properties.[12] Second, those who had a choice did not go to Israel; about 10,000 Iraqi-born Jews settled outside Israel in the 1950s. Later, many Iraqi Jews who had settled in Israel left for Europe and the United States.[13] Third, under regulations of the 1951 law, the Custodian was required to pay a legal maintenance allowance to persons maintained by a denaturalized person from his property. Fourth, Jews who left Iraq from 1 January 1948 were given two months to return to the country to have their frozen property restored. The sick, caretakers and students were excluded from that requirement. Finally, denaturalized persons could stay in the country for judicial or legal necessity.[14]

Israel lost no time responding to the 1951 Iraqi law and using it to exempt Israel from compensating Palestinian refugees. On 19 March 1951, nine days after the law's enactment, Sharett declared in the Knesset:

By expropriating the assets of tens of thousands of Jews who immigrated to Israel, the Iraqi government has incurred a debt to the state of Israel. Such a debt already exists between Israel and the Arab world, and that is the debt of compensation to those Arabs who left Israeli territory and abandoned their property ... The action now taken by the Iraqi kingdom ... compels us to link the two debts ... The value of the Iraqi Jewish assets that were expropriated will be taken into consideration when calculating the compensation we committed to pay Arabs who abandoned their property in Israel.[15]

Naeim Giladi, an Iraqi Jew who participated in 'Operation Ali Baba', reached a different conclusion. In his book, *Ben Gurion's Scandals: How the Haganah and the Mossad Eliminated Jews*, Giladi details a web of collusion and terror for which he holds Zionist leaders, in concert with Britain and weak, pro-western Iraqi government officials, responsible. He established a panel of inquiry in Israel to seek reparations for Iraqi Jews who had been forced to leave their properties in Iraq.[16]

Neither the United States nor the British government expressed surprise at or disapproval of the 1951 law, nor did they make any representation about it to the Iraqi government. The British Foreign Office commented in a letter to the British Embassy in Washington on 27 March 1951: 'We see no likelihood of getting the Iraqis to rescind the law freezing assets, since the Israelis themselves are by no means blameless in this respect.'[17]

JEWS FROM OTHER ARAB COUNTRIES

Of the estimated 700,000 Jews who left Arab countries from 1948 through the 1950s, approximately 500,000 went to Israel, with the remainder settling in Europe, the United States, Canada and Latin America. In addition to the 115,000–200,000 Iraqi Jews, the majority emigrated to Israel from Morocco (180,000), Yemen (60,000–70,000), Libya (35,000), Tunisia (20,000), Egypt (16,500) and Syria/Lebanon (12,000).[18]

Like the Iraqi Jews, Jews from other Arab countries emigrated voluntarily, in most cases prompted by an organized Zionist campaign. Most of those who left North African countries in the late 1950s did so in the context of their countries' independence struggles. Most who emigrated were poor or identified with and benefited from their association with the departing colonial powers. In general, those with means and a choice (including foreign nationality) did not emigrate to Israel. Interestingly, while global reference to Jewish properties left in Arab countries is integral to Israeli and

Zionist rhetoric on the issue, little evidence of properties from these other countries is provided.[19] In the case of Yemen's Jews who were airlifted in 1949 as part of 'Operation Magic Carpet', for example, Israel was strangely quiet about their properties, in contrast to its immediate expression of concern about the fate of Iraqi Jewish property. Shiblak explains:

> There have been suggestions that Israel offered the Imam [Yemen's ruler] financial inducements to allow Jews to leave the country ... but it is beyond dispute that all the immovable property of the departing Yemeni Jews was confiscated without compensation. They were allowed to bring with them the tools of their trade and their scrolls (*The Times*, 12 April 1950), arrangements which suggest that some measure of agreement had been reached between Zionist officials and the Imam.[20]

Three years after 'Operation Ali Baba', Mossad agents, in what became known as the 'Lavon affair', bombed American and British property in Egypt, forcing Ben-Gurion's resignation as prime minister. The anti-Jewish attacks by Zionists in an effort to force the emigration of the Egyptian Jewish community to Israel was modelled on the precedent of 'cruel Zionism' set in Iraq.[21]

In summary, emigration from Arab countries was voluntary and connected to events totally unrelated to the 1948 war. Perceived self-interest, and in most cases a concerted campaign usually involving 'cruel Zionist' tactics, motivated the emigration.

The flow of immigrants from Iraq, Yemen and North Africa, as well as from Eastern Europe from 1948 through the 1950s, enabled Israel to consolidate its claim on the territories it had seized in the war. As Don Peretz notes, the extensive properties left by the Palestinian refugees added a crucial element to Israel's economic development and ability to absorb such large numbers. The overwhelming financial support generated by the American Zionist propaganda of 'pogroms' further facilitated what turned out to be a major boon of funds and immigrants for the fledgling Jewish state.[22] Contrary to the Israeli government claim that the absorption of Jews from Arab countries strained Israel's economic resources, Israel clearly benefited economically from the 'ingathering' campaign orchestrated by the state and Zionist agents.

If one were to construct a balance sheet of gains and losses, Israel would clearly be the winner, while Arab Jews (despite their benefit from Palestinian refugee properties), the Arab countries from which they emigrated and certainly the Palestinian refugees would be the losers. Such as assessment is corroborated by British and US officials and independent observers of the period. But does a balance sheet offer an appropriate measure of the issues?

DECONSTRUCTING THE LINK

In 1951, Moshe Sharett disingenuously and inaccurately characterized Palestinian refugee claims as a 'debt' between Israel and the Arab world, and linked that debt to the counter-claims of Jewish properties left in Arab countries as a 'debt' owed to Israel by the Arab world. The myth of a 'population exchange' well served the purposes of Israel and the Zionist movement to divert the focus from Israel's responsibility for the Palestinian refugee problem, to reframe the refugee issue exclusively in terms of resettlement and balancing compensation claims, and to bury the Palestinian right to return and restitution. In a period of weak or colluding Arab governments, an ineffectual UNCCP and enabling or acquiescing superpowers Britain and the United States, the myth prevailed.

Despite the fact that countries like Britain and the United States accepted or acquiesced to a constructed balance of claims framed as an issue between Israel and the Arab countries, there are serious legal flaws in that formulation. From a legal and historical perspective, however, Jewish claims cannot be considered counter-claims to those of the Palestinians. Legally, a counter-claim is one arising 'out of the same transaction or occurrence as the original claim, and between or among the same parties'.[23] Clearly, the Jewish claims do not arise from the same occurrence or even the same time-frame as Palestinian refugee claims. Jewish losses were not at the hands of Palestinian refugees, nor did Arab Jews cause Palestinian dispossession, although they benefited from it. Moreover, as Arab states insisted in UNCCP compensation discussions, Palestinian refugee claims are individual claims against the state of Israel, not collective claims that can be settled between Israel and Arab governments. The simultaneous existence of individual and collective compensation claims among various parties does not mean that such claims can or should be handled in the same forum or that they balance each other out. Each individual or collective claim should be handled in its appropriate forum, represented by authorized parties, with responsible parties held accountable.

RESURRECTION OF THE MYTH

In recent years, the World Organization of Jews from Arab Countries (WOJAC) has resurrected the myth constructed by Moshe Sharett in 1951, adding that by its calculations, the properties Jews 'abandoned' in Arab countries are worth about five times the value of properties 'left' by Palestinians in Israel. The Israeli government, in contrast, has maintained a relatively low profile on the issue. That low profile, however, does not mean that Israel has dropped the issue from its global strategy on Palestinian refugees.

BADIL Resource Centre suggests that 'Israeli officials may be heeding the advice of legal experts who have frequently warned that raising Jewish claims against third parties in the official Israeli-Palestinian negotiations would open the Pandora box of Palestinian and Arab counter-claims ...'.[24] Such a move would also not be supported by WOJAC, which represents claims of Arab Jews who would not authorize Israel to represent them. In an intriguing parallel, the state of Israel has also taken a back seat to organizations such the World Jewish Restitution Organization regarding Holocaust assets.[25] As with the issue of Holocaust assets, however, it should not be assumed that Israel has abandoned the issue. On the eve of the Camp David II Summit in July, Joseph Alpher, as adviser to the Israeli prime minister, stated that Barak 'is prepared to suggest creation of a new international body to distribute compensation to refugees with land claims and claims for other lost possessions ... The new international mechanism would replace the authority of ... UNRWA on any Palestinian compensation issue, and also would deal with land and property claims by Jews forced to flee Arab countries in 1948 [*sic*]'. Israel, Alpher said, would contribute financially to the new body, which would be funded in large part by 'some of the world's wealthier nations'.[26] Such statements indicate that Israel's position has not changed since 1951, and that it still maintains the posited link between Palestinian refugee losses and Arab Jewish losses.

In the post-Oslo context, some analysts, including Palestinians, have suggested that Jewish and Palestinian compensation claims might be settled 'in tandem' or that Jewish property claims against Arab governments be 'thrown into the cauldron' of compensation calculations for Palestinian refugees.[27] Such pragmatic linkages are not simply legally and historically baseless. More ominously, they contribute to perpetuating a 50-year myth designed to undermine Palestinian refugee rights and to exempt Israel from its obligations. It is time, finally, to expose the myth and deconstruct the link.

NOTES

1. Joseph P. Schechtman, *The Arab Refugee Problem* (New York: Philosophical Library, 1952), p. 101.
2. Ze'ev Schiff, 'The IDF's New Take on the Refugee Problem', *Ha'aretz* (5 November 1999). Palestinian and independent historians put the percentage much higher.
3. Schechtman, *The Arab Refugee Problem*, pp. 27–8, and Don Peretz, *Israel and the Palestine Arabs* (Washington, DC: The Middle East Institute, 1958), pp. 110–12.
4. United Nations General Assembly Resolution 194 (III) of December 1948, paragraph 11, quoted from <http://www.un.org>.
5. Schechtman, *The Arab Refugee Problem*, p. 110. See also Peretz, *Israel and the Palestine Arabs*, pp. 192–202.
6. Peretz, *Israel and the Palestine Arabs*, p. 200.
7. Abbas Shiblak, *The Lure of Zion: The Case of the Iraqi Jews* (London: Saqi Books, 1986), p. 68.
8. Ibid., p. 69.
9. Ibid., p. 131.
10. Ibid., pp. 115–19. According to Israeli statistics, 124,646 Iraqi-born Jews arrived in Israel from 1948 to 1953.
11. Ibid., pp. 122–3. See also Elmer Berger, *'Who Knows Better Must Say So!'* (New York: The Bookmaker, 1955), pp. 32–8. The bombing campaign and its leaders were confirmed by Israeli sources including *Ha'olam Hazeh* (29 May 1966) and the *Black Panther* magazine (9 November 1972). Riots in 1941 in which several Jews were killed were also later linked to the Zionist movement in Iraq.

12. Shiblak, *The Lure of Zion*, p. 127, Berger, *Those Who Know*, pp. 37–8, and Ali Ibrahim Abdo and Khairieh Kasmieh, *Jews of the Arab Countries* (Beirut: PLO Research Centre, 1971), pp. 30–1. The majority of them left Iraq later, mainly for Europe and the United States, leaving about 300 Jews in the country by the 1970s.

13. Shiblak, *The Lure of Zion*, p. 127, and Abdo and Kasmieh, *Jews of the Arab Countries*, pp. 30–1.

14. Shiblak, *The Lure of Zion*, citing the regulations, Appendix 5, pp. 144–6.

15. Schechtman, *The Arab Refugee Problem*, p. 112, English translation of *Divre haKnesset*, III, 19 March 1951, pp. 1358–9.

16. Naeim Giladi, 'The Jews of Iraq', reprinted interview by *The Link*, 'Americans for Middle East Understanding' (16 March 1998).

17. As quoted in Shiblak, *The Lure of Zion*, p. 90.

18. Approximate figures cited in Abdo and Kasmieh, *Jews of the Arab Countries*, and Schechtman, *The Arab Refugee Problem*.

19. See, for example, Schechtman, *The Arab Refugee Problem*, p. 112, which mentions 'considerable property which was disposed of by the respective governments', but provides no citation.

20. Shiblak, *The Lure of Zion*, pp. 87–8.

21. Ibid., p. 123.

22. Don Peretz, 'The Question of Compensation', *Palestinian Refugees: Their Problem and Future* (Washington, DC: The Center for Policy Analysis on Palestine, October 1994), pp. 15–20.

23. Susan Akram, e-mail communication, 29 November 1999.

24. BADIL Resource Centre, 'What's New about the Israeli Position on the Palestinian Refugee Question?' BADIL press release (14 October 1999). It is interesting, for example, that a provision for pursuing Jewish claims in the Camp David Agreement with Egypt has never been used.

25. Marilyn Henry, 'Where Israel is Failing the Jews', *Jerusalem Post* (17 September 1999), p. 4B. Israel has refrained from taking a leading role in Holocaust compensation negotiations, apparently for diplomatic reasons and economic interests with the involved states.

26. Michael McGuire, 'Barak has Plan on Refugee Compensation, Aid Says', *Chicago Tribune* (13 July 2000). Note the inaccuracies in Alpher's formulation, including the characterization that Jews fled Arab countries in 1948, although the majority left in the 1950s in circumstances unrelated to the 1948 war, and the implication that UNRWA has authority for refugee compensation, which it does not.

27. See, for example, Rashid Khalidi, 'Toward a Solution', *Palestinian Refugees: Their Problem and Future* (Washington, DC: The Center for Policy Analysis on Palestine, October 1994), p. 24.

13 VALUING PALESTINIAN LOSSES IN TODAY'S DOLLARS

Atif Kubursi

1

The Palestinian economy, which Israel usurped in 1948, was a viable and thriving economy with a significant flow of output and income that sustained a growing population of approximately two million people. The Zionist claim that Palestine was an empty and barren land is contradicted by the substantive and authoritative works of R. Loftus (1944), R. Nathan et al. (1946) and The Survey of Palestine (1945–46), which estimated the Net Domestic Product of Palestine to have exceeded £P123 million in 1944, with commerce, manufacturing and agriculture contributing almost equal shares. This income in 1944 translates into a total wealth estimate of over £P3.1 billion using a modest 4 per cent real rate of interest. The Arab share of this wealth is roughly estimated at 51.2 per cent using Loftus' calculation of the Arab share in total Palestinian Net Domestic Product (NDP) at the time. It follows that the Arab share of this wealth is about £P1.6 billion. Translating these into 1998 prices using the exchange rate of an £P = $4.03 and the US inflation rate between 1947 and 1998, these estimates add up to $2.3 billion in income and $57.8 billion in wealth. Furthermore, taking into account the impact of a 4 per cent real rate of growth that was surpassed between 1944 and 1948, the Arab NDP in Palestine will rise to $19.2 billion and the corresponding Arab wealth will rise to $480 billion.

Regardless of how high these estimates are, a homeland is much too precious to be assigned a monetary value. No financial award, however large, could compensate fully for its loss. However, the Arab wealth in Palestine which was confiscated by the Zionists in 1948 was substantial, and an accurate assessment of these assets would serve, at least, to indicate the magnitude of the losses and the difficulties the Palestinians had to endure in their absence. It also helps define the range of values that might be considered as basis for compensation should they choose this alternative. Estimating the losses and the discussion of compensation, however, do not override the basic issue, which is the right of return of the refugees. Compensation estimates are only meaningful within the overall context of the empowerment of refugees and the preservation of their options and choices. Compensation is seen as a complement to the right of return and not as a substitute.

Surely, not all aspects of the traumatic loss of a homeland can readily be measured in monetary terms. The argument here is that monetary values may be assigned to these losses that might be acceptable to those who suffered as fair compensation. There are many precedents that can be used to delineate the range of values to put on such losses. We have opted to use the special documentation that was used by Jews in their submissions for compensation to the Federal Republic of Germany under the terms of the *Wiedergutmachung* programme, *Wiedergutmachung* meaning 'to make something good again', in this case, for the crimes of the Nazis.

Use of the Jewish submissions are based on many considerations, but primarily on the fact that the Palestinian submissions to Israel for compensation cannot legitimately be dismissed by the same party that used them to get compensated. Moreover, the Jews were successful in their bid for compensation for psychological suffering under the *Wiedergutmachung;* a precedent of considerable importance to the many Palestinians who suffered severe psychological and other non-property related hardships. We will attempt here to assign monetary values to the psychological and human suffering of the Palestinians using the same estimates and rules that governed the compensation of Jews by the Federal Republic of Germany under the terms of the *Wiedergutmachung* programme. The following passage is a quote from the *Wiedergutmachung* document that deals with the need to consider compensation for non-property losses:

After the war, the occupation powers in Germany enacted laws in their individual zones which restored property confiscated by the Nazis to the original owners (mainly Jews). These laws were restricted to real property. They did not encompass personal damage to the victims of Nazi persecution – physical and psychological suffering, or unjust deprivation of freedom, or injury to a person's professional or economic potential. Nor did these laws provide for assistance to the widows and orphans of those who had died as a result of Hitler's policies.[1]

The parallels with the Palestinian situation are evident. It is easy to see that if for 'victims of Nazi persecution', 'victims of Zionist persecution' was substituted, a similar situation should apply to the Palestinians. The German basis of compensation was all-inclusive and that is the precedent that is relevant here and should form the basis of any estimate of Palestinian losses.

This chapter has a number of objectives, but its main purpose is to assess both the physical and psychological Palestinian losses in 1948 and to convert these values into current dollars. Although this is not the first such attempt, it is perhaps the most comprehensive and precise assessment, based on valuation methods, data and procedures that were not available to previous studies.

THE THEORETICAL BASIS FOR COMPENSATION[2]

Economics is based on the fundamental postulate that human beings when unimpeded would seek to arrange their economic affairs in such a way as to obtain the greatest possible satisfaction. Any arrangement that does not produce this outcome is inadequate and will soon be displaced by one yielding a higher level of satisfaction (or 'utility'). That is, individuals will take advantage of any opportunities for exchange to achieve the greatest possible satisfaction where their willingness to trade is matched exactly by their opportunity to do so. Circumstances outside the objective conditions of the market that preclude such an outcome imply lower levels of utility – loss of welfare, as it is usually called. The size of this loss is indicated by the difference between the levels of satisfaction attainable in the two circumstances. Alternatively, it is equal to that monetary compensation that would permit the higher level of utility to be realized.

This conception of economic loss also suggests that social losses are the sum total of individual losses. This is true, however, only if all goods are private goods (those goods any individual's consumption of which reduces what is available to others in the market). In the case of public goods (those goods of which one individual's consumption does not diminish their availability to other members of the society), special adjustments would have to be made.

Essential to this analysis is the specification of each individual utility function and the determination of the effect on utility of the forced or imposed situations that lead to loss of welfare. Individual utility indices differ not only with respect to the arguments that define them, they also differ with respect to their nature. Typically all things that contribute to utility are included as arguments of those indices. This would make the list too long for any useful analysis. Alternatively, we may group these arguments under the following headings: private goods, public goods, individual psychological needs, and social psychological needs. Private goods include all the commodities and services desired and purchased by consumers; public goods include education, health services, etc.; individual psychological needs cover a wide spectrum comprising tranquillity, safety, absence of pain, family cohesiveness, etc.; and social psychological needs include national identity, cultural activities, etc.

Another widely used approach to measure the losses of injured parties is predicated solely on the income streams that would prevail in the absence of the injury as compared to that existing stream. This restricts the losses to purely income losses and diminishes the range of injuries and the way different people respond to them. The utility analysis is more general, allows for different valuations and is more inclusive. It is predicated on two main assumptions:

- Individuals shall be considered better off if they are in a position of their own choosing. Since we define utility as that which individuals attempt to maximize, it follows that they will choose rather more than less utility. An increase in utility can then be regarded as synonymous with being better off.

- An individual utility depends entirely on the volume of commodities and services they consume and on the needs they satisfy. They will always be assumed to choose to consume more, or at least not less, of a commodity and to satisfy more of their needs rather than less.

This manner of defining the welfare function severely limits the form which social value judgements can take. If the welfare of society is held to depend upon the utility level of the members of society, and upon nothing else, then the only further social value judgements to be made concern the welfare significance of each individual's utility index. In a totally egalitarian society each person's utility would count equally, though some form of interpersonal compatibility of utility in cardinal terms would be necessary to give substance to the judgement. Alternatively, it might be held that some members of society are more deserving than others, and their utility indices would be weighted more heavily in the welfare function.

Whichever form is specified for the social welfare function, it is clear that individual losses are translated into social losses and the social welfare function can be used to assign valuation of these losses. The concept of compensation as developed by Hicks and Kaldor is a case in point.[3] The concept underlying the compensation principle is that if a change in a situation would result in some persons being better off and others worse off, those who gain could compensate the losers in such a way that on balance everybody would be better off.

Consider the representation of an individual's utility map in Figure 13.1. The numeraire (or money) is measured on the vertical axis and the commodity X on the horizontal. Consider first an individual who receives income OM_2 and purchases OX_1 of X at price P_2, and attains equilibrium at point A on U_1. If price is reduced to P_1, he will purchase OX_4 of X, and be in equilibrium at point B on U_{11} is the increase in his satisfaction; the problem is to express this in money. Seen differently, the individual is maximizing his utility at point B and a forced situation (a more binding budget constraint) is imposed on him which forces him to point A on U_1. His loss of satisfaction is the difference between U_1 and U_{11} and the challenge is to assign a dollar value to this loss. This can be done easily along the following lines developed by Hicks.

Construct a line with slope P_1 tangent to U_1 (at D) to intersect the ordinate at M_1. If the individual income is reduced by M_1M_2 at the same time as the price is reduced, he will be just as well off at D as he was at A. The amount M_1M_2 is therefore a monetary measure of how much better off he is if the price falls and there is no change in his money income. Alternatively, M_1M_2

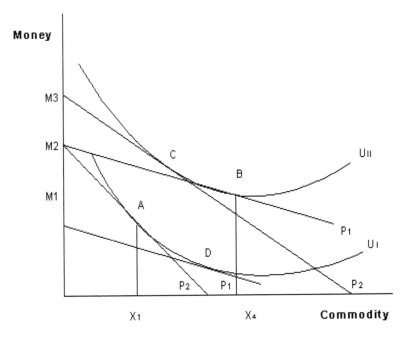

Figure 13.1 The Principle of Compensation

represents the financial compensation to be paid to the individual to take him back to his original utility level before the new imposed situation. M_1M_2 is called the 'compensating variation' for the price fall or for the forced situation.

Compensation is, therefore, synonymous with indemnification in the legal meaning of the undoing of damage done and losses suffered. *Total indemnification means in essence, a return to a situation which existed before the loss was incurred.* If it is done by way of restitution, the old situation is restored in specie. If it is done wholly or partially by way of compensation, the consequences of the damage are liquidated although the old situation is not restored in the true sense of the word.[4]

It is clear, however, that such a return to the old situation is possible only by way of total restitution or total indemnification and only when changes in the general financial, economic, social, and demographic situations are taken into account.

Previous Valuations of Palestinian Losses and their Deficiencies

A list of Arab losses in Palestine should include the following items:

Immovable property (real estate)

This includes all types of land (rural and urban) whether privately or collectively owned, publicly recorded premises (airports, harbours, railways, buildings, school, etc.), churches and mosques, etc.

Movable property

This includes a wide spectrum of commodities and assets ranging from consumer durable (appliances and furniture) to the tools and implements of industry, to human skills and education.

Lost opportunities

The income forgone due to loss of jobs and complementary inputs over a finite horizon constitutes a legitimate grievance that should be included in a comprehensive assessment of losses.

Psychological damage

Of special concern to human welfare are security, safety, identity, and self-realization. Any denial of these psychological 'commodities' would diminish the individual's equilibrium and happiness. In technical economic jargon it would force individuals to lower levels of utility.

The United Nations Palestine Conciliation Commission attempted to assess these losses, but it considered only a very small sub-set of these losses, and assigned the meagre sum of about £P120 million in 1951.[5] It is desirable and necessary, therefore, to re-examine the methodology used by the UN Land Specialist in 1951 and the work of the UN Land Expert in 1964,[6] and to re-evaluate these losses, adding to them the major components identified by broader considerations. We are emboldened to use this approach by a number of considerations:

1. the economic theoretic justification along the lines of the Hicks-Kaldor compensation principle noted above;
2. the settlement of Jewish claims by the Federal Republic of Germany, which included compensation for psychological damage and for denial of social needs.

Several other attempts have been made to identify and assess Palestinian losses. The UN Land Specialist's evaluation was indeed a major contribution to this literature. However, it was, as noted above, restricted to a small sub-set of the losses and assigned exceptionally low values to them (see Table 13.1).[7] There is also the study of the Arab Higher Committee (AHC), which was first published in Cairo in 1955 under the title *Palestinian Refugees: Victims of Imperialism and Zionism* and then in Beirut under the title *Statement* in 1961. The AHC assessments were substantially higher than those of the UN study and included several additional non-real estate assets (factories, jewellery, livestock, public transport facilities, etc.). Nevertheless, these estimates failed to include lost opportunities of income generation, the depletion of human capital stock, innumerable public and private assets (schools, airports), and private and social psychological damage. While it represented an improvement on the UN Land Specialist's study, it fell short of computing the full range of losses and used below-market indices in the evaluation of real-estate losses.[8]

A third assessment was carried out by the Arab League Expert Group and produced similar results to those of the AHC.[9] Finally, Professor Yusif Sayigh attempted to redress some of the omissions in the preceding assessments in his book *The Israeli Economy* (1964). His coverage was more extensive, his indices more realistic and generally in conformity with economic principles, and his analysis was more perceptive and original than all the preceding attempts. Again Professor Sayigh's estimates, although more extensive than preceding studies, did not cover the full range of lost assets and missed opportunities, and disregarded, for example, psychological damage. Besides, some of the figures used by Professor Sayigh were pure estimates that needed confirmation by collation with the results of hard surveys, particularly those relating to real estate.

Outline of the Chapter

A brief outline of the rest of the chapter is sketched here to set the tone for the development of our conclusions. The next section provides a detailed review of all past attempts at evaluating Palestinian losses, followed by a general overview of the Federal Republic of Germany's repatriation and compensation schemes for the victims of Nazi persecution as well as a reworking of the present value of these schemes in terms of today's prices. A special section is devoted to the examination of the typology of Palestinian losses excluding land, while a total section is devoted exclusively to the evaluation of rural and urban lands and housing. This is our major contribution and it was, therefore, felt necessary to devote a special section to the subject. Finally, we conclude with an overall estimate of the losses and an analysis of their significance and the way they differ or relate to earlier estimates.

A Synopsis of the Results

Full compensation for Palestinian material losses would amount to a sizeable total of £P743 million in 1948 prices. Translating this total into 1998 prices (adjusting only for the inflation rate between 1948 and 1998) in US dollars brings it to $20.9 billion. The inclusion of human capital losses raises the total compensation to $33.2 billion. If the modest real rate of growth of 4 per cent was included, these numbers rise to $148 billion and $236 billion, respectively. Indeed, the inclusion of compensation for psychological damage and pain, following the FRG compensation schemes to Jews, would raise this total to a staggering $281 billion.

2

The Topology of Palestinian Losses: A Re-evaluation

In 1944, Palestinian national income at market prices was estimated at
£P123 million. In Tables 13.1 and 13.2 we present estimates of national
income at different periods. It is clear from these tables that national income
in Palestine was significant and growing fast. Although inflation in the
1940s was high, it does not account for the full increase in national income
between 1939 and 1944, as is clear from the data in Table 13.3.

Given the prevailing real interest rate at the time (4 per cent), it is
legitimate to claim that the total wealth in Palestine (physical and human)
in 1944 was of the order of £P3.075 million. The Arab share of this wealth
is roughly 51.2 per cent, given the estimate of Loftus[10] of Arab net domestic
product of £P63 million in 1944. This translates into £P1,575 million.[11]
Since non-property income (labour income) then constituted about 50 per
cent of total income the value of non-human wealth should be around
£P787.5 million.[12] The refugees represent 55 per cent of the Arab
population of Palestine and, on the basis of this proportion, their share of
non-human wealth would be £P433 million in 1944 prices. Indeed, this is
a lower bound (minimum figure) because part of the human wealth was lost
as refugees also lost the complementary inputs that combined with their
labour to produce the output and income estimated above. Most of the
refugees were engaged in farming.[13] When they were deprived of their land,
their human capital was lost too. Refugees who were not farmers lost their
labour skills through unemployment. They were confined to camps by the
sheer economic force of being excess labour in already labour-surplus
economies.

Table 13.1: National Income of Palestine, 1939, 1942 and 1943 (£P million)

	1939	1942	1943
Agriculture, fisheries and forests	5.97	18.51	20.20
Manufacturing, mining, and private utilities	5.97	14.72	21.70
Contract building and construction	1.84	5.82	5.70
Housing	3.40	4.25	4.80
Transport and finance	4.59	9.33	11.00
Hotel, restaurant and domestic service	1.50	2.50	3.00
Other services	1.75	7.98	9.60
Government	3.47	5.81	7.20
Total	30.04	75.89	90.00

Source: Robert Nathan et al., *Palestine: Problems and Promise, an Economic Study*
(Washington, DC: Public Affairs Press 1946), p. 156.

If lost opportunity and deterioration of human capital, through lack of use or absence of complementary inputs, were to be valued, another £P300 million would have to be added to the losses of the refugees, bringing the total to £P733 million in 1944 prices.

Table 13.2: National Income of Palestine, 1944 (£P million)

Agriculture and livestock	28.257
Fisheries	0.850
Manufacturing and handicrafts	28.233
Housing	6.149
Building and construction	5.655
War Department airline employment	3.914
Palestine troops	2.270
Transport and communications	8.247
Commerce and finance	19.700
Government and local authorities	7.501
Hotels, restaurants and cafés	3.069
Domestic and other services	6.831
Overseas income	2.000
Total	123.023

Source: R. Loftus, *National Income of Palestine* (Jerusalem: Government Printer, 1944), p. 1.

Table 13.3: Inflation and Real Rate of Growth of GNP in Palestine, 1939–44

Year	Price	Nominal national income	Real national income in 1939 prices
1939	100	30.04	30.04
1940	131	—	—
1941	166	—	—
1942	211	75.89	35.97
1943	230	90.00	39.13
1944	248	123.02	49.61

Source: The price index is the cost of living index for Arabs and Jews from Palestine Year Book, p. 162. Nominal national income figures are from Tables 19.1 and 19.2 of this section. Real national income is calculated by dividing nominal NI by the price index.

Taking the lower of these figures as the working value of lost assets, a rough value of $20.6 billion (if the figures were adjusted for the inflation rate) and $146.2 billion (if the real rate of growth of 4 per cent was added to the inflation rate adjustment) will be required to compensate the Palestinian refugees for their loss of these assets and to put them in an economic position equivalent to that before they were driven out of their homeland in 1948.

The detailed enumeration of property losses by type of asset and by value is undertaken in the following sections. We begin with capital.

Ownership of Capital

There are a few countries for which estimates of national wealth have been compiled and few of them claim that they are anything more than rough approximations. Palestine is numbered among those countries, which have not attempted a complete enumeration of national wealth. Nevertheless, certain basic information is available and will be presented here.[14] Special care must be exercised to distinguish the shares of Arabs and Jews.

The additional problem of separating the relative shares of the two broad groups of the population in the wealth of the country has involved additional difficulties which have been overcome only by the use of the methods of approximation which must further widen the margin of error that limits the value of all such estimates.[15]

The enumerated capital includes: rural and urban land; industrial capital; agricultural capital; livestock; commercial and private vehicles; commercial assets; financial assets; private and personal wealth; infrastructure; forestry; natural resources.

Rural and urban lands are the main capital. Their valuation was realized through a thorough and detailed analysis, and a complete section is therefore devoted to this assessment. The remaining assets are assessed below.

Industrial Capital

The Palestine government's Census of Industry in 1943 covered a total of 3,470 establishments, of which 1,558 were Arab and non-Jewish interests. Of the five concessions which existed then, three were Jewish-owned: Palestine Electric Corporation, Palestine Potash Ltd., and Palestine Salt Co. The other two were Arab-owned: Jerusalem Electric and Public Service Corporation and Shukri Deeb and Son, Ltd.

The census did not cover the entire industrial sector but excluded, notably, small enterprises in printing and publishing, garages, laundries and small workshops, which were predominantly Arab-owned. The findings of this census are presented in Table 13.4.

Net output in manufacturing, mining, and private utilities was estimated in 1943 (see Table 13.2) to exceed £P21.7 million. The difference of about £P6.9 million between the national accounts estimate and that of the census may be accounted for entirely by the exclusion of small businesses from the 1943 census. Using an average capital/output ratio for Arab establishments of 1.197, we obtain a value of £P8.3 million as additional Arab industrial capital in this sector. This brings the total accumulation of capital invested in the industrial sector to about £P28.7 million. The Arab share works out as follows: £P2.1 million of capital invested in the census-included establishments; £P8.3 million of capital invested in the census-excluded establishments; £P2.5 million in the Arab-owned concessions. This gives a total of £P12.9 million in 1943 prices.

The 1948 value of Arab capital in industry, assuming a 10 per cent nominal growth rate per year between 1943 and 1948, is estimated to be approximately £P20.7 million.[16] The share of the refugees is again put at 55 per cent of the total, resulting in an approximate value of £P11.4 million.

Table 13.4: Ownership of Industry in Palestine, 1943

Item	Arab and Other non-Jewish	Jewish	Concessions	Total
Establishments No.	2,558	1,907	5	3,470
Capital invested £P	2,064,587	12,039,929	6,293,681	20,452,197
Horse power	2,625	57,410	133,673	194,708
Gross output £P	5,658,222	29,040,679	2,131,467	36,830,368
Net output £P	1,724,793	11,487,843	1,631,474	14,844,110
Persons engaged No.	8,804	37,773	3,400	49,977
Capital/output ratio	1.197	1.053	3.857	1.378

Source: A Survey of Palestine, p. 567.

Agricultural Capital

Three types of agricultural capital are to be distinguished here: first, agricultural implements of all sorts; second, the stock of livestock maintained by the farmer; and third, rural fixtures and houses (a special section will be devoted to that category).

The survey of Palestine values Arab agricultural capital at £P13.100 million in 1942 prices, divided as follows:[17] Arab rural housing £P9 million; Arab agricultural implements £P1 million; Arab livestock (at pre-war prices) £P3.100 million. This gives a total of £P13.100 million.

Translating these sums into 1948 prices, we get the following values: Arab rural housing £P15.9 million; Arab agricultural implements £P1.8 million; Arab livestock £P9.3 (assuming 300 per cent inflation). The total now becomes £P27.0 million.

However, a simple examination of the valuation of rural housing reveals that these figures seriously undervalue the premises. If the rental income of rural premises is used as a basis for valuation, a much higher capital value would have to be assigned to this item.

Annual rent on rural houses in 1948 averaged about £P30. If 10 per cent of this value is deducted for maintenance, a net value £P27 is left. Using the real rate of interest of 4 per cent as a basis of translating income into capital, an average value of £P675 is assigned to each house. Professor Sayigh estimates that 750,000 refugees had vacated 150,000 houses: 60,000 in urban areas and 90,000 in rural areas.[18]

Thus, total refugee losses in rural housing alone are valued at £P60.7 million, or five times more than the valuation of all Arab rural housing in the Survey. To point out the absurdity of the Survey's valuation we may look at the problem in a different manner and ask what implicit rental income could the Survey have assumed to reach the valuation of £P9 million. Using our 4 per cent real rate of interest, the implicit net rental income on rural property in the Survey's calculation is £P4 per year. Surely, this is a gross understatement of the average rental income from rural houses and fixtures.

Accepting the Survey's valuation of livestock and implements but adjusting the valuation of rural Arab houses and using the 55 per cent ratio of refugees to the total Arab population of Palestine, the following agricultural losses emerge: rural housing £P60.7 million; livestock £P5.1 million; agricultural implements £P1 million. These total £P66.8 million.

The distribution and valuation of Arab livestock in Palestine are presented in Table 13.5.

Table13.5: Estimated Number and Value of Livestock in Arab and Jewish Ownership

	Arab (1943)	Jewish (1942)	total 1942–43
Cattle	214,570	28,375	242,945
Buffaloes	4,972	—	4,972
Sheep over 1 year	224,942	19,120	244,062
Goats over 1 year	314,602	10,174	324,776
Camels over 1 year	29,736	—	29,736
Horses	16,869	2,152	19,021
Mules	7,328	2,534	9,862
Donkeys	105,414	2,322	107,736
Pigs	12,145	—	12,145
Fowls (excl. chickens)	1,202,122	669,506	1,871,628
Other poultry	16,394	74,259	90,653
Estimated total value at pre-war prices	£P3,100,000	£P1,440,000	£P4,540,000

Source: A Survey of Palestine, p. 568.

Commercial and Private Vehicles

In 1945 the Survey estimated that a total of 9,673 vehicles were on the road in Palestine with a value of £P3.2 million. The Arab share was £P1.3 million. Details are provided in Table 13.6. This valuation of Arab vehicles rises to

£P1.730 million when expressed in 1948 prices. Of this total the refugees account for £P952,000.

Table 13.6: Motor Vehicles, Number and Estimated Value in Arab (including other non-Jewish) and Jewish Ownership, 1945

| | Number | Value in £P'000 | | |
		Jewish	Arab and other	total
Omnibuses	1,342	566	377	943
Commercial vehicles:				
Light	921	106	57	163
Heavy	3,111	717	386	1,103
Taxis	1,248	150	183	333
Private	3,051	343	281	624
Total	9,673	1,882	1,284	3,166

Source: A Survey of Palestine, p. 568.

Commercial Capital and Stocks

Commercial activity covers both internal and external trade and finance. Internal trade in Palestine was strongly influenced by the availability of transport facilities, marketing channels, patterns of production, and size of the market. In rural areas and farming communities where primitive agricultural production was prevalent, and where transport facilities were limited or non-existent, the economic system was self-sufficient and only small commercial establishments were in operation.

On the other hand, in the areas where citriculture, horticulture, and industrialization prevailed, a network of retail and wholesale markets developed and a significant proportion of the domestic labour force was absorbed in this activity.

In 1944, trading establishments number 14,000,[19] and about 7,447 persons paid taxes on £P6 million of income derived from such trade activities. The average rental income on these premises was valued at £P175 per year. Again, assuming repairs and maintenance expenses to average 10 per cent of rental income, and dividing net rental income by the real rate of interest, the average capital value of such premises is £P3,937 per unit. Thus, a total of £P55.1 million represents the capital value of these premises in 1944.

Given that the net output of commerce in the national accounts was then £P19.7 million, this results in a reasonable capital/output ratio of 2.8. Since commercial activity is very sensitive to market size and the latter to population, it is possible to argue that the proportion of the Arab refugee population to the total population of Palestine is as good an indicator as any of their share in the total value of commercial premises. Thus, a total of £P30.3 million is deemed to be their share. In addition, the Survey assigns a value of £P1.951 million to commodity stocks owned by Arabs. Therefore, the total value of commercial fixed and circulating capital owned by the Arab refugees is £P31.4 million in 1944 prices or £P45.9 million in 1948 prices.[20]

Hotels and Restaurants

Professor Sayigh estimates a total of £P19 million as the value of Arab hotels and restaurants in Palestine in 1948.[21] Since not all of these premises were vacated after the Israeli occupation, only the usual 55 per cent can be assigned to the refugees. Thus, a total of £P10.5 million can be added to the losses of the Palestinians who were forced to abandon their restaurants and hotels.

The details of Professor Sayigh's estimations are as follows: 1,000 hotels × £P15,000/unit = £P15 million; 2,000 restaurants × £P2,000/unit = £P4 million. The total is £P19 million.

Financial Assets

Until the end of the nineteenth century money-lenders supplied the credit needs of the bulk of the population. In about the year 1900, a Jewish banking company was established to provide credit facilities to Jewish colonists. At the same time a number of credit cooperatives were formed to provide credit facilities to the Jewish settlers.

After the First World War, large-scale Jewish immigration accompanied by the import of large amounts of capital created the conditions for the emergence of modern banking. By 1935, a total of 113 banks were operating in Palestine of which 18 were classified as commercial banks; six of the total were foreign banks.[22]

Deposits totalled £P17.2 million on 20 June 1936 and by the same date in 1939 they had reached £P20.2 million.[23] Foreign banks accounted for about 64 per cent of the deposits in 1939.

From the outbreak of the war in September 1939 until about the end of 1941, war events dominated banking developments. Heavy withdrawals of deposits from local banks forced a number into liquidation. Thus, the total number of banks operating in Palestine was gradually reduced, so that by the end of the war the number of commercial banks had dropped to 25 comprising five foreign and 20 local.[24]

By July 1941, total deposits held by banks and credit cooperatives began to rise and this trend was maintained throughout the period 1941–45. On 31 October 1945, total deposits had reached the level of £P84.9 million. The distribution of these deposits was as follows: Arab deposits £P12.5 million; Jewish deposits £P67.5 million; other deposits (including government) £P4.9 million. This gives a total of £P84.9 million.

Several local banks developed rapidly during the war. Table 13.7 shows the paid-up capital, reserve funds, total deposits, and total advances and bills discounted at the Arab Bank Ltd and the Arab National Bank Ltd at the end of each year, commencing with the figures for the month of August 1939.

Table 13.7: The Arab Bank and the Arab National Bank Paid-Up Capital, Reserve Funds, Total Deposits, and Advances, 1939–45

Date	Paid-up Capital	Reserve Funds	Total Deposits	Total Advances and Bills Discounted
31. 8.39	209,494	32,205	376,180	456,186
31.12.39	209.506	34,309	299,223	462,617
31.12.40	209,790	37,848	245,619	412,064
31.12.41	209,818	38,577	532,515	499,790
31.12.42	213,634	40,859	1,330,953	992,377
31.12.43	480,508	148,971	3,430,197	2,392,268
31.12.44	1,120,000	559,731	5,067,421	3,311,176
31.10.45	1,415,752	977,877	6,970,728	5,256,214

Source: A Survey of Palestine, p. 559.

Total deposits in these two banks increased from £P376,180 in August 1939 to £P6,970,728 at 31 October 1945. This is generally explained by the fact that Arab farmers had enjoyed rising prices for their products and had accumulated substantial amounts in cash, some of which had been deposited with banks, and the remainder hoarded.

If we were to assume that the deposits at these two banks grew at half the rate of growth they had achieved between 1943 and 1945, total deposits in 1948 would have reached £P12.4 million.[25]

Deposits at other banks, particularly foreign banks, have been assumed to have totalled £P6.5 million; of which £P6 million were deposited at Barclay's and the Ottoman banks and the remainder spread over a number of smaller foreign banks.

On 20 July 1948, the Israeli authorities ordered that all credits belonging to refugees in all the banks in occupied Palestine should be frozen. The frozen accounts included demand deposits, savings accounts, guarantee funds, financial instruments of all sorts, jewels and other valuables in safety deposit boxes. The experts of the Palestine Conciliation Commission estimated these funds to amount to £P6 million owned by about 10,000 Palestinians including the assets of the Arab Bank and the Arab National Bank. Indeed, such an estimate is far below the actual deposits and paid-up capital in 1945.

Total Arab deposits were already over £P12.5 million in 1945. The outbreak of war in 1948 must surely have resulted in some withdrawals, but many refugees were forced to leave at short notice and many felt that their departure was temporary. Besides, the total value of deposits is only one item of many financial instruments left behind.

Even when a liberal allowance for withdrawals of 50 per cent of deposits by the refugees is entertained, the total remaining deposits would exceed £P9 million. If the customary 2:1 ratio of deposits to other financial instruments and liquid wealth (jewellery and gold) is accepted, then another £P4.5 million would have to be added to the £P9 million, giving a total of £P13.5; a more realistic assessment of financial losses sustained by the refugees.[26]

The Palestine Conciliation Commission called on Israel to release the funds and organize a committee of experts from both sides to work out the details of their release. Israel was reluctant to unblock the funds. Moreover, when they finally succumbed to international pressure they released only £1 million sterling. Even then, the Israelis had imposed a compulsory 10 per cent national loan on every account and the Israeli custodian charged exorbitant fees for administering the released funds.[27] The net outcome of all this is to reduce our estimates by £P1 million.

According to the Survey of Palestine over £P39.3 million of Palestine's foreign assets in 1945 were held by the Arab population.[28] These assets included £P29.2 million of net currency reserves and about £P9.3 million in net banking reserves. Indeed, a portion of these assets have not been recovered and could legitimately be added to other monetary losses. If only a third of these assets were lost, this would raise the net monetary losses to £P26.5 million.

The Arab Bank did liquidate and pay back all its depositors and the above figure must be adjusted in consequence. On 31 October 1945 the Arab Bank total deposits were about £P3.8 million. Deducting this amount in its entirety would leave a net monetary loss of £P22.7 million. The share of the refugees is again assessed at 55 per cent; this puts their share of the monetary losses at £P12.5 million.

Private and Personal Wealth

This wealth category includes all personal movable properties, whether physical or financial. We have already estimated the financial losses. Therefore, we shall now restrict ourselves to an assessment of personal effects and household furniture and fixtures. The UN Palestine Conciliation Commission Refugee Office concluded that it was unable to make such aggregate evaluation of Arab refugee movable properties, since some categories of movable property did not lend themselves to global evaluation and since there was no means of knowing what properties the refugees took with them and what they left behind.[29]

None the less, the Office adopted two methods. The first involved the use of the percentages adopted at the time of the Turkish/Greek exchange of populations, whereas the second stipulated the use of 40 per cent of the Arab share in national income at the time.

The Office took into account a long list of movable property such as: industrial equipment, commercial stocks, motor vehicles, agricultural implements, livestock, and household effects. It is clear, however, that the Office grossly underestimated these losses. This is evident on account of the fact that consumer expenditure studies show that in more countries an average of 16–20 per cent of total consumer expenditure generally goes on clothing, household equipment and furniture. In Table 13.8 we present data on different country groupings classified by per capita income level and the average share of total consumption allocated to clothing and household durable. The corresponding expenditures on these two items were 21.8 per cent in Greece, 14.6 per cent in Korea and 22.2 per cent in Israel.[30]

Table 13.8: Consumer Expenditures on Clothing and Household Durables

Per Capita Income (US dollars)	Clothing	Household Durables
100–500	0.074	0.074
500–1,000	0.138	0.092
1,000–1,500	0.109	0.093

Source: Constantino Lluch, Allan Powell and Ross Williamson, *Patterns in Household Demand and Saving* (Oxford: Oxford University Press, 1977), p. 52.

The major flaw in the UN Office's estimation procedure lies in its failure to distinguish between stocks and flows. Indeed, only 20 per cent or so is allocated yearly to expenditure on personal and household effects; but if household and personal items last for more than one year, as in fact they do, they need to be accumulated as a stock.

An easy alternative to accumulating these flows over time is to use the concept of permanent consumption out of permanent income and to convert permanent income into wealth. Thus, we begin by postulating a standard marginal propensity to consume of 80 per cent out of permanent income and a 20 per cent share of total consumption allocated to personal and household effects.

Let : *Permanent Income* $= \sum_{i=0}^{\infty} \lambda^i y_{t-i}$

where λ is the weight of current income in the formation of permanent income. It is generally less than one ($\lambda < 1$).

Permanent Consumption $= (0.8) \sum_{i=0}^{\infty} \lambda^i y_{t-i}$

Permanent consumption expenditures on clothing and household effects =

$$(0.2)(0.8)\sum_{i=0}^{\infty}\lambda^i y_{t-i}$$

The stocks of household effects and clothing are then =

$$\frac{(0.2)(0.8)\sum_{i=0}^{\infty}\lambda^i y_{t-i}}{r+d}$$

Where r is the real rate of interest and d is the depreciation rate of this stock. Assuming a constant real income of £P123 million, a real rate of interest of 4 per cent, and a depreciation rate of 10 per cent, our estimate of the stock of clothing and household effects in 1948 is £P196.8 million. The share of the refugees is 55 per cent or £P108.2 million, half of which they could have taken with them. Thus, a low estimate of £P54 million is assigned to these losses in 1948.

Infrastructure

Palestine enjoyed an efficient transportation system with all types of facilities: roads, railways, water and air transport. Development of these means was systematic and deliberate and served to avoid duplication and promote complementarity. By the early 1940s, Palestine had a number of communications facilities, which helped to mobilize factors of production and trade, and relayed information that was instrumental in accelerating economic growth. The total contribution of these facilities to national output reached £P8.3 million in 1944. Given the high capital/output ratio (usually 4 and higher) of this sector, a total of £P33.2 million could easily be assigned to these facilities. It may be necessary to deduct the capital value of vehicles from this to avoid double counting. This would reduce the capital valuation of £P30 million. Since the development of this infrastructure involved substantial time-lags, it may not be legitimate to impute only one-half of this value to the Arabs since they had paid more for it over the years than Jews who had come in large numbers only in the late 1930s to mid-1940s, and much of this infrastructure was built in the early 1930s. Nevertheless, only the lower proportion of 50 per cent will be used here: this results in a total valuation of £P15 million. The share of the refugees is again 55 per cent or £P8.3 million. Converting this value to 1948 prices results in a total of £P12.1 million.

Natural Resources, Water and Forestry

Although Palestine was not rich in natural resources, there were many that were or could have been developed. Palestine had chemicals from the Dead Sea (potassium, chlorine and bromine); limestone, clay, and sand for cement and brick production; phosphates; sand for glass manufacture; kaolin for pottery and ceramics; oil products; salt for food industries and tanning; water and a temperate climate for agriculture and tourism.

It is admittedly difficult to assign an accurate value to these resources in the absence of detailed information on prices, volumes, and cost of production. Therefore, our estimates of property losses undervalue the total losses actually suffered by the Palestinians inasmuch as we neglect to assign values to the loss of natural resources. If anything, the loss of water alone could be worth a substantial amount.

A Synopsis of Results

Palestinian losses in non-human wealth were staggering. We have managed to include at best a small sub-set of them. If losses in human wealth and the cost of psychological damage, pain and suffering were included, substantial new values would be added. Clearly, the largest Palestinian loss is that of land.

Excluding urban and rural land losses, a total of £P214.2 million has been identified as the cost to the Palestinian refugees of non-land losses in 1948. Agricultural capital accounted for the largest item of these losses with a total value of £P66.8 million. Private and personal property losses added another £P54 million. The smallest losses are associated with commercial and private vehicles. No estimate of losses in natural resources was made, for lack of any reliable data on volume and prices.

Indeed, the estimation of these refugee losses is generally sensitive to two factors. First, the proportion of refugees to the total Arab population of Palestine is assumed to be 55 per cent. Any higher proportion would raise the magnitude of the losses. Since there is good reason to believe that the refugees were principally the well-to-do people of Palestine, it is conceivable that the value of their share of property would be higher than their share in the total population. Second, the net product of Palestine in 1944 was assumed to be roughly divided between the Arabs and Jews. There are also strong grounds that suggest that the Arab share in the net domestic product of Palestine should be higher, since the Palestinians owned most of the resources of the country and numbers were very much greater than those of the Jews. Besides, the national accounting estimates would most likely understate their contributions, given the inevitable difficulties accounting procedures have in measuring non-market activities in traditional sectors.

As will be argued later, the summation of property losses would result in a capital valuation greater than that derived from capitalizing the Arab share of net domestic product. This discrepancy may be a strong indicator of a measurable underestimation of the Arab share in the net domestic product of Palestine in 1944.

Table 13.9: Alternative Valuations of Palestinian Physical and Human Losses (in £P million and US$ billion)

	Low (50 per cent)	Average (60 per cent)	High (68.61 per cent)
Physical Losses			
1944 prices	512.5	615.0	703.0
1948 prices	750.3	900.0	1,029.6
1998 prices (US$ billion)	21.1	25.3	28.9
1998 prices (US$ billion)	149.6	179.5	205.3
Physical and Human Losses			
1944 prices	812.5	915.0	1,003.0
1948 prices	1,189.5	1,340.0	1,468.5
1984 prices	33.4	37.6	41.2
1984 prices (US$ billion)	237.2	267.2	292.8

3

Valuation of Palestinian Urban and Rural Real Estate Losses

The purpose of this section is to identify and value rural and urban land and buildings vacated by Palestinian refugees in 1948. This is not the first time that such a valuation has been attempted. It is, however, the first systematic appraisal of these losses.

This section makes extensive use of a hitherto neglected set of UN records relating to real estate holdings in Palestine in 1946 and 1947. These records identify urban and rural properties by sub-district, village or town block and parcel number, by tax category of net annual value, by type of ownership and by ethnic background of the owner. We also draw on a second rich but neglected source of data relating to all property sales as registered in the official records of the government of Palestine between 1 January 1946 and 19 November 1947. Drawing on these two sources, records of sales, ownership, prices, and nature of property were coded for computer analysis. The results are the focus of this section.

In general, the basis for land appraisals is the selling price of the property. But when the recorded prices do not accurately reflect market prices, indirect tests are needed. First, the present values of the net streams of expected incomes of these representative farms were used as proxies for their capital values. Second, location and land fertility indicators were compared to sale values to determine the consistency of the two series.

The selling price of a unit of land in Palestine may understate its true value inasmuch as sellers and buyers have equal and common incentives to report lower values as they would both save on taxes and registration fees.

However, it is equally true that only prime parcels of land would generally be sold. Since the prices realized on the sales are generally used to estimate the values of comparable but unsold land, this procedure may overestimate the overall value of the land.

The use of the selling price as depicted in the realized sales therefore rests on the assumption that these two opposing forces (one to underestimate and the other to overestimate) would cancel each other out.

A Note on the Data

These types of data were collected, computer-coded and processed. These include data on sales of rural land and urban property and data on ownership patterns.

Over 4,000 recorded sales were identified and coded by sub-district, village, parcel number, block number, area of parcel, tax category, date of sale by day, month and year, share sold, value realized, private or public ownership, Jewish or Arab sale, and by type of sale.

More than one million records on urban areas were coded and stored. The following codes were used: urban area code, block number, parcel number, area of land, assessed price per metre, description of land, total number of rooms, total number of offices, shops, stables, huts, town halls, garages, storage rooms, area of buildings, price per metre of built-up area, net annual value, and finally the year of assessment. Similar codes were used for the rural areas.

Some gaps in the data, particularly the sales data, emerged in the course of their coding and processing. Complete data for all villages and tax categories only existed for very few sub-districts. The gaps are primarily the result of the absence of any recorded sales of particular grades of land in some villages or the total absence of any sale records for any tax category for an entire village.

Extensive coverage is noted for Acre, Beisan, Tiberias, Haifa, Tulkaram, Jaffa, Ramle, Nazareth, Safad and Jerusalem. Few records existed for Gaza, Nablus, Ramallah, Hebron and Jenin.

When gaps were identified, the following rules were used. First, Gaza was considered similar to Ramle, Hebron to Jerusalem, Jenin to Haifa and Tulkaram, Ramallah and Nablus to Jerusalem. Second, when no sales were recorded under a particular tax category in a given village, the average for the sub-district for the same tax category was used. Third, when a zero appears under a given tax category in a sub-district, the average for all sub-districts for the same tax category was used.

Urban land data proved to be more complicated, given their sheer magnitude. However, fewer gaps were encountered. The most glaring gap was the identification of a zero entry under a building area when an office or rooms were noted. This gap is significant inasmuch as it understates the areas of buildings and their values. To correct this gap, an average room size for the town was established and used to fill in the missing data.

Prices per metre of buildings provided another source of difficulty. They ranged from a low of about £P17 to a high of £P45. But these prices were apparently representative of cost before the Second World War. A major adjustment took place between 1940 and 1948 and so these prices had to be adjusted upward. The scale of the adjustment will be discussed in the latter part of this chapter.

Valuation of Rural Land

The consequence of using several methods and norms is naturally a multiplicity of values. However, these values are not substantially different from one another and indeed some procedures dominate over others.

Simple averages are seen to result in very high valuations which are not internally consistent. They are also generally sensitive to extreme values and when they are assigned equal weights they tend to generate extreme values. The weighted averages suffer from the same difficulty of being sensitive to extreme values but the weighting scheme infuses a proportionality criterion that moderates this sensitivity.

Although we shall present the results of using both simple and weighted averages, we have opted to use the lower but more realistic and defensible estimates generated by using weighted averages.

We shall present only four tables on rural land values in the text below; the rest of the results are in Part V of my contribution to Sami Hadawi's *Palestinian Losses in 1948*.[31] In Table 13.10, we present the results of using simple and weighted averages for each sub-district independent of tax category and village to assign values to rural losses. In the case of data gaps we used the corresponding averages of the remaining numbers.

Two valuations emerged. Using the simple average, a total of £P633.6 million was estimated, whereas using weighted averages a total of £P391.1 million resulted. Both valuations exclude the 12.5 million dunums[32] in Bersheeba which should add another £P25 million to each of these totals.

Alternatively, when the minimum values are assigned to the sub-district with no recorded sales, the simple averages result in a valuation of £P510 million, whereas the weighted averages result in a valuation of £P329 million.

The results of differentiating sale values by tax categories are presented in Table 13.12 for the weighted averages and in Table 13.13 for the simple averages. It is clear from these results that the total value of Arab rural land in Palestine in 1946/47 prices was of the order of £P30.4 million using weighted prices and £P million using simple averages of prices. Again a value of £P25 million should be added to these totals to include the valuation of the rural land in Beersheeba sub-district.

The robustness of the results for the weighted price under the different valuation schemes is another argument for their adoption. Several other criteria based on *a priori* expectations are used to substantiate this adoption.

1. the grade differentials of land appear to be preserved under this weighting scheme. In other words, it is to be expected that the value of citrus, banana, and fruit lands should dominate lower grades of land in tax categories 9–13, 14–15 and 16. This dominance is preserved.
2. Second, it is to be expected, for instance, that land near Acre, Jaffa, Haifa, and Jerusalem, which is uncultivable and capable of being used for building, should have higher values than comparable land in Nazareth, Tulkaram, Beisan and Tiberias. Again this expectation is fulfilled.

Another independent confirmation of the sale values may be obtained through a capitalization of the streams of net real incomes of farmlands. Since farming income is sensitive to location, climatic conditions, and type of crops, three representative farms located in different areas, and which were studied in detail in the Survey of Palestine are singled out for analysis here.[33]

Farm A is in the hills around Jerusalem and comprises 95 dunums of which only 30 dunums are used for plantation crops. The gross income of the farm is £P177,050, whereas net income is only £P100,400. The gross income from plantation crops is £P83,300. The details of production and income on the 30 dunums devoted to plantation crops are in Table 13.10.

Table 13.10: Income from Farm A: Plantation Crops

Crop	Area (dunums)	Yield (kg)	Value per kg (£P)	Gross Value (£P)
Olives	10	700	40	28.000
Figs	10	2,000 (dried)	9	18.000
Table grapes	5	2,500	5	12.500
Apricots	3	2,100	8	16.800
Almonds	2	160	50	8.000
Totals	30			83.000

Source: A Survey of Palestine, p. 281.

A total of 45 dunums are devoted to the production of annual crops. The gross income from this production is £P51.650. Given an annual cost of 450 mils per dunum, a net income of £P31,400 is identified. In addition to plantation crops and annual crops the farm derives a total of £P11,350 in net income from livestock.

The total annual net income of this farm is estimated to exceed £P100.400. It is derived as shown in Table 13.11.

Net income per dunum devoted to plantation crops is £P1.922 which when capitalized using a discount rate of 4 per cent yields an average value of £P48. This is almost exactly equal to the average dunum price used in valuing tax categories 5–13 in the Jerusalem area. The net income per dunum in the production of annual crops is about 698 mils which yields a capitalized value of £P17.444. The corresponding value used in Table 20.3 in Hadawi's book[34] for the same category of land in Jerusalem sub-district is £P19.456.

Table 13.11: Net Farm Income: Farm A

Details	Gross Income (£P)	Expenditures (£P)	Net Income (£P)
Plantation crops	83.300	25.650	57.650
Annual crops	51.650	20.250	31.400
Livestock	42.100	30.750	11.350
Total	177.050	76.650	100.400

Source: A Survey of Palestine, p. 284.

These figures are close enough to lend a measure of reliability to the estimates used in our tables, particularly those corresponding to the weighted averages. A similar analysis was carried out using information on Farm B located in Jenin sub-district. The area of this farm is 1.35 dunums of which 10 dunums are devoted to plantation crops and 120 dunums to annual crops in a three-course rotation. The details of income generated are presented in Table 13.12.

Table 13.12: Net Farm Income: Farm B

Details	Gross Income (£P)	Expenditures (£P)	Net Income (£P)
Plantation crops	28.000	7.000	21.000
Annual crops	137.500	66.000	71.500
Livestock	42.100	30.750	11.350
Total	207.600	103.750	103.850

Source: A Survey of Palestine, p. 286.

The net capitalized value for tax categories 9–13 in Jenin using the net stream of income of Farm B is £P39.450. This is slightly higher than the value of £P34.629 in Table 20.3 in Hadawi's book,[35] but close enough to make the number credible. We would in general prefer our estimates to be on the low side.

The value of £P304.4 million is chosen to represent a low estimate of Palestinian losses of rural land, exclusive of the losses in the Beersheeba sub-district. If the latter were included this estimate of the total loss would rise to £P329.4 million in 1946/47 prices. Applying the standard inflation adjustment raises the value to £P398.6 million in 1948 prices.

A third independent check uses the geographical details of each sub-district. The valuation of rural property village by village allowing for locational differences and grade differences results in a total valuation of £P329.4 million in 1946 prices. The inclusion of locational details in addition to the fertility differences resulted in the same total value for rural losses. This is another confirmation of the reliability of our estimates. This value rises to about £P398.6 million in 1948 prices.

Table 13.13: Valuation of Arab Urban Lands and Buildings in Palestine in 1947

Urban Area	Land Area (dunums)	Building Area (dunums)	Value of Land (£P)	Value of Buildings (£P)	Total Value of Buildings and Land (£P)
Acre	1,749	266	146,273	514,493	660,765
Beisan	590	72	85,709	125,712	211,421
Nazareth	4,585	310	212,469	715,217	927,686
Safad	1,053	191	104,215	371,240	475,455
Tiberias	611	127	283,040	364,928	647,968
Haifa	15,421	1,490	6,724,481	5,963,818	12,688,299
Jerusalem	10,798	1,043	4,902,832	11,754,215	16,657,047
Jaffa	9,683	1,035	3,504,084	4,500,730	8,004,814
Ramle	1,569	81	271,980	139,487	411,467
Lydda	3,210	167	556,453	287,570	844,023
Beersheba	3,256	169	90,680	290,802	381,482
Tel Aviv	1,970	190	752,225	511,239	1,263,464
Majdal	1,146	282	331,480	779,486	1,110,966
Shafa Amr	304	45	8,466	33,220	41,686
Total	55,675	5,468	17,974,387	26,352,157	44,326,544

Source: Hadawi (1988, p.176). Public lands are allocated according to population shares of land owned by Arabs and Jews and using the old vector of prices per metre of buildings as in Hadawi (ibid., Appendix XI, p. 316).

Valuation of Urban Property

Extensive information on urban land holdings and buildings in Palestine in 1947 was collected by the UN Land Expert. As noted above, these data formed the basis of our estimates of Arab urban property losses in 1947. Thirteen urban areas (or towns) are the focus of this section. More than 55,675 dunums of land and 5,468 dunums of buildings were identified to belong to Palestinians before 1948. These were lost following Israel's creation.The major losses, as is clear in Tables 13.13–13.17 are concentrated in Haifa, Jerusalem, Jaffa and Nazareth. The proportion of build-up areas on Arab urban lands varied from town to town, and those used were calculated from the UN data which were obtained from Hadawi (1988, Appendix XI, pp. 316–17). The highest proportions are in Majdal (24.7 per cent), in Tiberias (21 per cent) and in Safad (18.2 per cent). The overall effective average ratio of built-up area to land area is 9.8 per cent.

Table 13.14: Valuation of Arab Urban Lands and Buildings in Palestine in 1947

Urban Area	Land Area (dunums)	Building Area (dunums)	Value of Land (£P)	Value of Buildings (£P)	Total Value of Buildings (£P)
Acre	1,479	266	146,273	514,493	660,766
Beisan	587	71	85,273	123,966	209,239
Nazareth	4,585	310	212,469	715,217	927,686
Safad	1,049	191	103,820	371,240	475,455
Tiberias	673	139	311,761	399,347	711,108
Haifa	16,490	1,593	7,190,629	6,372,000	13,562,629
Jerusalem	10,636	1,027	4,829,276	11,629,748	16,459,024
Jaffa	9,613	1,028	3,478,752	4,554,040	8,032,792
Ramle	1,569	81	271,986	139,487	411,467
Lydda	3,210	167	556,453	287,570	844,023
Beersheba	3,341	173	93,047	297,560	390,607
Tel Aviv	1,648	179	705,640	481,510	1,187,150
Majdul	1,146	282	331,480	779,486	1,110,906
Shafa 'Amr	304	45	8,466	33,220	41,686
Total	56,530	5,552	18,325,325	26,698,884	45,024,209

Source: Hadawi (1988, p. 177). Public lands are allocated according to population shares of land owned by Arabs and Jews and using the old vector of prices per metre of buildings as in Hadawi (ibid., Appendix XI, p. 316).

The average price per dunum of land in the various urban areas was taken directly from UN statistics (see Hadawi, 1988, Appendix X, p. 315). Experts, familiar with market prices at the time, consider these prices to be somewhat on the low side. However, the discrepancies between market prices and these weighted averages are not considered to be substantial and so no adjustment was made to them. The fact that they are regarded as low has the advantage of refuting any charge that Arab claims are being exaggerated. In Tables 13.13–13.16, the weighted average price per dunum of land in each urban area is the same.

However, the average prices per square metre of buildings were found to understate grossly the true cost of replacement at the time. Thus, in Tables 13.13 and 13.14, the valuation of Arab urban buildings was undertaken using the UN data, whereas in Tables 13.15 and 13.16, a new set of prices per square metre of buildings that reflect the market values in 1947 was adopted. The difference in price by town is presented in Table 13.17.

Table 13.15: Valuation of Arab Urban Lands and Buildings in Palestine in 1947

Urban Areas	Land Area (dunums)	Building Area (dunums)	Value of Land (£P)	Value of Buildings (£P)	Total Value of Buildings and Land (£P)
Acre	1,749	266	146,273	2,660,000	2,806,273
Beisan	590	72	85,709	648,000	733,709
Nazareth	4,585	310	212,469	3,720,000	3,932,469
Safad	1,053	191	104,215	1,910,000	2,014,215
Tiberias	611	127	283,040	1,905,000	2,188,040
Haifa	15,422	1,490	6,724,481	29,800,000	36,524,481
Jerusalem	10,798	1,043	4,902,832	26,075,000	30,977,832
Jaffa	9,683	1,035	3,504,084	22,770,000	26,274,084
Ramle	1,569	81	271,980	810,000	1,081,980
Lydda	3,210	167	556,453	1,670,000	2,226,453
Beersheba	3,256	169	90,580	1,352,000	1,442,680
Tel Aviv	1,970	190	752,225	4,180,000	4,932,225
Majdal	1,146	282	331,480	2,538,000	2,869,480
Shafa 'Amr	304	45	8,466	405,000	413,466
Total	55,675	5,468	17,974,387	100,443,000	118,417,387

Source: Hadawi (1988, p. 178), public lands are allocated according to population shares of land owned by Arabs and Jews and using the old vector of prices per metre of buildings as in Hadawi (ibid., Appendix XI, pp. 316–17).

Naturally, major differences in the valuation of buildings emerge under the two price vectors. Since the lighter prices are more in line with the market norms in 1947, we have opted to use the estimates of Tables 13.15 and 13.16.

According to our figures, Arab urban losses in 1947 are evaluated at £P118.4 million. Of this total, almost £P18 million represents the value of vacated urban lands, and the remaining £P100.4 million the value of vacated buildings. In 1948 prices, these estimated losses rise to £P130.3 million.[36]

Table 13.16: Valuation of Arab Urban Lands and Buildings in Palestine in 1947

Urban Area	Land Area (dunums)	Building Area (dunums)	Value of Land (£P)	Value of Buildings (£P)	Total Value of Buildings and Land (£P)
Acre	1,479	266	146,273	2,660,000	2,806,273
Beisan	587	71	85,273	640,800	726,073
Nazareth	4,585	310	212,469	3,720,000	3,932,469
Safad	1,049	191	103,820	1,910,000	2,013,820
Tiberias	673	139	311,761	2,087,646	2,399,407
Haifa	16,490	1,593	7,190,629	31,858,680	39,049,309
Jerusalem	10,636	1,027	4,829,276	25,685,940	30,515,216
Jaffa	9,613	1,028	3,478,752	22,607,853	26,086,605
Ramle	1,569	81	271,986	810,000	1,081,986
Lydda	3,210	167	556,453	1,670,000	2,226,453
Beersheba	3,341	173	93,047	1,387,183	1,480,230
Tel Aviv	1,848	179	705,640	3,927,370	4,633,010
Majdal	1,146	282	331,480	2,538,000	2,869,480
Shafa 'Amr	304	45	8,466	405,000	413,466
Total	56,530	5,552	18,325,325	101,908,472	120,233,797

Source: Hadawi (1988, p. 179).

A number of observations should be made here to justify and validate the figure of £P130.3 million:

1. The land owned by the Arabs in the urban areas of Palestine includes that of Muslims, Christians, and other non-Jews lumped together. It is generally presumed, mistakenly, that the Arabs of Palestine are only those who profess the religion of Islam. The principle adopted here is to include all non-Jews at one group, which is considered as representative of Palestinian refugees.

2. The weighted prices of land were cross-classified against net annual values. The rank correlations were all higher than 0.72 (a perfect correlation coefficient is equal to one). This indicates that the vectors of weights and prices are consistent with a priori orderings of value as represented by net annual values.

3. The old vector of per metre prices of urban buildings was scaled upward using two principles – the relationship of one price to another is generally preserved in the two vectors and the blow-up scalars were calculated on the basis of changes in construction workers' wages and prices of construction materials between 1939 and 1947.

4. Whenever more than one estimate was made, the lower estimate was always adopted.
5. Several Arab households remained in their premises and so the total figure may overstate the magnitude of Arab urban property losses. However, our findings indicate that the proportion of urban lands and buildings that remained in the hands of Palestinians who opted to stay in Palestine in 1948 is only a tiny fraction of their original holdings. A case in point is Jerusalem, where it is estimated that at most 1,000 dunums of urban lands could be claimed to have remained in Arab hands after 1948. But given our modest estimates of the buildings on Arab land, and the adoption of the lower estimates of Arab shares in public lands, any overestimation in this regard is balanced, if not cancelled, by this source of underestimation.

Table 13.17: Prices per Metre of Urban Buildings in Palestine

	Old Price (£P)	New Price (£P)
Acre	1.944	10
Beisan	1.746	9
Nazareth	2.307	12
Safad	1.943	10
Tiberias	2.873	15
Haifa	4.000	20
Jerusalem	11.324	25
Jaffa	4.430	22
Ramle-Lydda	1.722	10
Beersheba	1.720	8
Tel Aviv	2.690	22
Majdal	2.765	9
Shafa 'Amr	0.737	9

Source: Hadawi (1988, p. 180).

In any case, even when the value of land owned by Arabs who remained in Palestine and retained ownership of their property is subtracted from the totals in Tables 13.13–13.16, the resulting figures are only marginally changed.

A Synopsis of Results

A total of £P528.9 million represents the value of Arab real estate losses in Palestine. By any standards this is a modest figure, even in 1948 prices – in fact it is an underestimate. But low as it is, it is still many times (over six times) higher than the valuation of these losses by the UN Refugee Office.

What is surprising about this discrepancy is the fact that we have used exactly the same UN data that should have formed the basis of their valuation. The only exception is the adjustment of building prices. But this exception can explain no more than 10 per cent of the discrepancy. The UN estimate of Palestinian real estate losses in 1948 is thus shamefully unrepresentative of their true market value.

4

Palestinian Losses: A Final Balance Sheet

A homeland is much too precious to be assigned a monetary value; and no people in history have been known willingly to trade their heritage for material benefits. No financial compensation – however attractive or substantial – could offset the effects of its loss. The loss of Palestine is principally a moral one, whose dimensions and costs stretch far beyond property and money.

The Palestinian wealth confiscated by the Zionists in Palestine was, however, considerable and the costs they imposed on the Palestinians exceeded their property losses. These costs must be assessed, despite the passage of time and despite the fact that no monetary value could ever equal or compensate the loss of a homeland. The principal reason for making the assessment is to document the scale and consequences of the calamity that has befallen the natives of the Holy Land. Its dimensions are not purely financial; they involve major psychological and human suffering that may only indirectly be assigned monetary values, like the Jewish claims against Germany under the *Wiedergutmachung*.

Palestinian property losses add up to a sizeable £P743 million in 1948 prices. When human capital losses are added, the total rises to £P1,182.2 million. When these sums are converted into 1984 prices, using the United States inflation rate between 1948 and 1984 and the prevailing rate of exchange of $4.03 to the British pound in 1948, the losses amount to a staggering $147,000 million for the all-inclusive wealth losses and $92,000 million for the restrictive physical property valuation.

It is legitimate to consider the appropriateness of using United States dollars and inflation rates. It is legitimate to ask whether it would be more appropriate to use British pounds and British inflation rates instead, given the close association between Britain and Palestine then. The 1984 value of the Palestinian losses using British inflation rates between 1948 and 1984 amounts to £48,900 million for the all-inclusive wealth valuation and £30,600 million for the valuation exclusive of human wealth.

The valuation in British pounds is significantly lower than in US dollars. But either valuation is indicative of major losses incurred by the Palestinians. The dollar valuation is perhaps more valid given the international standing of the dollar and its unequivocal dominance of the world financial markets. Most Arab economies of the area have broken their strong links with Britain and established new links with other trading partners using the dollar as the dominant international currency. The British pound has suffered major losses over the years and it is inconceivable that Palestine would have maintained its earlier ties to the British economy and the British pound, had it remained Arab and independent.

Distribution of Losses by Item

The losses of major items are presented in Table 13.18. The largest losses are those of rural land, accounting for 53.6 per cent of the total property losses. Urban and rural land losses together account for about 72 per cent of these losses.

Agricultural capital losses and losses of personal and household effects contribute £P66.8 million and £P54 million, respectively. Together they account for about 17 per cent of the total. The smallest losses are those of commercial and private vehicles.

Table 13.18: The Distribution of Palestinian Losses in 1948 Prices

Items	Value (£P million)
Industrial capital	11.400
Agricultural capital	66.800
Commercial and private vehicles	0.950
Commercial capital and stocks	45.900
Hotels and restaurants	10.500
Financial assets	12.500
Private and personal wealth	54.000
Infrastructure	12.100
Rural land	398.600
Urban property	130,259
Total	743.050

Human capital losses are real and substantial. The loss of complementary inputs reduced the productive Palestinian farmers to the status of surplus agricultural workers in the basically surplus labour economies of Jordan, Syria and Lebanon. Skilled Palestinian workers also had to compete with the indigenous workers in the host countries against several handicaps. A large number of them had to wait for months or years before they were able to find work, thereby wasting their potential and losing their proficiency.

The addition of human capital losses to property losses is justifiable and necessary. But the valuation procedure is not complete unless we add yet another sum to compensate for psychological suffering, dislocation, and loss of life and limb. The Jews were able to obtain enormous sums of money from the Federal Republic of Germany in compensation for these sufferings and losses. Merely on the basis of the proportion of the total compensation received by Jews from the FRG for these items, another $58.5 billion at least would have to be added to the total compensation bill in 1998 prices.

It has not been possible to find out how many Palestinians lost their lives or were injured during the creation of the state of Israel, and attempts to make a fair estimate have failed. However, the number is not inconsiderable since it was Zionist policy to terrorize the Palestinians into leaving their homes and country. Thus, before 15 May 1948 when the Jewish state was due to come into existence, the Zionists carried out a few calculated 'massacres' of the Deir Yassin type. This is confirmed from the following:

Sir John Bagot Glubb disclosed that a British officer of the Jordan Arab Legion under his command enquired of a Palestine government Jewish official 'whether the new Jewish state would not have many internal troubles in view of the fact that the Arab inhabitants of the Jewish state would be equal in number to the Jews'. The Jewish official is reported to have replied: 'Oh no! That will be fixed. A few calculated massacres will soon get rid of them.'

Arieh Yitzhaqi, Jewish historian and researcher, accused Palmach (the striking force of Hagana, controlled by the Jewish Agency) of operations similar to those of ETZEL (the Irgun Zvei Leumi led by Menachem Begin) and LEHI (the Stern Gang led by Yitzak Shamir). He wrote:

If we assemble the facts, we realize that, to a great extent, the battle followed the familiar pattern of the occupation of an Arab village in 1948. In the first months of the War of Independence, Hagana and Palmach troops carried out dozens of operations of this [Deir Yassin] kind, the method adopted being to raid an enemy village and blow up as many houses as possible in it. In the course of these operations, many old people, women and children were killed wherever there was resistance.[37]

Yitzhaqi then lists some of the Arab villages raided and the number of Arabs killed:

- Balad Esh-Sheikh – 60 killed, most of non-combatants.
- Sa'sa' – 20 houses were blown up over their inhabitants and some 60 Arabs were killed, most of them women and children.
- Katamon Quarter of Jerusalem – Arab women working as servants in the St. Simon Monastery were killed. (Note: Other deaths known to the writer who lived in Katamon Quarter were seven at Semiramis Hotel; and 14 buildings were blown up killing another three.)
- Lydda Town – orders were given to fire on anyone seen in the streets. In a few hours, going from house to house every moving target was fired at. According to the commander of Palmach's report, 250 Arabs were killed.

Arieh Yitzhaqi concludes: 'There were also the indiscriminate reprisal attacks on Arab civilian communications, in which many innocent citizens were killed.'[38]

Other large-scale massacres include:

- Deir Yassin – 250 men, women, and children.
- Ed-Dawayima – 200 killed, mostly between the ages of 70 and 90.

No figures are available for people killed in the major cities of Jaffa, Haifa and Jerusalem, or the smaller towns such as Acre, Nazareth, Ramle and Lydda, whose inhabitants were expelled. The numbers were none the less very large and the value of $23,000 million is surely a low estimate for these losses in human life and psychological damage.

The Capitalized Income Approach versus the Itemized Approach

When income is treated as the return on capital, a total valuation of £P634 million can be assigned to the property losses of Palestinian refugees in 1948. On the other hand, a total estimate of £P743 million is derived from a detailed enumeration of refugee losses in 1948. The two estimates vary by a total of £P109 million or 14.7 per cent. This difference could arise from a combination of the following factors:

1. because of a low estimate of the Palestinian share in net domestic product;
2. the share of labour income in net domestic product is overestimated;
3. the real rate of interest is overestimated;
4. the valuation of property losses is overestimated.

Factors 2–4 are not likely to explain the discrepancy because only the low estimates of property losses were used, labour income share in total net domestic product at the time could not possible have exceeded 50 per cent, given the nature of the Palestinian economy in 1948, and the real rate of interest is already low enough.

Factor 1 perhaps offers a better explanation of the difference between the two estimates of Palestinian property losses. There are strong grounds for believing that Loftus and other have exaggerated the share of Jews in net domestic product of Palestine in 1944/45. The financial and human capital that Jewish immigrants brought to Palestine in the 1930s and early 1940s was indeed substantial. However, the numbers of Jews in Palestine then and their share in total land ownership were so low that productivity differentials between them and Arab Palestinians could not possible justify or explain the high share of net domestic product assigned to them. Furthermore, there is always the possibility that national income accounting procedures which place heavy emphasis on organized market transactions could underestimate the products and income flows of traditional sectors. Consequently, the discrepancy could well be due to an underestimation of the Arab share in net domestic product which is derived primarily from traditional sector activities.

5

Conclusion

Although this is not the first attempt at assessing Palestinian losses, it is based on new, more comprehensive, consistent, and precise identifications and valuations, using the most recent methods and procedures and the rich data sets of the United Nations.

The basic premise of the valuation of Palestinian losses is that human beings when unimpeded would seek to attain the highest level of utility given their economic endowments and prices. Given the chance, individuals will take advantage of any exchange opportunity to move to their highest level of satisfaction where their willingness to trade is matched exactly by their ability to do so. Circumstances outside the objective conditions of the market that prevent the economic agents from reaching their preferred status and outcomes result in loss of satisfaction and welfare. The size of these losses is generally identified as the difference between the maximum level of satisfaction possible and that which is realized under the forced circumstances. Compensation is a mechanism to reinstate the individual to the situation he or she would have chosen before the damaging circumstances intervened.

Individual rights are at the heart of the compensation issue. Individuals or families have incurred the largest losses. The collective will as expressed by the Palestinian leadership can only theoretically forfeit collective rights. It is up to individuals to pursue their rights regardless of the Agreements the current Palestinian leadership may reach with the Israelis at this time, presumably on their behalf.

A homeland is too precious to be assigned a monetary value. This principle cannot be emphasized too strongly. Similarly, no financial compensation, however large, could make up for the loss of a homeland. Nor is there any compensation for the loss of human life, the dissolution of families, and the separation of loved ones. Our expression of these losses in financial terms does not mean that the figure we reached would compensate the Palestinians for the loss of Palestine. It is simply a historical and monetary valuation of the injustices inflicted on the Palestinians, no more and no less.

NOTES

1. Federal Republic of Germany. Focus on Restitution in Germany, No. 1, May 1985.
2. See J.R. Hicks, *A Revision of Demand Theory* (Oxford: Oxford University Press, 1951); and D.M. Winch. *Analytical Welfare Economics* (Baltimore: Penguin, 1971).
3. See Hicks, *A Revision*.
4. Nechmiah Robinson. *Indemnification and Reparation: Jewish Aspects* (New York: International Press, 1944), pp. 84–5.
5. The US dollar equivalent of this value is approximately $480 million at the then rate of $4.03 to the Palestinian Pound (UN Document A/Ac.25/W.81/Rev.2, Annex V dated 2 October 1961).

6. While the Land Expert who followed the Land Specialist in 1956 was appointed to carry out the work of identification and valuation of Arab losses in immovable property, he did not report the aggregate estimates in his Report of 1964 (UN Document A/AC.25/W.84/Appendix A).

7. The value of land for instance was derived as the capitalization of taxes. This has led to substantial underestimation inasmuch as these taxes were very low and were out of line with the market value of the assets.

8. The detailed assumptions made by AHC in assessing these losses will be dealt with in the next section.

9. Unfortunately, we do not have the full details of the methods and procedures used by this Expert Group.

10. Loftus, *National Income of Palestine* (Jerusalem: Government Printer, 1944).

11. The year 1936 is the only interwar year for which direct estimates of Palestine's product by ethnic origin are available.

12. This is based on the identification of 302,000 workers and average wage of about 500 fils per day. Survey of Palestine 1945–46, Jerusalem, p. 731.

13. Statistically, the man-farmer is the head of the family, but in point of fact, in the Arab world, the whole farming family, big and small, male and female, are engaged in the cultivation and harvesting of the produce.

14. See ibid., pp. 563–9.

15. Ibid., p. 563.

16. This is made up of 4 per cent real rate of growth and 6 per cent inflation.

17. Ibid., p. 569.

18. These figures were based on an estimated 5 persons per household.

19. Loftus, *National Income*, pp. 1–15.

20. A rate of 10 per cent was used.

21. Yusif A. Sayigh, *The Israeli Economy* (Beirut: PLO Research Centre, 1967), p. 108.

22. Said Himade, *The Economic Organization of Palestine* (Beirut: American University of Beirut, 1938), pp. 464–84.

23. Survey, p. 554.

24. Ibid., p. 556.

25. The annual rate of growth of deposits between 1943 and 1945 was 42.6 per cent. Half of it is 21 per cent, which is the assumed rate of growth here.

26. The assets of the Arab Bank and the Arab National Bank are not included and left to cover for any margin of error the estimates above might include.

27. See my chapter in Sami Hadawi (ed.), *Palestinian Rights and Losses in 1948* (London, Saqi Books, 1988).

28. Survey, pp. 565–6.

29. United Nations Conciliation Commission for Palestine. A/AC/.25/W.81Rev.2, p. 46.

30. Constantino Lluch, Allan Powell and Ross Williamson, *Patterns in Household Demand and Saving* (Oxford: Oxford University Press, 1977), pp. 40–1.

31. Hadawi, *Palestinian Rights and Losses in 1948*.

32. A dunum is 1,000 square metres.

33. Survey of Palestine, p. 555.

34. Hadawi, *Palestinian Rights and Losses in 1948*, pp. 170–1.

35. Ibid.

36. Yusif Sayigh, ibid., pp. 92–133.

37. Yediot Aharonot, *The Journal of Palestine Studies*, Vol. 1, No. 4 (Summer 1972), pp. 142–6.

38. Ibid.

14   A PROGRAMME FOR AN INDEPENDENT
       RIGHTS CAMPAIGN
Ingrid Jaradat Gassner

This chapter discusses the political circumstances in the 1967 occupied Palestinian lands and in 1948 Palestine/Israel which have led to the evolution of new, independent popular (grass-roots) initiatives for the defence of Palestinian refugee rights in the post-Oslo era. It summarizes the efforts at popular refugee organizing since 1994/95, as well as the principles and agenda defined in this process.[1]

We argue in this chapter that these independent, popular refugee initiatives present an opportunity for the development of a new model of issue-based activism. Under the condition that the backbone of such activism is formed by the popular, independent Palestinian refugee organizations and initiatives, it can help reconnect Palestinian grass-roots organizations with all those Palestinian (and non-Palestinian) activists, NGOs and professionals who are concerned about the future of Palestinian refugee rights, rebuild dialogue and cooperation between the Palestinian (refugee) community in the homeland and in exile, and become a strong tool of advocacy for refugees' rights of return, restitution of property and compensation.

While not wishing to simplify the complexity of the Palestinian struggle and its internal contradictions, since the establishment of the Palestine Liberation Organization (PLO) in 1964, we argue that the rift caused in the Palestinian National Movement by the signing and implementation of the Oslo Accords poses an unprecedented existential threat to the future of the Palestinian struggle. On the one hand, we are confronted with an extremely unfavourable balance of regional and international power and the division of the Palestinian people over its political programme (for or against Oslo). On the other hand, there is deep popular disappointment of and distrust in the political leadership, including both the Palestinian Authority (PA)/PLO and the unsuccessful Palestinian opposition. Popular disappointment and distrust in the historical party leadership and Palestinian intellectuals affiliated with it has led to an overwhelming 'crisis of representation' in the Palestinian struggle, a crisis which is the major reason for the failure of all initiatives aimed at rebuilding a unified Palestinian programme of action since Oslo.

Initiatives for a popular and independent refugee (internally displaced) campaign/movement – appearing on the political map of the 1967 occupied territories and in 1948 Palestine/Israel after the signing of the 1993 Oslo Accords – are an expression of the current crisis of representation, and a direct response of the refugee community to the exclusion of their rights from the political programme of the Palestinian leadership.

GRASS-ROOTS ACTIVISM IN PRE-OSLO PALESTINE

By the second half of the 1980s, the Palestinian popular uprising (the *Intifada*, 1987–91) in 1967-occupied Palestine shifted the focus of the Palestinian struggle to the West Bank and Gaza Strip. The PLO was thus temporarily extricated from the deep programmatic and organizational crisis it had entered due to its eviction from Lebanon in 1982.

Prior to that period, the role of the Palestinian national liberation movement in the occupied homeland (1967 and 1948) was defined mainly in terms of *Sumoud* (steadfastness), while the centre of action for the liberation of Palestine, via armed struggle and diplomacy, was based in the exile. Deep popular respect and admiration for the liberation fighters, as well as the hope created by the activities of the PLO among the Palestinian community in the homeland, facilitated the recruitment of popular strata to the organizational structures of the PLO in Palestine, especially in the late 1970s and early 1980s.

In 1948 Palestine/Israel, this resulted in the 'Palestinization of the Arabs of Israel' – a phenomenon much deplored by Israeli researchers and policy-makers at the time. The defence of land which had remained in Palestinian hands after the 1948 war became the focus of Palestinian organizing and mobilization in 1948 Palestine/Israel, especially after the brutal Israeli repression of the first large demonstration in March 1976 (Land Day). The Committee for the Defence of Arab Land, dominated by Palestinian members of the Israeli Communist Party and Abna' al-Balad (PFLP), remained the pillar of the Palestinian national struggle until 1990. The Committee became inactive, however, due to the weakening of the PLO as a result of the 1991 Gulf War, and the reshuffling of the Palestinian political forces in response to the Madrid/Oslo process. Since the early 1990s, the Arab Monitoring Committee (mainly Palestinian mayors and heads of local councils, Palestinian members of Knesset), which is characterized by a political orientation along the parameters set by the Israeli Labour Party much more than by the PLO/PA, has assumed a leadership role for the Palestinian community in 1948 Palestine/Israel.

The 1987 uprising (*Intifada*) in the 1967-occupied homeland was a spontaneous reaction of the popular strata against the heavy and humiliating Israeli repression in the 1980s (Rabin's 'Iron Fist' policy). Its transformation from spontaneous protest to organized resistance was facilitated by the presence of the organizational infrastructure set up earlier by the PLO member organizations.

The Palestinian *Intifada* defined itself as a popular resistance movement against the Israeli occupation in the 1967-occupied West Bank and Gaza Strip. The political programme of the Palestinian uprising, although maintaining the three historical pillars (liberation, self-determination, right of return), gave priority to the partial liberation of Palestine and self-determination, understood as the establishment of the Palestinian state in the liberated areas, over the earlier vision of total liberation and refugee return. This programme was shared by all PLO factions (whether as a tactical or strategic programme), and re-established a national consensus and unity which had been deeply eroded following the 1982 PLO withdrawal and destruction of its infrastructure in Lebanon.

The concreteness of the aims of the *Intifada*, and the popular belief in the achievability of its aims, gave rise to broad grass-roots support and credibility of the political leadership. The *Intifada* involved and united all social classes and strata of the Palestinian people in the 1967-occupied homeland, including its refugees. Palestinian refugee camps figured among the hard core of the struggle, and refugees, although existing as a special social category, did not represent a separate political category. The moral strength of the popular resistance movement in the 1967-occupied homeland also had a motivating and unifying impact on the otherwise politically divided Palestinian people and its organizations in exile.

THE POST-MADRID/OSLO PERIOD (1991–99)

Evolution of Independent Refugee Initiatives

The end of the Palestinian national consensus based on the programme of the *Intifada* came with the 1991 Gulf War and the subsequent Madrid Conference. The consensus was shattered completely by the 1993 Oslo Accords and the consequent implementation of the Israeli-Palestinian follow-up agreements.

Palestinians of 1948 Palestine/Israel already understood at the time of the 1991 Madrid Conference that they would, from now on, be excluded from the political programme of the Palestinian leadership. This caused large numbers of core activists to redirect their political efforts towards the struggle for equal citizens' rights in Israel, and strengthened the influence of Israeli Labour Party politics among the Palestinian community.

In the 1967-occupied homeland, the establishment of new institutions under the Palestinian Authority (PA), and its role as major employer among the popular strata, led to the destruction of the infrastructure set up by the popular resistance movement. Moreover, the gradual creation of a caricature of a Palestinian state, in parts of the 1967-occupied homeland, radically different from what had been the aim of the popular struggle, combined with economic difficulties caused by Israeli-imposed restrictions on freedom of movement, the continuation of human rights violations, and new PA clientalism and corruption, led to deep and broad disappointment among the Palestinian popular sector. Severe alienation of the popular strata from the political leadership (PA, as well as the unsuccessful opposition) and its unsuccessful national programme is the result.

Palestinian refugees in the homeland were especially struck by the negative effects of the Oslo process by the obvious exclusion of the Palestinian right of return from the political agenda of the dominant leadership group (PA) in the 1967-occupied lands. The process also led to the two-fold marginalization of the popular refugee sector from the scene of political action: first, in the framework of the general marginalization of the popular sector, and again, as a result of the exclusion of their central political concerns from the leadership's political debate and action.

Despite the radically different social and political realities of Palestinian refugees in the West Bank and Gaza (under Israeli occupation and PA rule) and refugees in 1948 Palestine (oppressed citizens of an exclusive Jewish state), both groups of refugees reacted along very similar lines. New, independent refugee initiatives designed as popular movements were established to lobby and pressure the respective authorities (PA, PLO, Israel) for the recognition of their legitimate rights, especially the right to return to their homes and properties in what is now Israel. Thus, for the first time in the history of the Palestinian struggle in Palestine, we are witnessing initiatives 'by refugees for refugees', that is, the evolution of refugees as a political category distinct from the Palestinian non-refugee population.

REFUGEE MOBILIZATION IN 1948 PALESTINE/ISRAEL

The establishment of the National Committee for the Defense of the Rights of the Internally Displaced in Israel (NCID) by activists and members of the displaced Palestinian communities in Israel came in reaction to the exclusion from the agenda of the Madrid Conference of 1948 Palestinians in general, and the concerns of the 200,000–250,000 internally displaced in particular. A first Action Committee (set up in 1992) recruited some 300 activists from community organizations and political parties, NGOs and Palestinian members of Knesset to its first popular conference held in Nazareth in March 1995. By 1999, the National Committee for the Internally Displaced, established at the 1995 Conference, represents some 60 uprooted Palestinian communities in Israel.

The NCID demands the implementation of UN Resolution 194 in regards to the internally displaced Palestinians as well as the refugees in exile, and lobbies for the inclusion of the file of the internally displaced in the context of the Palestinian refugee question. It organizes protest activities and voluntary workdays to maintain the holy sites in the depopulated villages, gathers demographic and property documentation, and lobbies in the Knesset for the approval of the return of internally displaced communities to their empty homes and properties. The NCID encouraged several

Palestinian displaced communities to form local action committees and registered associations, and succeeded to place the right of return of the internally displaced on the agenda of all Palestinian parties and the Arab Monitoring Committee in Israel.

REFUGEE MOBILIZATION IN 1967-OCCUPIED PALESTINE

The spark for the launching of the popular initiative for refugee rights was provided by an action programme developed in a meeting of political activists rooted in the refugee community. The meeting was held in the former Israeli prison compound of Al-Far'ah/Nablus District in December 1995; the action programme called for the formation of an independent refugee lobby, headed by refugee councils to be elected in a series of popular refugee conferences in the homeland and in the diaspora. The Union of Youth Activity Centres-West Bank (UYAC; a union formed by the Youth Activity Centres located in each refugee camp, in order to cope with the discontinuation of UNRWA support and protection) was chosen, in the absence of an appropriate political organization, to carry on this initiative.

Following a series of preparatory workshops in spring 1996, the first Popular Refugee Conference was held in Deheishe Refugee Camp in September 1996, directly followed by a similar conference in Gaza. The initiative failed to bring about the desired election of authentic refugee councils, mainly due to the intervention of sectarian party politics. Despite its failure on the organizational level, this popular refugee initiative was successful in defining the basic agenda and guidelines of the struggle for the defence of refugee rights in the 1967 occupied territories. (For details, see Recommendations of the First Popular Refugee Conference, Deheishe, September 1996 <www.badil.org/Refugee/Documents>.)

The initiative for the popular refugee conferences (and rumours around the formation of a Conference of Return in exile, as well as the prospect of the final status negotiations with Israel) led the PLO leadership to reactivate its Department for Refugee Affairs and to establish the Popular Service Committees as its presence in each refugee camp. While initially perceived as a threat and tool of control by the independent popular refugee initiative, the Popular Service Committees in the West Bank were rapidly integrated into the grass-roots network, because: 1) its members are authentic refugee activists; and 2) the PLO Department lacked the means (manpower, infrastructure and funds) required to build the Service Committees as an alternative to the independent initiative.

Throughout 1997–78, strategy debates, lobbying and protest activities carried out by activists affiliated with the UYAC, Popular Service Committees and local refugee committees continued; they were joined by members of the Palestinian Legislative Council (PLC), especially by the PLC/Refugee Subcommittee whose members were elected by a refugee constituency, and by activists in Palestinian institutions (unions, PNC, etc.). In early 1999, BADIL Resource Centre undertook a new effort to structure the debate among this loose network of activists and to define priorities and agenda by means of a series of strategy workshops (see Principles and Agenda, below). Despite the absence of a formal structure, the short history of the independent refugee initiative in Palestine can show achievements, among them the unification of the UYAC West Bank with the Youth Activity Centres in Gaza refugee camps into the Union of Youth Activity Centres-Palestine; the adoption by the PA of the stand that it represents, in legal terms, a 'host country' of the refugees in its territory; and, in 1999, the public expression of support for the independent, popular refugee campaign by the PLO Department for Refugee Affairs.

Principles and Agenda of the Independent, Community-based Campaign for Palestinian Refugee Rights

The following recommendations summarize the results of a series of strategy workshops of West Bank refugee activists and members of Palestinian institutions. The recommendations obtained the support of the PLO Department for Refugee Affairs. (Compiled by the BADIL Friends Forum, spring 1999.)

Organizational Principles

1. Given the current disarray of Palestinian partisan politics and the alienation of the refugee community from the PA and partisan political leadership, a broad and non-sectarian movement is the best organizational model to pressure and lobby for the protection of Palestinian refugee rights.

2. The backbone of the movement must be formed by Palestinian popular organizations and initiatives that express the genuine needs and demands of Palestinian refugees.

3. The movement must *be independent* from the PA/PLO bureaucracy bound by the Oslo programme and independent from partisan interests. It will work to pressure the PLO, in order to prevent a political compromise of the legitimate rights of Palestinian refugees, and assist and strengthen all those forces in the PA/PLO who take a positive stand on the Palestinian right of return.

4. The solution of the Palestinian refugee question is an extremely difficult task. It requires unity and mutual support, and must include the refugees in the homeland (1967 and 1948) and the diaspora in order to overcome the threat of geographic separation, and include Palestinian non-refugees in order to avoid sectarian activism.

Agenda

1. The campaign must focus on raising awareness and support for the Palestinian right of return in order to counter the position – held by Israel and powerful western governments – that this right is outdated. Palestinian organizations are called upon to raise UN Resolution 194

(Right of Return) in conjunction with UN Resolution 181 (UN Partition Resolution), because Israel continues to refer to the latter as representing the legal basis for the establishment of the Jewish state, while violating its obligation, under the same UN resolution, to guarantee freedom and rights of its non-Jewish population.

2. Recognition by Israel, of the right of return as a principle is a Palestinian precondition for negotiations over a concrete solution of the Palestinian refugee question. No concrete scenarios and mechanisms for a solution are to be advanced by negotiators, researchers and Palestinian institutions until Israel's acceptance of the principle of return.

3. Awareness raising and mobilization among the Palestinian refugee community must also address immediate refugee needs that result from the heavy economic pressure in the camps.

4. The Palestinian debate about the concrete meaning of the right of return in the current political context must be continued and intensified. Central questions must be clarified with the assistance of experts, in order to achieve a sound Palestinian consensus and the unification of Palestinian public speech. Among the central questions are: i) the complementary relationship of the right of return, restitution of property and compensation as part and parcel of Palestinian refugee rights to avoid addressing these rights as if they were mutually exclusive; ii) the implications of the right of return as both an individual (human) and collective (political) right: options of return must be explored on both levels; the debate about return with or without Palestinian sovereignty must be continued; iii) the development of concrete Palestinian scenarios for the option of return to 1948 Palestine/Israel (return to where, under which mechanism?); iv) exploration of the impact of Palestinian statehood on the right of return in its legal and political context; v) the difference, according to international law, between return to the PA areas and return to the original homes and lands. In order to prevent public confusion about the concrete meaning of the term, we recommend speaking about the 'right of return to homes and properties' (instead of using 'homeland' used by the PA to refer to the future state).

5. Palestinian pressure for maintenance and improvement of UNRWA services is important, not only because of the services provided by the Agency, but also because UNRWA is an expression of the international responsibility for the Palestinian refugee question.

6. The movement calls upon the PLO to prepare – with the help of experts – position papers for the negotiations with Israel. These papers should be presented to the Palestinian Council prior to disclosure in the negotiations. Since an agreement on the solution of the refugee question with Israel cannot be expected in the short term, a Palestinian strategy for dealing with the delay of this central question must be developed.

7. The movement calls upon the PLO to democratize its institutions dealing with the refugee question, especially the Department of Refugee Affairs

and the PLO Service Committees, in order to allow for the involvement of popular refugee activists and experts.

TOWARDS A PALESTINIAN-INTERNATIONAL CAMPAIGN FOR THE DEFENSE OF PALESTINIAN REFUGEE RIGHTS

By the year 2000, many of the central activists of the popular initiatives were connected in the BADIL Friends Forum (established in 1998), which – through BADIL Resource Centre – has begun to develop contacts and cooperation with Palestinians in Lebanon and the National Committee for the Internally Displaced and NGOs in 1948 Palestine/Israel.

Based on the principles and agenda defined for the local grass-roots campaign in Palestine, BADIL proposes an initiative for an International Campaign for the Defence of Palestinian Refugee Rights to NGOs and solidarity groups in Europe, the United States, Canada and Australia. This international campaign initiative aims to:

1. Build a solid international network for advocacy for Palestinian refugees' rights right of return, restitution and compensation.
2. Assist refugee grass-roots initiatives by means of professional expertise as well as logistic and financial support in: regional networking, service development, advocacy;
3. Raise international public awareness for Palestinian refugees' right of return, restitution of property, and compensation. The public awareness campaign should be designed in the context of the anti-racism campaign and highlight the fact that racism, discrimination, and ethnic-cleansing policies inherent in the Zionist model of the exclusive Jewish state represent both the cause of the massive Palestinian displacement in 1947–48 and the major obstacle to their repatriation in the framework of a just and durable solution in the future. Public education about the ongoing validity of the right of return must be the priority (return is legitimate according to international law; represents refugee choice; is practically possible without resulting in massive displacement of the Jewish population in Israel; is economically more feasible than payment of compensation; will be conducive to regional cooperation and development). International responsibility for Palestinian refugees (protection/UNHCR and assistance/UNRWA) can be highlighted in this context.
4. Develop tools (advocacy documents), strategies and logistics for efficient advocacy and lobbying among key policy-makers. (For details on BADIL's Campaign proposal, see BADIL Packet for Information and Mobilization for Palestinian Refugee Rights, 2nd edition, February 2000.)

NOTE

1. For a description of the socioeconomic situation of Palestinian refugees in the West Bank, Gaza, Lebanon, Jordan, Syria, Israel and Egypt, see *Country Profiles* (Bethlehem: BADIL Resource Centre, 2000).

15 TOWARDS CONVENING A CONGRESS OF RETURN AND SELF-DETERMINATION

Naseer H. Aruri

Despite the numerous meetings held between Palestinian and Israeli negotiators since the Oslo Declaration of Principles (DOP) was signed by Yasir Arafat and the late Yitzhak Rabin in the White House's Rose Garden, the input of the community of more than 5.5 million Palestinian refugees has never been sought or solicited. And despite Arafat's millions of miles of travel to meet leaders all over the world, not one single mile has been invested by the Palestinian leadership in consulting representatives of its refugee constituency. Thus it has become paramount that an all-Palestinian Congress of Return and Self-Determination be convened to reassert the right of return, among other fundamental rights. The future of these rights seems bleak under the US-brokered 'peace process' and the initial reluctant acquiescence of Arafat's Palestine Authority (PA) within that process.

The right of return for Palestinian refugees emerged as the single most important challenge facing Palestinian and Israeli negotiators during the year 2000, as they were summoned to reach a final status agreement prior to the end of Bill Clinton's presidency. Paradoxically, however, while the issue continued to bedevil negotiators, it seemed certain that it did not occupy a real place on the active agenda of the negotiations. Hence, Palestinians everywhere began to insist that peace was not possible without return. Thus, the issue has recently become a rallying point for Palestinians struggling for their fundamental rights. It has been placed on the public agenda not by the PA, the presumed heir of the sole legitimate representative of the Palestinian people (PLO), nor by the Arab League, and certainly not by the self-appointed guardian of the Middle East 'peace process' – the United States – but by various segments of Palestinian society. In particular, it has been grass-roots organizations – older ones and recently formed ones in the refugee camps, inside Israel and in the Palestinian diaspora – that have seized the initiative by restoring the right of return to a central place in the discourse about Palestine.

As an example, on 16 September 2000, two demonstrations attended by several thousand activists were held simultaneously in Washington and

London to promote the right of return. During the same period, similar demonstrations, most of which coincided with the eighteenth anniversary of the massacres at the Sabra and Shatilla camps in Lebanon, were staged in the Lebanese refugee camps and in Palestine. Numerous conferences, workshops and rallies were held in and outside the region bringing together community leaders, activists and scholars to discuss various strategies for reviving the right of return and ensuring a prominent place for it on whatever agenda of whatever peace talks dealing with the question of Palestine. Such gatherings, mass rallies, symposia and public protests are likely to be repeated again and again in various cities and refugee camps, in the region and around the world, until the right of return is dealt with in a fair and legal manner in any future settlement.

A HISTORICAL OVERVIEW

Since the 1948 Palestinian catastrophe (*nakba*) and its concomitant creation of the Palestinian refugee crisis, the issues of return, compensation and restitution have taken a back seat in the discussions on the overall question of Palestine. During the better part of the past five decades since the creation of the refugee problem, the issue of refugees has been rendered secondary and even tertiary, despite the fact that Israel's admission to the United Nations was made contingent on its compliance with the UN General Assembly Resolution 194 of December 1948. Resolution 273 of 11 May 1949 made Israel's admission conditional on an unambiguous commitment by Israel to respect 'unreservedly' UN resolutions pertaining to the Arab-Israeli conflict, including Resolution 194. Article 11 of that resolution resolved that Palestinian refugees wishing to return to their homes and live in peace with their neighbours should be permitted to do so at the earliest practicable date, and that compensation should be paid for the property of those choosing not to return and for loss of or damage to property, which, under principles of international law or in equity, should be made good by the governments or authorities responsible.

As we know, Israel was admitted to the United Nations without complying, thus keeping alive and exacerbating the refugee crisis we face today. Resolution 194 has been ritualistically reaffirmed more than 100 times. However, the will to make that reaffirmation a reality is not on the international agenda.

Israel's non-compliance had impelled the General Assembly to adopt other resolutions calling on it to meet its obligations to the refugees. For example, Resolution 3236 of 1974 upheld the 'inalienable right of the Palestinians to return to their homes and property from which they have been displaced and uprooted'; and in 1997, Resolution 52/62 reaffirmed that the 'Palestine Arab refugees are entitled to their property and to the income derived therefrom, in conformity with the principles of justice and equity'.

With the emergence of the PLO and resumption of armed struggle during the 1960s, the issue of the refugees, rather than becoming the central human dimension of the revolutionaries' struggle to reverse the *nakba*, was relegated to a humanitarian-charitable issue better left to the likes of UNRWA. The armed struggle thesis posited that the refugees would be naturally accommodated in the future democratic secular state – the stated goal of the PLO.

The 1967 war exacerbated the refugee crisis by creating a new generation of refugees. At the same time, the crisis disappeared from the PLO agenda. The overarching objective of the PLO was global recognition of its status as sole legitimate representative of the Palestine people. Subsequently, throughout the 1960s and 1970s, PLO legitimacy and Palestinian self-determination became intertwined, indistinguishable goals. Moreover, once it became the anchor and unifier of Palestinians scattered throughout the diaspora, the PLO perceived discussion of the plight of the refugees as a distraction from the 'important' issues. True, the refugees remained a humanitarian concern, especially for showcasing the 'social' institutions of the PLO in Lebanon. Yet from the perspective of political rights, the refugee question continued to have no political content or force.

After 1972, as the armed struggle gave way to a new form of diplomatic programme, the refugee question became dormant. The new definition of 'struggle', formulated in Arab summit conferences in Algiers, Rabat and Cairo, encouraged the PLO to promote itself together with a programme of 'self-determination' in a mini-Palestinian state in the West Bank and Gaza. In return for supporting the 'new' PLO with its truncated objectives in capitals around the globe, the Arab governments demanded an unwritten *quid pro quo*. The PLO would drastically scale down its guerrilla operations and cease its rhetoric about a democratic secular state in all of historic Palestine. In return, not only would the PLO be 'rewarded' with Arab diplomatic support in far-flung countries, the Arab governments would also increase economic assistance to the organization.

Thus, for the next two decades, until the signing of the Oslo Accords in 1993, that unwritten agreement was to occupy the combined energies of Palestinians and Arabs. During that period, all matters relating to refugees were removed from the PLO's public agenda. The PLO quest for international recognition, as the sole legitimate representative of the Palestinian people and as a solid bargaining partner for the creation of a mini-state, claimed the lion's share of Arab and Palestinian resources while refugee rights and interests were set aside.

While the PLO achieved its goal of becoming the focal point of the Palestine question, ironically, it became the first Arab party to sign an agreement that effectively denied the refugees their internationally recognized rights. Indeed, the PLO, the supposed national organization of the dispersed Palestinian people seeking to achieve their inalienable national and political rights, has for all practical purposes signed away the right of return.

The downgrading of the core problem, the refugee crisis, in favour of making the PLO 'sole legitimate representative' was an unsound decision.

The current re-emergence of the right of return in such a vigorous manner, after almost a quarter of a century of dormancy, signifies a belated vote of no confidence in PLO policies towards the refugees as well as a people's movement seeking redress.

THE 'PEACE PROCESS' AND THE RIGHT OF RETURN

If there were ever the slightest hope that the refugees could attain even a modicum of their internationally recognized rights within the context of the Oslo framework, such hopes have been dashed. Under the unwritten rules of the 'peace process', it is considered a sign of intransigence were Arafat or any of his negotiators to bring up the right of return, Resolutions 194 or the 29 November 1947 Partition Resolution 181. The return of refugees is a *real* demographic threat to Israel. This is logical since they insist, juridically and in every other way, that the state of Israel should remain exclusively Jewish. That would not be possible if there were not a Jewish majority. This ethos is prevalent amongst large segments of the Jewish-Israeli 'peace movement'. The Palestinian refugees' right of return is not only absent from the agenda of official Israel and the Israeli Jewish public; it is actively and vociferously opposed. For example, 33 prominent members of the Israeli Jewish peace movement addressed a message to the 'Palestinian leadership' in a front-page advertisement in *Ha'aretz* (2 January 2001). They stated, in part:

We recognize the true and urgent need to resolve the problem of the 1948 refugees, and we recognize the part of the State of Israel, also, in the creation of the problem. The refugees will have the right to return to their homeland, Palestine, and settle there. But, we want to clarify that we shall never be able to agree to the return of the refugees to within the borders of Israel, for the meaning of such a return would be the elimination of the State of Israel.

One of the signatories, Amos Oz, wrote an article in the *New York Times* (6 January 2001) in which he praised Ehud Barak's government for offering to let the Palestinians govern themselves, as he put it, while describing the PA as the real 'obstacle to peace', for having raised the issue of the right of return.

Implementing the Palestinian 'right of return' would amount to abolishing the Jewish people's right to self-determination. It would eventually make the Jewish people no more than an ethnic minority in the country, just as fundamentalist Islam would have it.

The Israeli public thus seems united in its rejection of international law, as it pertains to the rights of the Palestinian refugees. And yet, of all the issues to be addressed in the so-called final status negotiations – borders, Jerusalem, settlements, water, refugees – the issue of the refugees is certainly not only the most thorny, but also unique in that it is the only issue that links 1948 to 1967. Israel has been acting in the 'peace process' as if the conflict began in 1967 and not in 1948; therefore, the borders of 4 June 1967 constitute Israel's frame of reference for resolving the final status issues. Paradoxically, those borders, known as 'the green line', have continually been eroded by successive Israeli governments. It is really the ever-elusive 'green line' which may, in real terms, not exist at all.

The question of refugees, however, clearly encompasses the fate of the 5.5 million Palestinians who lost their homes in the 531 villages and towns in Palestine in 1948 and in 1967. It does not only concern the 3.7 million, who are registered with the United Nations Relief and Works Agency (UNRWA) and who live in the more than 60 camps in four Arab countries and in Palestine.

Refugees also include those who live in the area on which the Jewish state was set up in 1948. They are internal refugees, who can see their land, but cannot live on it or make use of it. They are what Israel refers to as present absentees. Many of them live in the so-called 'unrecognized villages'. These villages exist, but cannot be found on any official map. They receive no municipal services whatsoever, despite the fact that their inhabitants are tax-paying Israeli citizens. They are not entitled to water and electricity, schools and health facilities, paved roads so that they can reach their villages or many other facilities. Instead, the ubiquitous bulldozer is ever threatening most of these villages. The present absentees and the citizens of the unrecognized villages certainly qualify for the status of refugees.

The displaced Palestinians, who are citizens of the state of Israel, number between 150,000 and 200,000. They constitute a significant sector of the Palestinian community who have Israeli citizenship in Galilee and Naqab and in what are known as the 'mixed' towns, that is where there is no Jewish hegemony, towns such as in the Haifa and Lydda areas.

According to an article by Ori Nir (*Ha'aretz*, January 2001) about half of Nazareth's Arab residents are internal refugees and their descendants and more than half of Umm al Fahm's residents belong to this group. The article cites the work of Professor Hillel Cohen, who put the number of the abandoned villages at 162.

Conscious of Arafat's propensity for making repeated concessions, these internal refugees have organized themselves and refused to have the PA assume responsibility for their future. According to Nir, Attorney Wakim Wakim, secretary of the National Council for the Defence of the Rights of Displaced Persons in Israel, has said that he and his colleagues do not wish to have the PA incorporate their cases into the 'peace' talks. Instead, they want the internal refugees themselves to wage their own legal, public and political struggle within the framework of the state of Israel:

We don't want a situation to arise in which we end up being forgotten, and not included in an arrangement on the refugee problem. On the other hand, if such an arrangement is one in which the Palestinian leadership makes concessions about our basic rights, we wouldn't want any linkage between the diplomatic negotiations and our struggle as Israeli citizens.

It must also be kept in mind that new refugees are being created as Israel's campaign of ethnic cleansing, underway since 1967, in and around Jerusalem continues, progresses and escalates. Residency cards are confiscated at will; and building permits are all but denied to Palestinians in all parts of the West Bank. This includes what they call 'greater Jerusalem' – a concept that has no juridical meaning and would appear to be a euphemism for Jewish land expansion and ownership via expropriation, eminent domain policies and other methods of land theft. Palestinian homes are being demolished on a wholesale basis (and have been for a long time; see the history of this policy during the previous *Intifada*). The bulldozer is, it appears, a more lethal weapon of war against the Palestinian people (in 1948 Palestine as well) than any other – at least in the long run.

All these categories of refugees constitute the overwhelming majority of the overall Palestinian population. Yet they are excluded from the decisions that will bear materially not only on their lives and future and on the way they can exercise their rights, but on the future and character of the Palestinian nation. One must not forget that their rights are collective and individual. And one must never forget that they are inalienable. No one can take them away – not Arafat, not the United States, not Barak or Sharon. They are firmly enshrined in humanitarian and other international law and morality.

One primary challenge facing the Palestinian people today is thus essentially juridical. In addition to their dispersal, dismemberment, dispossession and disenfranchisement, a legal vacuum has paralysed the Palestinian question. The body of UN resolutions adopted during the past five decades, together with international law provisions on the right of civilians under military occupation, constitute a jurisprudence for the Palestine question. But due to the recent hegemony of what has become known as the peace process, particularly since the Madrid conference in 1991, that legal framework has been marginalized and maligned by the self-appointed catalyst for peace in the Middle East: the United States.

The September 1994 letter by the then US ambassador to the United Nations, Madeleine Albright to all UN members declaring all UN resolutions on Palestine 'contentious, irrelevant and obsolete', is a case in point. Ironically, the Palestinian people had thus been placed in jeopardy of losing the basic legal framework defining their rights by the 'peace-broker'. The injection of the Oslo Declaration of Principles (DOP), under the charade of the 'peace process' into the apparent vacuum, began to obfuscate the global consensus, which had sustained and preserved these rights, for many decades. The global consensus now effectively belongs to a bygone era, while the sole legitimate representative of the Palestinians has switched roles from the presumed guardian of Palestinian rights to accomplice in the suppression of those rights.

Having effectively accepted the role of Israel's warden and subcontractor, the PA is hardly the national embodiment and address that the PLO once was for the Palestinian people. Even the Palestine National Council (PNC), presumed to be a Palestinian parliament-in-exile for four decades, has effectively become an instrument doing Israel's bidding at the behest of Arafat. At a special meeting in April 1996, urged by Shimon Peres, the PNC 'voted' to nullify the articles of the Palestinian National Covenant, which Israel has long deemed offensive.

That action will probably go down as one of the most infamous acts in modern Palestinian history. To have been unwilling to hold a meeting to debate the DOP was strange enough; but to convene two and a half years after the signing of the DOP, under Israeli occupation, and for the express purpose of ratifying the negation of Palestinian rights is certainly unique.

THE REFUGEES AND THE YOSSI BEILIN–ABU-MAZIN AGREEMENT

In the aftermath of the Israeli-Palestinian Interim Agreement on the West Bank and Gaza, concluded on 24 September 1995 (Oslo II), which divided the West Bank into three zones (A, B and C) Israel and the PA began to study possible modalities for a framework for the final status issues as mandated by the DOP. A secret agreement was forged between Arafat's next in line (Mahmoud Abbas, known as Abu-Mazin) and Yossi Beilin, a Meretz bloc leader close to Shimon Peres, which envisaged solutions to the refugee question, among other final status issues. That agreement, however, was pushed to the sidelines when Peres lost the election in the spring of 1996. The resurfacing of the agreement and the publication of the full text in *Newsweek* in September 2000 came in the wake of the unsuccessful Camp David II talks in July 2000.

Dated 13 October 1995, the ' Framework for the Conclusion of a Final Status Agreement between Israel and the Palestine Liberation Organization' was regarded by its two authors as paving the way for a ' lasting and comprehensive peace'. It was deemed essential in the sense that it declared 'null and void any agreement, declaration, document or statement which contradicts this Framework Agreement'. Presumably, it nullifies *ipso facto* not only Resolution 194, but also all other international instruments and provisions of refugee law, human rights law and humanitarian law in which refugee rights are enshrined, including Article 13 of both the Universal Declaration on Human Rights and the 1949 Fourth Geneva Convention, which provide that 'Everyone has the right to leave any country, including his own, and to return to his country.' Moreover, it also negates fundamental rights guaranteed by the International Covenant on Civil and Political Rights, which provides that 'no one shall be arbitrarily deprived of the right to enter his own country'; and the International Convention on the Elimination of All Forms of Racial Discrimination, which provides that a state may not deny, on racial or ethnic grounds, the opportunity 'to return to one's country'.

Surely, it does not take much legal research to discover that what Abu-Mazin carelessly signed on behalf of the 5.5 million refugees relinquishes fundamental rights that are well established in numerous international instruments. Such instruments are well known to international lawyers and international law students. It is hard to imagine that they are not known to Abu-Mazin, who, it would appear, is inclined towards a political rather than a juridical agenda.

The Beilin–Abu-Mazin Framework has now become an important pillar for a set of 'understandings' reached secretly at Camp David II in July and August 2000. Anxious to conclude an Israeli-Palestinian peace that would ensure his place in history, Clinton invested heavily in those talks, and lashed out mercilessly at Arafat when the latter refused to surrender in absolute terms. With the failure of Camp David II and the infamous and provocative 'visit' of Ariel Sharon to al-Haram al-Sharif on 28 September 2000 (undeniably with the active acquiesence of Barak), it was a matter of only one day before a full-scale uprising took place. Meanwhile, the outlines of an agreement on the refugee question was leaked to *Newsweek*.

To the extent that the Beilin–Abu-Mazin agreement constitutes a significant portion of the Camp David II 'understandings', we need to examine its references to the Palestinian refugees. Section I of Article VII of the Framework commits the Palestinian side to reconsider the refugees rights under international law in light of the changing realities on the ground since 1948:

Whereas the Palestinian side considers that the right of the Palestinian Refugees to return to their homes is enshrined in international law and natural justice, it recognizes that the prerequisites of the new era of peace and coexistence, as well as the realities that have been created on the ground since 1948 have rendered the implementation of this right impracticable. The Palestinian side, thus, declares its readiness to accept and implement policies and measures that will ensure, in so far as this is possible, the welfare and well- being of these refugees.

Clearly, it could not have occurred to Abu-Mazin, a refugee himself, now accustomed to a life of luxury, that the 'welfare and well-being' of 'these refugees', who constitute 67.7 per cent of the eight million Palestinians in the world, includes their right of return. Pragmatism is certainly carried to new dimensions in this agreement. And what is really striking is the lack of subtlety and what is generally known as 'constructive ambiguity' that might enable the PA to maximize its diplomatic position in future talks.

In Section 2 of Article VII, Israel acknowledges 'the moral and material suffering caused to the Palestinian people as a result of the war of 1947–1949', but that imposes neither legal nor moral responsibility for that 'suffering' on Israel itself. In conformity with Oslo I, which transfers all responsibility for injuries sustained during the Israeli occupation to the PA, this Framework also places the burden of redress on the PA:

It [Israel] further acknowledges the Palestinian refugees' right of return to the Palestinian state and their right to compensation and rehabilitation for moral and material losses.

The right of return as articulated by international law is, therefore, declared null and void in this clause, inasmuch as its implementation falls on the shoulders of the PA, with Israel shirking any of *its* responsibility (recognized, as we have said, by a myriad of international instruments) for the plight of the refugees. Moreover, the right to compensation and restitution – another Israeli responsibility under international law – will be dealt with, according to this Framework, by an International Commission for Palestinian Refugees (ICPR). The Commission is charged with the responsibility to fund raise, distribute payments, adjudicate claims disputes and develop 'rehabilitation and absorption programmes'. Its decisions will be final and subject to no appeal.

The ICPR would, in effect, shield Israel from its obligations under international law, and look elsewhere for means of redress. It would also protect Israel from any international litigation. The Palestinian 'state', truncated as it may be, the Arab states and international donors anxious to terminate the conflict are, in effect, summoned by this Framework agreement to assume Israel's liabilities.

Not only will this obstruction of the judicial process be unusual and improper, but its mechanism could never provide the refugees reasonable redress. Their right of return to their homes and property will have been forever surrendered, and the most Israel would be willing to do is to admit into Israel proper fewer than 100,000 refugees strictly on a 'humanitarian basis', and under full peace conditions (peace after all is defined by the victor, which in the scenario under discussion is Israel).

The refugees' claims for compensation and restitution will be satisfied only to the extent that fund-raising efforts are successful and a proper judicial mechanism is available, with the capacity to operate in such a constricted legal environment. Not a single aspect of the Nazi Holocaust precedent for compensation and restitution, established through the diligent efforts of major Jewish organizations in cooperation with Israel and its tributaries in the world Zionist movement, will have any application here.

Prime Minister Barak, in fact, confirmed the gist of the Framework regarding a final settlement of the refugee claims as he was departing for the negotiations of Camp David II. As if to declare in advance that peace had no chance without Palestinian capitulations to Israel's demands, he assured his constituents in a published message (*Yediot Aharonot*, 11 July 2000) that Israel's red lines still applied:

Separation – us here, them over there; no return to the 1967 borders; Jerusalem united under our sovereignty; no foreign army west of the River Jordan; most settlers under Israeli sovereignty in the final status Arrangement; *Israel will not recognize any moral or legal responsibility for the Palestinian refugee problem.* (emphasis added)

Thereafter, the Clinton administration tried to force Arafat to sign a peace treaty with Israel that would finesse the issue of refugees but in fact deny them the right of return forever. President Clinton was proposing that both sides recognize the right of Palestinian refugees to return either to 'historic Palestine' or to 'their homeland'. Yet under the proposal there is no specific right of return to what is now Israel. Instead, the refugees may choose to go the 'State of Palestine', to areas in one of the proposed 'land swap' schemes under discussion; or to be resettled in Arab and/or other countries.

Clinton's eleventh hour attempt to put his seal on a Palestinian-Israeli peace settlement did not recognize the right of refugees to return to their original homes as mandated by international law. It also violated the maxims of refugee law and human rights law, and rendered any protection clauses superfluous and irrelevant.

TOWARDS CONVENING A CONGRESS OF RETURN AND SELF-DETERMINATION

Tampering with the legal framework of Palestinian rights has placed the Palestinian people in a serious dilemma. What can the Palestinians do to escape the fate of other native people who have been subjected to genocide and forced onto reservations into Bantustans and other forms of quarantined and marginalized areas? To avoid becoming perpetual captives in isolated Gaza, or to remain forever a disenfranchised community, or left to wander in exile, living at the sufferance of hostile Arab governments, they may consider taking action along the following lines.

First and foremost, they must cling tenaciously to the legal framework, which has been surrendered on their behalf, but without their consultation or authorization. The state of legal limbo inflicted on them must be terminated and their internationally guaranteed rights must be reaffirmed. They should recall Wakim's reminder that no one must be allowed to dictate undesired terms. To that end, an assemblage of the representatives of the 5.5 million living in the diaspora and the two million in the West Bank and Gaza, would begin to undo the implied surrender, reclaim their national rights and render all acts denying them these rights – implicitly or explicitly – in transitional arrangements or final status talks, null and void.

The Congress of Self-Determination and Return, as it may be called, is the irreducible minimal step which the Palestinian people can take as they embark on rectifying the wrongs of Oslo. Whereas concluding the DOP had involved less than half a dozen confidants of Arafat, meeting in secret with Israelis outside the parameters of the public scrutiny, the Conference of Return would be an open forum for all Palestinians from all walks of life, meeting within the rules of accountability. It would be a culmination of a grass-roots effort with decisions by local committees and regional groupings moving from the bottom up in a democratic process and in an egalitarian spirit. It would be a non-partisan, non-ideological, non-sectarian project, aiming to uphold the right of return and self-determination. These rights, enshrined in the Universal Declaration of Human Rights and UN Resolutions 194 and 3236, and long supported by an international consensus, must be placed high on the agenda of any peace talks taking place at any time and in any place.

The conference would serve as a constituent assembly to remedy the legal vacuum which plagues the Palestinian nation. For neither the PNC in its present form, nor the so-called Legislative Council, representing the West Bank and Gaza, is qualified to fulfil that function. The PNC was last re-formed in 1991 and repackaged in the spring of 1996 to suit specific requirements conflicting with Palestinian rights and injurious to Palestinian interests. The 'Legislative Council', on the other hand, is a product of the DOP and its derivative Agreements, and is, therefore, part of the problem and not part of the solution.

The omission from the DOP of the right of return within the meaning of Resolution 194 is the single most serious impediment to genuine redress of the refugees' grievances. How can a council representing two million Palestinians in the so-called self-rule areas, leaving the bulk of the Palestinian populations out, most of whom are refugees, negotiate momentous issues with Israel, under Israeli occupation and according to inequitable conditions imposed by Israel itself?

It is not unreasonable to assume that an independent PLO, rather than the Legislative Council and Arafat's executive, must be charged with negotiating the question of the refugees. Despite serious damage inflicted on the PLO at Oslo, it is still theoretically the only valid representative of the entire Palestinian people, including the refugees. It is still the proper address and the national embodiment of Palestinian nationalism. Care, therefore, must be exercised to insure that PA agreements with Israel are not perceived as being those of the PLO, as has been the case with Oslo and the Beilin–Abu-Mazin agreement.

Moreover, the representative character of the Legislative Council is limited to a single segment of the Palestinian people – those based in the West Bank and Gaza. It is the only sector of the Palestinian nation for whom Israel is willing to accept some obligation, albeit in return for giving Israel total exemption from all responsibilities for breaches and crimes committed against the Palestinian people. Under the present rules, the Legislative Council and Arafat's executive would not be able to deal substantively with the right of self-determination and the right of return. Israel views the DOP as granting the Council neither judicial nor legislative powers, only powers having to do with modalities for limited self-governance for residents of the West Bank and Gaza, not even those of Jerusalem, were granted to the Council.

To make matters worse, the question of return is further marginalized by the fact that it has already been considered by the DOP as a regional matter affecting *all* refugees, including Jews who left property in Arab countries. That is why both Camp David and the DOP have called for a committee consisting of Israel, Jordan, Egypt and the Palestinian Council to settle that problem, with Israel retaining an effective veto.

The proposed Congress of Return would be inclusive, rather than exclusive, comprehensive rather than segmental, and people-oriented rather than elitist. Its legitimacy is derived from the entire Palestinian nation and from the relevant international declarations and UN resolutions, which the United States and Israel are feverishly trying to render ineffective and superfluous. The Congress would be able to undo the negations of Albright and voice an eloquent reply to her decree that the UN resolutions are 'contentious and obsolete'.

Representatives of the Palestinian people from all walks of life, from the refugee camps of Lebanon, Jordan and Syria, from the West Bank and Gaza, from Israel proper, the United States, Australia and elsewhere, would reaffirm their rights under these resolutions. They would re-establish the right of a reconstituted PLO to resolve the refugees question with Israel. They would declare in unison that they and not the handful of operatives who met in Oslo, Cairo, Taba and other such places have the right to claim and relinquish rights. It would be an experience that would initiate the process of redress, the process of real confidence-building, democratization, and the process that can give a real voice to the voiceless.

16   LESSONS OF HOLOCAUST COMPENSATION
Norman G. Finkelstein

Soon after the Nazi Holocaust, Jewish organizations and the government of Israel negotiated substantial compensation agreements with Germany. In the past decade, new compensation agreements have been negotiated with Germany as well as with other European governments. These agreements constitute an important precedent for Palestinian material claims against Israel.

In the early 1950s Germany entered into negotiations with Jewish institutions and signed a series of indemnification agreements.[1] With little if any external pressure, it has paid out to date some $60–80 billion. The German government sought to compensate Jewish victims of Nazi persecution with three different agreements signed in 1952. Individual claimants received payments according to the terms of the Law on Indemnification (*Bundesentschädigungsgesetz*). A separate agreement with Israel subsidized the absorption and rehabilitation of several hundred thousand Jewish refugees. The German government also negotiated at the same time a financial settlement with the Conference on Jewish Material Claims against Germany, an umbrella of all major Jewish organizations including the American Jewish Committee, American Jewish Congress, Bnai Brith and the Joint Distribution Committee.

The sums paid out by the postwar German government significantly affected Jewish life. During the first ten years of the agreement (1953–63), the Israeli historian Tom Segev reports:

the reparations money funded about a third of the total investment in Israel's electrical system, which tripled in capacity, and nearly half the total investment in the railways, buying German diesel engines, cars, tracks, and signaling equipment. Equipment for developing the water supply, for oil drilling, and for operating the copper mines ... was bought in Germany, as well as heavy equipment for agriculture and construction – tractors, combines, and trucks.[2]

Germany earmarked the Claims Conference monies (approximately $1 billion in current values) for victims of Nazi persecution who were not adequately compensated by the German courts. As it happened, the Claims Conference used the monies mostly for other purposes, for example, subsidizing Jewish communities in the Arab world and Jewish cultural institutions such as the Yad Vashem Holocaust museum in Israel.

Beginning in the early 1990s mainly American Jewish organizations cooperating with Israel opened a new round of 'Holocaust compensation' negotiations with various European countries. The first target was Switzerland.[3] The Swiss stood accused of directly and indirectly profiting from the Nazi persecution of Jews. Acting at Israel's behest, the World Jewish Restitution Organization mobilized officials at the federal, state and local levels in the United States to press Switzerland for Holocaust compensation. A senior official in the Clinton administration, Stuart Eizenstat, conscripted twelve federal agencies for this initiative. A major international conference was convened in London. The House and Senate banking committees held multiple hearings. Class action lawsuits against Switzerland were filed in American courts. State and local legislatures across the United States implemented economic boycotts. In the end, Switzerland agreed to pay some $1.5 billion in compensation.

For our purposes, the merits of the case against Switzerland (dubious at best) are less important than the legal and moral precedents it set. The chairman of the House Banking Committee, James Leach, maintained that states must be held accountable for injustices even if committed a half-century ago: 'History does not have a statute of limitations.' Eizenstat deemed Swiss compensation to Jewry 'an important litmus test of this generation's willingness to face the past and rectify the wrongs of the past'. Although they couldn't be 'held responsible for what took place years ago', Senator Alfonse D'Amato of the Senate Banking Committee acknowledged that the Swiss still had a 'duty of accountability and of attempting to do what is right at this point in time'. Publicly endorsing the Jewish demand for compensation, President Clinton likewise reflected that 'we must confront and, as best we can, right the terrible injustice of the past'. 'It should be made clear', bipartisan Congressional leaders wrote in a letter to the Secretary of State, that the 'response on this restitution matter will be seen as a test of respect for basic human rights and the rule of law'. And in address to the Swiss Parliament, Secretary of State Albright explained that economic benefits Switzerland accrued from the plundering of Jews 'were passed along to subsequent generations and that is why the world now looks to the people of Switzerland, not to assume responsibility for actions taken by their forbears, but to be generous in doing what can be done at this point to right past wrongs'. Noble sentiments all, but nowhere to be heard – unless they are being actively ridiculed – when it comes to Palestinian compensation for the dispossession of their homeland.

In negotiations with Eastern Europe, Jewish organizations and Israel have demanded the full restitution of or monetary compensation for the pre-war communal and private assets of the Jewish community.[4] Consider Poland. The pre-war Jewish population of Poland stood at 3.5 million; the current population is several thousand. Yet, the World Jewish Restitution Organization demands title over the 6,000 pre-war communal Jewish properties, including those currently being used as hospitals and schools. It is also laying claim to hundreds of thousands of parcels of Polish land valued in the many tens of billions of dollars. Once again the entire US political and legal establishment has been mobilized to achieve these ends. Indeed, New York City Council members unanimously supported a resolution calling on Poland 'to pass comprehensive legislation providing for the complete restitution of Holocaust assets', while 57 members of Congress (led by Congressman Anthony Weiner of New York) dispatched a letter to the Polish parliament demanding 'comprehensive legislation that would return 100% of all property and assets seized during the Holocaust'.

Testifying before the Senate Banking Committee, Stuart Eizenstat deplored the lax pace of evictions in Eastern Europe: 'A variety of problems have arisen in the return of properties. For example, in some countries, when persons or communities have attempted to reclaim properties, they have been asked, sometimes required ... to allow current tenants to remain for a lengthy period of time at rent-controlled rates.' The delinquency of Belarus particularly exercised Eizenstat. Belarus is 'very, very far' behind in handing over pre-war Jewish properties, he told the House International Relations Committee. The average monthly income of a Belarussian is $100.

To force submission from recalcitrant governments, those seeking Jewish restitution wield the bludgeon of US sanctions. Eizenstat urged Congress to 'elevate' Holocaust compensation, put it 'high on the list' of requirements for those East European countries that are seeking entry into the OECD, the World Trade Organization, the European Union, NATO and the Council of Europe: 'They will listen if you speak ... They will get the hint.' Israel Singer, of the World Jewish Restitution Organization, called on Congress to 'continue looking at the shopping list' in order to 'check' that every country pays up. 'It is extremely important that the countries involved in the issue understand', Congressman Benjamin Gilman of the House International Relations Committee said, 'that their response ... is one of several standards by which the United States assesses its bilateral relationship.' Avraham Hirschson, chairman of Israel's Knesset Committee on restitution and Israel's representative on the World Jewish Restitution Organization, paid tribute to Congressional cooperation. Recalling his 'fights' with the Romanian prime minister, Hirschson testified: 'But I ask one remark, in the middle of the fighting, and it changed that atmosphere. I told him, you know, in two days I am going to be in a hearing here in Congress. What do you want me to tell them in the hearing? The whole atmosphere was changed.'

'Were it not for the United States of America', Eizenstat aptly observed in his paean to Congress, 'very few, if any, of these activities would be ongoing today.' To justify the pressures exerted on Eastern Europe, he explained that a hallmark of 'Western' morality is to 'return or pay compensation for communal and private property wrongfully appropriated'. For the 'new democracies' in Eastern Europe, meeting this standard 'would be commensurate with their passage from totalitarianism to democratic states'. Yet, judging by the claims of Palestinians, it would seem that a main US ally has yet to make the transition.

Apart from the moral link joining Jewish claims against Europe, on the one hand, and Palestinian claims against Israel, on the other, a direct material link potentially joins the respective demands. When Israel first entered into negotiations with Germany for reparations after the war, the Israeli historian Ilan Pappe reports, Foreign Minister Moshe Sharett proposed transferring a part to Palestinian refugees, 'in order to rectify what has been called the small injustice (the Palestinian tragedy), caused by the more terrible one (the Holocaust)'.[5] Nothing ever came of the proposal. A respected Israeli academic, Clinton Bailey, recently suggested using part of the funds from the Holocaust settlements with Switzerland and Germany for the 'compensation of Palestinian Arab refugees'.[6] Given that almost all survivors of the Nazi holocaust have already passed away, this would seem to be a sensible proposal.

One cautionary note should be entered. Elsewhere I have documented that Jewish organizations misappropriated much of the monies earmarked for the Jewish victims of Nazi persecution.[7] It would be regrettable should monies earmarked for the Palestinian victims of Israel's establishment also end up in undeserving hands. Indeed, if only to avert yet another injustice befalling the refugees, it is vital that Palestinians set up accountable democratic institutions.

NOTES

1. For background, see especially Nana Sagi, *German Reparations* (New York, 1986), and Ronald W. Zweig, *German Reparations and the Jewish World* (Boulder, 1987).
2. Tom Segev, *The Seventh Million* (New York, 1993), p. 241.
3. For details, see Norman G. Finkelstein, *The Holocaust Industry* (New York, 2000), chapter 3.
4. Ibid.
5. Ilan Pappe, *The Making of the Arab–Israeli Conflict, 1947–51* (London, 1992), p. 268.
6. Clinton Bailey, 'Holocaust Funds to Palestinians May Meet Some Cost of Compensation', *International Herald Tribune*; reprinted in *Jordan Times* (20 June 1999).
7. Finkelstein, *Holocaust Industry*.

NOTES ON THE CONTRIBUTORS

Jan Abu Shakrah teaches sociology and peace studies at Portland Community College, Oregon. She founded and directed the Palestine Human Rights Information Centre in Jerusalem from 1986 to 1995.

Salman Abu-Sitta is a researcher and author of over 50 papers on Palestinian refugees. He has been Director of international development projects and is a former member of the Palestine National Council and founder of Palestine Land Society.

Susan M. Akram is Associate Professor at Boston University School of Law, where she teaches Immigration Law, Comparative Refugee Law, and supervises in the Boston University Civil Litigation Program. She is a founding director of both the Immigration Project at the public interest law firm of Public Counsel in Los Angeles and the Political Asylum/Immigration Representation (PAIR) Project in Boston. She was Fulbright Senior Scholar for the academic year 1999–2000, teaching at Al-Quds University/Palestine School of Law in Jerusalem.

Naseer Aruri is Chancellor Professor Emeritus (Political Science) at the University of Massachusetts, Dartmouth. His latest book is *The Obstruction of Peace: The US, Israel and the Palestinians* (1995). He is editor of *Occupation: Israel over Palestine* (1988) and co-editor of *Revising Culture, Reinventing Peace: The Influence of Edward W. Said* (2001). He is a former member of the boards of Amnesty International USA and Human Rights Watch/Middle East. He is currently chair of Trans-Arab Research Institute, Boston.

Noam Chomsky is Institute Professor in the Department of Linguistics and Philosophy at the Massachusetts Institute of Technology. His recent publications include *The New Military Humanism: Lessons from Kosovo* (2000), *Rogue States: The Rule of Force in World Affairs* (2000), and *Fateful Triangle* (1999, updated edition). He is the recipient of many awards and prizes, including the Kyoto Prize for Basic Science (1989), the Distinguished Scientific Contribution Award of the American Psychological Association, the Helmholtz Medal, and others.

Norman G. Finkelstein received his doctorate from Princeton University for a thesis on the theory of Zionism. He is the author of several books, including *Image and Reality of the Israel-Palestine Conflict* (1995) and most recently *The Holocaust Industry: Reflections on the Exploitation of Jewish Suffering* (2000). He teaches political theory at the City University, New York.

Nahla Ghandour is currently Director of Habilitation Pre-school at the Ghassan Kanafani Cultural Foundation. She is a Pediatric Occupational Therapist and Special Educator, Consultant and Trainer in the field of Childhood Education and Habilitation for Children with Multiple Disabilities. She is an active member in disability organizations in Lebanon.

Alain Gresh is editor-in-chief of *Le Monde diplomatique*. His previous publications include *PLO: The Struggle Within* (1986); *Palestine 1947, un partage avorté* (1987); *Golfe: Clefs pour une guerre annoncée* (1990); *An A to Z to the Middle East* (with Dominique Vidal, 1990); *Un Péril islamiste?* (1994); and *Actualités de l'Etat palestinien* (with Didier Billion, 2000).

Ingrid Jaradat Gassner was born in Austria and is a graduate of the Hebrew University, Jerusalem (1981) and University of Salzburg, Austria (1987). She has lived and worked in Bethlehem since 1988. She is a founding member of the BADIL Resource Centre for Palestinian Residency and Refugee Rights, established in cooperation with refugee organizations in the West Bank.

Elaine C. Hagopian is Professor Emerita of Sociology, Simmons College, Boston. She was one of the founders of the Trans-Arab Research Institute and one of the organizers of the Right of Return Conference, whose presentations are the basis of this volume. She has held special appointments with UNICEF and with UNESCO. Her publications range from studies of Arab-Americans to analysis of particular issues in the Palestine/Israel conflict.

Atif Kubursi is Professor of Economics and Regional Science at McMaster University, Canada. He has also taught and lectured at Purdue University, Indiana, University of Cambridge and Harvard University. In 1972 he formed Econometric Research Limited which he serves as president. In 1982 he joined the United Nations Industrial Organization as senior development officer. As a consultant, he specializes in the fields of impact analysis and regional planning with special emphasis on industrial development.

Nur Masalha is a Palestinian historian from the Galilee, currently based in the Centre for Islamic and Middle Eastern Law, SOAS, University of London; St Mary's University College, University of Surrey, UK. His books include *Imperial Israel and the Palestinians: The Politics of Expansion* (2000), *A Land without a People: Israel, Transfer and the Palestinians 1949–96* (1997) and *The Concept of 'Transfer' in Zionist Political Thought, 1882–1948* (1992).

Joseph Massad is assistant professor of modern Arab politics and intellectual history at Columbia University. He is the author of *Colonial Effects: The Making of National Identity in Jordan* (2001) and has published many articles on the Palestinian–Israeli conflict.

Ilan Pappe is a senior lecturer in the Department of Political Science in Haifa University, Israel. He is also the academic head of the Institute for Peace Research in Givat Haviva, Israel. He is the author of books and articles dealing with the Palestine question, among them *The Making of the Arab-Israeli Conflict, 1947–1951* (1992) and the editor of the *Israel/Palestine Question* (1999).

Michael Prior is a Principal Lecturer in Biblical Studies at St Mary's College, Strawberry Hill (University of Surrey, England). He was Visiting Professor in Bethlehem University, and Scholar-in-Residence in Tantur Ecumenical Institute, Jerusalem (1996–97). His books include *Paul the Letter Writer and the Second Letter to Timothy* (1989), *Jesus the Liberator. Nazareth Liberation Theology (Luke 4.16–30)* (1995), *The Bible and Colonialism. A Moral Critique* (1997) and *Zionism and the State of Israel: A Moral Inquiry* (1999).

Edward W. Said is currently University Professor of English and Comparative Literature at Columbia University. His publications include *Orientalism* (1978); *Culture and Imperialism* (1993); *Representations of the Intellectual* (1994); *Peace and its Discontents* (1993); *Out of Place* (1999); *The End of the Peace Process* (2000) and *Reflections on Exile* (2000).

Wadie Said is an attorney in New York and a member of the New York Bar. He received his JD from Columbia University School of Law where he served as articles editor of the *Columbia Human Rights Law Review*. He was a Fulbright Scholar in Egypt, 1994–95, and worked as an advocate and translator for various NGOs in Palestine in 1995–96. He was a summer law clerk at the Shehadeh law firm, Ramallah in 1997 and most recently was law clerk to the Hon. Charles P. Sifton, Chief District Judge, EDNY 1999–2000.

Jaber Suleiman was born in Palestine in 1945 and now works as an independent researcher in Lebanon. He was visiting research fellow at the Refugee Studies Programme, University of Oxford (1997–98). He is a co-founder of *Ai'dun* (Those Who Will Return). He has written extensively in the field of refugee studies; his most recent publication is 'The Political, Organizational and Security Situation in the Palestinian Refugee Camps of Lebanon', *Journal of Palestine Studies* (August 1999).

INDEX